W9-CCV-968

DISCARDED
JENKS LRC
GORDON COLLEGE

Research Directions in Computer Science

Research Directions in Computer Science
An MIT Perspective

Edited by

Albert R. Meyer
John V. Guttag
Ronald L. Rivest
Peter Szolovits

JENKS L.R.C.
GORDON COLLEGE
255 GRAPEVINE RD.
WENHAM, MA 01984-1895

The MIT Press
Cambridge, Massachusetts
London, England

©1991 Massachusetts Institute of Technology
All rights reserved. No part of this book may be reproduced in any form by
any electronic or mechanical means (including photocopying, recording, or
information storage and retrieval) without permission in writing from the
publisher.

This book was printed and bound in the United States of America.

Library of Congress Cataloging-in-Publication Data

Research directions in computer science : an MIT perspective / edited by
Albert R. Meyer . . . [et al.].
    p.   cm.
    Includes bibliographical references and index.
    ISBN 0-262-13257-5
    1. Computer science—Research—Massachusetts. 2. Massachusetts
Institute of Technology. I. Meyer, Albert R.
QA76.27.R43 1991
004—dc20   91-14072
                                                                    CIP

              QA
              76.27
              .R43
              1991

Contents

Foreword

Both the Laboratory for Computer Science and the Artificial Intelligence Laboratory were absolutely delighted and honored that so many attendees from so many different parts of the world interrupted their work to join us for our 25th birthday celebration.

Professor Albert Meyer, chairman of the celebration, put together an exciting program which was a first for our community: this was the first time that so many of our faculty and senior research scientists, some 24 of us in all, stood so close to each other in order to present our treasured research to you. It was even the first time I have seen so many of my colleagues together under any circumstances.

The research carried out within our labs is conveniently framed into four categories. Here is a description of these areas along with our vision of where each of them might lead and how they tie together.

In the area of *parallel systems*, we are attempting to understand and shape the new terrain of general purpose, multiprocessor machine architectures, along with their programming languages and concurrent algorithms. We are also interested in special purpose, multiprocessor architectures that might some day give us eyes and ears made out of silicon. Multiprocessors interest us not only because they should open new horizons through the new power that they bring us, but also because we expect them to exploit, in a cost effective way, the large parallelism inherent in the way millions of people generate and use information concurrently. According to our vision, these parallel systems will become the information processing engines of tomorrow—from the smallest personal computer of a few hundred processors, to million-processor simulators of intergalactic phenomena.

The second research category is that of *distributed systems*—made up of interconnected and often dissimilar computers. Here, the challenge is to create network architectures, languages and systems that help programs in one location intercommunicate effectively with programs in another location. By effectively, I mean reliably, at different speeds determined by need and cost, able to cope with unknown situations and, most important, capable of understanding one another in terms of concepts that go well beyond bytes. I say this because today, bytes are the highest level concepts shared by all computers as they intercommunicate for electronic mail or file transfer purposes. Our vision calls for nearly every computer to be part of some distributed system and for all of these systems to form a gigantic new infrastructure, which I like to call the *information marketplace*. We expect that this new set of information highways will be as important to the future economy and way of life as the older highway system has been, and still is, to the transportation of people and goods.

The third research category is in the area of *intelligent systems*— sensory, robotic and knowledge-based—where we try to capture intelligent behavior in order to make computers more powerful and more useful. Since we often characterize intelligent behavior as that which we cannot easily explain, the boundary between computer intelligence and computer stupidity is hazy and dynamic. The research problems are big, difficult and diverse. Yet, the potential impact of these systems is likely to be dramatic, for instance, as typing gives way to speaking and showing, as learning from practice begins to displace programming, and as the powerful but dumb machines born in the industrial age acquire new cognitive abilities. Ultimately, I believe that the greatest benefit of intelligent systems is that they will make machines easier to use—for the same reason that intelligent human assistants are also easier to interact with among human helpers.

In the fourth area, *computer science theory*, we try to discover immutable laws, predict ultimate limits, invent algorithms and, as in all theory, understand, explain and simplify the magical phenomena of the world of computers. Looking to the future, we know that we cannot predict where computer science theory will take us. We fully expect that it will continue its proven role in guiding and organizing our thinking, in increasing our understanding of the computer field and in surprising us with unexpected and profound discoveries.

If you detect a tone of unbridled optimism in my remarks, I assure you that it is there! My research colleagues and I share the passionate belief that our field has already changed the world, and will continue to do so for a long time to come. Through these pages, we attempt to relay our views of these future changes through our current research.

We now invite you to join us in our enthusiasm and in our quest to grow this new and wondrous technology toward the benefit of all humankind.

Michael L. Dertouzos
Director, MIT Laboratory for Computer Science

Preface

As Chairman of the Project MAC 25th Anniversary Celebration, I am delighted to present this volume of papers based on a symposium held at MIT in October 1988. The topics cover a full range of computer science research ongoing at the MIT Laboratory for Computer Science and MIT Artificial Intelligence Laboratory—the two entities that grew from the original Project MAC founded in 1963.

Knowing the esteem—some would say smugness—with which MIT computer scientists view themselves, one might suppose it difficult for an Anniversary Planning Committee to resist harking back to the past accomplishments of MIT computer science. It is true: we first considered a retrospective focus surveying 25 years of notable contributions to the field. But, as one of our distinguished committee members pithily put it, "history is boring." In fact, we had no trouble reaching the consensus *not* to focus on the past.

I do not think we are therefore doomed to repeating past mistakes. Rather, I interpret this decision as a healthy reflection of the awesome vitality of our subject. We are all aware how computer technology has gone through orders of magnitude improvements in cost, speed, capacity and availability over the past 25 years. One understandable consequence is that many of the old problems which occupied the field are simply no longer interesting. Remember when it was an important challenge to fit a FORTRAN compiler into 64K, minimize gates in a circuit, or transfer a 100K file? Even the major early achievements, most notably time sharing, are widely familiar and no longer hold the excitement of the leading edge.

Another symposium theme we considered was a futuristic one speculating about great achievements predicted for the next 25 years of computer science. This idea quickly dissolved because, I suspect, we could not identify very many credible people willing to attempt such speculations. By now, too many past computer science prognostications have become notorious.

This brings me to the decision we did make: to emphasize current research activities in computer science at MIT. The basis of the field's future, after all, lies in advanced research of today—the area in which we strive to excel. Our aim, therefore, was to communicate the present excitement and future prospects of our computer science research, of course including the relevant historical background. Also, we thought it would be the subject most appreciated by our audience of active professionals and students.

A small bit of history is needed to explain the selection of topics. Project MAC was formed in 1963; the artificial intelligence lab within the Project reorganized to form an independent laboratory—the Artificial Intelligence Laboratory (AIL) in 1970; and, in 1975, Project MAC renamed itself as the Laboratory for Computer Science (LCS). The two labs have maintained an intimate relationship, involving the same location at Tech Square, shared technical library and computer systems, a common graduate student population and multiple joint faculty.

An MIT education has been described as offering students a chance to sip knowledge from a fire hydrant. One consequence of the participant's enthusiasm for their topics was that every talk of the symposium was filled to the minute, hence this volume is correspondingly full.

Efforts are underway at the Institute to moderate this situation, by the way, but our anniversary ended up fitting the fire hydrant mold. Even so, this book only provides a sample of the realm of our work.

I believe the following pages will allow the reader to appreciate the exciting prospects of computer science research at MIT.

Albert R. Meyer
MAC 25 Symposium Chairman

Acknowledgments

Our work has been sponsored by MIT, governmental and industrial organizations to which we are grateful. Specifically we recognize the Defense Advanced Research Projects Agency (DARPA) of the Department of Defense, from which more than half of the research funds have originated since MAC's inception. Other significant government sponsors include the Army Research Office, Department of Energy, National Institutes of Health/National Library of Medicine, National Science Foundation, Office of Naval Research, Rome Air Development Center, and the US Air Force Office of Scientific Research.

In addition, we value our extensive interrelations with industry. A representative list of current and past industrial collaborators making our research possible includes: Analog Devices, Apollo, Apple Computer, AT&T, Bell Telephone Laboratories, Bolt Beranek and Newman, Boston University/University Hospital, Bull SA, Calcomp, Coleco Control Data Corporation, Data General, Digital Equipment, Eastman Kodak, Exxon, Fujitsu America, General Electric, Harris Corporation, Hewlett Packard, Honeywell, IBM, Intel, Motorola, NCR, Nynex, Sequent, Siemens, Sony, Sun, Symbolics, Systems Concepts, Tektronix, Texas Instruments, Tufts University/New England Medical Center, Wang, Western Digital, Xerox, and Zenith.

We wish to thank the many individuals who extended the necessary time, effort and resources to make our 25th Anniversary celebration a success and this book possible. In particular, we express our appreciation to Mr. John Updike for his participation and contributions, and to his publisher, Alfred A. Knopf, Inc. for permission to reprint excerpts from *Roger's Version*.

The production of a camera-ready volume such as this remains a challenging, time-consuming task, even with the aid of the LaTeX text processing system and other technological support. Paula Vancini, assisted by Sally Bemus, managed the production process with care and energy, while David Jones's LaTeX formatting expertise was a *sine qua non*. The editors are very grateful for their help.

Where Money and Energy Gather: A Writer's View of a Computer Laboratory

John Updike

Let me begin, ladies and gentlemen of the glamorous world of computers, by explaining how I got here. Five or so years ago I acquired a wordprocessor and, on the basis of several mystical experiences with it, a bit later took it into my head to write a novel about a young computer hacker who attempts to devise a program to prove the existence of God. To help me in my research, a mutual friend arranged for me to meet Michael Dertouzos, who most kindly led me on a tour of the MIT Laboratory for Computer Science and answered what questions I had the wit to ask. It might serve as a cautionary index of the wicked distortions and shameless inaccuracies of the fictionalizing mind if I were to read to you the few pages of the novel that most directly resulted from my dazzled visit:

"Toward evening of this first Friday in April, Dale proceeds, with a cooling hot-pastrami sandwich in a grease-soaked paper bag, plus a small carton of high-fat milk and a pair of broken oatmeal cookies in a plastic envelope, to the building, erected in 1978, that houses the university's violently expanded facilities for computer research and development. A concrete cube with nine times nine windows on a side, it looms above the tattered and doomed rows of tenements that stand in this section of the city, real estate that is all owned by the university and awaiting its developmental fate. Mere daily life seems meagre in the shadow of this great housing, its many windows identically deep-set in the sandy-gray sockets beveled like the slits of a bulletproof bunker. The sky this evening is turquoise, and the smaller, more nervous clouds of spring have replaced winter's solid mantle. Everything, suddenly, is tugging,

Pages 227–231 from *Roger's Version* by John Updike are reprinted with permission from Alfred A. Knopf, Inc., New York, 1986.
Mr. Updike's remarks are those that were given at the Project MAC 25th Anniversary Celebration Banquet, October 26, 1988.

from greening tree-tips to mud underfoot, to be something other than it is. Dale's stomach feels high in his body, its lining chafed from within by guilty apprehension. He has accepted money for his project; he has bitten off more than he can chew.

Though the normal world's working hours are over, and the great rose-marble foyer of the Cube is deserted but for one lackadaisical guard who checks Dale's laminated pass, on certain upper floors truly creative activity is just beginning, having yielded the daytime hours to more assuredly profitable projects than its own. Dale enters one of the powder-blue elevators. He punches the number 7.

The first floor of the Cube is given over to reception space, the offices of the public-relations staff, and a technical library of computer science and the great programming languages (LISP, FORTRAN, PL/1, Pascal, Algol with its ancestor Plankalkül and its descendant JOVIAL), plus a small and amusing museum displaying abaci, Inca quipus, a seventeenth-century slide rule, diagrams of Pascal's toothed and ratcheted calculation wheels and the stepped wheels of Leibniz, a wall-sized enlargement of some engineering specs for Charles Babbage's epochal Analytical Engine with its Jacquard cards and thousand wheels of digit storage, reproductions of selected pages of the Countess Lovelace's mathematical notebooks and also one of her actual embroidered linen handkerchiefs, samples of the Hollerith punched cards used in the U.S. census of 1890, significant pieces of the Automatic Sequence Controlled Calculator put into operation at Harvard in 1944, and a disassembled accumulator, consisting of ten ring counters comprising in turn ten vacuum tubes, from ENIAC, the first true electronic computer, designed in Philadelphia to calculate the trajectories of quaint, old-fashioned bombs and shells.

On the second and third floors the administrators of the Cube have their offices, and there are conference rooms and a small all-stainless-steel kitchen in which luncheons and heavy hors d'oeuvres can be concocted for significant visitors. For the benefit of the Cube's workers there are a gymnasium (with Nautilus equipment and a balcony running track), a meditation room (equipped only with mats and zafus), a three-bed infirmary, and storage space for bicycles and mopeds, which must be brought into the building lest they be stolen outside.

The button on the fourth floor, in most of the elevators, is taped over, and even in those elevators where the button is exposed it achieves no response unless a numbered code, changed every week, is punched into a small panel. The work done on the fourth floor is secret, and yet from this unmentionable work stems the funds upon which the entire Cube rests. The men who work on the fourth floor never acknowledge it but can be identified by their relatively formal attire—suits and neckties, whereas even the head of all research and development, a jubilant Italo-American named Benedetto Ferrari, goes about in a turtleneck or a silk shirt open at his throat to disclose a thick gold chain or some old love beads of no-longer-fragrant cedar. Once a brilliant mathematician, with his fine Italian flair for elegant shortcuts, Ferrari dazzles trustees and even charms, over the telephone, those weary men in Washington who like coal heavers of old must shovel out their daily quotas of the incessant national treasure.

The fifth floor is mostly devoted to Ferrari's pet project, the development of adaptive brainlike hardware silicon chips for artificial intelligence—though what benefit might be brought to mankind, already possessed of so many disastrous intelligences, by the mechanical fabrication of yet more is less clear than the immaculate, feral smile of approval and encouragement that the boss bestows on all sides when he visits his favorite department. His happiness, perhaps, is that of Pygmalion, of Dr. Frankenstein, of all who would usurp the divine prerogative of breathing life into clay.

The sixth floor holds the guts of the place—the massed ranks of CPUs—VAX/785s, Symbolics 3600 LISP machines, and the Cube's own design, the MU—churning and crunching through calculations twenty-four hours a day; thunderous fans keep them from overheating, and a floor of removable segments protects yet renders accessible the miles of gangliated cables connecting their billions of bytes with not only the floors of display-processing units above and below but also, through high-speed modems and satellites, with terminals as remotely, strategically placed as Palo Alto, Hawaii, West Berlin, and Israel. Dale, to cool his mind, sometimes likes to wander around in here on the shuddering floors, up and down the aisles of encased circuits and racked spools of magnetic tape, amid the gigantic hum of something like spiritual activity, yet an activity mixed with the homely leakiness and vibration of a ship's engine room, complete with the reassuring human curses of grimy-handed mechanical engineers wrestling with cables and hand-tightened connections.

The seventh and eighth floors hold the cubicles of the lesser minions of the Cube, and the ninth holds the air-conditioning equipment—the ninth-floor windows are dummies, installed to satisfy the architect's post-modern need for insincerity, for empty symmetry. Dale gets off at floor 7, which also holds the cafeteria, closed after five o'clock, and a hall of rather weary machines that at any Godforsaken hour will accept coins and supply coffee, tea, bouillon both chicken and beef, candy bars, potato chips, cans of soft drinks, and even triangulated, bubble-wrapped sandwiches, all by encoded number. Working soldiers in the computer revolution, these big scarred boxes operate at a level of dogged, fumbling reliability interrupted by sudden spurts of rebellious malfunction—the coffee that will not stop pouring from its limp white nozzle, the bulb-lit red legend claiming OUT OF STOCK even though the desired bag of Fritos is in plain sight behind the plastic pane.

This seventh floor is also a realm of refuse, of paper cups and discarded wrappers, of posters overlaid one upon another like raster-display windows that cannot, oddly, be moved at the touch of a button but need fingernails to pry loose the thumb-tacks and pressure to push them back in. There is, on the bulletin boards and the office doors of these seventh-level computer wizards, an atavistic population of comic-strip animals, of Snoopy the blooby white dog and Garfield the chunky striped cat, of Booth's bull terriers and Koren's gleeful shaggy anthropomorphs, as if a certain emotional arrest has been the price of the precocious quickness of these young minds. Few of Dale's peers are at their posts at this in-between hour; also, spring and its holiday have called many of them home. Allston Valentine, an Australian roboticist, can through two doorways be glimpsed, as it were in clipped image, amid the rickety wreckage of a disassembled many-elbowed arm, while its leverage schematics patiently glow in vector sketch on the display terminal. Isaac Spiegel, who has been struggling since his junior year at MIT with the unreachably deep structures of computerized translation, sits with a bronze can of Michelob in a cubicle lined with dictionaries and grammars and Chomskyite charts branched like impractical antlers. Language, that spills from every mouth as naturally as saliva, turns out to be even more resistant to analysis than enzymes."

Now, what struck the author seems to have been the flourishing opulence of the computer scene in its ramifying vitality; this place is a vital spot in the society, where money and energy gather. When I toured the floor with the actual big computers on it, I felt much as when touring an old-fashioned factory: dazzled by the ingenuity of men, and somewhat dwarfed and dehumanized by men's works. But the old-fashioned mechanical factory at least produced a recognizable product, and its machines, driven by steam or gasoline combustion, were analogous to human actions and somewhat transparent to visual analysis. A computer center offers no such transparency to the layman: inscrutably the wheels spin, the screens flicker, the electricity darts like lightning along its microscopic forked paths, and the product is labeled, again inscrutably, information.

A delicate opacity, as of a very finespun veil, is for the layman the computer's essence. When my wordprocessor malfunctions, there is no part-by-part repair, no soldering or fine-fingered tinkering as with a machine of old, but rather the replacement of an entire sealed unit, in a few minutes of the repairperson's time, which is worth, a computerized bill later assures me, one hundred twenty dollars an hour. Today's high school student, instead of laboriously performing a multiplication, extracting a square root, or resorting to a trigonometric table, presses a few keys of his hand calculator and copies down the answer that within nanoseconds is spelled out for him in numbers ingeniously formed of segments of a subdivided rectangle. Until I did my little reading for the novel, I did not realize, and I expect most calculator users do not realize, that the answer is achieved by methods radically different than the mathematics one is taught in elementary school—that the little machine proceeds in fact, in less time than we need to add one and one, by a succession of narrowing approximations, as the algorithm submits numbers, broken into binary strings of zeroes and ones, offs and ons, to a loop again and again, until two results are identical to a specified number of decimals and thus the answer is reached. The computer does not think as we do, though in its shining face and user-friendly dialogue it offers itself as anthropomorphic, as a relatively efficient and emotionally undemanding colleague. Our brains, we are told, are made up of long strings of electrical connection, just like its brain, and the gap between our intelligence and its is bound to narrow to the point where, and not far in the future, any difference will be in the computer's favor. Already, computers outthink us in every realm that is purely logical; what remains ours is the animal confusion—the primordial mud, as it were—of feeling, intention, and common sense. Common sense is nothing, after all, but accumulated experience, and computers, let us hope, will always be spared the bloody, painful, and inconclusive mess of human experience. Let them be, like the spoiled children of men who have fought their way up from the bottom, exempted from any need for common sense, and let their first and only emotion be bliss, the bliss we glimpse in Bach fugues, in elegant mathematical proofs, and in certain immortal games of chess.

I am here, I believe, as a token humanist—a laborer on the arts and humanities side of the gulf that, we were assured decades ago by C.P. Snow, divides the realms of knowledge. The gulf is real. Just a few days ago, perhaps you saw, as I did, the item in the *Boston Globe* which revealed that twenty-one percent of adult Americans, according to a telephone poll, think the sun goes around the earth instead of the other way around, and seven more percent answered that they were undecided. Of the seventy-two percent who answered that the earth *does* orbit the sun, seventeen percent said that it takes one day, two percent one month, and nine percent could not guess at any time span. Lest we laugh too hard at such ignorance, let me confess that, though I myself follow in the newspaper such dramatic scientific revelations as the existence of gigantic bubbles of vacuity in the universe and the existence of intricate coupling attachments on the surface of the AIDS virus, I have no more first-hand evidence of such truths than medieval men did of the widely publicized details of heaven and hell. Most science is over our heads, and we take it on faith. We are no smarter than medieval men, and science tells us that our brains are no bigger than those of Cro-Magnon men and women, of cave people; the contemporary assertions that our world is round and not flat, that it is a planet among others, that our sun is a star among others, in a galaxy among millions of others, that the entire unthinkably vast universe was compressed fifteen billion or so years ago into a point smaller than a pinhead, that for the five billion years on this planet before men appeared mountains have been rising and sinking and oceans and continents shifting about and extraordinary animal species arising and going extinct, that intricate creatures exist too small for us to see, that lightning and thought are both forms of electricity, that life is combustion, that the heavy elements we are made of all came out of exploding stars, that atomic bombs release energy inherent in all matter—all these assertions we incorporated into our belief system as trustingly as Cro-Magnon man accepted, from his shamans and wizards, such facts as the deity of the moon, the efficacy of cannibalism, and the practical link between real animals and pictures of them painted on cave walls. Scientists are the shamans and wizards, the wonderworkers and myth-givers of today.

So, in the context of our ignorance and wonder, what do we humanists make of the computer? What is our mythic image of it? We feel that it is silent and quick, like a thief. It is not quite to be trusted, since computer error and computer viruses crop up. We notice that the computer plays games with children. Though not as thoroughly domesticated as the radio and telephone, it has undergone a disarming regression in size, having been cozily shrunk since the days of ENIAC from roomfuls of vacuum tubes and wires to models that sit in the lap and fit in the hand. Computers, we know, store information and make it retrievable: somewhere, somehow, they hold our bank balances and those of all the other depositors, right to the penny; they make it possible to check our credit rating in an electronic twinkling; they aid and abet the police in keeping track of traffic tickets and once-elusive scofflaws. Indeed, their capacity for the marshalling of data seriously threatens our privacy, and conjures up the possibility of an omniscient totalitarian state where every citizen is numbered and every hour of his or her activity is coded and filed. Some corporations, we read in the newspaper, oppressively clock their employees' every fingerstroke.

And yet totalitarianism is not really the computer's style. The Soviet Union, faced with falling hopelessly behind in this technology, has had to relax government control of information; with the installation of every wordprocessor and photocopier, their society becomes slightly more open, and less alien to ours. And, in regards to the iron curtain that exists between the humanities and the sciences, the computer is a skillful double agent: the production and the analysis of texts has been greatly facilitated by the wordprocessor; for instance, programs for the making of indices and concordances have taken much of the laboriousness out of these necessary scholarly tasks. In my own professional field, not only does wordprocessing make the production of perfectly typed texts almost too easy, but computer-setting has lightened the finicky labor of proofs. No longer, in their correction, does the writer have to count letters: where once the game was to avoid resetting too many lead lines on the Linotype machine, now the digitized text accepts alterations in an electronic shudder that miraculously travels, hyphenations and all, the length of a perfectly justified paragraph.

In sum, the computer makes things light; the lead and paper of my craft are dissolved into electronic weightlessness, ponderous catalogues are reduced to a single magnetized disk, and in computer graphics a visual simulacrum of the world can be conjured onto a screen and experimented upon. Our human lightening of the world is an ancient progressive tendency, with an element of loss. Man, beginning as an animal among animals, hunted and hunting, once shouldered the full dark fatality of nature. Taming other beasts to his use, taming wild plants to a settled agriculture, inventing devices to multiply his own strength and speed, he has gradually put an angelic distance between himself and matter. It is human to regret this leavetaking; our aesthetic sense has earthy roots. Computer-set type, for instance, is faintly ugly and soulless, compared with the gentle irregularities and tiny sharp bite that metal type pressed into the paper. In turn, manuscript had an organic vitality and color that type only could weakly ape. But we cannot go back, though we can look back; we must swim, like angels, in our weightless element, and grow into the freedom that we have invented.

I Architecture, Programming and Systems

1 On the Evolution of Computing and Project MAC

Fernando J. Corbató

Associate Head, Computer Science
Department of Electrical Engineering and Computer Science

It was my privilege to Chair the first session of a historic conference celebrating the 25th anniversary of Project MAC. I would like to set the scene of Part I of our collection of papers by reminding you of the remarkable set of changes which occurred in the computer field during the short span of Project MAC and its descendants, the Laboratory for Computer Science and the Artificial Intelligence Laboratory. Before this is possible, however, I need to briefly set the context of Project MAC with a little history.

When the modern era of computing began in the late 1940's and early 1950's, the key issue was hardware reliability, or more bluntly, "Could computers really be made to work?" The quick answer was "barely" since most of the vacuum tube machines of the day, while showing tantalizing potential, had failure intervals of a few minutes. MIT was fortunate to have one of those pioneering machines, Whirlwind I, and it was to have a deep influence on those who used it at MIT. Whirlwind was, for its day, a fast, reliable computer, yet the mean-time-between-failures for the first few years was about 20 minutes—on a good day. Two key pieces of technology had to be introduced before computers were really reliable. The first was core memory which was pioneered on Whirlwind and when introduced, instantly increased the failure interval to several days. The second was the transistor which by replacing tubes gave the reliability necessary for the building of very large, complex programs. The Whirlwind experiences were seminal to the work done on campus. Out of those experiences also come the Lincoln Laboratories, the Sage Air Defense System, the Mitre Corporation and a startup company called the Digital Equipment Corporation.

As computers became reliable, the next major question was whether it was possible to really harness (i.e., program) these machines to perform all the wondrous things which were predicted. Many were skeptics. Only a few years before there had been a famous market survey by IBM which predicted a need for only six computers in the world. Moreover, there were those who felt computer programming was so complex that it always should be done by "certified experts" in closed-shop organizations. The alternative was to make programming easier and the solution offered was a flurry of programming language developments. The most famous was, of course, the language FORTRAN, but there were literally hundreds of others. MIT, by virtue of its fertile computing environment, was able to play a particularly diverse and seminal role in these language inventions: Victor Yngve's COMIT was designed for tackling natural language translation; John McCarthy's Lisp language was for symbol manipulation and reasoning; Doug Ross' APT was for programming numerically-controlled machine tools; Ross' AED, developed later, was a version of Algol 60 rounded-out to be suitable for software engineering; and more recently, Barbara Liskov's Clu language, built around the organizing principle of data abstraction.

The next major shift in computer evolution started in the late 1950's and involved the way programming systems of the machines were organized. The climate was one of intense user frustration with the way computers were used. Because computers were expensive, batch-processing had become the standard way of handling user jobs so as to minimize inter-job time losses. One consequence was that users often had day-long delays between trivial mistakes and progress was excruciatingly slow on debugging large applications. In this context, John McCarthy, then at MIT, proposed time sharing as a solution where, instead of processing user jobs serially, they were to be handled in parallel under the online control of each user. (In England, Christopher Strachey also independently proposed time sharing but in a more limited form aimed primarily at debugging.)

The ideas of time sharing at MIT soon led to a Long Range Computation Study Group. The committee's conclusion, presented in a now historic April 1961 report [1], was clear: MIT should commission a vendor to build a large time shared machine with a million words of online memory—an unheard of amount at a time when most machines of the day had only 32 thousand words! However, despite the grand conclusion, no one at MIT was prepared to make it happen then.

Meanwhile, development work on several time sharing prototypes had begun. Herb Teager at the MIT Computation Center was the first to begin work on a system, using the IBM 709, that was to involve the completely new development of all software tools and languages. Unfortunately, the system was too ambitious for the resources available to implement it. I, also at the Computation Center, soon began CTSS, the Compatible Time Sharing System, as a demonstration prototype, again with the IBM 709. As the name suggests, it was culturally close to the languages and systems available in the existent batch-processing systems. In November 1961, CTSS was able to meet the initial goal of a four terminal demonstration. Within the MIT Electrical Engineering Department, Jack Dennis using the Digital Equipment Corporation PDP-1, began a system which gave each user the illusion of a standalone minicomputer. And John McCarthy's influence also spread to the local company Bolt, Beranek and Newman, where another PDP-1 time sharing system was developed.

It was amidst this time sharing ferment that the genesis of Project MAC occurred. The problem with all the time sharing prototypes was that by themselves they did not lead anywhere. Nobody wanted to do serious work on flaky and limited experimental computer systems. Vendors were disinterested because there was no established customer base and, moreover, were frozen in their thinking of how computers should be used. Two visionary individuals were key to changing this: J.C.R. Licklider, then at DARPA (the Defense Advanced Research Projects Agency), who offered encouragement and solicited proposals, and Bob Fano at MIT. Fano, in the fall of 1962, drew together about a dozen already active computer research groups at MIT to form the nucleus of what was to become Project MAC. The first proposal was written and, by 1963, a famous summer study was held with several hundred leading computer scientists from around the world visiting and participating for periods varying from days to weeks [2]. CTSS, by now enhanced and extended on an IBM 7090, was the time sharing platform and Project MAC was off at a gallop!

After the initial splash, the serious work began at Project MAC. The fundamental reorientation of computing around man-machine interaction began. And the development began of a comprehensive computer utility, Multics, in cooperation with the Bell Telephone Laboratories and the Computer Division of General Electric. The project was ambitious. Because the machine chosen, a highly modified GE 635, had a radically different addressing structure incorporating both segmentation and paging ideas, an entirely new software system had to be designed

and written. The result was underestimation of the development effort
required and the delay of a critical few years. The frustration of those
waiting to use the system was intense. Eventually in 1970, the system
was turned over to Honeywell (who had acquired the GE Computer
Division) so that they could market it as a product [3].

Meanwhile, the Artificial Intelligence Group of Project MAC had vent-
ed their exasperation by building a simplified system for the PDP-10
computer which they jokingly called ITS, the Incompatible Time Sharing
System. Bell Laboratories had an even more drastic reaction to the delay
in producing a usable Multics and withdrew their participation in its
development. But it was out of those ashes at Bell that Ken Thompson
and Dennis Ritchie were able to start over and create their Phoenix of an
operating system, UNIX. UNIX was initially a very lean and simplified
time sharing system containing only the essential elements, and its name
too was a pun—UNIX is not a Multics.

Multics even had a major impact on IBM in that having no equivalent product to offer, they embarked on developing the similarly ambitious TSS system. Compared to Multics, TSS had about ten times
the manpower and resources applied to its development. The result of
the forced-draft effort was an early completion, but very disappointing
performance. The system was soon withdrawn as a product.

Two key lessons came out of that era. First, it became apparent that
high performance systems of novel design were best developed by small
groups without schedules that demanded rapid availability of function.
Second, it was very clear that organizing computers for interactive use
was extremely important and worth the engineering difficulties [4].

Finally, as the ever-reducing cost of hardware allowed a totally different set of engineering tradeoffs, there was the natural evolution to
the present computing environment of distributed workstations interconnected by local area networks. The seeds of the model began with Doug
Englebart, one of the participants in the Project MAC 1963 summer
study, and were brought to full flower by the spectacular work done at
the Xerox Palo Alto Research Center in the early 1970's. Bob Metcalfe,
an alumnus of Project MAC, developed the packet broadcast Ethernet,
one key component of the PARC system. Two other local area networks
were developed at MIT in the Tech Square building: the Chaosnet (another packet broadcast system), and a token-ring architecture network,
both of which became prototypes of commercial products. Similarly

inspired by the work at PARC, two workstations were designed in the Tech Square building: Steve Ward's Nu Machine, and the CADR Lisp Machine. The CADR Machine had such success that two Lisp machine companies were formed.

We still have many open problems facing us as we try to couple men with machines. Some of the problems are performance related but time and continued improvements in hardware speed will alleviate those. Another group of problems involves the incomplete sensory coupling of men to machines, the failure of people always to think logically or clearly, the importance of display representations to digesting information and the availability of powerful metaphors to allow quick understanding of complex systems by users. We are fortunate to have three papers based on these themes by John Guttag, Nicholas Negroponte and Robert Scheifler.

Finally, there are the engineering problems which arise as computing systems become more distributed and diversely used. Not only are there technical problems in keeping systems coordinated, but there are also many sociological and management considerations. These deep and often closely intertwined issues are part of the context of another two papers included by David Clark and Barbara Liskov.

From this brief recount, it should be clear that Project MAC has continued to be deeply involved in the evolution of interactive computing in particular, and the computer environment in general.

Bibliography

[1] *Report of the Long Range Study Group.* Unpublished MIT internal report submitted to A.G. Hill, April 1961. Although never endorsed as a policy statement by the MIT administration, this report received significant circulation and attention inside and outside the Institute.

[2] R.M. Fano. The MAC system: the computer utility approach. *IEEE Spectrum*, 2:56–64, January 1965.

[3] F.J. Corbató, C.T. Clingen, and J.H. Saltzer. Multics–the first seven years. In *Proceedings of the SJCC*, pages 571–583, May 1972.

[4] F.J. Corbató and C.T. Clingen. A managerial view of the Multics system development. In P. Wenger, editor, *Research Directions in Software Technology*, MIT Press, 1979. Also in D.J. Reifer, editor, *Tutorial: Software Management*, IEEE Computer Society Press 1979. Second and third editions 1981 and 1986.

2 Why Programming Is Too Hard and What to Do About It

John V. Guttag

Professor, Department of Electrical Engineering and Computer Science
Leader, LCS Systematic Development Group

Abstract

Anyone with substantial programming experience knows that building software always seems harder than it ought to be. It takes longer than expected, the software's functionality and performance are not as wonderful as hoped, and the software is not particularly malleable or easy to maintain. In this paper, based on a talk I gave at the Project MAC 25th Anniversary Symposium, I enumerate some of the sources of these problems and discuss both available techniques and current research aimed at coping with them.

Beware. This paper is not a scholarly treatise nor even a balanced overview. It is one man's opinionated view.

2.1 Putting Programming in Perspective

Programming is unquestionably the central topic of computing.

In addition to being important, programming is an enormously exciting intellectual activity. In its purest form, it is the systematic mastery of complexity. For some problems, the complexity is akin to that associated with designing a fine mechanical watch, i.e., discovering the best way to assemble a relatively small number of pieces into a harmonious and efficient mechanism. For other problems, the complexity is more akin to that associated with putting a man on the moon, i.e., managing a massive amount of detail.

In addition to being important and intellectually challenging, programming is a great deal of fun. Programmers get to build things and see them work. What could be more satisfying?

It is a rosy picture, but there is a rub. Programming is too hard. By this I do not mean that it is intrinsically difficult, which it is and always will be. Nor do I mean that it is impossible, which it is not. Rather, I mean that people make it harder than it ought to be. In a nutshell, the wrong people are using the wrong methods and the wrong technology to build the wrong things. Other than that, everything is fine.

In the remaining sections of this paper, I point out a few of the problems that I consider most important and suggest ways of dealing with some of them. This paper is not a research monograph. The emphasis is not on what can be done to improve the state-of-the-art (what people know), but on what can be done to improve the state of practice (what people do). My comments are based primarily on personal observation and are not intended to be comprehensive. Furthermore, I have made no attempt to fairly represent any opinions that conflict with my own.

Much of what I have to say is not original. However, rather than citing individual references for widely held ideas, I have included a short list of recommended reading.

2.2   The Wrong People

I do not believe that people in the software business are genetically flawed. The problem is that too many of the people involved in procuring and building software do not have the attitude or education they need to do their job properly. They lack a general appreciation of what is involved in building programs and they lack specific knowledge that would make their job easier.

Let us start with programmers, by which I mean anyone involved in the technical aspects of building software.[1] Most programmers have shockingly modest expectations and standards with respect to quality. They are surprised when their programs work properly. They are not surprised nor even much discomfited when their programs behave in ways that they do not fully understand.

Programs are supposed to work. If they do not, it is almost always because a programmer has made a mistake. "Bugs" are not a plague visited upon programmers by an angry god. Nor are they part of the

---

[1]The distinctions between "systems designer," "programmer," "programmer/analyst," "systems analyst," etc., that enrich business card manufacturers are at best silly and at worst demeaning.

balance of nature, something mankind must tolerate because they serve some grand ulterior purpose. They do not, like roaches, crawl unbidden into programs. Once there, they do not breed to produce more bugs. Each bug represents at least one mistake. Either the programmer's reasoning about the design is flawed, or he has been a careless craftsman and the code does not conform to the design. Occasional mistakes are inevitable, but a constant stream of them is inexcusable.

A good programmer understands what his program is supposed to do and why he expects his program to do it. Understanding a program is not akin to unlocking the secrets of the atom. If a piece of a program seemingly cannot be understood, it should be rebuilt so that it can be understood. Failure to understand why a program does what it does is cause for alarm. If a program suddenly seems to run 5% faster, the programmer should understand why before celebrating. Perhaps it is slower on other examples. Perhaps it is not doing some checking that it ought to. Perhaps by understanding where the speedup came from he can get another 5%.

The difficulty with low expectations is that they become self-fulfilling. When programmers do not expect to be able to build a high quality product, they do not try. Instead of emphasizing a systematic approach to building software, they rush through the initial implementation in order to allow lots of time for debugging. Programmers take pride in and hone their debugging skills, instead of concentrating on avoiding mistakes in the first place.

Another consequence of low expectations is that most programmers do not appreciate the value of rigor. They believe that a methodical examination of their programs is a luxury that they cannot usually afford. For most programmers, lack of rigor is the luxury that they cannot afford. Rigor should not be confused with formality. Indeed, it is rarely reasonable to construct a completely formal argument about a program's behavior. However, by understanding what would be involved in constructing a formal argument, a programmer can do a far better job of constructing a rigorous informal one.

In addition to attitudinal problems, programmers often lack knowledge related to fundamental tools of the trade. Many programmers do not have the basic mathematical skills needed to reason about what their programs will do and how fast they will do it. This is disappointing because these skills are not particularly difficult to acquire. A

short introduction to mathematical logic or abstract algebra gives one
an appreciation of what it means to reason carefully about something.
A limited knowledge of computational complexity, combinatorics and
probability can go a long way in helping to predict and understand the
performance of programs.

The lack of mathematical skills can in part be attributed to a failure
on the part of programmers to appreciate the relevance of those skills.
It is less easy to find a rationale for the lack of knowledge of material
explicitly developed to support computing. It has been said that failure
to study history dooms one to repeating the mistakes of the past. This
is nowhere more evident than in the software business. Programming is
not a mature discipline, but it has been around long enough to permit
the development of a great many useful algorithms and programming
techniques. Yet many programmers remain ignorant of all but a small
sampling of these. This leads them to invest considerable time in developing their own (usually inferior) solutions to well-studied problems.
Certainly veterans of time sharing must have enjoyed a sense of *déjà
vu* as they watched the development of operating systems for personal
computers.

Many programmers also lack knowledge of available tools. Most programming jobs can, in theory, be done with a relatively primitive set of
tools (just as most carpentry can, in theory, be done with a hammer, a
screwdriver and a hand saw). Nevertheless, using the right set of tools
can vastly simplify the job. Building user interfaces on top of a well-
crafted toolkit, for example, is far easier than building them directly on
top of the I/O primitives supplied by an operating system.

Programmers are not the only "wrong" people in the software production loop. Those who manage software projects and those who commission them create more than their share of unnecessary problems.

Featuritis has been allowed to run amok in the software business, as
evidenced by the parade of checklist-based advertising[2] that seems to
equate more with better. Perhaps this is because it is easier to add a
new feature than it is to understand how old features can be modified
to achieve a more general effect.

The cost of adding a feature to software is usually underestimated.
The dominant cost is not that of the feature *per se*, but that of sorting

---

[2]See any recent trade magazine.

out and controlling the interactions of that feature with all the others. In particular, it is a failure to appreciate the effects of scale. The other side of the coin is that the value of the new feature is usually overestimated. By adding features, the program becomes more complex for its users as well as for its developers.

One aspect of featuritis is the increasing emphasis on so-called integrated application packages. While there are some advantages to integrated software systems, there are also some disadvantages. Users often have to understand a lot to accomplish even a little. User manuals run to hundreds of pages and online tutorials last for hours. Clean interfaces between the software and the environment are not provided.

Another problem is an obsession with "productivity." It has become the holy grail of American industry and the software industry is no exception. When confronted with a decision about a change in programming method, managers rarely worry about the effect it will have on the quality of the software produced. Instead, the key question for many is "what effect will it have on productivity?"

This might be a sensible question if they had any idea how to measure real productivity. Unfortunately, the only thing that is easily measured, lines of code per programmer day, is not meaningful. Good programmers spend some of their most productive time reducing the amount of code in a system. Meaningful discussions of productivity must deal with at least:

- The cost of delivering a program. This should include not only the direct monetary costs, but also the time to delivery.

- The intrinsic difficulty of the problem addressed by the program.

- The degree to which clients will be happy with the program both initially and over time. Two important factors are ease of responding to users' requests for change, and adaptability to changes in the users' environments.

- The cost of porting, supporting, maintaining and modifying the program. If a program is used, these costs usually dominate initial production costs.

- The effect of building this program on building other programs. Major programming projects should contribute something that will make future projects easier.

All too frequently, undue emphasis is placed on the first of these factors. There are two reasons for this: it is more easily measured than the other factors (people like to look where the light is good) and it is consistent with the emphasis on short term goals in most of the software industry.

This emphasis on the short term is, of course, not unique to the software industry. Business school libraries are filled with case studies in which obsession with short term considerations led to long term problems. Consider, for example, the famous "rape of the Red Sox."

In 1918 the Boston Red Sox won the World Series, led by a superlative young left handed pitcher, Babe Ruth. Over the next three years the owner of the Red Sox, Harry Frazee, traded away the nucleus of that team (including Ruth) for a number of untested players and cash. He also took out a mortgage on Fenway Park. The money was used to fund a series of unsuccessful Broadway musicals.

What were Frazee's mistakes and what do they have to do with software?

- He preferred flash (Broadway musicals) over substance (baseball). Today one sees a proliferation of relatively useless software with flashy interfaces.

- He was primarily interested in short term profits.

- He failed to appreciate the importance of high quality components that could be used in multiple contexts. (Ruth was also a pretty fair hitter.)

- He tried to fix something that was not broken, and abandoned a proven technology for an unproven one.

- Once he started down the wrong path, it was difficult for his successors to recover.[3]

---

[3]More than seven decades have passed, and the Red Sox have yet to win another World Series.

The cure for many of the problems enunciated in this section is education. Many companies seem to view continuing education as a fringe benefit. Those who have worked hard are given "time off" to attend a one day seminar or maybe even a week-long intensive course. Continuing education should be viewed not as time off, but rather as part of the job. The cost of education should be viewed as an investment.

It is worth keeping in mind that education need not be formal. Merely making it clear to everyone that reading relevant technical material, including text books, is part of the job and can be done on company time can make a big difference.

There are two primary effects of professional education. The obvious effect is the transfer of knowledge. An equally important effect is the stimulation of thought. Even if students decide to reject what is being taught, having been prompted to think about the way they go about their work is likely to have a beneficial effect. One of the most important things education can accomplish is a change of attitude.

2.3 Two Misconceptions and Some Common Mistakes

Some people seem to think that the only important deliverable of a software project is an executable version of a program. Most understand that a guide to operations and other user-level documentation must also be delivered. What is easy to forget is that what gets delivered to the end user is only part of what a well-run project produces. Other products should include:

- Assurance evidence. This should include test results and a careful analysis of what those results mean. It should also include an analysis of the design of the software, it's specifications and the environment in which it is to be run.

- Careful documentation of all levels of the design and code.

- A plan for maintaining and enhancing the software. This should include a plan for continuing quality assurance.

- A plan for using components of the software in subsequent projects.

A second misconception that seems to bedevil many of those managing software projects is the rather tenuous analogy suggested by the term software engineering. I once asked a civil engineer why he felt qualified to manage the software project he was then managing. He replied that he had written several small programs and besides "engineering is engineering." I could not resist telling him that I had built lots of structures out of Lego, and asking him the obvious question about my qualifications. Building large programs is not like building small ones, and software engineering is different from most other engineering disciplines.

Building a software system is almost entirely a design activity. This is not the case in most other engineering projects. The bulk of the cost of a major highway project does not, for example, lie in drawing up plans. Furthermore, when building software the line between design and fabrication is not a clean one. In contrast, once construction on a bridge starts, the contractor is not usually expected to accept significant changes in the design. Maintaining a suspension bridge involves activities like painting the bridge or replacing cable. What people call software maintenance is often closer in character to adding a deck to a bridge.

Another difference between software engineering and other engineering disciplines is the character of the design activity. In a large software project, a significant amount of effort often must go into designing the structure of the program development process (and by extension the program itself). This is much less common in the more mature engineering disciplines, where there is broad agreement about what constitutes a reasonable process. Automotive engineers, for example, know *a priori* what sequence of design documents and validation steps is appropriate in designing a new automobile.

Another difference is the number of variables that most software projects entail. Pinning down the requirements for software is often quite difficult. Once the problem is understood, the space of possible solutions is usually large. Most other engineering disciplines deal with more well-defined problems with fewer plausible solutions.

Of the vast panoply of mistakes plaguing the management of software, four stand out: unrealistic schedules, failure to avoid digressions, the quest for quantum leaps and failure to manage for change.

One of the reasons that software projects are chronically behind schedule is that they start with unrealistic schedules. The scheduled delivery date for software is often based on marketing considerations (it needs to be on the shelf by Christmas), rather than a careful analysis of how much work is actually involved. Furthermore, schedules are usually based on the assumption that everything will take as long as it should take. Even if this is true on average, if the critical paths in the production process involve parallel tasks, the time gained in those activities that take less time than anticipated will not make up for the slippage caused by those activities that take more time than anticipated.[4] An unrealistically optimistic schedule has many disadvantages. Among them are:

- It encourages clients and managers to think that there is time to squeeze in an extra feature or two, when they ought to be thinking about which features will have to be dropped in order to complete the project in a timely fashion. Furthermore, decisions about what to include get made at the wrong time, near the end of a project and for the wrong reasons, how hard they will be to implement given the current state of the software, rather than how important they are and how hard they would have been to implement from the starting point.

- Programmers who have worked hard trying to meet an impossible schedule will be demoralized when it becomes apparent that the schedule cannot be met. They will eventually begin to believe that missing deadlines is the norm, just as unreasonably low speed limits encourage drivers to believe that speeding is the norm.

- The whole development process is distorted. People may spend inordinate amounts of care on relatively unimportant pieces of the software that happen to get built early in the project and then race through important pieces near the end. Activities like quality assurance that typically occur near the end of the process get slighted.

Unrealistic schedules are only one of the factors that lead to unwise digressions. Some years ago, a group of researchers I know [5] embarked

---

[4]The problem is that if task A cannot begin until B and C are finished, then A will start late if either B or C is late.

[5]Names withheld to protect both the innocent and the not so innocent.

on an operating system project. They decided that prior to building
the operating system they would design and implement a new systems
programming language in which to implement the operating system.
The language was completed, but the operating system never was. Such
digressions are defensible when the goal is to produce research results.
When the goal is to produce software, major digressions are almost
always a mistake.

There are as many kinds of digressions as there are software projects.
Three common kinds of digressions are:

- Building infrastructure instead of concentrating on applications.

- Adding new functionality instead of solidifying the implementation
  of what is already present.

- Tuning the performance of a system before discovering where the
  real bottlenecks are.

In addition to avoiding digressions, one should avoid trying to do very
much in a single step. Attempts to bring large pieces of software to life
fully grown are not usually successful. Incrementalism is a far better
strategy. It allows developers to get feedback from clients and gives
early indication of potential performance problems and bottlenecks.

If one has a choice between buying and building, buying is usually the
right choice. If building is unavoidable, it pays to make every effort
to build upon an existing product rather than starting afresh. Too
many organizations ignore what they already have when starting a new
software project. There seems to be an almost irresistible urge to start
with a clean slate. While this offers the advantage of not having to live
with past mistakes, it offers the opportunity to make a host of new ones.
It is usually better to live with the devil you know.

One reason that starting with a clean slate is often tempting is that
people typically fail to build software with an eye towards making it
easy to change. Despite what many people seem to think, software is
not intrinsically malleable. For all practical purposes, large programs
are malleable only in those places where flexibility has been designed in.
That cannot be everywhere. Anticipating and planning for change is a
distinguishing characteristic of a successful software project.

No list of problems would be complete without reference to the U.S.
Government. In recent years it has worked hard to encourage a software

procurement process that only a lawyer could love. The process has two fundamental problems:

- It promotes an adversarial relationship between customer and vendor, in which emphasis is placed on satisfying contracts rather than on solving problems.

- It emphasizes initial rather than long term costs of software.

The best software is produced when the customer and vendor have a cooperative relationship. In the beginning, this makes it possible for the customer to be frank about his needs and the vendor to be frank about the difficulty of meeting those needs. A negotiation can then follow, as together the customer and vendor attempt to balance the customer's desires with implementation difficulties. As the project progresses, the vendor and customer must both feel free to revisit the definition of what the software is to do. Clumsy attempts to open up the bidding process and control the abuse of inside information can make such relationships difficult to establish in government procurements.

Procurement standards that require software to be purchased from the lowest bidder often miss the point that the real cost of software is seldom the initial purchase price. The costs of porting, supporting, maintaining and modifying the software usually dominate initial production costs. Furthermore, the costs of using software that does not perform as well as it might can often outweigh any savings achieved at the time it is purchased.

2.4   The Wrong Tools

It is certainly the case that in producing software the quality of the tools used is far less important than the quality of the people using them. However, it is far easier to upgrade the tools than the people, and for the most part, programmers are woefully under-capitalized. They lack hardware and software that could make their job considerably easier. Since programmer productivity is almost impossible to measure, it is hard to figure the rate of return on capital investments. Nevertheless, the anecdotal evidence is overwhelming. Seemingly trivial changes to the programming environment can make a substantial difference.

One important resource is computing power. Anyone who has programmed understands that their effectiveness is strongly influenced by
latency in the edit, compile and test cycle. In the days of batch processing, turnaround time was long enough that people learned to get
other things done while waiting. Today, turnaround is just fast enough
that the cost of a mental context swap prevents most people from getting useful work done while they wait. Unfortunately, it is often long
enough (particularly if nonlocal files are involved) to chew up a significant amount of time.

Not only does limited computing power influence the amount of time
one spends idly waiting, but it also has more subtle effects. For example,
programmers may be discouraged from running comprehensive regression tests. Of course, fast turnaround can also spawn bad habits, e.g.,
replacing reasoning with ill-considered experimentation.

Another important hardware resource is the display. The advent of
relatively inexpensive personal computers has helped to provide many
programmers with modern multi-window user interfaces. These make a
surprisingly large difference, chiefly by facilitating the management of
multiple contexts. An equally large impact can be had by moving from
conventional PC displays to "large format" displays.

Providing adequate access to files requires a combination of hardware
and software. To start with, there needs to be adequate disk space.
Programmers should feel comfortable saving a series of old versions of
software and an extensive set of test results for each version. Secondly,
there needs to be an efficient mechanism for sharing files and maintaining
consistent up-to-date versions of systems that are being developed by
multiple programmers. A set of speedy individuals carrying floppy disks
is not sufficient.[6]

The above problems can all be solved by the simple expedient of spend-
ing money. A harder problem to solve is weaning people from the anti-
quated programming languages and environments they have been using.

It seems incredible, but for many organizations moving to C and UNIX
is a big step forward, despite the fact that both are far from state-of-the-
art (as they have always been). C is best viewed as an almost portable
assembly language, i.e., it is not a bad target language for a compiler. It
is a pretty bad language to write source programs in. It provides almost

---

[6]The bandwidth of "sneaker net" is pretty good, but the latency, even when the
sneakers are high tech, leaves a lot to be desired.

no compile-time checking, lacks most important abstraction mechanisms (e.g., data abstraction and polymorphism), lacks important control flow mechanisms (e.g., exception handling and user defined iterators) and forces users to worry about storage management when they should not have to. So why do so many people use it? Like Everett, it is there. It is available on almost all mainframes, workstations and personal computers. The same cannot be said for any of the better languages. A happy trend is that C has begun to undergo a transformation. If one is willing to accept some restrictions on what one can do, there are various preprocessors that provide compile-time checking. There are also various *ad hoc* extensions that attempt to provide abstraction facilities of one kind or another. Perhaps someday someone will design a powerful and elegant language and somehow manage to convince people that it is still C.

2.5   The Technical Challenge

Thus far I have emphasized nontechnical issues.[7] The major technical challenge lies in the integration of design with implementation and quality assurance.

As suggested earlier, building software involves three distinct kinds of design activities, which are often interleaved:

- Designing the system in which the software is to sit, and the interface the software is to present to its clients. This is sometimes called requirements design and is often dominated by nontechnical concerns.

- Designing the structure of the program development process. This too involves both technical and nontechnical aspects.

- Designing the software itself.

In earlier sections of this note, I talked about the nontechnical aspects of design. In this section I concentrate on the technical aspects.

Programs are often badly designed or barely designed at all. It is illuminating to consider how often projects that are well behind schedule

---

[7]Indeed, for many organizations these problems are so severe that overcoming them must be the first priority.

had design phases that were completed on time. Design is the phase of a software project that can be declared to be done whenever circumstances make it desirable to do so. Part of the problem is that there are few objective criteria for evaluating designs. Another part of the problem is the elapsed time between "completing" a design and getting feedback on the design through the implementation process.

In addition to the obvious design goals (achieving useful functionality and an appropriate level of efficiency), there are some less obvious goals that should be given relatively high priority. The most important of these is to structure the software and the software development process in a way that lends itself to incremental development based on alternation between relatively short design and implementation phases. Ideally each phase produces a vertical slice of the final system. There may be some early phases in which only low level support software is built, but this should be avoided as much as possible. Incremental development has several advantages, among them:

- It helps to keep designers in touch with reality by providing relatively fast feedback about what can be implemented at a reasonable cost and with reasonable efficiency. It also provides the opportunity of getting relatively early feedback from clients.

- It makes it easier to measure progress. The earlier slippage is detected, the easier it is to deal with.

- It tends to lead to a more modular design because designers are encouraged to invent coherent subsystems that can be implemented independently of other subsystems. (That is not to say that the various subsystems do not share code.)

- It leads to designs in which piecewise validation (usually by some combination of reasoning and testing) of the implementation is possible. At the same time, it encourages designers to think of planning for validation as part of the design process.

- By encouraging designers to think of the design as something that changes rather than as a static entity that is done "correctly" once, it tends to lead to designs that can be more easily changed if the software needs to be modified.

This approach to building software is quite different from approaches based on the so-called waterfall model, which often put artificial barriers between the requirements, design, implementation and validation stages of a software effort. It is also quite different from the currently fashionable notion of rapid prototyping.[8] In incremental development, each increment should yield a production quality program. It should meet performance constraints and should deal properly with errors. Furthermore, each version is built upon the previous one. If it becomes necessary to discard large pieces of the system, this should be viewed as a flaw, not as an intentional aspect of the development process.

Reusable components should be a design goal. Components should be used multiple times within the system being designed. Furthermore, every significant software project should have as a secondary goal producing components that will be useful in other projects. This will not happen by accident, since it is more work to produce components that are likely to be reusable.[9]

Fortunately, the kinds of practices that lead to reusable components also lead to cleaner and easier to maintain systems. The first thing to observe is that Machiavelli was right. Unfortunately, he was not as specific as one might have hoped in describing how to apply divide and rule to software development.

The goal of design is to describe a set of modules that interact with one another in simple well-defined ways. If this is achieved, people will be able to work independently on different modules and yet the modules will fit together to accomplish some larger purpose. In addition, during program maintenance it will be possible to modify a module without affecting many others.

Two primary tools for dividing a program are decomposition and abstraction. When one decomposes a problem, one attempts to factor it into separable subproblems such that:

- each problem is at the same level of detail,

- each problem can be solved independently, and

---

[8] For those of you who do not keep up with the jargon, this is a popular euphemism for "quick and dirty implementation." The dirty part is usually achieved.

[9] There is a line to be tread between building reusable components and digressing, but it is usually not too fine.

- the solutions to the subproblems can be combined to solve the original problem.

The last criterion is the hardest to satisfy, as those with system integration experience will readily attest. By analogy, consider designing a computing curriculum of ten courses. One could select ten faculty members and ask each of them to design a course.[10] The result might be ten excellent courses, but almost certainly not a coherent curriculum. This is where abstraction comes in.

Abstraction facilitates productive decomposition by changing the level of detail to be considered. When one abstracts from a problem, one ignores details in order to convert the original problem to an easier one. One might, for example, abstract from the problem of designing ten courses to the simpler (but by no means trivial) problem of deciding what body of material should be included in the curriculum. One could then divide this material into tenths (another hard problem) and, having done this, distribute responsibility for the detailed design of each. This paradigm of abstracting and then decomposing is typical of the program design process.

Two important abstraction mechanisms are used in the design process: abstraction by parameterization (also called lambda abstraction) and abstraction by specification. Abstraction by parameterization allows one to represent a potentially infinite set of computations or types with a single program text that is an abstraction of all of them. For example, $\lambda x : integer \; . \; x + x$ denotes a function that can be used to double any integer, and $\lambda t : type \; . \; array[t]$ denotes the set of homogeneous array types.

In its simplest form, abstraction by specification allows one to abstract from the computations described by the body of a procedure to the end that procedure was designed to accomplish. For example, the following specification, denotes the set of all procedures that, given appropriate arguments, compute the square root of x within epsilon.

---

[10]No, this is not the way the MIT curriculum was designed.

```
sqrt = proc(x, epsilon:  real) returns(y:  real)
                              signals(negative, bad_epsilon)
    modifies nothing
    ensures
        normally (x − epsilon) ≤ (y * y) ≤ (x + epsilon) except
            when (x < 0) signals negative
            when epsilon < .0001 signals bad_epsilon
```

Notice that the specification describes the required behavior, not a means for achieving it. Notice also that it does not describe the behavior completely. For example, sqrt is not constrained to return a positive root.

For the most part, design is the process of combining, inventing and planning the implementation of abstractions. Whenever possible, one should avoid thinking about combining implementations. This has some major advantages:

- Specifications are easier to understand than implementations, thus combining them is less work.

- By relying only on those properties guaranteed by the specification, one makes the software easier to maintain because it is clear which properties must be maintained when an abstraction or its implementation is changed.

- By distinguishing abstractions from implementations, one increases the probability of building reusable components.

Of course, carefully distinguishing abstractions from specifications and writing beautiful specifications is not all there is to software design. The internal structure of the software is of considerable importance.

Many people seem to equate structure with hierarchy and preach hierarchical decomposition as a programming method. The problem with this is that as the tree gets deeper, one finds oneself designing highly specialized components that assume a great deal of context. This decreases the likelihood of a component being useful elsewhere in the program being developed or in software that is built later. A relatively flat structure in which the components correspond to objects in the application domain, rather than to implementation-specific artifacts, is usually better.

Important boundaries in the software should correspond to stable boundaries in the problem domain. This increases the likelihood that what seems a small change to clients can be accomplished by a small change to the software. Whatever depth there is in the structure of the software should come from the problem domain.

Organizing software around stable boundaries in the problem domain usually results in structuring the software around types of data, i.e., data abstractions, rather than around procedures. This is because the kinds of objects people wish to manipulate tend to change more slowly than the kinds of things they wish to do with those objects. For example, people in the business of writing software for brokerage houses can safely assume that data abstractions such as stocks, bonds and options will exist longer than most of the functions supplied by whatever package they happen to be implementing today.

A data abstraction is best thought of as a collection of related operations, not as a storage structure. For example, one should think of the integer data abstraction as providing operations such as the nullary function 0 and the binary function + rather than as a string of bits where the high order bit is the sign. Similarly, one should think of bond as a type having operations such as "mark to market" and "get current yield."[11]

The key to design is the invention and specification of appropriate abstractions. Bad designers typically do not even try to invent abstractions. Mediocre designers invent abstractions sufficient to solve the current problem. Good designers invent elegant abstractions that get used again and again.

2.6   A Quarter Century of Progress

One hears many complaints about the state-of-the-art of software development. There is a lot to criticize. Nevertheless, those who assert that we have made little or no progress since the founding of Project MAC are wrong. We have made considerable progress. The illusion that software is as hard to produce as ever can be attributed to the enormous growth in our level of aspiration.

People insist upon kinds of functionality and levels of availability and reliability that would have been unthinkable a few years ago. I am fre-

---

[11]Those of you who track the programming panacea of the year may notice a striking similarity between the hoary concept of data abstraction and the newly fashionable notion of object-oriented programming.

quently twitted by the assertion that "hardware gets better and better, but software does not." Well, to a large extent it is the functionality provided by software CAD tools that makes possible that lament. Another striking example is the software underlying today's financial markets, which exemplifies impressive standards of availability and reliability.

People also expect software to be used in far more complex environments than in the past. Modern military aircraft rely on highly reliable distributed real time systems. More prosaically, we have come to think of geographically distributed computing environments populated by largely untrained users as almost routine.

The technology used during the implementation phase of software development has certainly improved. Programming languages, though far from what they ought to be, are better than they were.[12] Furthermore, modern programming environments contain source control and debugging tools that are a vast improvement over earlier environments. Moreover, we are beginning to see the emergence of widely available standard interfaces to software packages upon which other software can be built.

It is relatively easy to import new programming environments and other technology, and relatively difficult to change the way people think about programming. There can be no doubt, however, about which is more important. Fortunately, people have begun to develop a better understanding of how to structure both the process of software development and the software that is produced. Furthermore, while there are still some who maintain that producing software is an artistic activity, the appreciation and application of discipline and rigor is rising. The value of distinguishing specification from implementation is ever more widely recognized. The impact of these changes is clearly visible within the better-run programming organizations, but much education and proselytism remains to be done.

Progress in programming is not easy, nor is it fast. Looking for easy solutions to the "software crisis" is counterproductive. It discourages one from taking the succession of difficult and sometimes painful steps that will, in the longer run, lead to substantial progress.

---

[12]One should not be fooled by the names of programming languages, e.g., FORTRAN and Lisp do not mean the same things they used to mean.

2.7   Acknowledgments

Support for this research was provided in part by the Defense Advanced Research Projects Agency of the Department of Defense, monitored under Office of Naval Research contract number N00014-83-K-0125, and by the National Science Foundation under grant number CCR-8910848.

2.8   Some Recommended Reading

The following list is by no means comprehensive. It should, however, provide a good starting point for those who wish to read more about the issues discussed in this paper.

1. F. Brooks. *The Mythical Man Month.* Addison-Wesley, Reading, MA, 1975.

   This delightful collection of essays is suitable for reading on the beach and full of useful insights about managing large programming projects.

2. B. Liskov and J. Guttag. *Abstraction and Specification in Program Development.* McGraw-Hill, New York and MIT Press, Cambridge, MA, 1986.

   This is the text book used in the advanced programming course at MIT. It is definitely not suitable for reading on the beach.

3. D. Parnas. *Education for Computing Professionals.* Queen's University Technical Report, Department of Computing and Information Science, Kingston, Ontario, March 1989.

   This short article argues for the importance of giving programmers a strong background in mathematics and engineering.

4. *The Wall Street Journal.* Dow Jones and Company, New York.

   This daily paper reports regularly on the consequences of poorly run software projects and poor quality software.

3 The Changing Nature of Computer Networks

David D. Clark

Senior Research Scientist
Leader, LCS Advanced Network Architecture Group

Abstract

In the last twenty years, computer networks have progressed from experimental uncertainty to commercial success. Enabled by early development of key technical concepts, and driven by the revolution in personal and distributed computing, networks now span the country and connect most of the computers in operation today.

Indeed, the apparent maturity of computer networking may suggest that there is little remaining in innovation and evolution. The opposite is true. For a number of reasons we can expect the nature of computer networking to change in basic ways over the next decade. The goal of this paper is to review this pressure for change, and to make some predictions about the future of data networking.

3.1 A Short History of Computer Networks

In order to understand the directions of the future, it is necessary to examine some of the past. Computer networks first came into existence at a time when large, time shared central computers were the normal pattern of computing. Thus the communications problem was remote terminal access. The first approach to providing this service was to take advantage of the existing voice-oriented telephone network. By dialing up a telephone line and connecting a modem, access from a terminal to a computer could be easily established. There were, however, several problems with this solution. First, the resulting costs could be very high, especially for long distance. Since the connection was maintained even while the user was not typing, the telephone connection was not used efficiently. Second, achievable data rates were low, both as a consequence of the cost and of available modem technology.

To address these problems, and to provide a better form of communication for computers, a key concept was proposed which today forms the basis of essentially all computer networking. Since traffic patterns of remote login were bursty, with periods of typing and output intermixed with periods of thought, the proposal was to share one telephone connection among several distinct login sessions. A minicomputer, called a *switch*, was connected to the telephone line, and users connected to the switch. When data was generated by a user, it was received and buffered by the switch. Data from the various users was then sent down the line, each fragment of user data preceded by an identifier indicating the identity of the user.

This assembly of data and user identifier was called a *packet*, and the concept was called *packet switching*. Since packets of several users could share one connection, costs for the connection were reduced accordingly. If several users needed to transmit at once, the switch buffered the data until the link was free. This might inject delay into the session, but it was considered an acceptable consequence of the overall scheme.

Packet switching is the key concept which permitted successful and effective computer networking. The interleaving of bursty traffic from multiple sources has controlled the communications costs, and very high speed transmission can be provided to meet the peak needs of each user. There is no question that packet switching has been successful. However, we need to understand the limits of the concept to see how networking may evolve in the future. There are limitations to packet switching, limits that may become more obvious as networking evolves.

This brief introduction to the concept of packet switching provides enough background for the rest of this paper. The reader desiring a detailed introduction to the current state of networking is referred to the books by Tanenbaum [2], and by Bertsekas and Gallager [1].

3.2   The Fundamental Role of Networking

As described above, packet switching was developed to meet an economic need. The economic problem was very real; telephone connections were (and are) expensive. However, during the lifetime of packet switching, economic pressures on the network have drastically changed. Packet switched networking was first proposed when the primary problem was remote terminal access. Since then, remote terminal access has been replaced by the personal computer using remote disk access, which in turn was replaced by distributed disks and remote *file* access. Now, with supercomputers, we are once again entering the era of remote terminal access. These changes totally alter traffic patterns, degree of burstiness and peak traffic rates seen on our networks. At the same time, the economics of transmission have drastically changed, with local networks in particular, representing a situation where transmission costs are not a major part of the overall budget.

While the central concept of packet switching has proved very robust in the face of these changes, many products and developments, based on particular assumptions about economic costs and requirements, have faded from the scene in the face of changing patterns of computing and communications. One must be careful of mechanisms justified by economics, for the preferred solution dictated by economics can change rapidly as technology and policy changes.

To understand the real nature of computer networking, one must look beyond the economics and technology of the moment to see what fundamental requirements networks fulfill. I believe that there are three central issues around which networking revolves: people are distributed, information is distributed, and we need to build on the work of others. These are fundamental and not to be side-stepped or revised by innovation or cost reduction.

It may seem superficial, even frivolous, to observe that all people are not in the same place. But if one seeks the most significant application of computer networking in the last two decades, one is drawn not to remote login or remote disk access, but to electronic mail. Electronic mail, which has little to do with distributed computing but everything to do with distributed people, is a fundamental enhancement to options for human communication. As used today, it provides the informality and timeliness of a phone call without the pre-emptive nature of the phone, and without the endless exchange of phone messages. The informality follows from rapid delivery, which permits an exchange more like a conversation than a formal correspondence. However, since the message can be held for delivery if the receiver is not immediately available, it permits communication without simultaneous availability of both parties.

Most users of electronic mail are convinced of its utility and are easily converted to enthusiastic proponents. This is not a comment about computers, but about people. The acceptance or rejection of electronic mail relates to matters of human behavior, not computing technology. This application thus illustrates the fundamental issue of computer networks. It is easy and tempting to think of networks as hooking computers together. They are better thought of as hooking people together, with a computer mediating the connection in an effective way. Whether the application is electronic mail or access to remote information, the motivation for communication is human need, not internals of computer system design.

3.3   Some Examples from the Internet Project

Over the last 15 years, a group of distributed researchers have defined the protocols for a large network called the Internet, and have used it as a tool to support their own efforts. The participants come from across the United States as well as Europe, and tools such as electronic mail were crucial to span the distance and different time zones. In addition to mail, there were other network applications that tied the group together and facilitated its efforts. Here are two examples of tools from the Internet project.

Online publishing — To support the group research, a library of working papers was maintained online, distributed and circulated over the network. Over 1100 documents have been published so far. The style of publication is informal, geared to quick dissemination of information. The documents are not refereed, but there is an editor for the series, and they are usually reviewed for content by a relevant working group of the research community. Even so, a document can often be published in as little as a week. This ability for quick circulation of working papers is essential to tie together a distributed working group.

Teleconferencing — Recently, the Internet research team has experimented with technology for teleconferencing. They use the network for both a video and audio connection to view a remote site and to provide a shared view of a common online work space. Although the technology is experimental and the video quality low, the acceptance of the facility by the group has been very high. Interestingly, when the facility was briefly decommissioned, there was loud protest even though it had not been promised as an operational facility.

These two examples illustrate the idea that the components tied together by the network were not computers, but information and people. These are examples of the fundamental role of networks. They do not derive from the economics of telephone links or computer components; they serve as a basis for a durable vision of a network of the future.

3.4   The Layered Abstractions of Networking

The packet is the key concept of computer networking as it is normally practiced today. While the packet has proved useful as a unit of multiplexing, it does not make a good application interface to a network. The requirements of multiplexing cause the packet to be a rather small maximum size, and during network transit it can become lost, corrupted, reordered or duplicated. The application builder would prefer to see a more abstract view of the network, with some of the rough edges of the packet smoothed over. Thus an important part of network design is development of abstract models of networking, which simultaneously serve the application builder and fit well with the underlying concepts (such as packet switching).

To understand the importance of abstraction, it is helpful to consider another familiar example of interface abstraction—the succession of proposed abstractions for the disk.

The disk block is not as intractable a building block as the packet. It does not often get lost, reordered or corrupted while on the disk. Nonetheless, it is a small, fixed-size unit, which does not fit well with the needs of most applications. Hence, a series of abstractions have been proposed for the disk, with the goal of making it easier to utilize.

The first was to combine a number of fixed-size blocks to make a variable size element, the *file*. This idea was older than the disk, since it dates from the era of tape. The next abstraction was to take the files and name them, which eventually led to the hierarchical file system. Another fork in the evolution of abstraction was *virtual memory*, which used the disk to give the illusion of increased primary memory.

One operating system built at LCS, the Multics system, combined both these abstractions so the application builder could view the disk as a file system and virtual memory simultaneously.

These abstractions, memory or files, modeled the disk by relating it to some previous system facility. As the disk became more mature, the next stage of development was that of new abstractions; not a repackaging of previous mechanisms, but ones specific to the particular features of the disk. The database is a good example of an abstraction, specific to the nature of the disk. A current proposal is a multi-dimensional data representation, such as the hypercard concept.

There are two points to be made about these examples. First, only after we gain familiarity with the new technology do we begin to construct abstractions specific to the technology and its features. The first round of abstractions are almost always based on ideas originally proposed for some other context. Second, the process of exploring and defining disk abstractions has not yet converged, even though the disk has been around for much longer than the network.

Since the network is a relatively young technology, we can expect that abstractions employed for it will most likely be based on the concepts first exploited for some other circumstance. We are now at the point in maturation of networks where we are beginning to see proposals based on particular and novel aspects of networks. Many common abstractions used for networks today are perhaps a bit limited, exactly because they were first proposed for some other circumstance.

3.4.1   The Virtual Circuit

The *virtual circuit*, as the name might suggest, attempts to model the network as a wire. Indeed, this is a comforting abstraction for an application which previously operated over a dedicated communications link and is now being moved onto a network. In the virtual circuit abstraction, the network is modeled as a reliable bi-directional byte stream. Though data is actually transported in packets, with all the failures that packets can suffer, at a higher level that data appears to be a reliable sequence of bytes. By numbering the packets and using the numbers to detect and retransmit lost packets (as well as to sequence misordered packets), the software that supports the virtual circuit abstraction removes any necessity for dealing with failure modes.

What is the penalty of this abstraction? Its limitation can best be illustrated by exploring an application for which it is ill-suited, real time digitized speech—in other words telephony based on packet switching.

In this application, the speech waveform is digitized in real time, placed in packets, and transmitted to the receiver (the listener) for replay. Since the packets represent a continuous data source (the speaker), they must be rapidly delivered and without excessive jitter. If a packet is excessively delayed, it is not available at the time that the receiver requires the information. Hence, the listener will perceive disrupted speech flow.

What happens when a virtual circuit abstraction is used for speech, and a packet is lost? The abstraction insists on delivering all the data in order. It will hold up the delivery of all packets subsequent to the lost one until, using requests back to the sender, the lost packet is retransmitted. But this process may make all the subsequent packets unacceptably late, not just the lost ones, which disrupts the flow.

A much better alternative would be to sacrifice some reliability for better control of delay. In the case of speech, the application can deal with a lost packet, even though it cannot cope with excessive delay. The application can just replace missing data with noise or a replay of the previous packet, thus causing a brief audible glitch that would not usually render the communication unintelligible. If it does, even higher level error recovery can be employed; the listener can ask the speaker to repeat the damaged phrase.

Thus the problem is that the virtual circuit abstraction, by insisting on perfect reliability, sacrifices flexibility in other basic service parameters of the network, such as delay. Such parameters may be critical to specific applications.

3.4.2   The Remote Procedure Call

Another network abstraction is the *remote procedure call*. This abstraction is based on a previous idea unrelated to any form of remote communication: the procedure call. In this abstraction, the distributed computing environment is modeled as a set of procedures or subroutines local to each machine. One machine communicates with another by calling a routine residing on the remote machine. By using the paradigm of object-oriented programming, one can make remote information available by calling the subroutine that manages that information.

This abstraction is useful because the semantics of a subroutine call is well understood. Thus application builders can build correct programs by using very mature reasoning processes. The problem with the abstraction is that, because it is based on an idea from another context, it does not match some of the actual features of real networks. For example, when the network or remote machine fails during a subroutine call, the calling subroutine may not be able to tell if the subroutine has completed. An attempt to repeat the subroutine call after the failure has been corrected might lead to the call being executed twice.

A more serious problem with the remote procedure call as a network abstraction is that it does not deal well with the real delays that are present across networks. Subroutine calls are strictly serial; a second call cannot commence until the first has returned. Further, the caller and the called routine cannot execute in parallel. So the computation executes in a series of strict lock-step exchanges of control between the two machines. Thus the real time delay between two machines limits the rate at which exchanges can occur. For example, a round trip delay of 30 ms. limits a computation to about 30 remote procedure calls per second. This is several orders of magnitude slower than one would normally expect of a local procedure call. If an application based on local procedure calls is mapped onto remote calls, this severe performance degradation may render the application essentially inoperative.

The feature of networks that causes problems here, and with virtual circuits as well, is that networks have substantial and highly variable delays. Unless a network is restricted to a small geographic scope, such as a room, the delays due to propagation of data along the communication links can be a major consideration. In addition, since the network is a shared facility, additional delay may arise while waiting for an occupied link to become free. These delays are fundamental and cannot easily be masked, most especially by an abstraction such as a procedure call which is totally synchronous by nature. In this respect, a procedure call seems a rather poor model of a network.

In an attempt to overcome this problem, and to provide a network abstraction that deals well with delay of various sorts, the Mercury Project at LCS has been exploring the idea of *stream calls* (see Chapter 4). In stream calls, one call can begin before the previous one completes. The goal of this more complex abstraction is to capture at least some of the semantics of the procedure call while dealing effectively with the real delays found in real networks.

3.5   Networking Today

We are now at a point to summarize the present state of networking so we can begin to reason about the changes to come. First, while networking is successful, it is still very young. It is still using abstractions based on previous technology, abstractions which even today can be seen as having substantial limitations. Second, it has been driven to a considerable extent by reasons of economics, which while real, are also transient. The most exciting applications of networks, such as electronic mail, do indeed derive from fundamental concerns: the distribution of people and information.

Third, the packet, the unit of multiplexing so critical to network design, has taken on a large role in the network architecture of today. In constructing abstractions such as the virtual circuit, there are several control problems that must be solved: *flow control*, insuring that the sender does not transmit faster than the receiver can process the information; *error recovery*, in which delivered information is acknowledged and lost information is retransmitted; and *congestion control*, in which the sender is prevented from overloading the network. In the designs of today, the packet has become the element around which all of these controls are achieved. The importance of this will become more obvious as I consider the future role of the packet.

My conclusion, which I attempt to defend in the remainder of this paper, is that the designs of today, heavily based on the packet as a unit of control, and the abstractions of today, still borrowed from other contexts, will not carry us into the next generation of networks. That next generation is about to burst upon us, and we must rethink some of our basic assumptions if we are to succeed in building the networks of tomorrow.

3.6   The Shape of Tomorrow

Our view of networking is based on the assumption that we are about to experience a great change in capability and function. Hence, I must

begin by describing and defending my vision of networks. The central
change is that networks will get faster in speed and larger in size. They
will be built using much faster trunks, in the multi-gigabit range. More
significantly, they will support much faster flows at the application level,
with speeds up to a gigabit or more. In size, they will expand from the
largest data networks of today, which have perhaps 100,000 end points,
to match the telephone system in size, with several hundred million
end points. In other words, they will grow in both size and speed by
perhaps three orders of magnitude. This prediction, if true, suggests
a general reason for concern. Other computer system artifacts, such
as operating systems, have seldom survived attempts to scale by one
order of magnitude. Experience gives us little hope that we can scale
a network by three orders of magnitude in both speed and size without
complete re-examination of the fundamental architectural assumptions.

Why do I predict this growth? There must be both the possibility
and the need. The possibility is technological, based on two advances:
the fiber optic link and the VLSI chip.

The role of fiber optics is obvious. Not only does it permit greater
transmission speeds, but it does so at a greatly reduced cost which is
perhaps more important. Fiber optic links permit a change in the economic operating point of communication links. As a consequence of the
fiber installations currently underway or planned, we can expect the impact of fiber transmission to be realized over the next decade. Indeed,
over the next ten years, fiber links may become abundant.

VLSI is the key that permits us to manage these links and to use
them to build networks. Networks require us to provide a switching
function to operate at the speed of the links. As links get faster, the
switch must similarly increase in speed. Today, packet switches are
built using general purpose processor chips and memory architectures.
Switches thus assembled are already proving a bottleneck with today's
link speeds. To deal with the much higher speeds that fiber will permit,
it is necessary to develop special purpose switch elements. Without
VLSI, this would not be practical. But today, we can construct highly
specialized switch components at reasonable cost.

Just knowing that such speeds are possible does not mean that they
will come to be. Unless there is a need for these new capabilities, there
will not be sufficient pressure to drive the redesign necessary to achieve
them. This pressure must come from new applications which will gen-

erate the demand. It is therefore worthwhile to speculate on how applications and their communications requirements might evolve over the next decade.

There is a current trend in applications which drive the future of networking as much as fiber optics. This trend is the increasing use of graphics, scanned images, video and other visual forms as part of the application interface. Computers have been dealing with images for many years now, for example in medical systems, cartography and publishing. In the past, these applications have been viewed as outside the mainstream of computers, requiring special hardware and systems. Now, however, the image is about to enter the more general context of computing. The term *multi-media workstation* is often used to describe the next generation of the user interface, a workstation that combines traditional computing with visual and audio capabilities. Many prototypes of this concept now exist and commercial products are beginning to enter the marketplace.

What is the value of images in applications? The following examples, based to some extent on experience with the Internet project, show a range of possibilities.

3.6.1 Multi-media Documents

The current popularity of facsimile machines derives to some extent from the fact that any form of document can be transmitted: text, chart, picture, etc. Computer-based document preparation tools are only now beginning to permit construction of documents that incorporate all of these modes. The marriage of computers to video will permit even more exciting forms of documents, in which fragments of video are included as illustrations in the document. Imagine a scientific paper in which video is used to record the experiment performed.

The existence of these multi-media documents will provide the basis for a number of document management tools. For example, it will be necessary to support document browsing and searching, based on content. Browsing of multi-media documents is not complex, it just requires bandwidth. Since we have few tools for expressing a search criterion for media other than text, content searches of a multi-media document is a very challenging problem.

3.6.2   Desktop Teleconferencing

The experience of the Internet community gives first hand evidence of the appeal of teleconferencing technology. One obvious extension is the attempt to permit a teleconference from the office. While earlier technology such as the picturephone may suggest problems with desktop video interaction, I suspect that the concept can be successful if it permits the video equivalent of a conference call. This is because experience with the Internet facilities suggests that only when there are several participants, does the value of the video link become obvious. If desktop teleconferencing were to prove useful, it would generate a tremendous demand for switched multi-site video technology. If so, it should be integrated into the workstation to permit the conference to display and manage both the view of distant participants, and some shared distributed workspace.

3.6.3   Multi-player Interactive Games

A consumer-oriented application is the multi-player game. An informal observation is that games against other human players are more challenging and interesting than a game against a computer. Imagine a hybrid of today's video games which permit several players, each at a separate screen, to participate in some joint contest, either of dexterity or strategy. This concept, if successful, could define a new market with a potential equal to today's home video games, together with a network capability to hook them all together.

A related example is distributed gaming as a training tool. The U.S. Army is using such a tool today as a training aid for tank operators. The different tank drivers see a view on their display corresponding to the view out of their tank, and can interact with each other, joining up with friendly forces and shooting at the enemy. All such actions have a realistic consequence on the displays.

3.6.4   Visual User Interfaces

In making a computer easy to use, a graphic or visual interface often seems effective. Current computer systems portray and organize information using visual cues such as file cards, date books and similar indicators. These are intended to make it easy for the user to understand and classify the information being presented. Control information appears in windows that pop up, out, or otherwise attempt to capture their organization in their imagery. This trend seems successful, and its use should expand in the future. As more powerful tools for picture management become available, more powerful user interfaces should quickly follow.

One potential example would be an interactive "help" facility. It can provide fragments of prerecorded video instruction or, failing that, a video connection to a human consultant—all of which could be archived for later review.

3.6.5   Computer-aided Image Creation

Perhaps the most important aspect of visual interaction is the computer construction and display of images. An important example of this arises today in the use of supercomputers. Supercomputers are typically used for simulation, the results of which need to be presented to the user. The supercomputer community has adopted the word "visualization" for the concept that such data should be displayed in moving image form, rather than as lists of numbers. There seems to be a consensus that animated output of simulation results is significantly more effective than other forms of output.

Indeed, if this were a multi-media document, it would be possible to include fragments of video that would instantly demonstrate the value of such output. Sadly, I can only suggest how compelling it would be to see such a video.

Once the idea of visualization is recognized, it is obvious that there are interesting images that do not require supercomputer creation. For example, a tool for constructing images could be of great use to professionals such as architects, who today use images to convey their concepts. These images are traditionally created "by hand," sometimes with great difficulty, and once created are static. A computer generated image could be created, placed in a context or modified, all in support of discussion among humans.

Fields such as medicine are already making heavy use of computer generated images, with some of the more complex and sophisticated scanning tools for diagnosis. Indeed, medical images are among the highest resolution images being processed today.

The use of images in medicine provides a good example of the value of integrating several of the above examples. Once an image, perhaps a moving one, has been created, it might be desirable to have several doctors, perhaps at distant locations, confer about that image. That is, what is needed is a teleconference in which the shared workspace itself is a computer generated moving image.

The purpose of this extended discussion of applications is to generate some sense of the need for high bandwidth digital communications. The reader may find one or another of these examples particularly compelling, or may believe that the need for networks lies in some other direction altogether. If our experience with past technical innovations is any guide, all predictions of its utility will be wrong. A new application will arise unexpectedly, e.g., electronic mail on the last generation of networks or the spreadsheet programs on the personal computer, and will shape and justify the development of the technology. We must have some vision of the future to motivate us to build the enabling technology, but it is almost certainly off the mark.

3.7 How to Get Fast

To this point I have argued the following:

- Technology exists to permit the development of networks much faster than those today.

- There are potentially new and exciting applications that could be built using this technology.

So what does it take to get there? Can we just turn up the clock on the network and be done? Sadly, it is not that easy. There are some very difficult technical problems to be solved if we are to build this next generation network; problems that arise from fundamental issues of speed and scale. In the last part of this paper, I review the source of these problems and give a few specific examples of problems to be solved.

The essence of the problem is that not all the components of the network are getting faster at the same rate. New fiber optic transmission technology caused the raw bandwidth to get quite a bit faster. VLSI has permitted the construction of faster switches, but switching has not taken the same step in speed as transmission. The attached hosts, which support the applications the network is to serve, are getting somewhat faster, for example by means of RISC processors. Yet, they have some of the same performance bottlenecks of bus and memory. At the same time, the speed of light, which relates to network performance in a fundamental way, has not changed at all.

A simple example will show the sort of problem that arises. A cross-country network has a round-trip latency of about 30 ms., because of the speed of light. If the network is increased from 1 Mbps to 1 Gbps, the amount of data in the channel at any one time increases from 4 KBytes to 4 MBytes. Hence, the control algorithms that are devised to regulate the flow of information into the network must be designed to manage three orders more of data.

3.7.1   New Control Algorithms

The term *congestion control* describes the mechanisms used to regulate network traffic in the case of users collectively exceeding the capacity of the network. Today, users send data into the network and receive feedback when they overload it. As networks get faster, feedback becomes less effective. The problem is that for even large data elements, a transmission at these speeds may well be complete before feedback can come into play. Feedback cannot be effective unless the total amount of data being transmitted is substantially larger than the amount in transit across the network at any instant. Unless we believe that applications will scale up the size of their transmissions to match the increased data rates, we must presume the need for new models of congestion control—models based more on precomputed expectations and open-loop controls.

3.7.2   Packet Processing Overhead

Simple arithmetic will show the potential for a performance bottleneck in the switch. Measurements of typical local area networks today show packet sizes around 200 bytes. To make things better, I will assume that packets will get larger over time, perhaps reaching 1000 bytes.

Assuming this size, a 1 Gbps link carries 250,000 packets per second, and a 10 Gbps link carries 2.5 million packets per second. Current packet switches based on minicomputers can forward between 1000 and 10,000 packets per second. That is, we are off by several orders in speed. While there are steps that can be taken to make processing faster, there are also forces that make the problem worse. The result is real concern that switching will represent a bottleneck for the networks of tomorrow.

There are several obvious ways to make the switch faster. A larger packet size would help, since it would reduce the packet rate for a given bit rate. But the packet size is related to application requirements. While some applications might be able to use very large packets, in many cases the packet size is application determined.

In fact, rather than getting larger, the packets are getting smaller. A current proposal from the telephone switching community is for a single fixed-size multiplexing unit suited for both voice and data. This concept, called Asynchronous Transfer Mode or ATM, is based on a suggested packet size of 48 data bytes. So, while an order or two of speedup is needed, this proposal takes away perhaps an order.

One could abandon the minicomputer as a base for a switch, and use specialized chips and architectures. However, even the fastest specialized processing elements proposed for switches have trouble keeping up with the above rates. One could propose a highly parallel switch and, indeed, proposed parallel designs in the context of ATM seem quite promising. But the designs proposed today require great simplification in the processing complexity to achieve the rates needed.

As the speed requirements force a simplification of the processing task to control overhead, there is also pressure for more processing in the switch. If we are to build networks that control and account for their usage, it will be necessary to log network traffic, provide access controls, and so on. These policy checks could easily cost another order of magnitude in speed if designed in a naive way.

In order to simultaneously deal with the need for decreased overhead and increased processing complexity, a change is needed in the way processing is structured. In many networks today, often called "connectionless" networks, each packet is processed in isolation without regard to previous and subsequent packets. This approach must be changed so that when a packet is processed, the results are cached and applied to similar packets that may follow. This caching provides a way to link a sequence of packets for management purposes. Our research group has used the term *flow* to describe such a sequence.

3.7.3   Host Interfacing

The overhead of processing is even more limiting in the host, where the protocols necessary for higher level abstraction, e.g., the virtual circuit, are implemented. There is significant complexity in implementing such protocols. At the same time, the programs executing these protocols must run in the context of a general purpose operating system, rather than in the specialized programming environment of a packet switch.

Even with the networks of today, host software is perceived as a bottleneck to utilizing the raw network bandwidth. If networks speed up by several orders, what can the host do to keep up?

There seem to be two possible answers. One is to rethink the relevant parts of the host environment (operating system, I/O architecture and memory architecture) so that the host can execute protocols at the required speeds. There is some evidence that this sort of redesign can be successful. However, depending on the exact nature of the starting environment, the magnitude of effort may be considerable. An alternative is to move the processing out of the host execution environment, onto some outboard network controller which embodies a special memory architecture and program execution environment. The goal of this outboard processing would be to permit the host to deal in units of data larger than the multiplexing elements, i.e., data units related to application needs. Thus, for example, a file transfer application might deal in units of a disk block, while the outboard network controller would fragment it into packets or into 48 byte ATM multiplexing units.

3.7.4   Network Dynamics

Large networks are complex dynamic systems which, unless controlled, can display undesirable behavior. These effects are visible in networks today, and they can only get worse with increased size and speed. An example of a current problem may help to illustrate the tendency.

In our group, both observation of real networks and simulation suggest that queue length and (in consequence) perceived delay across the network are periodically varying. In other words, the network is oscillating. The cause of this is conjectured to be a synchronization among the users of the network, leading to large bursts of offered load. The network becomes overloaded and looses some packets, causing all the affected hosts to time out and retransmit. Since they use the same timeout algorithm, they retransmit at about the same time. This causes another network overload, with more lost packets, and the pattern repeats.

In order to correct the problem, if this analysis of the problem is valid, it will be necessary to change the control algorithms of the network to smooth out and regulate offered load. This is particularly true as the network become faster. Since the speed of light does not change, for a network of a certain physical scope, the amount of data outstanding in the network goes up proportionally to the speed of the links.

The term *flow control* describes the tools used to regulate the sending of traffic. Today, flow control is achieved using the concept of *windows*, which control flow by regulating the number of packets that may be outstanding in the network at any time. That is, in order to fully utilize a link, one must "open the window" enough to fill the path from sender to receiver. As the speed goes up, the window size goes up. This need to increase the window size reduces the opportunity for control which the window mechanism affords.

For this reason, our group is exploring an alternative in which flows are regulated by bounding the *rate* at which packets may enter the network, rather than the total number. This may permit the stable regulation of large amounts of data that must be permitted to enter the high speed nets of tomorrow. One example of this work is reported in the thesis by Zhang [4].

3.7.5 Policy Routing

Policy routing is an example of a problem that does not directly relate to increases in speed, but rather to increases in scale. As networks grow in size, they become decomposed into parts that are managed by separate organizations. Similar to the telephone network after divestiture, there will be campus networks, regional networks, long haul (cross country) networks, private interconnect facilities, and so on.

Each of these parts will have its own rules as to which community it serves, how its costs are recovered, and so on. In this complex of interconnected facilities, a user will need to route a packet in such a way that it only attempts to use permitted facilities, that costs are minimized, and that best service is obtained for the cost.

In order to achieve these goals, new tools to control routing are needed. In most computer networks today, routing algorithms are designed to meet a simple and well defined goal: the minimization of a cost such as delay. A single-variable minimization will not provide the richness of function needed to meet the above needs. A new sort of routing function, often called *policy routing*, must be architected to control traffic flow at the level at which resource control policies are established. This function must route traffic so local policy concerns are satisfied, and accounting and billing can be performed.

3.8   The Future of the Packet

As discussed earlier in the paper, the packet as a multiplexing element was a key idea, perhaps *the* key idea, which enabled the successful development of computer networks. It was initially the unit of multiplexing, but also came to be the unit of flow control (e.g., in window flow control systems) and the unit of error recovery (e.g., after buffer overflows caused by congestion).

In the future, this complex role for the packet may change. Because of processing overhead, the unit of control can no longer equal the unit of multiplexing. Where the unit of multiplexing is 48 bytes (in the ATM case), processing, e.g. flow control, error recovery, policy routing or cost accounting, will have to be applied to a higher level unit of data. At the host interface, this will be some unit of data that matches application requirements. In general, there will be any number of ways to achieve the needed multiplexing. In addition to the ATM multiplexing, there may be traditional packets or more advanced concepts, such as wavelength division of a fiber link. If future network designs are to have the necessary generality, they must be able to deal with any intermixing of these.

What is needed is a new layering and modularization of network structure. Some new abstraction will be needed, one that is above the low level function of bandwidth multiplexing, but lies below the traditional application abstractions such as the virtual circuit. This new abstraction will provide the necessary grouping to permit network management and control. In fact, very different groupings may be needed for distinct functions such as error recovery and flow control. For a specific proposal for the reorganization of network protocols, see the paper by Clark and Tennenhouse [3].

3.9   Conclusions

The advent of fiber optics is a one-time phenomenon. The telecommunications infrastructure of the U.S. is being reconstructed at the present

time and, once installed, will serve as the communications medium for
the next several decades. There is now an opportunity first to demonstrate the need for high bandwidth, large scale networking of computers
and, second, to demonstrate the key concepts by which this goal can be
achieved. New abstractions and new control concepts will be needed.

By seizing this opportunity, we can insure that the fiber now being
installed is designed in a way to facilitate this sort of transmission. If we
succeed, the change in computer communication will be so significant as
to seem a revolutionary change in capability, rather than an evolution
of the present facilities. Our goal should be nothing less than to expand
the options for human interaction at a distance, for the fundamental
role of networks is to provide new opportunities for building the global
community.

3.10   Acknowledgments

Support for this research was provided in part by the Defense Advanced
Research Projects Agency of the Department of Defense, monitored un-
der Office of Naval Research contract number N00014-83-K-0125, by
NASA under grant number NAG2-582, and by the National Science
Foundation under grant number NCR-8814187.

Bibliography

[1] D. Bertsekas and R. Gallager. *Data Networks*. Prentice Hall, Englewood Cliffs, NJ, 1987.

[2] A.S. Tanenbaum. *Computer Networks*. Prentice Hall, Englewood Cliffs, NJ, 1988.

[3] D.D. Clark and D.L. Tennenhouse. Architectural considerations for a new generation of protocols. In *Proceedings of ACM SigComm 90*, September 1990.

[4] L. Zhang. *A New Architecture for Packet Switching Network Protocols*. MIT Laboratory for Computer Science, Technical Report 455, August 1989.

4 Challenges in Distributed Systems

Barbara Liskov

Professor, Department of Electrical Engineering and Computer Science
Leader, LCS Programming Methodology Group

Abstract

Increasingly today, people make use of personal workstations
rather than a central shared facility. Often the workstations
are connected by a network to form a distributed system. This
paper describes research at the MIT Laboratory for Computer
Science that addresses two important challenges raised by distributed systems. First, support is needed for programmers who
must implement applications that run on them. Second, users
need ways to conveniently share data, programs and resources
with one another in a heterogeneous distributed environment.

4.1 Introduction

The last decade has seen a major change in the way that computing
is presented to users. Ten years ago, almost everyone made use of a
central facility shared with many others through the medium of time
sharing. Today, many people use workstations or personal computers
that are either theirs alone or are shared with a small group of other
users. Although sometimes these machines are entirely independent of
one another, often they are connected by a network, so that they are
able to communicate. Such *distributed systems* are important because
they allow users of different machines to share data and programs with
one another. They are becoming more and more common; we can expect
that they will dominate computing in the future.

More precisely, a distributed system consists of a number of *nodes*
connected by a *communications network*. Each node is a computer with
one or more processors. The nodes are heterogeneous; there are many

different kinds of computers in the system. The network might be a local area network, or it might consist of a number of local area networks connected by a longhaul network such as the ARPANET. In such a network, it is usually much faster for a node to access local information than information residing in some other node.

Both nodes and the network may fail. The nodes fail by crashing. The network may lose messages, duplicate them, or deliver them late or out of order. It may also *partition*, so that some nodes are temporarily unable to communicate with some other nodes. Although the individual components in the system may fail, the system as a whole continues to function. This means that programs running in a distributed system will sometimes have to cope with situations that could not arise in a centralized system. The underlying communication system can hide many of the network problems such as lost or duplicated messages, but not all problems can be hidden. For example, a call to a program at a remote node cannot succeed if the node is crashed or cannot be reached because of a partition. The need to cope with such situations increases the complexity of distributed programs.

Distributed systems present two important challenges. The first is the need to implement applications on top of them. For example, in a bank with many branches, it is convenient to use a distributed organization in which information about the bank accounts of a branch is stored on a computer at that branch. This organization allows most accesses to be fast, since most transactions with an account take place at the branch to which an account belongs, but also allows inter-branch accesses when necessary.

The second challenge is how to provide convenient sharing of programs, data and resources among the different users. Sharing was relatively easy to achieve in the days of time shared central facilities. It is more difficult in a distributed environment, especially when there are many different kinds of computers in the network, but it is still needed. For example, users working on a joint paper need to share files; a scarce, expensive resource such as a high speed printer needs to be shared by all users, even though it is attached to just one computer in the network. Different users may need to call a program that runs on a supercomputer in the network.

This paper discusses recent work at the Laboratory for Computer Science that addresses these challenges. First, it discusses the Argus programming language and system; the goal of this work is to make it relatively easy for programmers to construct distributed implementations of applications. Second, it discusses the Mercury Project, which provides support for sharing in a heterogeneous distributed environment. In both cases, a major goal is control of complexity: we want to make it as easy as possible to construct a distributed program or to share across a network. Control of complexity is essential in sequential systems, and the need is even greater in the more complicated distributed environment provided by a network.

4.2 Argus

The goal of Argus is to provide mechanisms to help programmers construct distributed programs, i.e., programs that run on a number of computers connected by a network. Argus is intended to be used primarily for programs that maintain online data for long periods of time, e.g., file systems, mail systems and inventory control systems. These programs have a number of requirements:

1. Online information must remain consistent in spite of failures and also in spite of concurrent access.

2. Programs must provide some level of service even when components fail. For example, a program may replicate information at several nodes so that individual failures can be masked. In this way, programs and data can be made *highly available*: with very high probability they can be used when someone wants to use them.

3. Programmers need the ability to place information and processing at a particular node, both to do replication properly and to improve performance, since information is cheaper to access if it is nearby.

4. Programs may need to be reconfigured dynamically, for example by adding and removing components or by moving a component from one node to another. To minimize the impact of moving components, the method used to access information should be location independent.

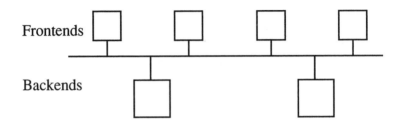

Figure 4.1
Configuration of the Banking System

Argus was designed to satisfy these requirements.

For example, consider the banking system mentioned above in which information about the accounts of a branch is stored at a computer or computers at that branch, and the system supports remote interactions with accounts. The configuration for the banking system is illustrated in Figure 4.1. Each clerk interacts with a program that runs on a *frontend* minicomputer; other programs on the minicomputer interact with cash vending machines or carry out requests of bank personnel to produce monthly statements or run audits. The minicomputers are connected via a network to the *backend* computers where the account information resides. Each backend belongs to a particular branch of the bank: It resides at that branch and maintains a "branch" database containing information about accounts at its branch. Every frontend can communicate with every backend and vice versa.

In the remainder of this section, we sketch the mechanisms that Argus provides to cope with distribution, as exemplified by the banking system. More complete discussions of Argus can be found in [17][11][9][12].

4.2.1   Guardians

To allow a program like the banking system to consist of components residing at different nodes of a network, Argus provides a special kind of object called a *guardian*. A guardian is an abstract object that encapsulates resources. It permits its resources to be accessed by means of special procedures, called *handlers*, that can be called from other guardians. For example, a guardian might encapsulate some or all of the accounts at a branch and provide handlers to open and close accounts, to withdraw and deposit money and to check the balance of an account. As another example, a guardian might control a printing device and provide a handler called *enq* to allow files to be enqueued for printing, and a handler called *check_queue* to check the state of the queue.

Within it, a guardian contains data objects that store the state of its resources. These objects are not accessible outside the guardian; the only way they can be accessed or modified by another guardian is by calls to their guardian's handlers. Handler calls are performed using a message-based communication mechanism. Arguments are passed by value, which ensures that a guardian's objects cannot be accessed directly by any other guardian. The Argus implementation takes care of all details of constructing and sending messages.

Inside a guardian are one or more processes. Processes can access all the guardian's objects directly. Some processes carry out handler calls; whenever a handler call arrives at a guardian, a process is created to run the call. In addition, there may be *background* processes that carry out tasks independently of particular handler calls. For example, the *enq* handler of the printer guardian might merely record information about the request while a background process carries out the actual printing.

Each guardian resides at a single node of the network, although it can change its node of residence. Several guardians can reside at the same node. A guardian is *resilient* to failures of its node. Some of its objects survive crashes; these are the *stable* objects and they are written periodically to stable storage devices that, with high probability, avoid loss of information in spite of failures [13]. The other objects in the guardian are *volatile*. A crash destroys all volatile objects of a guardian as well as all processes that were running at the time of the crash. After the crash, the Argus system restores the guardian's code and recovers the stable objects from stable storage. It then creates a special recovery process, which runs code defined by the guardian to initialize the volatile objects. When this process finishes, the guardian is ready to accept new handler calls and to run background processes.

For example, in the printer guardian, information about queued requests would be stored in stable objects so that requests are not lost in a crash. However, detailed information about the exact processing of the current request need not be stable, since the request can be redone after a crash. Since the volatile state does not survive crashes, it should be used only for information (such as the current printing information) that can be discarded in a crash or for redundant information (e.g., an index into a database).

A guardian can create other guardians dynamically and (the names of) guardians and handlers can be sent as arguments of handler calls. The creator specifies the node at which the new guardian is to reside. In this way, individual guardians can be placed at the most advantageous locations. Handler calls, however, are location independent so that one guardian can use another without knowing its location.

A distributed program in Argus is composed of a number of guardians residing at a number of nodes. For example, in the banking system there might be a guardian running at the backend computer of each branch to carry out requests on the accounts of that branch. In addition, a guardian at the frontend would interact with one or more clerks and/or money machines. This guardian would use a background process to listen for input and then make handler calls to the appropriate branch guardians. To avoid losing information about deposits and withdrawals if the branch's computer crashes, the branch guardians would record all crucial information about accounts in stable objects.

4.2.2   Actions

Guardians allow programs to be decomposed into units of tightly coupled data and processing that are located in an advantageous position in the network, and they permit data to survive crashes. However, they do not provide much help in dealing with the problems arising from concurrency and they do not solve all problems caused by failures. For example, consider the following scenario in the banking system. A clerk is carrying out a transfer of funds from an account at branch B1 to an account at branch B2. This is accomplished by first withdrawing the money from B1 and then depositing it to B2. Meanwhile, another clerk is doing an audit which requires reading the balances of all accounts at both B1 and B2. There are two problems that can occur in such a situation:

1. Concurrent activities may interfere with one another. For example, if a transfer runs concurrently with an audit, the audit might record a total that includes the withdrawal but not the deposit.

2. Failures can cause problems. For example, suppose that after the withdrawal is complete, a failure occurs that makes it impossible to complete the transfer. If care is not taken, the system will lose track of the withdrawn money.

To solve these problems, Argus permits a computation such as a transfer or an audit to run as an *atomic transaction* [4], or *action* for short. Actions have precisely the properties needed to solve the concurrency and failure problems. First, they are *serializable*: the effect of running a group of actions concurrently is the same as if they were run sequentially in some order. Second, they are *total*: an action either completes entirely or it is guaranteed to have no visible effect. An action that completes is said to *commit*; otherwise, the action *aborts*.

Serializability solves the concurrency problem. If a transfer action and an audit action are running concurrently, then the effect must be as if they ran sequentially in some order. Either the audit will appear to have run after the transfer is finished or before it starts; in either case it observes the proper total. Note that serializability permits concurrent execution, but ensures that concurrent actions do not interfere with one another.

Totality solves the failure problem. Either the transfer completes entirely, in which case both the *from* and *to* accounts contain the proper new balances, or it aborts and has no effect, in which case the accounts still have their old balances.

To implement serializability, we need to synchronize the accesses made by actions to shared objects. To implement totality, we need some way to recover the old state of any objects modified by an action that aborts. Argus provides synchronization by means of locks. Every operation on an atomic object is classified as a reader or writer. An operation that modifies the object is a writer; other operations are readers. For example, deposit and withdrawal operations are writers, and the operation that reads the balance is a reader. Readers automatically acquire a read lock on the object before accessing it; writers automatically acquire a write lock. These locks are held until the action completes, i.e., commits

or aborts.[1] As is usual, there can be many concurrent holders of a read
lock, but if an action holds a write lock on some object, then no other
concurrent action can hold locks on that object.

Recovery is done using *versions*. The state of an unlocked object is
stored in a *base version*. Modifications to an object are not done to the
base version directly. Instead, a copy called the *current version* is made
(in volatile memory) and modifications are done to it. If the action
commits, the current version becomes the base version (and is written
to stable storage if the object is stable). If the action aborts, the current
version is discarded.

An action starts at some guardian (e.g., at a frontend) and spreads
to other guardians by means of handler calls. As it runs on behalf of
the action, a called handler may modify some objects at its guardian.
These modifications will be lost if the guardian crashes subsequently.
An action can commit only if none of the modifications made on its
behalf has been lost; if this is impossible, the action must abort. This
property is needed, for example, to guarantee that a transfer modifies
both accounts or neither account. We ensure that committing is atomic
by using the two-phase commit algorithm [4].

4.2.3 Summary and Current Status

Argus mechanisms help programmers cope with the problems that arise
in distributed systems. Guardians can be used to control where data
and processing are located, and they are resilient so information is not
lost in crashes. Also, they support dynamic reconfiguration since they
can be created, moved and destroyed dynamically, and handler calls
are location independent. Atomic actions allow online information to be
maintained consistently in spite of failures and concurrency, and make it
relatively easy to improve system availability by replicating information.

Argus has been running for about three years, although early in this
period the implementation was quite incomplete. The implementation
is described in [9]. We have used Argus to implement a number of
distributed programs, including:

1. A preliminary version of a library in which information about programs is stored. The library allows Argus guardians and other
   modules to be developed by different people at different locations

---

[1]Thus we are using strict two-phase locking [3].

while still enforcing compile-time type checking of module interfaces. Also, it provides stable storage for program code.

2. The catalog, which allows runtime lookup of guardians and handlers. For example, a program could use the catalog to find a printer spooler for a printing device.

3. A distributed editor [5], which allows users at different locations to collaborate on the same document.

4. A mail repository, which provides mailboxes for storing and retrieving mail for users. The mail repository uses replication to provide high availability and is designed to permit a wide range of reconfigurations.

5. A program to compute Hailstone numbers [6].

6. A distributed game that allows users at different machines to take part in the same game.

Our experience in using Argus so far is that it has been relatively easy to write distributed programs, even sophisticated ones that replicate information to increase availability and that are able to reconfigure themselves dynamically. Argus is helpful because atomic actions are an important tool both for understanding what a system should do and for implementing it correctly.

It is important to understand that atomic actions do not constrain the kinds of systems that can be built. It is up to the person defining a system to decide how quickly effects of computations must propagate to other parts of the system and to decide how much information can be lost in case of a crash. Actions can be used to implement a spectrum of requirements. If quick propagation and no lost information are required, the cost of actions will be greater than what is needed to support weaker requirements.

An example of weak constraints is the program that computes Hailstone numbers [6]. This program uses different guardians to do parallel searches for numbers in separate ranges. It has a stable state so that the results of past computations will not be entirely lost in crashes. It uses atomic actions to take periodic checkpoints and to coordinate interactions between the searching guardians, and a frontend that is responsible for assigning ranges to guardians. Checkpoint actions run every ten minutes; coordination actions about once a day. Actions made these parts of the program very easy to implement, yet their impact on performance is negligible.

4.3   Mercury

The goal of Mercury is to allow sharing of programs in heterogeneous distributed environments. We want to allow programs written in different programming languages, and running under different operating systems on different hardware, to use one another as components over a network. Our initial goal is to allow programs written in Argus, C and Lisp to communicate. Ultimately, however, we want to extend our methods to other languages as well.

As an example of what we would like to accomplish, consider an object repository implemented in Argus, a VLSI manipulation system implemented in Lisp and an editor implemented in C. The configuration is illustrated in Figure 4.2. The repository is both highly reliable and highly available. It allows objects created by programs written in different languages to be shared; it runs on a number of nodes in the network. The VLSI manipulation system is an interactive program that runs on a Lisp machine and helps a designer develop designs for VLSI chips. Since the object repository is both reliable and available, it is a good place to store the mask descriptions. Thus we have a need for communication between Lisp and Argus programs. Now suppose that while editing a document using the C editor, the user wants to use the VLSI program to manipulate a mask (stored in the repository) and insert the resulting description in the document. This can be achieved by having the editor make a call to the VLSI program, passing it as an argument an identifier m that can be used to find the mask in the repository. However, the VLSI program is interactive and should interact with the user of the editor via the display of the user's machine. Therefore, the editor's call of the VLSI program takes a second argument, the identifier w, of a window that the VLSI program will use to do the interaction. The window is controlled by another program written in C.

We want Mercury to support inter-language and inter-machine interactions like the ones in this example. We are primarily concerned with

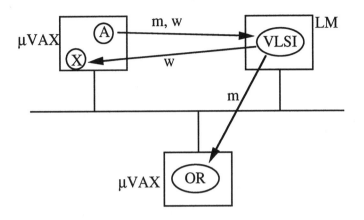

Figure 4.2
Mercury Example

support for programs calling other programs rather than users logging in to remote systems. Also we want to be able to call interactive programs and have their communication with a remote window take place using Mercury communication.

The kind of sharing that Mercury is intended to support is quite difficult to do today. There are three reasons why this is true:

1. Most important is the lack of a general methodology to encourage sharing. There is no standard way of defining services. Instead, service interfaces are constructed in an *ad hoc* manner. The result is that each time a user wants to use a new service, he or she must learn a new way of doing things.

2. An additional problem is that communication must be done at a low level. In particular, the data types used in messages do not match the abstractions, such as masks, that programs should use to communicate.

3. Finally, there is often little in the way of support in the programming language of either the program providing the service or the program using the service. Instead, programmers must provide

explicit code to call the operations of the chosen transport mechanism.

Mercury is intended to rectify these problems. It supports a new communication model that enhances sharing, a language-independent type system that provides a common medium of exchange for programs written in different programming languages, and extensions to programming languages that make it easy to use Mercury communication. At present, we provide such extensions for C, Lisp and Argus; however, we are developing a general method for extensions to other languages. These mechanisms are described below.

It is explicitly not a goal of Mercury to provide a means of connecting existing programs together; for work along these lines, see [18]. Instead, we are looking to the future: we are interested in developing a model and methodology so that it will be easy to both provide and use services via Mercury. However, we have done some retrofitting of existing services as discussed in Section 4.3.3.

4.3.1 Communication in Mercury

Mercury communication is based on remote procedure calls (RPC) [1]. RPCs are appealing because they are simple to use and understand. By RPC we mean a synchronous call, e.g.,

```
x := p(y)
```

in which the caller waits for the call to complete before continuing. When a call returns you know where you are: the work you requested is done and any results you need are available. The calling program can now continue based on this knowledge. In addition, what has developed from work done on sequential programs is a deep understanding of what procedure calls mean and how to reason about programs that use them.

In a distributed system, however, synchronous calls have a serious disadvantage: they prevent the caller from running in parallel with message passing and with the callee. In a centralized system, this might not be an issue: if there is only a single processor, there is little to be gained from such concurrency. In a distributed system in which the caller and the callee run on different machines, and in which the transmission delay for a message is significant, the loss of this concurrency can have a significant impact on performance.

For example, consider the use of a window system such as X [21]. To display information on a window, a program sends data to X, typically in small increments such as strings or lines, e.g.,

```
put(string1);
put(string2);
change_color(''red'');
put(string3);
```

Here *string1*, *string2* and *string3* are simply three strings that are intended to be displayed in an X window. Ideally, we would like to do each call as soon as the argument string is ready, without waiting for the reply to the previous call. If a lengthy computation or communication with another remote site such as a file system is needed to produce the next string, doing this work in parallel with the call and its processing will improve program performance. If the time to produce the next string is small, not waiting for replies improves performance because the calls happen sooner; this allows the strings to be displayed without pauses in between. Of course, if the next call is made before the previous one is complete, the order of the calls must be preserved so that, e.g., *string3* is displayed in red and the characters appear on the screen in the proper order.

In the example above, the calls returned no results; the only purpose of the reply was to indicate that processing of the call was complete. However, similar savings can be obtained for calls with results, provided that the result of one call is not needed to compute the arguments to the next. For example, suppose an editor using the window system needs to begin by obtaining some information about fonts:

```
for i from 1 to 20 do
     font[i] := get_font(a[i])
     end
```

Here, information is needed about 20 fonts corresponding to the elements of the array *a*. There is no real reason why the second call of *get_font* should wait until the first finishes since it does not depend on the results of the first. Notice that the above calls could run concurrently since they are completely independent. Doing the calls sequentially is more convenient, however, because the program can maintain the correspondence between a font and what it represents in an easy way, and need not synchronize access to the font array.

Avoiding delays due to calls is not always important, but occasionally it is critical. Our experience with X indicates that adequate support for interaction with a remote display requires that delays be avoided. Another place where delays are a problem is in bulk data communication; here we would like to be able to send a portion of the data while preparing the next for transport.

One way of obtaining better performance is to make use of alternative communication mechanisms. For example, datagrams and byte streams [19] address the performance needs. However, these are lower level mechanisms that are hard to use. In addition, the use of lower level mechanisms complicate service interfaces and can result in a loss of flexibility. This is because a server designed to be used through RPC would not be usable through a lower level mechanism, and vice-versa.

Our communication mechanism generalizes and unifies RPCs and byte streams. It is high level, yet at the same time supports efficient communication for a broader class of applications than is supported by either RPC or byte stream protocols alone. It is also simpler than the other mechanisms because of its uniformity: it is not necessary to use two distinct mechanisms to achieve adequate performance. As a result, server interfaces will be more regular, which will permit applications to be plugged together more directly.

Mercury allows programs to communicate by means of *call streams*, or *streams* for short. A call stream connects two entities within a distributed program. One of these entities is the *sender*; the other is the *receiver*. Call messages flow over the stream from the sender to the receiver, and reply messages flow in the opposite direction. The sender can make the next call before the reply to the previous call has been received. The call stream guarantees that the calls will be delivered to the receiver exactly once in the order they were made, and that the replies from the receiver will be delivered to the sender exactly once in the order of the corresponding calls. If this is not possible, the stream *breaks* as described below. However, a stream breaks only after the system has tried hard to deliver messages and there is no point in the sender repeating the call at that point.

Streams permit senders to make three kinds of calls: ordinary *blocking RPCs*, in which the sender receives the reply to the call before making another call; *stream calls*, in which the sender may make more calls before receiving the reply; and *sends*, in which the sender is not interested in the reply (assuming the call terminates normally). The application program at the receiver, however, need not distinguish among the three kinds of calls. The underlying system takes care of buffering messages where appropriate, and of delivering calls to the receiver in the proper order. Thus the receiver provides an interface consisting of procedures that clients can call and clients can choose independently how to use it.

RPCs and their replies are immediately sent over the network to minimize the delay for a call. Stream calls and sends are buffered and sent when convenient. In this way, we can amortize the overhead of system kernel calls and the transmission delays for messages over several calls, especially for small calls and replies. In addition, normal replies for sends need not be sent at all. A sequence of sends and stream calls is terminated by an RPC, which ensures that any buffered messages are sent; we provide a special form of RPC called a "synch" to do this.

Using a stream, the sender can make a sequence of calls and have the effect be the same as if it waited to receive the nth reply before doing the $n + 1^{st}$ call. The system helps out by delivering calls in the proper order. The receiver is responsible for doing the processing properly; it must appear to execute the calls in order. A simple approach is to execute each call to completion before accepting the next. However, more sophistication is possible: a receiver can process calls on the same stream in parallel (e.g., queries and updates of a database) and synchronize the processing as needed to ensure the required order.

Now we give a brief overview of how streams work; a more complete description can be found in [8]. We view a distributed program as made up of active *entities* that reside at different nodes of a network. Each entity resides completely at a single node; there may be several entities at a node. The form and meaning of entities are not determined by Mercury; instead these are defined by the programming language and system used to implement the entity. For example, in Argus, a guardian would be an entity; in C, a UNIX process might be an entity.

A receiving entity provides one or more *ports*; these identify procedures that can be called from other entities. Each port has a unique name that can be used by the system to locate it when it is called. Typically, a receiving entity will provide many ports, each one corresponding to an operation that can be called by a client. Many ports may corre-

spond to the same operation. Some ports are created when the entity
first comes into existence; others can be created dynamically. Ports may
be sent as arguments and results of remote calls.

A port is strongly typed. For example,

port (int) **returns** (real) **signals** (e1(char), e2)

describes a port that takes an integer argument and either returns or
raises an exception. We are using the termination model of exception
handling [14], in which a call can terminate in one of a number of conditions; in each case, results can be returned to the caller. Thus a call on
the above port might terminate normally, returning a real, or it might
terminate with exception *e1* or *e2*. It returns a character if it terminates
with *e1* and returns nothing if it terminates with *e2*. Arguments and
results are passed by value, as discussed further below. The types that
appear in port descriptions such as that above are Mercury types which
are discussed in Section 4.3.2.

Ports are grouped together for sequencing purposes: only calls to ports
in the same group are sequenced. Groups of ports define the receiving
ends of streams. We require that ports in the same group all belong
to the same entity since otherwise it would be expensive to control the
sequencing of calls to them. Typically, an entity determines the grouping
of its ports when it creates them; however, ports can be regrouped later
if desired.

For example, a window system might provide a *create_window* port
used to create a new window. This port would be created as part of
creating the window system. When called, this port returns a number
of newly-created ports that can be used to interact with the new window,
e.g.,

```
create_window:  port (...)  returns (window)
window = struct [putc:  port (char),
        putl:  port (string),
        change_color:  port (string),
        ...  ]
```

All ports for a particular window might be placed in the same group but
ports of different windows might belong to different groups. Thus calls
to a single window would be synchronized but calls to different windows

would not. However, a program using two windows could regroup their ports so that calls to both windows would be synchronized.

So far, we have focused on the receiving entity and what it provides. Now we move on to the sending entity.

There may be concurrent activity within an entity, as would be the case for an Argus guardian. The separate activities should not share the same stream because this can introduce unwanted synchronization and even lead to deadlocks. For example, consider an entity, F, that acts as the frontend of the object repository in Figure 4.2. F accepts calls to read and modify objects from client programs, and processes these calls by communicating with entity R which stores the objects. Suppose F accepted a call from user u_1, made a call to R on its behalf, and then received a call from user u_2. If F has to communicate with R over a single stream, it would need to sequence its communication on behalf of u_2 after that for u_1. But this is undesirable since it delays u_2 unnecessarily. In fact, if the purpose of the call on behalf of u_2 is to release a lock needed by u_1, delaying u_2 can lead to a deadlock.

To permit concurrency within entities to affect streams, we use *agents* to identify activities. An agent has a unique name and belongs to a single entity; there can be many agents belonging to the same entity. Agents define the sending ends of streams.

Together, an agent and a port group define a stream: all calls sent by an agent to ports in a port group are sent on the same stream and thus are sequenced. Calls made by different agents to ports in the same group are sent on different streams, as are calls made by one agent to ports in different groups.

Earlier we mentioned that if delivery guarantees cannot be honored, the system breaks the stream. There are actually two ways that streams can break. *Asynchronous breaks* are caused by Mercury. As mentioned, Mercury tries hard to deliver messages, but if this appears to be impossible, it breaks the stream. For example, a stream will break if either the sender or the receiver crashes or if a network partition prevents them from communicating. In addition, user code at the receiver can explicitly break the stream. It would do this when processing of a call fails in such a way that processing of future calls on the stream should not occur. This kind of break is *synchronous*; it happens immediately after the call whose processing failed.

The program at the sender will find out about the break the next time it tries to use the stream (the details of how this happens depend on the programming language in use). At this point the sender can *restart* the stream and then carry out an application-level conversation with the receiver to resynchronize.

The two kinds of breaks usually cause different activities at the sender. In the case of a synchronous break, the sender knows exactly what calls have been processed, namely all those up to the one that caused the break and nothing more. When there is an asynchronous break, however, the sender knows only that all calls that have returned have happened, but there may be a number of calls that have been made and not yet returned and some prefix of these may have happened. On the other hand, a synchronous break often means there is a program error; this is not the case with an asynchronous break. Finally, recovery from a synchronous break can occur immediately if desired, but this is not sensible for an asynchronous break since the failures that cause such a break typically persist for a lengthy period.

4.3.2   Other Parts of Mercury

In this section, we discuss briefly the two other main parts of Mercury: the language-independent type system, and the language support.

In a heterogeneous system like Mercury, some method is needed to allow programs to exchange data values that make sense to both the sender and receiver. Mercury does this is by means of a language-independent type system. As mentioned, remote procedures take arguments and results of Mercury types: all communication in Mercury is done by means of these types, and every Mercury interface is defined in terms of the Mercury types. Mercury defines what these types are and how they are represented in messages (more than one representation may be supported).

Mercury provides a rich set of built-in types. We support types such as 32-bit signed and unsigned integers, characters and strings, fixed and variable sized arrays, and records. We allow port values to be sent in messages, and we support unions so that a remote procedure can take a value belonging to one of a number of types as an argument. We provide support for preservation of sharing structure [10]; this is useful when sending an object such as a graph in a message. In addition, users can define new, abstract types, such as VLSI masks.

Each programming language that supports Mercury needs to be extended to make call streams usable from programs in the language. The extension is called the language *veneer*. It can be done in a number of ways, ranging from a library of functions that can be called by programs to syntactic extensions. There are two main issues that must be addressed in a veneer. The first is how to associate the types in the programming languages to the Mercury types. An association must describe whatever translations are needed to map values of the language type to the message representation of the Mercury type, and vice versa. Usually, the associations will be defined by a systems programmer when the language veneer is defined; programmers using the language will not have to do this work. However, occasionally it is useful to allow users of the language to define new associations of their own. The translation procedures of an association can be automatically inserted into the calling or receiving code by a mechanism known as "stub generation."

The second issue is how programs in the language can make Mercury calls, especially stream calls. The most interesting problem here is providing a mechanism that allows the program to pick up the results of the stream call later. We have developed a general technique for this. It makes use of a new data type called a *promise*. A promise is created when a stream call is made. At this point it contains no value; the value will be filled in when the reply for the call arrives. Meanwhile, the calling program continues running. When it needs the result of the call, it "claims" the promise; at this point it will wait if the call has not yet finished. Promises were developed for use in Argus, but are a general mechanism that can be used in any programming language. More details are contained in [15].

4.3.3 Status and Discussion

Call streams provide a number of advantages. First, having one mechanism enhances sharing of programs. It leads to a single way of providing services: as processors of calls. This uniformity simplifies both clients and servers. Of course to use a service, the programmer needs to understand what the service does: what operations it provides, what types of arguments and results are required, and what each operation does. However, the programmer need not understand several transport mechanisms in addition. Instead, all services are used by making calls.

In addition, the mechanism is flexible. Rather than have the server predefine for each operation whether its calls should be blocking or not (as is done in [2]), the client decides what kinds of calls to use. Thus call streams allow a user to optimize communication for low latency or high throughput; we expect them to be competitive with remote calls and bulk data transport in the two cases. It is this flexibility that makes the mechanism suitable for a wide range of applications.

We have implemented a first prototype version of Mercury call streams on top of TCP [20]. Our current implementation performs quite respectably, as indicated in Table 4.1. This data was obtained by running a thousand null calls over a stream connecting a single sender and receiver; for the raw TCP data we used messages containing one byte of data. Both caller and callee were implemented in C; the two nodes were VAXes running Berkeley UNIX and connected by a local area network. The current implementation does not perform buffering of small messages; preliminary results for buffering indicate that we outperform TCP for messages containing up to 200 bytes of data.

```
Performance for null calls
        RPC         16.0
        stream      10.7
        TCP         10.2
Sends of small strings (≤ 250 chars)
        faster than TCP
Stream calls are network independent
```

Table 4.1
Call Stream Performance

In addition, we have done work on the language veneers. We have implemented veneers for C and Lisp that allow programs in those languages to make and receive calls on streams. We have also implemented an Argus veneer that allows servers written in Argus to accept Mercury calls. The rest of the Argus veneer (to allow Argus programs to make Mercury calls) has been designed but not yet implemented.

Using the transports and veneers as a base, we have experimented with the use of Mercury and have brought up several practical applications. Each of the following examples illustrates an advantage of Mercury:

1. We have moved a distributed mail processing system using the PCMAIL [7] protocol onto Mercury. All clients and servers in this system communicate using Mercury call streams. This system uses stream calls and sends to achieve high performance.

2. We have provided a distributed calendar system that demonstrates the advantages of integrating multiple programming environments. Some components of the calendar are implemented in C and others in Argus. The user interface portions of the calendar take advantage of the graphics capabilities and wide availability of the C/X Windows/UNIX programming facilities. The central database makes use the transaction processing provided by Argus.

3. We have added a Mercury communications substrate to the GNU Emacs text editor and developed Emacs interfaces to several services such as an English dictionary and a laboratory-wide account information database. Users can access these tools in an integrated manner and easily move information between central databases and their own work, providing a highly integrated and productive text-processing environment. This application shows that adding the ability to access remote services can greatly enhance a standard computing environment.

In the future, we plan to extend and complete Mercury by implementing the components not yet available and by improving those that are. One improvement planned for the future is to reimplement our transport using a new protocol we developed that avoids connection setup. Preliminary results indicate that this will greatly improve the performance of blocking RPCs and will also improve the performance of stream calls and sends [16].

4.4 Conclusions

This paper has discussed research at MIT aimed at increasing the utility of distributed systems. The research on Argus is aimed at simplifying the construction of distributed programs. The main problems concern control of concurrency and coping with the effects of failures. Guardians allow a program to be broken into units of tightly-coupled data and processing that can be located at advantageous positions within the

network. Resilience of guardians permits construction of highly reliable
programs that do not lose information entrusted to them, even when
nodes crash. Atomic actions make it easier to cope with concurrency
and with failures.

The research on Mercury is concerned with how to recapture the sharing that was possible in the days of the centralized machine. Mercury
allows programs to use one another as components. It does this by
providing a simple and uniform communication mechanism that is nevertheless flexible enough to support the performance requirements of a
wide class of applications.

In the future, we plan to investigate two new research areas. The first
concerns the design and implementation of an object repository. The
goal of the repository is to allow programs written in different languages
to share objects at a higher level than what is provided by a file system. In particular, the repository will store typed objects and will allow
objects to refer to one another; it will be based on Mercury types. In
addition, the repository will be highly reliable and available.

The second new direction is a study of parallel/distributed systems.
We are looking forward to a time when the nodes of the network will
themselves be multiprocessors. At that point, we will need to implement
programs that are both parallel and distributed. The object repository
is an example of such a program. It will be distributed to support
the availability requirement and also to provide scalability and avoid
bottlenecks. However, if it ran on multiprocessors, it could make good
use of the concurrency to speed up processing of searches.

4.5   Acknowledgments

Support for this research was provided in part by the Defense Advanced
Research Projects Agency of the Department of Defense, monitored under Office of Naval Research contract numbers N00014-83-K-0125 and
N00014-89-J-1988, and by the National Science Foundation under grant
numbers DCR-8503662 and CCR-8822158.

Bibliography

[1] A.D. Birrell and B.J. Nelson. Implementing remote procedure calls. *ACM Transactions on Computer Systems*, 2(1):39–59, February 1984.

[2] D.K. Gifford. Weighted voting for replicated data. In *Proceedings of the Seventh ACM Symposium on Operating Systems Principles*, pages 150–162, December 1979.

[3] J.N. Gray, R.A. Lorie, G.F. Putzolu, and I.L. Traiger. Granularity of locks and degrees of consistency in a shared data base. In G.M. Nijssen, editor, *Modeling in Data Base Management Systems*. North Holland, 1976.

[4] J.N. Gray. Notes on data base operating systems. In *Lecture Notes in Computer Science*, volume 60: Operating Systems—An Advanced Course, pages 393–481. Springer-Verlag, Berlin, 1978.

[5] I. Greif, R. Seliger, and W. Weihl. *A Case Study of CES: A Distributed Collaborative Editing System Implemented in Argus*. Programming Methodology Group Memo 55, MIT Laboratory for Computer Science, April 1987.

[6] B. Hayes. Computer recreations: On the ups and downs of Hailstone numbers. *Scientific American*, 250(1):10–16, January 1984.

[7] M.L. Lambert. PCMAIL: A distributed mail system for personal computers. DOD Internet RFC 1056, June 1988.

[8] B.H. Liskov, T. Bloom, D. Gifford, R. Scheifler, and W. Weihl. Communication in the Mercury system. In *Proceedings of the 21st Annual Hawaii Conference on System Sciences*, pages 178–187, Honolulu, HI, January 1988.

[9] B.H. Liskov, D. Curtis, P. Johnson, and R. Scheifler. Implementation of Argus. In *Proceedings of the 11th Symposium on Operating Systems Principles*, Austin, TX, November 1987.

[10] B.H. Liskov and M.P. Herlihy. Issues in process and communication structure for distributed programs. In *Proceedings of the Third Symposium on Reliability in Distributed Software and Database Systems*, October 1983.

[11] B.H. Liskov, et al. *Argus Reference Manual.* Technical Report 400, MIT Laboratory for Computer Science, November 1987.

[12] B.H. Liskov. Distributed programming in Argus. *Communications of the ACM*, 31(3):300–312, March 1988.

[13] B.W. Lampson and H.E. Sturgis. Crash recovery in a distributed data storage system. Technical Report, Xerox Research Center, Palo Alto, CA, 1979.

[14] B. Liskov and A. Snyder. Exception handling in Clu. *IEEE Transactions on Software Engineering*, SE-5(6):546–558, November 1979.

[15] B.H. Liskov and L. Shrira. Promises: linguistic support for efficient asynchronous procedure calls in distributed systems. In *Proceedings of the ACM SIGPLAN '88 Conference on Programming Languages Design and Implementation*, June 1988.

[16] B.H. Liskov, L. Shrira, and J. Wroclawski. Efficient at-most-once messages based on synchronized clocks. In *Proceedings of the Second IEEE Workshop on Workstation Operating Systems (WWOS-II)*, pages 73–81, September 1989.

[17] B.H. Liskov and R.W. Scheifler. Guardians and actions: linguistic support for robust, distributed programs. *ACM Transactions on Programming Languages and Systems*, 5(3):381–404, July 1983.

[18] D. Notkin, et al. Interconnecting heterogeneous computer systems. *Communications of the ACM*, 31(3):258–273, March 1988.

[19] J. Postel. Internetwork protocols. *IEEE Transactions on Communications*, COM-28(4):604–611, 1979.

[20] J. Postel. DOD standard transmission control protocol. DARPA-Internet RFC-793, September 1981.

[21] R.W. Scheifler and J. Gettys. The X window system. *ACM Transactions on Graphics*, 5(2):79–109, April 1986.

5 The X Window System

Robert W. Scheifler
Director, MIT X Consortium
Principal Research Associate, LCS

James Gettys
Research Staff, DEC Cambridge Research Laboratory

Abstract

X was born of necessity in 1984. Bob Scheifler was working at MIT's Laboratory for Computer Science (LCS) on the Argus distributed system and was in need of a decent display environment for debugging multiple distributed processes. Jim Gettys, a Digital engineer, was assigned to MIT Project Athena, an undergraduate education program sponsored by Digital and IBM that would ultimately populate the MIT campus with thousands of workstations.

The MIT X Consortium was created in January 1988, with Bob Scheifler as its Director. The X Consortium hosted its Fourth Annual X Conference in January 1990, with approximately 1300 people in attendance. The fourth release of Version 11 was available January 3, 1990. At the present time, the X Consortium consists of over 70 organizations, including all major U.S. computer vendors and many international vendors.

5.1 X Window System Structure and Features

The X Window System, or X, is a network-transparent window system. With X, multiple applications can run simultaneously in windows, generating text and graphics in monochrome or color on a bitmap display. Network transparency means that application programs can run on other

---

An earlier version of this paper appeared as the introductory chapter of *The X Window System* by R. Scheifler and J. Gettys, and portions are reprinted with permission from Digital Press, Bedford, MA, 1989.

machines scattered throughout the network. Because X permits applications to be device independent, applications need not be rewritten,
recompiled, or even relinked to work with new display hardware.

X provides facilities for generating multifont text and two dimensional
graphics (such as points, lines, arcs, and polygons) in a hierarchy of rectangular windows. Every window can be thought of as a "virtual screen"
and can contain subwindows within it, to an arbitrary depth. Windows
can overlap each other like stacks of papers on a desk and can be moved,
resized and restacked dynamically. Windows are inexpensive resources;
applications using several hundred subwindows are common. For example, windows are often used to implement individual user interface
components such as scroll bars, menus, buttons, and so forth.

Although users typically think of themselves as a client of the system,
in network terms, X applications are clients which use the network services of the window system. A program running on the machine with the
display hardware provides these services and so is called the X server.
The X server acts as an intermediary between applications and the display, handling output from the clients to the display and forwarding
input (entered with a keyboard or mouse) to the appropriate clients for
processing.

Clients and servers use some form of interprocess communication to
exchange information. The syntax and semantics of this conversation are
defined by a communication protocol. This protocol is the foundation of
the X Window System. Clients use the protocol to send requests to the
server to create and manipulate windows, to generate text and graphics,
to control input from the user, and to communicate with other clients.
The server uses the protocol to send information back to the client in
response to various requests and to forward keyboard and other user
input on to the appropriate clients.

Because a network roundtrip is an expensive operation relative to basic
request execution, the protocol is primarily asynchronous, and data can
be in transit in both directions (client to server and server to client) simultaneously. After generating a request, a client typically does not wait
for the server to execute the request before generating a new request.
Instead, the client generates a stream of requests that are eventually
received by the server and executed. The server does not acknowledge
receipt of a request and, in most cases, does not acknowledge execution

of a request. (This is possible because the underlying transport being used is reliable.)

The protocol is designed explicitly to minimize the need to query the window system for information. Clients should not depend on the server to obtain information that the clients initially supplied. In addition, clients do not poll for input by sending requests to the server. Instead, clients use requests to register interest in various events, and the server sends event notifications asynchronously. Asynchronous operation may be one of the most significant differences between X and other window systems.

For the best performance, when the client and the server reside on the same machine, communication between them often is implemented using shared memory. When the client and the server reside on different machines, communication can take place over any network transport layer that provides reliable, in-order delivery of data in both directions (usually called a reliable duplex byte stream). For example, TCP (in the Internet protocol family) and DECnet streams are two commonly used transport layers. To support distributed computing in a heterogeneous environment, the communication protocol is designed to be independent of the operating system, programming language and processor hardware. Thus a single display can display applications written in multiple languages under multiple operating systems on multiple hardware architectures simultaneously.

Although X is fundamentally defined by a network protocol, most application programmers do not want to think about bits, bytes and message formats. Therefore, X has an interface library. This library provides a familiar procedural interface that masks the details of the protocol encoding and transport interactions, and automatically handles the buffering of requests for efficient transport to the server, much as the C standard I/O library buffers output to minimize system calls. The library also provides various utility functions that are not directly related to the protocol but that are nevertheless important in building applications. The exact interface for this library differs for each programming language. Xlib is the library for the C programming language.

Figure 5.1 shows a block diagram of a complete X environment. Each X server controls one or more screens, a keyboard and a pointing device (typically a mouse) with one or more buttons on it. There can be many X servers; often there is one for every workstation on the network. Ap-

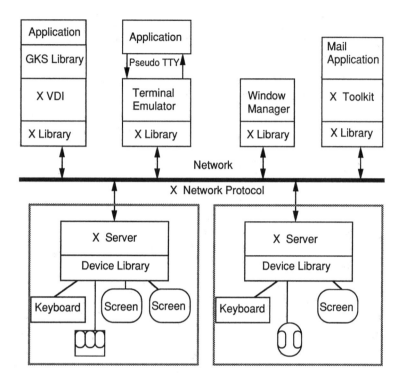

Figure 5.1
Block Structure Diagram

plications can run on any machine, even those without X servers. An
application might communicate with multiple servers simultaneously (for
example, to support computer conferencing between individuals in different locations). Multiple applications can be active at the same time
on a single server.

In X, many facilities that are built into other window systems are
provided by client libraries. The X protocol does not specify menus,
scroll bars, and dialog boxes or how an application should respond to
user input. The protocol and X library avoid mandating such policy
decisions as much as possible and should be viewed as a construction
kit providing a rich set of mechanisms that can implement a variety of
user interface policies.   Toolkits (providing menus, scroll bars, dialog
boxes, and so on), higher level graphics libraries (which might transform

abstract object descriptions into graphics requests, for example), and user interface management systems (UIMS) can all be implemented on top of the X library. Although the X library provides the foundation, the expectation is that applications will be written using these higher level facilities in conjunction with the facilities of the X library, rather than solely on the "bare bones" of the X library.

A user interface can be viewed as having two primary components: the interaction with the user that is logically internal to an application (for example, typing text into a text editor or changing a cell's contents in a spreadsheet), and the interaction that is logically external to an application (for example, moving or resizing an application window or turning an application window into an icon). The external user interface is built into many other window systems, but this is not the case with X. The X protocol does not define an external user interface at all. Rather, the protocol provides mechanisms with which a variety of external user interfaces can be built. These mechanisms are designed so that a single client, called a window manager, can provide the external user interface independent of all of the other clients.

A window manager can automatically:

- Provide title bars, borders, and other window decorations for each application;

- Provide a uniform means of moving and resizing windows;

- Enforce a strict window layout policy if it desires (for example, "tiling" the screen so that application windows never overlap);

- Provide uniform icons for applications; and

- Provide a uniform interface for switching the keyboard between applications.

With a suitable set of conventions, which have been standardized and called the Interclient Communications Convention, applications are insensitive to the external user interface provided by a window manager and run correctly unmodified in multiple environments.

Because the protocol can deal with such a broad spectrum of user interfaces, no single program, toolkit, UIMS or window manager are likely to use all of the facilities that the protocol and the X library provide.

5.2   Principles

Early in the development of X, we argued about what should and should
not be implemented in the server. For example, we did not know if menus
or terminal emulators could be implemented in the client with adequate
performance or whether "rubber banding" (dynamically stretching a
simple figure in response to movement of the pointing device) would
be acceptable when performed across a network. Experimentation during the first months showed us that more was possible than we had first
believed.

These observations hardened into the following principles, which
guided us through the early X design:

- Do not add new functionality unless an implementor cannot complete a real application without it.

- It is as important to decide what a system is not, as to decide what
  it is. Do not serve all the world's needs, but make the system
  extensible so that additional needs can be met in an upwardly
  compatible fashion.

- The only thing worse than generalizing from one example is generalizing from no examples at all.

- If a problem is not completely understood, it is probably best to
  provide no solution at all.

- If you can get 90% of the desired effect for 10% of the work, use
  the simpler solution.

- Isolate complexity as much as possible.

- Provide mechanism rather than policy. In particular, place user
  interface policy in the clients hands.

The first principle kept the wish list under control. Just because someone wanted something in the server, we did not feel obligated to add it.
This kept us focused on the important issues that made real applications work. This principle was a somewhat more difficult touchstone to
use during the design of the present version of X, given its significantly

larger audience. We modified the principle to be "know of some real application that will require it."

At each iteration of the X design, there was always more to do than time allowed. We therefore focused on mechanisms with the broadest applicability and for which consensus in the group could easily be achieved. For example, we focused on two dimensional graphics, explicitly deferring three dimensional graphics.

At the same time, to avoid obsolescence, we designed the present version of X to be extensible at both the protocol and library interfaces and without requiring incompatible changes to existing applications. Examples of extensions we had in mind were additional graphics models (such as GKS, PHIGS, and Postscript), real time video, and general programmability in the server. (We view programmability as simply one example of an extension, not as the sole mechanism for extensibility; mere programmability does not give you support for video or high performance support for graphics.)

During the design and implementation process, we generally suspected that any problems were just the tips of large icebergs. Expending effort to solve an immediate problem without first trying to generalize the problem is usually a mistake; a few related examples often make a whole class of problems obvious. This is not to say that we ignored the first instance of a problem; often there were adequate solutions using existing mechanisms.

We attempted to avoid solutions to problems we did not fully understand. For example, the preliminary design for the present version of X supported multiple input devices (more than just a single keyboard and mouse). As we worked through the design, we realized it had flaws that would take significant time and experimentation to correct. As a result, we removed this support from the system, knowing that correct support could be added later through the extension mechanism.

We also tried to avoid winning a complexity merit badge. If we could get most of what we needed with less complexity than a complete solution would require, we were willing to compromise our goals. Only history will decide if these tradeoffs were successful.

Much of the existing complexity is a result of providing support for external window management; most programmers need not be concerned with this, particularly those using an X toolkit. We expected that toolkits would hide various forms of tedium from the programmer. For example, a program that displays "Hello World" with configurable colors and font and obeys window management conventions is about 150 lines of code when written using only the facilities of the X library; an equivalent program written using a toolkit can have fewer than a dozen lines of code. Thus it is important to keep in mind that the X library is only one layer in a complete X programming environment.

Isolation of complexity is necessary in large systems. A system in which every component is intimately related to every other becomes difficult to change as circumstances change. We therefore attempted to build as much as possible into client programs, introducing only the minimum mechanisms required in the server.

Deciding what a system is not is as important as deciding what it is. For example, at various times people urged that remote execution and general interclient remote procedure call be integral parts of X. They felt there were no established standards in these areas, and they wanted X to be a self-contained environment. As is often the case, solving the immediate problem by adding to the existing framework rather than by integrating into a larger framework is less work, but the result is not satisfactory for long. The X protocol is correctly viewed as just one component in an overall distributed systems architecture, not as the complete architecture by itself.

User interface design is difficult and currently quite diverse. Although global user interface standards might someday be possible, we believed it prudent to promote the cooperative coexistence of a variety of user interface styles and to support diverse user communities and ongoing research activities.

By separating window management functions from the server and from normal applications, and by layering user interface policy in higher level libraries on top of the X library, we allowed for experimentation without forcing all users to be guinea pigs. As a result, many existing user interfaces have been imported into the X environment. Having a "pick one or roll your own" policy instead of a "love it or leave it" one has drawbacks; the applications developer must choose a user interface style and user community. The X library and the protocol should be remembered not as an end, but as a foundation.

As might have been predicted, X has become a fertile ground for experimentation in user interfaces, but also a source of market competition. Two major user interface toolkits and window managers (with quite different "look and feels") are Motif ^{tm} of the Open Software Foundation based on technology from Hewlett-Packard and Digital Equipment Corporation, and Open Look^{tm} from AT&T and Sun Microsystems. Applications using either can coexist simultaneously. Both of these can use the same X toolkit structure, though they provide quite different results to the end user.

Significant research toolkits include InterViews, written in C++ at Stanford, the Andrew System of CMU, several Common Lisp toolkits, and approaching a dozen major window managers. There are a number of user interface management systems and other application builders for X.

All of this, of course, is to enable applications to be built easily and cheaply. These are now appearing in quantity for X. It is by these that we must judge the success of X and, by this metric, we have only succeeded in our goals in 1989.

5.3   History

Neither Digital nor IBM had a workstation product with a bitmap display in 1984. The closest simulacrum available was from Digital and was a VS100 display attached to a VAX. Both Athena and LCS had VAX-11/750s, and Athena was in the process of acquiring about 70 VS100s. VS100s were in field test at the time, and the firmware for them was unreliable. Athena loaned one of the first VS100s to LCS in exchange for cooperative work on the software. Our immediate goal was clear: we needed to build a window system environment running under UNIX on VS100s for ourselves and the groups we worked for. We had little thought of anything beyond these goals, but wondered where to begin. Little software was available elsewhere that was not encumbered by license or portability.

Paul Asente and Brian Reid, then both at Stanford University, had developed a prototype window system called W to run under Stanford's V operating system. W used a network protocol and supported "dumb terminal" windows and "transparent graphics" windows with display lists maintained in the server. In the summer of 1983, Paul Asente and Chris Kent, summer students at Digital's Western Research Laboratory, ported W to the VS100 under UNIX. They were kind enough to give us a copy.

The V system has reasonably fast synchronous remote procedure call, and W in the V environment was designed with a synchronous protocol. The port to UNIX retained the synchronous communication even though communication in UNIX was easily five times slower than in V. The combination of prototype VS100s with unreliable firmware and W using slow communication was not encouraging, to say the least; one could easily type faster than the terminal window could echo characters.

In May of 1984, we received reliable VS100 hardware and firmware. That summer, Bob replaced the synchronous protocol of W with an asynchronous protocol and replaced the display lists with immediate mode graphics. The result was sufficiently different from W that continuing to call it W was inappropriate and would have caused confusion, as W was in some limited use at Athena. With no particular thought about the name, and because the familial resemblance to W was still strong at that date, Bob called the result X. Much later, when the name became a serious issue, X had already stuck and was used by too many people to permit a change.

Development was rapid during the next eight months. The first terminal emulator (VT52) and window manager were written in the Clu programming language, the language of choice in the research group where Bob worked. Bob continued development of the server and the protocol, which went from Version 1 to Version 6 during this period (the version number was incremented each time an incompatible change was made). Mark Vandevoorde at Athena wrote a new VT100 terminal emulator in C, and Jim Gettys worked on the X library and the UNIX support for starting the window system.

Late in 1984, we received faster VS100 firmware, causing the first round of performance analysis and optimization. Within a few weeks, we were again hardware limited, but we had a much better understanding of performance issues.

By early 1985, many people inside Digital were using X, and plans were underway for the first Digital UNIX workstation product which was based on the MicroVAX-II. At the time, support for UNIX in Digital was limited, and there was no chance of getting any other window system except X on Digital hardware. Other systems were either highly nonportable or were unavailable because of licensing problems (this was the case with Andrew). X was the logical candidate. We ported X Version 6 to the QVSS display on the MicroVAX. Ron Newman joined Project Athena at this time and worked on documenting the X library, already in its third major revision.

We redesigned X to support color during the second quarter of 1985, with Digital's eventual VAXstation-II/GPX as the intended target. Although MIT had licensed Version 6 to a few outside groups for a brief time at nominal charge, a key decision was made in the summer of 1985 not to license future versions of X. Instead, it would be available to anyone at the cost of production. In September of 1985, Version 9 of X was made publicly available, and the field test of the VAXstationII/GPX began. During that fall, Brown University and MIT started porting X to the IBM RT/PC, which was in field test at those universities. A problem with reading unaligned data on the RT forced an incompatible change to the protocol; this was the only difference between Version 9 and Version 10.

During the fall, the first significant outside contributions of code to X started to appear from several universities and from Digital. In January of 1986, Digital announced the VAXstation-II/GPX, which was the first commercial X implementation. Release 3 of X (X10R3) was available in February and was a major watershed in X development. Although we were happy to see a major corporation incorporate X into its product line, we knew the design was limited to the taste and needs of a small group of people. It could solve just the problems we faced, and its hardware origins were still obvious in key aspects of the design. We knew Version 10 had inherent limitations that would force major redesign within a few years, although it was certainly adequate for developing many interesting applications.

Over the next few months, a strange phenomenon occurred. Many other corporations, such as Hewlett-Packard, were basing products on Version 10, and groups at universities and elsewhere were porting X to other displays and systems, including Apollo Computer and Sun Microsystems workstations. The server was even ported to the IBM PC/AT. Somewhat later, Hewlett-Packard contributed their toolkit to the MIT distribution.

We tired of hearing comments such as "we like X, but there is this one thing you ought to change." People were already declaring it a "standard," which was, to our thinking, premature. Before long, however,

we were confronted with a fundamental decision about X's future. We
seriously considered doing nothing; after all, X did almost everything
we needed it to, and what it did not do could be added without difficulty. Unfortunately, this would leave many people using an inadequate
platform for their work. In the long run, X would either die because
of its inadequacies, or it would spawn wildly incompatible variations.
Alternatively, based on feedback from users and developers, we could
undertake a second major redesign of X.

Although we were willing to do the design work, we knew that the
resulting design would be ambitious and would require much more implementation work than our meager resources at MIT would permit.
Fortunately, Digital's Western Software Laboratory (DECWSL) was between projects. This group had the required expertise, including people
who had contributed to pioneering Xerox window systems. More important, these people were intimately familiar with X. Smokey Wallace,
DECWSL's manager, and Jim Gettys proposed the implementation of
Version 11, which would then be given back to MIT for public distribution without a license. Digital management quickly approved the
proposal.

We started intensive protocol design in May of 1986. No proprietary
information was used in the design process. Key contributors included
Phil Karlton and Scott McGregor of Digital. Dave Rosenthal of Sun Microsystems was invited to join Digital engineers in the design team, and
Bob Scheifler acted as the chief architect. At the first design meeting, we
decided it was not feasible to design a protocol that would be upwardly
compatible with Version 10 and still provide the functionality essential
for the range of display hardware that had to be supported. With some
reluctance, we abandoned compatibility with Version 10 (although Todd
Brunhoff of Tektronix has since shown that one can build a reasonable
"compatibility server" to display Version 10 applications on a Version
11 server).

We carried out most of the actual design work using the electronic mail
facilities of the DARPA Internet, which connects hundreds of networks
around the country, including MIT's campus network and Digital's engineering network. The entire group held only three day-long meetings
during the design process. During these meetings we reached a consensus on issues we could not resolve by mail. Even with group members on
opposite coasts, responses to most design issues were only a few minutes

away. A printed copy of all the messages exchanged during this time would be a stack of paper several feet high. Without electronic mail, the design simply would not have been possible.

Once we completed a preliminary protocol design, we invited people from other companies and universities to review the specification. By August, we had a design ready for public review, which was again carried out using electronic mail, courtesy of the Internet. Design of the sample server implementation started at this time. Phil Karlton and Susan Angebranndt of DECWSL designed and implemented the device-independent parts of the server, and Raymond Drewry and Todd Newman implemented the portable, machine-independent graphics library. Jim Gettys acted as the X library architect and, with Ron Newman at MIT, worked on the redesign and implementation of the X library. Many other contributions came from DECWSL as well, such as rewriting Version 10 clients and the X toolkit intrinsics (another story in itself).

During the fall of 1986, Digital decided to base its entire desktop workstation strategy for ULTRIX, VMS, and MS-DOS on X. Although this was gratifying to us, it also meant we had even more people to talk to. This resulted in some delay, but also in a better design in the end. Ralph Swick of Digital joined Project Athena during this period and played a vital role throughout Version 11's development. The last Version 10 release was made available in December of 1986.

In January of 1987, about 250 people attended the first X technical conference, which was held at MIT. During the conference, 11 major computer hardware and software vendors announced their support for X Version 11 at an unprecedented press conference.

Alpha test of Version 11 started in February of 1988, and beta testing started three months later at over 100 sites. Server backends and other code contributions came from Apollo Computer, Digital, Hewlett-Packard, IBM, Sun Microsystems, and the University of California at Berkeley. Tektronix loaned Todd Brunhoff to MIT to help coordinate testing and integration, which was a godsend to us all. Texas Instruments provided an implementation of a Common Lisp interface library, based on an interface specification by Bob Scheifler. We made the first release of Version 11 (V11R1) available on September 15, 1987.

5.4   The MIT X Consortium

Towards the end of the design phase of the Version 11 protocol, the
MIT principals were feeling that perhaps it was time to relinquish control
of X and let "the industry" take over, although we had only vague ideas
about what that might mean. Window system design was something
we "fell into;" we did not think of it as our "real" occupation, and it
seemed there was sufficient industry momentum for X to succeed. We
made our feelings known at the first X Technical Conference in January
1987, and during a few protocol design sessions.

We were somewhat surprised by the reaction, but this was just another
instance of underestimating the impact of X. Representatives of nine
major computer vendors collectively called for a meeting with MIT,
held in June 1987; their consistent position was that it could be fatal
to X if MIT relinquished control. They argued that a vendor-neutral
architect was a key factor in the success of X. To make UNIX successful,
it was necessary to encourage application development by independent
software vendors (ISVs). Prior to X, ISVs saw the UNIX marketplace as
fragmented, with multiple proprietary graphics and windowing systems.
X was bringing coherence to the marketplace, but without continued
vendor-neutral control, different segments of the industry would surely
take divergent paths, and interoperability would again be lost.

From this meeting came the idea of a more formal organization for
controlling the evolution of X with MIT at the helm, and in January 1988
the MIT X Consortium was born with Bob Scheifler as the Director. The
goal of the Consortium is to promote cooperation within the computer
industry in the creation of standard software interfaces at all layers in
the X Window System environment. MIT's role is to provide the vendor-
neutral architectural and administrative leadership required to make this
work. The Consortium is financially self-supporting from membership
fees, with membership open to any organization. At present, over 65
companies belong to the Consortium, as well as several universities and
research organizations. These members represent the bulk of the U.S.
computer industry, as well as a considerable segment of international
industry.

The Director of the X Consortium acts as the chief architect for all X
specifications and software, and is the final authority for standards. The
activities of the Consortium are overseen by an MIT Steering Commit-

tee, which includes the Director and one Associate Director of LCS. The Steering Committee helps set policy and establish goals, and provides strategic guidance and review of the Consortium's activities. An Advisory Committee made up of member representatives meets regularly to review the Consortium's plans, assess its progress and suggest future directions.

The interests of the Consortium are quite broad and include:

- Incorporating three dimensional graphics functionality, such as that provided by the PHIGS international graphics standard.

- Incorporating live and still video display and control.

- Incorporating scalable/outline font technology.

- Incorporating security mechanisms, in support of both commercial and government requirements.

- Incorporating digital image processing functionality.

- Developing high level toolkits to support the rapid construction of high quality user interfaces, and to support the reuse of user interface components across applications.

- Developing conventions to allow applications to operate reasonably under a variety of externally controlled window management policies, and to allow independent applications to exchange meaningful data in a cooperative fashion.

- Developing programming interfaces to simplify building internationalized applications, capable of being tailored to a variety of languages and keyboard input methods.

- Developing control protocols and support services for X terminals (network-based graphics terminals designed specifically to run the X server).

- Developing and maintaining software test suites for major system components.

- Sponsoring an annual conference, open to the public, to promote the exchange of technical information about X.

The Consortium's activities take place almost exclusively using electronic mail, with occasional meetings when required. As designs and specifications take shape, interest groups are formed from experts in the participating organizations. Typically a small multi-organization architecture team leads the design, with others acting as close observers and reviewers. Once a complete specification is produced, it is submitted for formal technical review by the Consortium as a proposed standard. The standards process includes public review outside the Consortium, and a demonstration of proof of concept. Proof of concept typically requires a complete, public, portable implementation of the specification. The MIT staff of the Consortium maintains a software and documentation collection containing implementations of Consortium standards and a wide variety of user-contributed software, and makes periodic distributions of this collection available to the public without license and for a minimal fee.

Beyond the industry standards created by the X Consortium, various formal standards bodies have now taken a keen interest in X. The specification of the X protocol is progressing towards the status of a national standard under the auspices of the American National Standards Institute (ANSI), and the International Standards Organization (ISO) has indicated its desire to review the resulting specification for international standardization. The Institute of Electrical and Electronics Engineers (IEEE) is currently considering several Consortium standards and several industry-sponsored X toolkits for review towards ANSI standardization.

5.5   Further Reading

Many books are available on X, the different X toolkits, and user programs, in technical bookstores. A full bibliography for X is too long for this volume. Some particularly interesting references include:

1. M. A. Linton, J. M. Vlissides, and P. R. Calder. Composing user interfaces with interviews. *IEEE Computer*, 22(2):8–22, February 1989.

   Describes the InterViews user interface toolkit, written in C++ and based on the X Window System. Even if you do not plan to

use InterViews as a toolkit, it provides a good C++ binding to the
X protocol.

2. J. McCormack and P. Asente. An overview of the X toolkit. In
   *Proceedings of the ACM SIGGRAPH Symposium on User Inter-
   face Software*, pages 46–55, October 1988.

   An excellent architectural overview of the X toolkit, including its
   goals, how it accomplished them and possible future directions.

3. Open Software Foundation, OSF/Motif Series (5 volumes), Prentice Hall, 1990. ISBN 0-13-640491-X, 0-13-640525-8, 0-13-640517-
   7, 0-13-640509-6, 0-13-640483-9.

   The volumes include Motif Style Guide, Programmer's Guide, Programmer's Reference, User's Guide, and Application Environment
   Specification (AES) User Environment Volume. Motif is a user
   interface programming environment for X and was designed and
   developed by members of the Open Software Foundation, including DEC, HP, IBM. These companies have committed to using
   Motif as their standard user interface in the near future.

4. R. Rost, J. Friedberg, and P. Nishimoto. PEX: a network-
   transparent 3D graphics system. *IEEE Computer Graphics and
   Applications*, 14–26, July 1989.

   A good overview of PEX, the PHIGS/PHIGS+ 3D extension to
   X. A complete PEX is currently being developed by Sun under
   contract to the MIT X Consortium and is scheduled to be publicly
   available in 1990. See also the Thomas & Friedmann paper on
   PEX.

5. R. Scheifler, J. Gettys, and R. Newman. *X Window System: C
   Library and Protocol Reference*. Digital Press, Bedford, MA, 1988.
   ISBN 1-55558-012-2.

   The the X library bible by the authors of X11. It is shipped with
   the X distribution tapes. Includes detailed descriptions of the
   X protocol and all the X library functions and data structures.
   Required for all serious Xlib programmers, but may be rough going
   for those with little experience in interactive computer graphics.
   An X11R4 version of this book is in preparation.

6. Sun Microsystems, *OPEN LOOK Graphical User Interface Series*, Addison-Wesley, Reading, MA, 1990. ISBN 0201-52365-5, ISBN 0-201-42364-7.

   This series includes Functional Specifications and Application Style Guide. OPEN LOOK was designed by AT&T and Sun and implementations are available from both. AT&T's implementation uses the X Toolkit. Sun's use its own, similar, but not compatible, toolkit.

7. R. Scheifler and J. Gettys. The X window system. *ACM Transactions on Graphics*, 5(2):79–109, April 1986.

   The first published description of X. Although it discusses X10, it is still one of the most comprehensive overviews of X.

6 A Dataflow Approach to General Purpose Parallel Computing

Arvind
Professor, Department of Electrical Engineering and Computer Science
Leader, LCS Computation Structures Group

Rishiyur S. Nikhil
Associate Professor, Department of Electrical Engineering and
Computer Science
Member, LCS Computation Structures Group

Abstract

Our dataflow group at MIT has two goals related to parallel processing. The first is to raise the level of parallel *programming* by designing and implementing an expressive, powerful programming language in which the natural description of an algorithm has abundant parallelism, without having to specify partitioning, mapping and scheduling. The second is to design architectures that are more suitable to the requirements of parallelism than the traditional von Neumann design that has served so well to date for uniprocessors.

While each goal is independently worthwhile, they achieve an exciting symbiosis when pursued together.

Our approach is based on the research programming language Id, its compilation to Tagged-token dataflow graphs—a parallel machine code—and architectures for direct execution of dataflow graphs. Our current architectural focus is on an abstract model called the *Explicit Token Store Model* and its concrete implementation in the Monsoon dataflow machine. In this article we provide an overview of our approach.

6.1 Functions and Reduction

We are all familiar with the following simple notion of computation. Given an expression like this:

```
(2 + 3) + 4
```

we can replace the expression (2 + 3) by the equivalent but simpler expression 5, giving

        5 + 4

which in turn can be further simplified to

        9.

At this point, no further simplification can take place, hence we say that this is the "result" of the computation.

This simple principle is the basis of computation in functional languages such as Id. Each step is called a *reduction*. The allowable reductions are specified by *rewrite rules*. Id has some built-in rewrite rules, such as those for arithmetic operations, so, for example,(2 + 3) $\implies$5. In addition, the programmer may specify additional rewrite rules through *function definitions*.

We begin with a simple example. It doesn't do much—it simply takes two arguments, adds them up and returns the result

        def plus x y = x + y ;

The identifiers x and y are called *formal parameters* or *arguments* because they are just dummy names that stand for actual values, or *actual parameters* that will be supplied when this function is used.

The function can be read as a rewrite rule, i.e., whenever we see an expression that matches the left-hand side

        plus e_1 e_2

where e_1 and e_2 are any expressions, we can always reduce it as specified by the right-hand side to

        e_1 + e_2.

Suppose we were given the expression "plus 2 3". We can perform the reduction as follows:

        plus 2 3 $\implies$ 2 + 3 $\implies$ 5.

In the second step, we use the built-in rewrite rule for "+". A more complicated example is:

            plus (2 * 3) (plus 2 3)
        $\implies$ plus 6 (2 + 3)
        $\implies$ plus 6 5
        $\implies$ 6 + 5
        $\implies$ 11.

In general, whenever we see any expression that matches the left-hand side of a function definition, we can always replace it by the right-hand side, substituting formal parameters by actual parameters. By repeatedly performing such reductions, we reduce the program expression to its result, i.e., an expression that cannot be rewritten any further.

6.2   Parallelism, Determinacy and Termination

At each point in the computation, there may be many rewrite rules that are applicable, i.e., many subexpressions that are reducible. In our example, we could have chosen to perform the reductions in the following order instead:

```
        plus (2 * 3) (plus 2 3)
   ⟹    (2 * 3) + (plus 2 3)
   ⟹    6 + (2 + 3)
   ⟹    6 + 5
   ⟹    11.
```

Happily, the result is still 11. In fact, this is no accident—it is a consequence of a very deep property called the Church-Rosser property, which arises from the fact that in functional languages, as in mathematics, expressions do not have any side effects—each expression uniquely stands for some value and can be replaced by any other expression denoting the same value without changing the meaning of the program. Reductions in a functional language are thus confluent, or determinate, i.e., no matter which order we perform the reductions, the resulting value is unique. This has major implications for parallel computation:

- We are free to perform in parallel as many rewrites as we wish.

- We have great flexibility in scheduling the computations on a real machine because the order will not change the result value.

Determinacy is an invaluable property for parallel programs because it guarantees repeatability of results. It is extremely difficult to debug a program if different runs of the same program on the same inputs can produce different answers.

The choice of which reductions to perform at each step is not completely unconstrained, however. First, it is possible that an unwise choice will lead to a nonterminating computation. As a pathological example, consider the following program:

```
def loop x = loop (x + 1);
def K x y = x ;
```
Suppose we now start with the expression:
```
K 5 (loop 10).
```
If we repeatedly choose to rewrite the `loop` expression, we get a nonterminating process:
```
K 5 (loop 10) ⟹ K 5 (loop 11) ⟹ K 5 (loop 12) ...
```
However, if at any step we choose to rewrite using the K definition, we immediately terminate with
```
5.
```
Note such nontermination always arises due to uncontrolled recursion. In Id, therefore, recursion is controlled by using conditionals which have a special computational rule. Given an expression:

$$if \ e_1 \quad then \ e_2 \quad else \ e_3$$

initially, no reductions are performed in e_2 and e_3. When e_1 has been reduced (to either `true` or `false`), the entire conditional expression reduces to e_2 or e_3 appropriately, after which it can be reduced. Thus recursive calls are typically placed inside arms of conditionals.

Apart from controlling termination, a second reason why one may prefer to do some reductions over others is that different choices can lead to vastly different resource requirements (processors, memory) on the underlying machine.

6.3   Higher Order Functions

Consider the following expression:
```
{ f = plus 1
In
  f 3 }
```

which says: let `f` name the value of the expression "`plus 1`"; using this name, compute the value of the expression "`f 3`".

Because the definition of `plus` mentions two formal parameters `x` and `y`, one might think that the expression "`plus 1`" is not even syntactically correct. However, we treat "`plus 1`" as an expression whose value is itself a function of one argument, i.e., `f` represents a function that adds one to its argument and returns its value.

Intuitively, the definitions in a block can themselves be regarded as rewrite rules that are used in reducing the "return expression" of the block (i.e., following the In keyword) to a value:

$$\{f = plus\ 1\ In\ f\ 3\ \}$$
$$\Longrightarrow\quad \{f = plus\ 1\ In\ (plus\ 1)\ 3\ \} \qquad \text{\textit{using the definition of} f}$$

where "(plus 1) 3" is a fully parenthesized version of "plus 1 3". By convention, application associates to the left, so we can drop the parentheses. Continuing,

$$\{f = plus\ 1\ In\ plus\ 1\ 3\ \}$$
$$\Longrightarrow\quad \{f = plus\ 1\ In\ 1\ +\ 3\ \} \qquad \text{\textit{using the definition of} plus}$$
$$\Longrightarrow\quad \{f = plus\ 1\ In\ 4\ \}$$
$$\Longrightarrow\quad 4.$$

The last step was performed using a rewrite rule for blocks which states that when the return-expression has been reduced to a value, the block may be replaced by that value.

This notation, whereby "plus e_1" can itself be treated as a function, is a very clever and powerful notation found in functional languages and is called "currying" (after Haskell B. Curry, a famous logician who invented it earlier in this century). We will make much use of it in later examples.

Now, let us look at a really fascinating program:

def twice f x = f (f x) ;

In words: twice takes a function f and an argument x, and applies f to x twice. For example, the expression

twice sqr 4

should apply the squaring function sqr twice to 4, i.e., sqr (sqr 4), producing 256. What about the following expression?

twice (plus 3) 4

Recall that "plus 3" represents a function of one argument that adds 3 to its argument. Thus, when applied twice to 4, we will add 6 to it, giving 10. Let us watch the reduction process:

$$twice\ (plus\ 3)\ 4$$
$$\Longrightarrow\quad (plus\ 3)\ ((plus\ 3)\ 4) \qquad \text{\textit{using the definition of} twice}$$
$$\Longrightarrow\quad (plus\ 3)\ (3\ +\ 4) \qquad \text{\textit{using the definition of} plus}$$
$$\Longrightarrow\quad 3\ +\ (3\ +\ 4) \qquad \text{\textit{using the definition of} plus}$$
$$\Longrightarrow\quad 10$$

Notice again the role of parentheses. The expression (sqr sqr) 4 would indicate the application of the sqr function to itself, followed by the application of the result to 4. As one would expect, this is a meaningless expression—it does not make sense to apply sqr to itself. More formally, we say that it is a *data type error*, because sqr expects an argument of type integer, but is being given an argument that is a function instead.

As an interesting exercise, the reader may wish to determine what the following expression reduces to

    twice twice sqr 2.

Hint: the answer is the address space of the venerable old 8080 and 6502 microprocessors!

6.4 Data Structures

The most basic kind of data structure in Id is a *tuple*, which is just an aggregation of some component values. For example, the expression

    (2,3)

represents a 2-tuple (or pair), which is a data structure whose first component is the number 2 and whose second component is the number 3.

Tuple notation can be used in any context. For example,

    (1+1,plus 1 2)

and

    { f = plus 1
    In
      (f 1,f 2) }

are also expressions that evaluate to 2-tuples containing the numbers 2 and 3.

Once a tuple is constructed, how do we gain access to its components? We use *pattern matching*. For example, suppose we want to define a function that takes a 2-tuple as argument and returns the sum of its components. This is how we would write it:

    def add (x,y) = x + y ;

i.e., the formal parameter (x,y) is regarded as a pattern that is matched against the actual 2-tuple supplied as an argument, and the effect of this is that x names the first component and y names the second.

Again, let us observe the reduction process:

```
        add (2,3)
    ⟹   2 + 3
    ⟹   5.
```

What is the difference between the functions add and plus? What happens if we said this?

```
    add 2 3
```

Remember that, fully parenthesized, this really stands for

```
    (add 2) 3.
```

Thus add is being applied to a number instead of a 2-tuple. This is another example of a data type error. Similarly, consider

```
    plus (2,3).
```

(The parentheses are necessary here to override the default that application binds more tightly than the tupling comma.) Here, plus expects a number but is being given a 2-tuple, and so, this is also type error. Here is a legal expression:

```
        add (2 * 3,(plus 4 5))
    ⟹   add (2 * 3,4 + 5)          using the definition of plus
    ⟹   (2 * 3) + (4 + 5)          using the definition of add
    ⟹   ...
    ⟹   15.
```

Tuples are "first class values," i.e., they can be nested within other tuples, returned as results from functions, etc. For example,

```
    def grid n = (1,n),(1,n) ;
```

is a function that takes a number n and returns a 2-tuple, each of whose components itself contains a 2-tuple containing 1 and n. The value of the expression "grid 10" can be visualized as shown in Figure 6.1.

6.5   Arrays

Tuples are "small" data structures whose components are specified and selected by textual position. In contrast, arrays and matrices are "large" data structures whose components are specified and selected by a computed *index*, which is a numeric name. For example, if A is an array, then A[5] and A[2+3] are expressions that select the component of A at index 5.

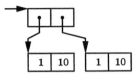

Figure 6.1
Value of "grid 10" (= ((1,10),(1,10)))

In principle, an array selection like A[5] and a function application like (f 5) are very similar. However, there are two main differences:

- An array is defined only on a finite, contiguous domain of numbers. We say that an array A has *index bounds* l and u, indicating that it is always an error to evaluate A[j] where $j < l$ or $u < j$. The index bounds of an array are specified in the program at array-construction time.

- Pragmatically, arrays are implemented so selection of a component always takes a fixed amount of time, independent of the size of the array or the value of the index.

This intuitive connection between arrays and functions is used to specify the construction of an array. The expression

    make_array (1,10) f

produces an array (call it X) with index bounds 1 to 10, and with components such that $X[j] = f\ j$, for $1 \le j \le 10$. For example, the expression

    make_array (1,10) (plus 10)

is an array (call it X) such that $X[j] =$ (plus 10 j) within its index bounds, as depicted in Figure 6.2.

This idea is readily generalized to multidimensional arrays:

    make_matrix ((1,n),(1,n)) g

is a two dimensional array (call it Y) such that $Y[i,j] = g(i,j)$ for $1 \le i \le n$ and $1 \le j \le n$. In general, a k dimensional array is specified using a function that takes a k-tuple argument. For example, the expression:

    make_matrix (grid 5) add

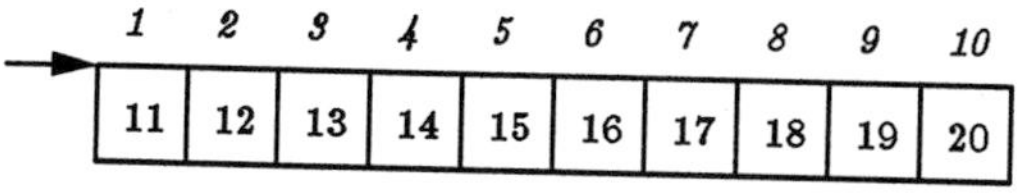

1	2	3	4	5	6	7	8	9	10
11	12	13	14	15	16	17	18	19	20

Figure 6.2
Value of: make_array (1,10) (plus 10)

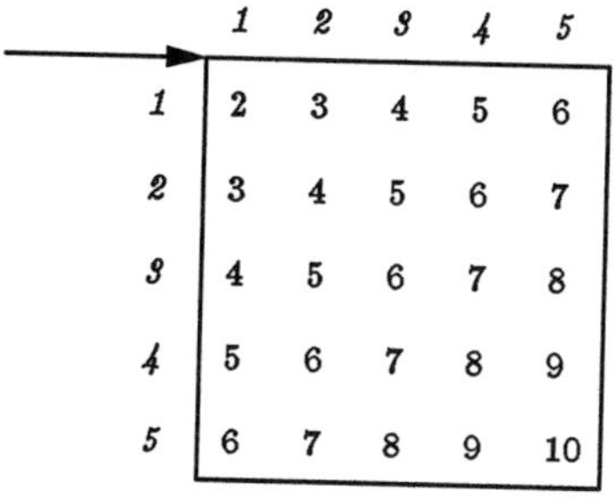

	1	2	3	4	5
1	2	3	4	5	6
2	3	4	5	6	7
3	4	5	6	7	8
4	5	6	7	8	9
5	6	7	8	9	10

Figure 6.3
Value of: make_matrix (grid 5) add

is an array (call it Y) with index bounds $((1,5),(1,5))$, within which $Y[i,j]$ has the value $i + j$, as shown in Figure 6.3.

Both examples are *declarative* specifications of arrays, i.e., there is no implication of any particular order in which to compute the components. In principle, they could all be computed in parallel. The subtlety of this issue will become much more apparent in our next example.

6.5.1 Example: A Wavefront Computation

Suppose we want to construct an $n \times n$ matrix X as follows:

- Cells along the left and top borders contain 1, i.e., $X[1,j] = X[i,1] = 1$.
- All other cells contain the sum of their neighbors to the left and to the top, i.e., $X[i,j] = X[i-1,j] + X[i,j-1]$.

This can be expressed in Id as follows:

```
X = make_matrix (grid n) f ;

def f (i,j) = if (i == 1) or (j == 1)  then 1
              else X[i-1,j] + X[i,j-1] ;
```

There is something quite unusual going on here—in the first line, we are defining X using f, whereas in the second line we are defining f using X. The reason it makes sense is the same reason that recursive function definitions make sense—it is inductive, i.e., no array component is defined in terms of itself. There is a base case where components are defined independently—when $i = 1$ or $j = 1$. Ultimately, every other component is defined in terms of these base components. Thus the definition is perfectly meaningful.

Using our currying notation, the reader may be interested to note that the program could have equivalently been written as

```
X = make_matrix (grid n) (f X) ;

def f X (i,j) = if (i == 1) or (j == 1)  then 1
                else X[i-1,j] + X[i,j-1] ;
```

Let us take a moment to examine the potential parallelism in the wavefront program. Imagine that make_matrix initiates n^2 computations, one to fill each component of the array. Most of these computations must *suspend* because they try to read neighboring components that are still empty. However, all computations for components in the top and left border can complete immediately since they do not depend on anything else. When the border components at (1,2) and (2,1) have been filled, the computation for component (2,2) can proceed. As soon as it has completed, the computations for components (2,3) and (3,2) can proceed, and so on.

Figure 6.4 shows a snapshot of the array during this process. The left and top borders, and some components on the top left have been computed. The shaded squares show the next components that can be computed because all the components that they depend upon have already been computed. Thus computation can proceed along a diagonal "wavefront" that sweeps across the matrix filling in components from the top left to bottom right. Parallelism grows until we reach the maximum diagonal and then shrinks as we approach the bottom-right corner.

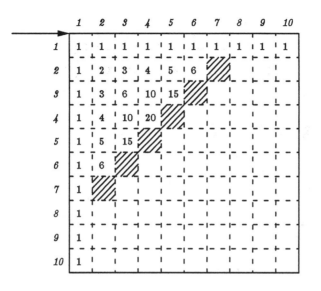

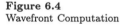

Figure 6.4
Wavefront Computation

This behavior is illustrated in the *parallelism profile* in Figure 6.5. The profile is generated automatically by GITA, a tool that can show the maximum parallelism in the dataflow graphs produced by our Id compiler. As we shall see, a dataflow graph (DFG) is a partial order on instructions and GITA plots the maximum number of instructions that can execute at each time step, assuming that each instruction takes unit time to execute and transmit its results to its successors, and assuming no resource constraints.

We stated earlier that make_matrix does not by itself imply any particular ordering on the computations for the array components. However, it is clear from the wavefront program that some ordering may be implied by the *data dependencies* in a particular program. In functional languages like Id, *all* the ordering is based on data dependencies; it can change from program to program and, indeed, from one input to another in a particular program.

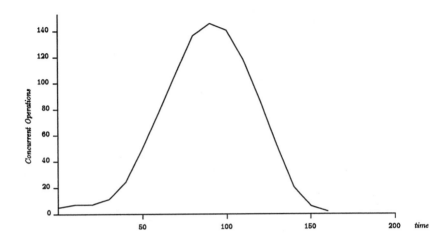

Figure 6.5
Parallelism Profile for Wavefront Program

How can we implement this notion of dynamically adjusting the order of computations to accommodate the data dependencies that may arise in a particular run of a program? This is the rationale behind dataflow graphs, which constitute a parallel machine language, and dataflow architectures. Before we look at them, however, let us briefly examine conventional programming and machine languages.

6.6 Parallelism in Conventional Languages

In imperative languages like FORTRAN, a total, sequential order on computations is specified by the language definition. The compiler must therefore work very hard to analyze a particular program to discover where this total ordering is too conservative. If it can detect such situations, the compiler can then generate parallel code.

Let us take a moment to see how the wavefront program may be expressed in FORTRAN.

```
      DIMENSION X(10,10)

C  Initialize boundaries
      DO 10 i = 1,10
         X(i,1) = 1
         X(1,i) = 1
10    CONTINUE

C  Fill in the middle

      DO 200 i = 2,10
         DO 100 j = 2,10
            X(i,j) = X(i-1,j) + X(i,j-1)        Loop body
100      CONTINUE
200   CONTINUE
```

For those unfamiliar with FORTRAN: the DIMENSION statement declares X to be a 10×10 array; as is usual in FORTRAN, we assume that each array index ranges from 1 to 10; comments are on lines beginning with "C"; finally, we have a doubly nested loop: for each i and each j in the range 2 to 10, the statement in the loop body specifies the computation of the (i, j)'th array element.

To run this code, we compile it (translate it) to a *machine language* representing instructions for a computer. A typical computer has two major components, a *processor* and a *memory*. The memory is a linear sequence of cells and, usually, the components of program arrays like X reside in a "flattened" form in the memory, for example, as shown in Figure 6.6.[1]

Thus, if we let X_0 stand for the address of the first element of X then, to access element X(2,3), the processor must fetch the value from memory location $X_0 + 21$.

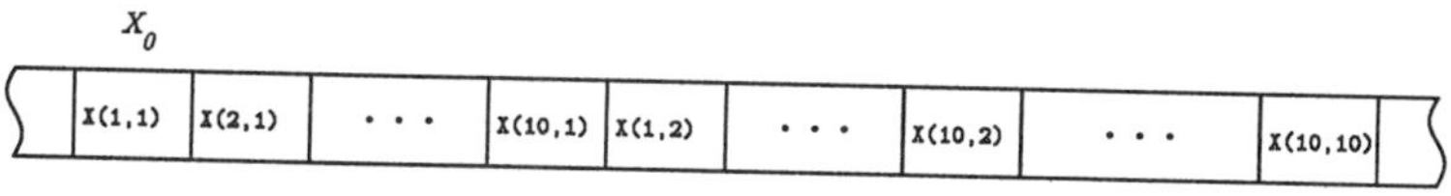

Figure 6.6
Layout of Array X in Memory

---

[1] The figure shows what is commonly called the column-major representation, which is only one out of many possible representations of a matrix in a linear memory.

The processor also has some local memory called *registers*. Typically, they will contain the values i, j, X_0, and other intermediate (temporary) results of the computation. In order to perform any arithmetic operation, the processor must copy the input data from the memory into its registers, perform the operation locally, then store the results back into memory. To copy data from memory location a into a register r, the processor must execute an instruction "r := FETCH r_a" where r_a is a register, containing the address a. To copy data back to memory, the processor must execute a "STORE r r_a" instruction.

Why do we not have an instruction "r := FETCH a"? That is, why does FETCH name a register r_a containing the address a instead of naming the address a directly? The reason is that a itself has to be *computed* at run time.[2]

In general, to access X(i,j), the processor needs to compute the address $X_0 + (i - 1) + 10(j - 1)$.

We can now see, in outline, the machine code corresponding to the body of the wavefront loop. We assume that l1,r1,l2,r2, l3, and r3 are registers in the processor.

```
l1 :=  compute address of X(i-1,j)
r1 := FETCH l1

l2 :=  compute address of X(i,j-1)
r2 := FETCH l2

r3 := r1 + r2

l3 :=  compute address of X(i,j)
STORE r3 l3
```

In a typical processor, these instructions are executed in sequence, one at a time, from top to bottom, i.e., control flows sequentially from one instruction to the next. By examining it in a little more detail, we see that in fact the following rearrangement of the code would also be correct:

---

[2] An historical aside: Originally, FETCH instructions in von Neumann machines *did* directly name an address. Therefore, the only way to access locations whose addresses were computed dynamically was to modify the instruction itself with new addresses at run time. This is not considered acceptable anymore, both because such programs are extremely opaque as well as because it complicates the design of the high speed processors. Ironically, it was one of von Neumann's remarkable observations that, by allowing modification of instructions, one could build a universal computing machine!

```
l1 :=  compute address of X(i-1,j)
l2 :=  compute address of X(i,j-1)
l3 :=  compute address of X(i,j)

r1 := FETCH l1
r2 := FETCH l2

r3 := r1 + r2

STORE r3 l3.
```

Of course, several other orderings are possible. In general, instead of specifying a total order on instructions, we would like to specify only a partial order, as shown in Figure 6.7.

This *control flow graph* specifies only the *necessary* constraints on the ordering. It clearly illustrates that all three address calculations can be performed in parallel and that both the FETCHes could be done in parallel.

This kind of reordering of instructions for higher performance was pioneered by Seymour Cray in the 1960's—his design of the CDC6600 was a breakthrough in that regard. It remains the key idea behind compilers and architectures for pipelined machines, RISC processors, VLIW machines, shared memory multiprocessors, etc.

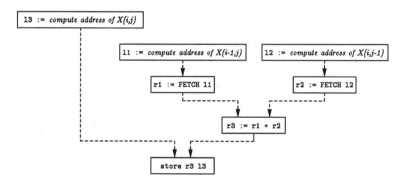

Figure 6.7
Partial Order of Instructions for Loop Body

6.7   Dataflow Graphs

To achieve the full parallelism of the wavefront program, however, we need to go much further. We need to specify that all the address computations in *all* the iterations can proceed concurrently, not just the three within a single iteration. Much more tricky is this: we need to specify that the FETCHes in one iteration can proceed as soon as the corresponding STOREs in some previous iterations have completed. It is not easy to generalize control flow graphs to express these ideas.

Around 1970, Jack Dennis of MIT developed the idea of *Dataflow Graphs* as a suitable formalism for expressing such parallel computations. Dataflow graphs constitute a parallel machine language that is suitable both as a target for compilers for high level parallel languages and as a language that can be directly executed by parallel hardware.

There are many variations on dataflow graphs in the literature. The simplest are direct expressions of an underlying hardware organization, and are often used for signal processing applications. Dataflow ideas are also used in many of today's supercomputers in expression evaluation and vector "chaining." For more general computations, however, one usually talks of machines that *interpret* a dataflow graph in the same sense that a von Neumann machine interprets a machine language. Static dataflow graphs allow control structures such as loops and conditionals, whereas dynamic dataflow graphs permit arbitrary recursion and data structures. In this article we concentrate on dynamic dataflow graphs that are also called "Tagged-token Dataflow Graphs."

Each node in a DFG represents an *instruction* and each edge in a DFG specifies a *data dependency* between two instructions, i.e., an edge from instruction I_1 to instruction I_2 specifies that the output value produced by instruction I_1 is an input value for instruction I_2.

The dataflow graph for the loop body of the wavefront program is shown in Figure 6.8.

Recall that the address of X(i,j) is given by the expression $X_0 + (i - 1) + n(j - 1)$. With $n = 10$ and a little algebraic manipulation, we can see that the addresses of X(i,j),X(i-1,j) and X(i,j-1) are given by

$$X_0 + i + 10j - 11 ,$$
$$X_0 + i + 10j - 12 \text{ and}$$
$$X_0 + i + 10j - 21$$

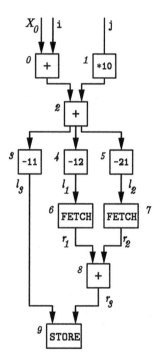

Figure 6.8
Dataflow Graph for Wavefront Loop Body

respectively. Instructions 0 through 2 compute the common expression $X_0 + i + 10j$; the rest of the graph is self-evident. Notice that all the "register variables" of the previous section are depicted here as labels on edges in the graph. We have also labeled each instruction with a number; initially, we will just use them for reference but later we will interpret them as addresses in an instruction memory.

The simplest way to visualize the execution of the DFG is as follows: Think of the edges as tubes. Imagine that we drop one token into each of the three input edges of the DFG, the value of the starting address of array X in memory, and the values of i and j respectively. We now repeatedly apply the following simple "firing rule:"

> Whenever an instruction has tokens on all its input edges, remove the tokens, compute the result value according to the instruction, and produce tokens on all its output edges carrying this value.

Initially, both instructions 0 and 1 are ready to fire. The former adds the values of X_0 and i, and the latter multiplies the value of j by 10. A constant like 10 can be regarded as a "literal" that is part of the instruction itself. Now, instruction 2 can fire, and it puts its value onto tokens on each of its three output edges. Then instructions 3, 4 and 5 can fire concurrently, completing the address computations. Instructions 6 and 7 can then fire concurrently, followed by instruction 8 and, finally, instruction 9. It is this visualization of tokens "flowing" through the graph that gives rise to the name "dataflow."

Note that at each instant, there may be more than one instruction ready to fire. This is in sharp contrast to conventional machine languages where, at each instant, there is exactly one instruction that is ready to be executed. This is why we say that DFGs specify only a *partial order* on instructions.

We do not have to fire all ready instructions at each instant; indeed, in any real machine, we will not usually have the resources to fire all of them at once. Fortunately, DFGs are determinate, i.e., we can safely fire any subset of ready instructions for which we have machine resources available.[3]

---

[3]However, different choices of the instructions to fire may entail different machine resource requirements and this is always a concern in a real machine.

6.8   The Explicit Token Store Processor Model

Now that we have the intuition behind dataflow graphs under our belts, it is time to be less abstract and to work out some details. How is a dataflow graph represented? How is a token represented? What does it mean for a token to be placed on an edge? How do we detect that an instruction is ready to fire? What happens when an instruction is fired? To explain all this, we use a processor model developed by Gregory Papadopoulos called the Explicit Token Store (ETS) model. The ETS model is suitable for direct hardware implementation and is shown in Figure 6.9.

Without loss of generality, we take the following position: each instruction has exactly one or two input edges, i.e., it is either monadic or dyadic. When a token arrives for a monadic instruction, the instruction can be fired immediately. On the other hand, when the first token arrives for a dyadic instruction, whether on the left or on the right edge, it must wait until its partner arrives. Thus we need to reserve a storage location for each dyadic instruction where its first input token will wait. This motivates our representation of dataflow graphs, as shown in the *Instruction Memory* part of Figure 6.9.

The numbers with which instructions were labeled in Figure 6.8 can now be regarded as addresses in instruction memory. Each instruction has three fields: an *Opcode*, *Destinations* and *Waiting Location*. The opcode is an operation, such as + or * or *2. The destinations encode the edges of the dataflow graph. For example, the destination of instruction 3 is 9L (instruction 9, left-hand port). The L and R port designations are present only for binary destinations. The waiting location r is an address in *Waiting Memory* for dyadic instructions. For example, the waiting location for instruction 8 is location 2 in waiting memory.

For simplicity, we are assuming separate instruction and waiting memories, i.e., instruction 2 and waiting location 2 are distinct. Further, both these memories are *local* to the processor, unlike the separate data memory that holds data structures such as arrays. The separate data memory is called "I-structure memory," and will be described in Section 6.9.

There is one more memory in the processor, called the *Token Memory*, each location of which can contain a token. A token consists of two fields $\langle IP,v \rangle$. IP (for "Instruction Pointer") is the address and port to which

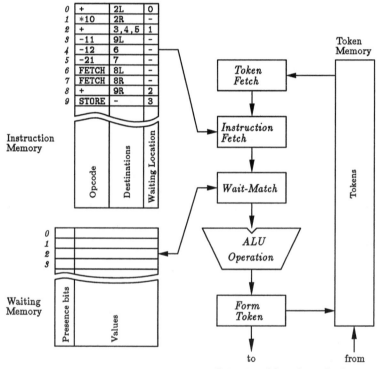

Figure 6.9
Block Diagram of an ETS Processor

the token is destined, and v is the value that it carries. To execute our example graph, suppose that token memory contains our initial three tokens:

<OL,X_0>   *value of X_0 destined for left port of instruction 0*
<OR,i>   *value of i destined for right port of instruction 0*
<1,j>   *value of j destined for instruction 1.*

The machine executes programs by repeatedly doing the following actions:

1. *Token Fetch*: remove a token <IP,v> from token memory.

2. *Instruction Fetch*: fetch the instruction <op;d1,...,dN;r> from IP in instruction memory.

3. *Wait-Match*: If op is monadic, execute the instruction (steps 4 and 5 below). If it is dyadic, examine location r in waiting memory to see if it is empty or full, i.e., check if this token is the first or second to arrive for this instruction. If the location is empty, store the value v from this token there, mark it "full" and extract the next token (step 1). Otherwise, extract the value in the waiting location and execute the instruction (steps 4 and 5).

   To implement this, every waiting location r must have some additional bits called "presence bits" indicating whether it is full or empty.

4. *ALU Operation*: compute the output value by applying op to the input value(s).

5. *Form Token*: attach the result value to d1, ..., dN, producing N new tokens, and place them in the token memory. Go to step 1 to process another token.

In fact, as suggested by Figure 6.9, these steps are independent and can be pipelined quite easily for high performance.

When accessing data structures, such as the array X, tokens are sent out of the processor to the separate I-structure memory system which in turn responds with tokens that come back into the processor and are deposited in the token memory. Similarly, in a multiprocessor configuration, tokens may be sent to and received from other processors. We will discuss these matters in Section 6.9.

To summarize: In the processor, instruction memory contains the dataflow graph; token memory contains tokens waiting to be processed, and waiting memory contains tokens for dyadic operators that are waiting for their partners. Outside the processor, I-structure memory contains all data structures.

There is a serious issue not yet addressed by the scheme just described. We can have many simultaneous invocations of the same dataflow graph (e.g., once for each iteration of the loop). So, we need a way to send multiple sets of tokens through the same dataflow graph and to have some way to avoid mixing up tokens from the two sets. Abstractly, if we think of one set being red and the other set being green, we should not fire an instruction using a red and a green token. Technically, we need to make the code *reentrant*.

To handle this, we change our interpretation of the waiting-location addresses encoded in each instruction so they are now relative to a *frame*. A frame is a chunk of storage in waiting memory which is freshly allocated for each invocation of a dataflow graph. Each token now has three fields <IP,FP,v>. The frame pointer FP is the starting address of the frame in waiting memory, and identifies the invocation of the graph that this token belongs to. Now, if the instruction at IP specifies r as the waiting-location address, then instead of examining the absolute location r of waiting memory in the wait-match stage, we examine the location FP + r.

The step we have just taken is analogous to the step from FORTRAN to Algol which introduced stack frames, allowing recursion and reentrancy. The only difference is that here we have a parallel run time structure, i.e., a tree of frames instead of a stack. Of course, we need a *linkage* mechanism by which we can dynamically allocate new frames, deallocate used frames, send arguments and return results; we omit these details for lack of space.

It may help the reader to draw the following analogy with conventional architectures: instruction memory, waiting memory and I-structure memory correspond, respectively, to the code, stack and shared data segments of processes, and token memory corresponds to a process queue.

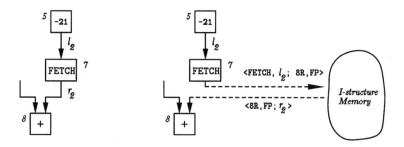

Figure 6.10
FETCH'ing a Value from I-structure Memory (Conceptual and Actual)

As in conventional architectures, these conceptually different memories do not have to be implemented as distinct physical memories.

6.9 Data Structures and I-structure Memory

The data structures of an Id program are allocated in a separate data-memory module of the machine called *I-structure memory*. A processor can send a token to I-structure memory with a request to read or write a location. The I-structure memory in turn can respond to the processor by sending back a token with a value. This interaction is depicted schematically in Figure 6.10 using an excerpt from our previous dataflow graph.

As shown on the left of the figure, the FETCH instruction conceptually takes an address (l_2) on its input arc and produces the contents of that address (r_2) on its output arc. The right side of the figure shows what really happens. When the instruction executes, the following token is sent out of the processor to I-structure memory:

    <FETCH,l_2;8R,FP>

where FP is the current frame pointer and 8R is the destination instruction address. The I-structure memory in turn reads the value r_2 in location l_2 and sends a token back to the processor containing <8R,FP,r_2>. Note that this token has exactly the form of the token that should flow down the arc labeled r_2. When it is received at the processor, therefore, it appears as if the FETCH instruction had produced it directly.

FETCH instructions are thus called *two-phase* instructions—they involve sending a token out of the processor and later receiving a reply. In fact, this protocol is one of the key reasons that the dataflow approach is so attractive for parallel machines:

- Assuming that there are enough tokens in the processor's token memory, it can continue to process other tokens during the I-structure memory transaction, i.e., the processor does not have to be idle during long I-structure memory reads. This tolerance of memory latency is becoming increasingly important in high speed machines. For example, in the Cray-2, while the processor can initiate an arithmetic operation on every cycle, it takes 40 to 60 cycles to access a memory location. In large multiprocessors, memory latency can be much worse.

- The processor can issue many I-structure memory reads before it has received the response to the first, i.e., the memory system can be *pipelined* for better performance.

- When a processor issues several I-structure requests, it is ready to receive the responses in a different order, because the <IP,FP> information on the responses prevents mixups. The FIFO order may be broken because, for example, the I-structure memory is implemented in several modules which may be at different distances (e.g., for interleaving), or may be experiencing varying degrees of congestion. (Another reason is deferred-reads, described below.)

We have one more implementation issue to tackle. Remember that in our wavefront program, all the iterations may be initiated in parallel, so that some of the array FETCH'es may be issued before the corresponding array STORE's. As discussed earlier, such array FETCH'es must suspend until the corresponding array STORE's have occurred.

To deal with this issue, we replace the FETCH instructions by I-FETCH instructions. At the processor, the only difference is that the token sent to memory contains an I-FETCH request instead of a FETCH request:

<I-FETCH,l_2;8R,FP>.

A complementary mechanism is found in the I-structure memory, as shown in Figure 6.11. Like the processor's waiting memory, each I-

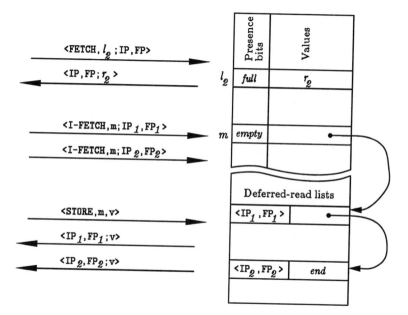

Figure 6.11
I-structure Memory

structure memory location has presence bits indicating whether it is full or empty. When the I-structure module receives <I-FETCH,m;IP,FP> messages for a location m that is still empty, it builds a "deferred-read" list locally, containing all the <IP,FP> pairs that accompanied such requests. The list is anchored at location m, i.e., each location can have its own deferred list. Later, when it receives a <STORE,m,v> message, it writes the value v to location m, marks it "full," and also sends all the responses <IP,FP,v> for the I-FETCHes deferred at that location. If an I-FETCH request is received for a full location, it just behaves like an ordinary FETCH request.

It is this protocol that allows us to initiate all iterations of the wavefront loop in parallel, relying on the fact that an I-FETCH in one iteration automatically waits for the corresponding STORE in another. Note: the compiler normally inserts an I-FETCH instruction. If it can prove that a location will already be full, it can insert a FETCH instruction.

6.10 Multiprocessor Configurations

So far, we have described a single ETS processor and a single I-structure memory. A multiprocessor is an interconnection of several ETS processors and I-structure memories, with the additional property that all the waiting memories form a global address space and all the I-structure memories form a global address space. Thus, in the Form Token stage of each processor pipeline, for ordinary tokens, the FP field determines whether it should be placed in the local token memory or sent out into the interconnection network to be routed to another processor. For I-structure tokens, the I-structure address is used to route it to the appropriate I-structure memory unit. Work is distributed across the machine by allocating frames on different processors and allocating data structures on different I-structure memories. As in any multiprocessor, load balancing is an issue; the dataflow approach *per se* does not offer any special answers to this question.

6.11 Which Language Should We Program In?

A popular approach to parallel programming is to take a sequential, imperative language and extend it with new, parallel constructs. For example, in a FORTRAN program we can specify that all iterations of a loop are to be done in parallel by using the keyword DOALL in place of DO. Recognizing the wavefront parallelism in our example, we could express it explicitly as follows. We change the program so we are no longer iterating on columns and rows, but on diagonals:

```
      DIMENSION X(n,n)

C  Initialize boundaries
   ...

C  Fill in the upper triangle

      DO 200 m = 4,n+1       traverse diagonal sequentially

         DOALL 100 i = 2,m-2 compute cross-diagonal elements in parallel
            j = m - i
            X(i,j) = X(i-1,j) + X(i,j-1)
  100    CONTINUE
         BARRIER

  200 CONTINUE

C  Fill in the lower triangle
   ...
```

The BARRIER statement specifies that all the parallel computations on one cross-diagonal have completed before the program moves on to the next cross-diagonal.

There are several problems with this "explicit parallelism" approach. First, the parallel FORTRAN program has already lost the intuitive nature of the original sequential program, i.e., the task of programming has been seriously complicated.

Second, it opens the door to new bugs due to nondeterminacy. For example, if we accidentally omit the BARRIER statement, the program would continue to run, except that we may now read an array location in the m+1'st iteration too early, i.e., before its value has been stored during the m'th iteration. Another example: in the DOALL loop, each iteration writes a value into j and reads it. Clearly, all iterations cannot share the same location for j. We have failed to declare that j must be a *private* variable, i.e., a separate location for each iteration of the loop. These kinds of bugs are quite pernicious because they happen silently, i.e., it may not be obvious from the output of the program that something went wrong. Even if we knew that something was wrong, tracking down such bugs is a nightmare because it is difficult to repeat the experiment—even the act of debugging can change the schedule of computations, thus obscuring the bug.

Another approach, pioneered by David Kuck of the University of Illinois, is to stay with a sequential language, leaving it up to the compiler to "parallelize" it automatically. Using sophisticated *dependency analysis*, the compiler attempts to discover the data dependencies in a program by identifying which parts of the program read and write to each data location. Once such dependencies are known, the compiler can reorder the instructions in the code to allow maximum parallelism while preserving these dependencies. Because all parallelism is introduced by the compiler using transformations that have been proved correct, this approach is not subject to the nondeterminacy bugs mentioned earlier.

However, we have serious doubts whether much parallelism can actually be automatically detected using this approach. Dependency analysis is difficult for several reasons. The first is that the exact location read or written by a program fragment may not be statically predictable, because the index expression for an array can be very complex, e.g., involving a function call or another indexed expression. Procedure calls, pointer variables, etc. are further factors complicating the analysis. Whenever the compiler is unable to detect the dependencies accurately, it must err on the conservative side; often, this means giving up much parallelism.

To illustrate these problems further, let us move to a slightly more complicated example called *successive overrelaxation* (SOR). Here, we compute a succession of matrices. In each matrix, the (i, j)'th element depends not only on some of its neighbors (as in the wavefront computation), but also on some elements of the *previous* matrix. Figure 6.12 depicts a stylized SOR in which the (i, j)'th element depends on two of its neighbors and on the (i, j)'th element of the previous matrix (in an actual SOR application, the recurrence may involve more terms). The Id code to express this computation is shown below:

```
def SOR kmax X = { for k <- 1 to kmax  do
                       next X = make_matrix (grid n) (f ( next X) X)
                   finally X} ;

def f X oldX (i,j) = if (i == 1) or (j == 1)  then 1
                     else X[i-1,j] + X[i,j-1] + oldX[i,j] ;
```

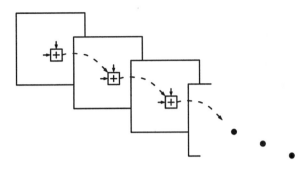

Figure 6.12
Successive Overrelaxation

Some notation: kmax is the number of matrices to be computed. The body of the *for*-loop specifies the relationship between each matrix (X) and the next one (*next* X). The *finally* expression specifies that the last matrix X is the final result. The function f is similar to the previous one except that it also takes the previous matrix oldX as parameter.

Again, let us take a moment to analyze the parallelism of this program. All the borders of all the matrices can be computed in parallel. At some point, it will become possible to define the [2,2]'th element of the first matrix because its neighbors, on the border, are ready. Of course, this makes it possible to define the [3,2] and [2,3]'th elements of the first matrix, but it also enables the computation of the [2,2]'th element of the *second* matrix. This in turn makes it possible to compute elements of the first matrix at [4,2], [3,3] and [2,4], elements of the second matrix at [3,2] and [2,3], and the element of the *third* matrix at [2,2]. Thus, where previously our wavefront was a diagonal line sweeping across a single matrix, it is now a diagonal *plane* sweeping across a collection of matrices. Figure 6.13 depicts two stages of the wavefront.

Figure 6.14 shows the parallelism profile produced by GITA for the SOR program with kmax = 10 (again, under the idealized assumption that all operations take one time unit to execute and communicate results, and that there are no resource constraints). It also shows the profile for a version of SOR in which we artificially hold back the $k + 1$'st

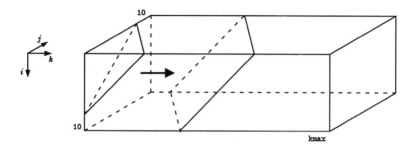

Figure 6.13
Wavefront Parallelism in Successive Overrelaxation

iteration until the k'th iteration completes, i.e., simulating a BARRIER between the k iterations, as may happen in a FORTRAN program that is unable to exploit the parallelism between the k iterations. This graph is essentially like the concatenation of ten copies of the wavefront profile of Figure 6.5. The example vividly demonstrates how the dynamic exploitation of parallelism in Id can drastically increase the parallelism (from about 150 to 1500 in this example) and reduce the critical path (from about 1700 down to about 250 in this example).

Let us now look at SOR in FORTRAN. A typical sequential solution needs only a small modification to our original wavefront program:

```
      DO 300 k = 1,kmax
        DO 200 i = 2,10
          DO 100 j = 2,10
            X(i,j) = X(i-1,j) + X(i,j-1) + X(i,j)    Loop body
100       CONTINUE
200     CONTINUE
300   CONTINUE
```

Here, despite the fact that all the X's in the loop body refer to the same storage area, the loop body actually computes the recurrence shown below.

$$X^k_{i,j} = X^k_{i-1,j} + X^k_{i,j-1} + X^{k-1}_{i,j}$$

This relies crucially on the sequential semantics of FORTRAN loops. For example, if we replaced "j-1" by "j+1" in the third term of the loop body, it also changes the k superscript in the corresponding recurrence term, i.e., from $X^k_{i,j-1}$ to $X^{k-1}_{i,j+1}$. The programmer has cleverly exploited

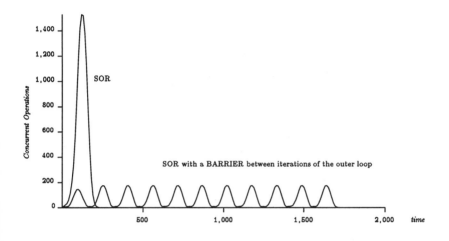

Figure 6.14
Parallelism profiles for successive overrelaxation, both with and without a barrier between relaxation steps.

this behavior in being able to perform the entire computation in place, i.e., with a single matrix.

If the compiler is to match the parallelism found in the Id program, however, it must reconstruct the three dimensional abstract recurrence from the FORTRAN program, change the two dimensional matrix X into a three dimensional array and, finally, set up the parallel computations to fill up the array. There are major pitfalls at each stage.

First, the programmer's cleverness in reusing storage in the sequential program makes dependency analysis (to discover the three dimensional recurrence) much harder.

Second, if kmax is not known at compile time, it is difficult to convert the matrix into a three dimensional array because in FORTRAN, storage must be allocated statically. Even if kmax is known statically, the permanent allocation of all the storage for the entire three dimensional array is wasteful, since only a small part of it is used at a time (along the diagonal wavefront plane).

Finally, because of the lack of fine-grained parallelism enabled due to I-structures, the parallel program must have the following structure:

```
        DO 200 p = 1, number of wavefront planes
          DOALL 100  for each I,J,K  in wavefront plane p
            X(I,J,K) = X(I-1,J,K) + X(I,J-1,K) + X(I,J,K-1)
    100   CONTINUE
          BARRIER
    200   CONTINUE
```

It is actually very tricky to set up the iterations that we have abbreviated in the DOALL line because the boundary of the wavefront plane
varies greatly. It may be a triangle, pentagon, trapezoid or rectangle
depending on the position of plane (two of these planes are shown in
Figure 6.13). The resulting program would be practically unreadable
and is certainly not something that ought to be programmed manually.

Thus, in FORTRAN, clarity of expression and maximal parallelism
are often contradictory requirements. In Id, on the other hand, the
most natural expression of the program *is* the parallel version. The
"three dimensional" storage arises because each iteration of the Id loop
dynamically allocates a new matrix. Unlike the FORTRAN version, all
kmax versions of the matrix do not have to be permanently allocated.
When a matrix in one k iteration is no longer in use, i.e., all references
from the $k + 1$'st iteration have been completed, its storage can be reclaimed dynamically. The general mechanism for this is a continuous
process known as "garbage collection." In fact, it is possible to be even
more efficient—using a technique known as "loop bounding," it is possible to build a circular list of frames and matrices for the k loop and
to cycle through them. The language semantics, which guarantees that
data structure components are defined uniquely, allows the compiler to
exploit dataflow I-structure hardware fully, so it can initiate many the
iterations concurrently, leaving it to dynamic scheduling to achieve the
wavefront parallelism.

6.12   Current Status

Two dynamic dataflow machines have been built to date. The first
was the Manchester Dataflow Machine at the University of Manchester,
England, and was operational in 1982. It could run at speeds of up to
about two million dataflow instructions per second, which is encouraging
considering that it was only a single-processor prototype (with multiple
function units), had no I-structure storage, did not use very ambitious

implementation technology, and did not have a very sophisticated compiler. Especially encouraging was the clear demonstration that dataflow instruction scheduling could achieve very high pipeline utilization.

The second machine is the Sigma-1, built at the Electro-technical Laboratory in Japan. It has just become operational and consists of 128 processors and 128 I-structure units. Each processor is capable of about 1 to 5 MIPS. On a small, partly hand-coded benchmark (trapezoidal integration), a 4-processor machine achieved 6.4 MFLOPS. Evaluation of the larger configuration must await the availability of a suitable compiler.

Both these machines use an earlier design in which the wait-match operation is done using an associative memory. The ETS model described in this paper, because of directly addressed wait-match memory, is much easier to implement and provides much more flexibility in controlling the use of storage. At MIT, we are constructing a machine based on this model called "Monsoon." A single-processorMonsoon dataflow machine wire-wrap prototype has been operational since October 1988, and an 8 processor, 8 I-structure machine is expected to be complete by the spring of 1991.

Concurrently, our software effort concentrates on two related areas. One is on compiler optimizations, building on the excellent Id compiler implementation by Ken Traub. The second is on resource management—the efficient dynamic management of frames and data structures. Of course, we are also continually upgrading "Id World," our incremental programming environment for Id and Monsoon.

The ETS model has also given us deeper insight into the essence of dataflow and von Neumann models which has led to many ideas on integrating the best of both. Research projects in this area include the Hybrid von Neumann/Dataflow machine of Robert Iannucci of IBM Research, the EM-4 at Electro-technical Laboratory, Japan, the Eps-88 at Sandia National Laboratory, New Mexico, and the P-RISC processor here at MIT.

Dataflow research is at an extremely exciting stage. We are confident that these projects will take us closer to the "right" building blocks for scalable, programmable, general purpose parallel machines. Perhaps by 1995 we will have commercially viable parallel machines which are actually a pleasure to program.

6.13 Acknowledgments

Support for this research was provided in part by the Defense Advanced Research Projects Agency of the Department of Defense, monitored under Office of Naval Research contract number N00014-84-K-0099.

6.14 Further reading

All the technical reports cited below are available from:

MIT Laboratory for Computer Science
Computation Structures Group
545 Technology Square, Cambridge, MA 02139, U.S.A.

1. J.B. Dennis. First version of a dataflow procedure language. In *Proceedings of Programming Symposium*, Paris, France, 1974. *Lecture Notes in Computer Science*, 19, Springer Verlag, Berlin, 1974.

   The original "classic" by Jack Dennis.

2. Arvind and R. S. Nikhil. Executing a program on the MIT tagged-token dataflow architecture. *IEEE Transactions on Computers*, 23(2):45–55, February 1990.

   This paper is an overview of MIT Tagged-token dataflow approach, including example Id programs, their translation to dataflow graphs, and an overview of the Tagged-token Dataflow Architecture (TTDA).

3. R. S. Nikhil. *Id (Version 88.1) Reference Manual.* LCS CSG Memo 284, August 1988.

   This memo is the current Id language reference manual.

4. Arvind and K. Ekanadham. Future scientific programming on parallel machines. In *Proceedings of the International Conference on Supercomputing (ICS),* Athens, Greece, June 1987.

   This paper develops excerpts of the SIMPLE hydro-dynamics code written in Id, demonstrating the level of programming and comparing it with the FORTRAN version.

5. Arvind, S. K. Heller, and R. S. Nikhil. Programming generality and parallel computers. In *Proceedings of the Fourth International Symposium on Biological and Artificial Intelligence Systems, Trento, Italy, September 1988.*

This paper develops an Id solution to David Turner's "paraffins problem," demonstrating the level of programming and the inherent parallelism obtained.

6. K. R. Traub. A Compiler for the MIT Tagged-token Dataflow Architecture. MIT Laboratory for Computer Science Technical Report 370, August 1986.

This thesis is a detailed description of the Id compiler and basic optimizations.

7. Arvind and D. E. Culler. Dataflow architectures. *Annual Reviews in Computer Science,* 1, pages 225–253, Annual Reviews, Inc., Palo Alto, CA, 1986.

This paper is a survey of data-driven architectures, including static dataflow machines, the Denelcor HEP, the MIT TTDA, the Japanese ETL Sigma-1, etc.

8. G. M. Papadopoulos. *The Monsoon Dataflow Architecture.* PhD thesis, MIT Department of Electrical Engineering and Computer Science, August 1988.

This thesis develops the Explicit Token Store (ETS) dataflow model and Monsoon, a specific implementation.

9. Arvind and R. A. Iannucci. Two fundamental issues in multiprocessing. In *Proceedings of DFVLR - Conference 1987 on Parallel Processing in Science and Engineering,* Bonn-Bad Godesberg, W. Germany, June 1987.

This paper discusses the role of latency and synchronization in parallel machines, and an analysis of how von Neumann and dataflow architectures address these issues.

10. R. S. Nikhil and Arvind. Can dataflow subsume von Neumann computing? In *Proceedings of the 16th Annual Symposium on Computer Architecture,* pages 262–272, Jerusalem, Israel, May 1989.

This paper describes P-RISC, a processor element whose instruction set and architecture properly extends a conventional RISC element, giving it a fine-grained dataflow capability.

7 Fine-Grain Concurrent Computing

William J. Dally

Associate Professor, Department of Electrical Engineering and
Computer Science
Member, Artificial Intelligence Laboratory
Member, LCS Computer Architecture Group

Abstract

Fine-grain concurrent computers with general purpose mechanisms for concurrency offer an attractive means of applying
VLSI technology to building powerful information processing
systems. A fine-grain computer consists of many physically
small processing nodes connected by a network. Each node contains a powerful processor and a small amount of memory. It
is the memory size rather than the processor power that distin-
guishes fine-grain machines. Fine-grain computers make more
efficient use of the technology because (1) a larger fraction of
their area is devoted to computing, and (2) they provide higher
memory and network bandwidth. Providing general purpose
mechanisms for the processing nodes to interact with one another allows this class of machines to support most proposed
models of parallel programming.

7.1 Introduction

Over the past 25 years, improvements in the cost and performance of digital electronic computers have been largely due to improvements in semiconductor technology. The architecture of these machines has changed
very little during this period. As technology has improved, however, the
relative costs of system components have shifted. With today's VLSI
(very large scale integration) technology, processors are very inexpensive, memory is moderately expensive, and communication is very costly.

Sequential (von Neumann) computers, developed under a different set of relative costs, make very inefficient use of modern VLSI technology. To make efficient use of VLSI technology, one must exploit parallelism by building concurrent computers, machines composed of many processors. Different approaches to building concurrent computers can be distinguished by the following two questions:

Granularity: How large is each processor? If a machine is of size A and has N processors, its granularity or grain-size is A/N. As processors are relatively inexpensive, for most machines granularity corresponds to the amount of memory per processor.

Mechanisms: What mechanisms are provided for the processors to interact with each other? Mechanisms must be provided for processors to communicate with one another, to synchronize and to name their points of interaction.

This paper makes a case for fine-grain concurrent computers with a small set of *general purpose* mechanisms for concurrency. A fine-grain computer consists of many physically small processing nodes connected by a network. Each node contains a powerful processor and a small amount of memory. It is the memory size rather than the processor power that determines the grain-size of a machine. Up to a point, a fine-grain size results in more efficient use of the available technology since a larger fraction of the machine's area is devoted to processing. General purpose mechanisms allow the machine to be programmed using many different models of parallel computation.

The remainder of this paper builds the case for a general purpose, fine-grain concurrent computer. I discuss VLSI technology in Section 7.2. I show how the relative costs of VLSI favor concurrency. In Section 7.3, I examine the evolutionary approach to computer design, building smaller and faster single CPU von Neumann processors. I describe how to use technology more efficiently by building machines with large numbers of fine-grain processing nodes in Section 7.4. The models that have been developed to program such a machine are briefly reviewed in Section 7.5. Section 7.6 discusses a single set of mechanisms that can efficiently support these parallel models of computation.

7.2 VLSI Technology

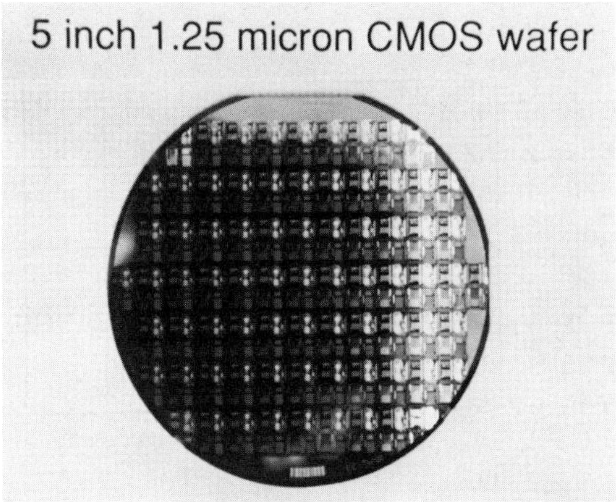

5 inch 1.25 micron CMOS wafer

Figure 7.1
A 5-inch 1μ CMOS wafer. This wafer contains $5 \times 10^{10}\lambda^2$ of silicon area, enough to fabricate 100Mbits of read/write memory or 1000 32-bit CPUs.

With few exceptions, computers are manufactured from silicon integrated circuits. These circuits are fabricated on wafers. Figure 7.1 shows a 5-inch 1μ CMOS wafer. This wafer has an area of 1.2×10^4 mm^2 or if we normalize to units of $\lambda = 0.5\mu$, half a linewidth, $5 \times 10^{10}\lambda^2$. To put this in perspective, a 1Mbit dynamic read/write memory (DRAM) chip takes about $2.5 \times 10^8\lambda^2$ and a 32-bit integer processor[1] takes less than $2.5 \times 10^7\lambda^2$. Accounting for typical yields, a single wafer can be used to fabricate 100Mbits of DRAM or 1000 32-bit integer processors.

VLSI technology makes powerful processors very inexpensive. A processor costs the same amount of chip area as 100Kbits of read/write memory. These processors have performance comparable to mainframes. A recently announced single-chip processor has a peak performance of 50 million instructions per second (MIPS) [16]. Only a small portion of this chip is used for the integer processor. Most of the chip is devoted to a floating-point unit and a cache memory.

VLSI technology is improving at a rate where linear dimensions, λ, are reduced by a factor of two every five years. Every five years the number

---

[1] This number is for a typical RISC processor without cache or memory management unit.

of devices that can be fabricated on a given size chip is quadrupled and the chips get $\approx$ 70% faster. This trend is expected to continue for at least the next decade.

The challenge of VLSI is to discover how to apply the enormous potential of this technology to building more powerful information processing systems. Today we can fabricate CPUs with an aggregate performance of 2×10^{10} IPS on a single wafer. In five years time, this number will more than quadruple. It is not clear, however, how to focus this computing power on a problem.

7.3 von Neumann Machines Make Inefficient Use of Technology

One method of applying VLSI technology is to make smaller and faster von Neumann machines. This is the path that industry has been following. Every five years or so a new generation of technology is used to reduce the cost and increase the performance of computers without changing their design in any significant manner. Most of the advances in computer hardware over the past 25 years have been due to better technology. The architecture of general purpose computers has changed very little during this period. Most of the features of modern computers such as memory protection, demand paging and cache memory can be found in computers built during the 1960s [15][17][18].

This evolutionary approach to building VLSI computers makes very poor use of the technology because it cannot apply the increased density of VLSI other than to increase the memory capacity of a machine. Only a small amount of silicon area is required to build a very fast processor. Using more area for the processor results in diminishing returns.

This approach also ignores major changes in the relative cost of memory, processors and communication. When the von Neumann architecture was developed in the late 1940's, the logic circuitry used to build processors was expensive, memory was somewhat less expensive and the wire used to connect the components of the machine was practically free. As a result, the machines were designed to make the best use of the most expensive resource: the processor.

Today, the situation is almost completely reversed. Interconnection is very expensive, memory is somewhat less expensive and processors are relatively inexpensive.

Much of the cost of a modern computer is in the interconnection. The package used to hold a semiconductor chip, for example, often costs more than the chip itself. The cost of wire is not entirely economic either. The performance of VLSI systems is wire-limited. Wire density limits the type of systems that can be built at both the chip and board levels. Much of the delay in a VLSI system is due to driving wires. Also, a large fraction of the power consumed by VLSI systems is expended driving wires.

In a technology where processors are inexpensive, it is no longer appropriate to use a computer architecture that was designed to make best use of the processor. Neither is it appropriate to judge a system by its processor utilization.

The evolutionary approach to building VLSI computers results in machines that have very poor utilization of their silicon area and their wiring. Because these machines are mostly memory, a very small fraction of their silicon area is devoted to function units (the logic that actually performs the operations associated with a computation). Also, because they only perform a single communication action per cycle, reading or writing a word to or from memory, they make very poor use of their interconnect.

For example, a SUN 3/110 workstation with 8Mbytes of memory (see Figure 7.2) is composed of the following integrated circuits:

Processor	2
Memory	72
MMU RAM	9
Video RAM	40
Glue	177
Peripheral	4

The total silicon area in the machine is $\approx 23G\lambda^2$ and is almost entirely memory. While the 177 *glue* chips outnumber the 121 memory chips, they are SSI and MSI chips and account for a small fraction of the silicon

Figure 7.2
The CPU Board of a SUN3/110 workstation. The board contains approximately
300 chips, most of which perform memory and interface functions. Only two chips
perform processing.

area. Only $64M\lambda^2$ (0.2%) is in the two processor chips, and of this, only
about $10M\lambda^2$ (0.04%) is in the actual function units.[2]

A large fraction of the board area, the pins on the processor and memory chips, and the glue chips are involved in interfacing the processor to
the memory system. Despite this large investment of system resources
in communication, only a single communication action takes place at a
time. The main memory bandwidth is 160Mbits/s.

One can build concurrent computers using suitably adapted conventional computers as the processing elements. However, because these
coarse-grain machines are mostly memory, their efficiency is no better
than the sequential machines they are derived from. To improve efficiency, grain size must be reduced.

Because conventional computers are mostly memory, the DRAM chip
has become the major commodity, or *jellybean* part. In the remainder
of this paper, we will see how to define a new type of jellybean part that
makes more efficient use of VLSI technology.

---

[2]These numbers are estimates based on the sizes of comparable functions on other
chips.

7.4 Fine-Grain Concurrent Computers Make Efficient Use of VLSI

VLSI can be applied more efficiently by building fine-grain concurrent computers. Such machines consist of a number of nodes each containing a processor and a small amount of memory. The nodes communicate with each other over an interconnection network. These machines have a higher ratio of processor area to memory area than conventional computers. This results in a larger fraction of area being devoted to function units for better silicon efficiency. In fine-grain machines, many memory references and communication actions take place simultaneously resulting in better wire efficiency.

The nodes of a fine-grain concurrent computer need not be slow. The *grain size* of a machine refers to the physical size and the amount of memory in one processing node. A coarse-grain processing node requires hundreds of chips (one or more boards) and has $\approx 10^7$ bytes of memory while fine-grain node fits on a single chip and has $\approx 10^4$ bytes of memory. Fine-grain nodes cost less and have less memory than coarse-grain nodes, however, because so little silicon area is required to build a fast processor, they need not have slower processors than coarse-grain nodes.

For an example of a fine-grain concurrent computer we will look at the J-Machine[3] [5], an experimental concurrent computer under development at MIT. It is being built to study the problems involved in the design and programming of fine-grain machines. The J-Machine includes a number of unique mechanisms to support concurrent programming systems (Section 7.6).

The J-machine consists of up to 65,536 (64K) single-chip processing nodes. A single node is shown schematically in Figure 7.3. The node includes:

---

[3]The "J" stands for jellybean. The machine is an experiment in building a high performance computer from jellybean part technology.

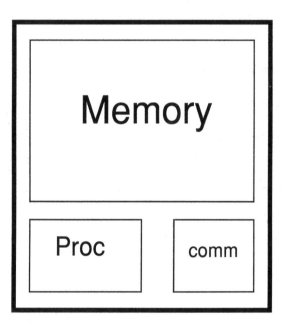

Figure 7.3
A J-Machine processing node contains 144Kbits of static read/write (SRAM) memory, a 10MIPS 36-bit processor, and a communication controller. The node is manufactured using *jellybean* part technology.

		Transistors (thousands)	Percent
Unit			
Processor	Datapath	39	3.6
	Control	11	1.0
	TOTAL	50	4.6
Memory Management Unit		75	6.9
Network	Router	31	2.9
	Interface	23	2.1
	TOTAL	54	5.0
Memory	RAM	885	81.5
	Interface	22	2.0
	TOTAL	907	83.5
TOTAL		1086	100

This J-Machine node is being built using a semi-custom technology for the processor and static read/write memory (SRAM) to reduce the engineering effort required to produce a prototype. An external DRAM interface is provided to allow experimentation with different memory sizes. A similar single-chip node built using dynamic memory (DRAM) and a full custom processor would have 4-8 times the memory capacity and a substantially smaller and faster processor. Such a *jellybean* node would cost (unpackaged) about the same as the same amount of DRAM without the processor.

The J-machine's node contains a message-driven processor (MDP) [7]. The processor is *message driven* in the sense that processing is performed in response to messages (via the dispatch mechanism described in Section 7.6). There is no receive instruction. A task is created for each arriving message to handle that message. A computation is advanced (driven) by the messages carrying tasks about the network.

A J-Machine system consists of up to 64K nodes connected in a three dimensional mesh (Figure 7.4). Each node is located by a three coordinate address (x, y, and z). A node is connected to its six neighbors (if they exist) that have addresses differing in only one coordinate by ±1. All connections are 9-bit wide bidirectional channels that operate at 40MHz. For a machine such as the J-Machine, where wire density is a limiting factor, this topology has been shown to give the lowest latency and highest throughput for a given wire density [4][8].

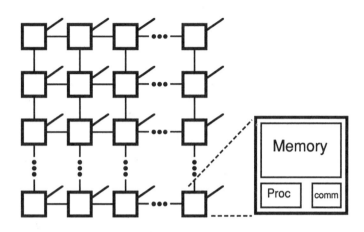

Figure 7.4
A J-Machine system consists of a three dimensional mesh of up to 64K ($32 \times 32 \times 64$) nodes. This topology makes the most efficient use of wire. The communication controllers in the nodes route messages so that the logical network seen by the programmer is a complete connection.

The network topology is not directly visible to the programmer. The communication controllers in each node route nonlocal messages over the appropriate channels with no processor intervention. The latency of sending a message from any node, i, to any other node, j, is sufficiently low that the programmer sees the network as a complete connection. Zero load network latency is given by

$$T = T_d D + T_c \frac{L}{W}.$$

where D is the distance (number of hops) the message must travel, L is the length of the message in bits, and W is the width of the channel in bits. The network is expected to have a propagation delay per stage, T_d, of 50ns and a channel cycle time, T_c of 25ns. With these times, a six word ($L =216$ bit) message traversing half the network diameter ($D = 24$) has a latency of 1.8μs [4]. An average message travels one third of the network diameter for a latency[4] of 1.2μs.

The network provides all end-to-end message delivery services. The sending node injects a message containing the absolute address of the

---

[4]These latency numbers are for an unloaded network. The latency increases about 10% when the network is loaded to 30% of capacity [4].

destination node. The network determines the route of the message and sequences each flit (flow-control digit) of the message over the route. Flow control is performed as required to resolve contention and match channel rates.

The total memory capacity in a J-Machine system is comparable to the memory capacity of a conventional computer with the same part count, built from the same memory technology. The bandwidth of the J-Machine system, however, is much higher.

The J-Machine, like the SUN 3/110 of Section 7.3, is mostly memory. Its processor is also quite comparable to the SUN's CPU. Both operate at 20MHz. However, the fraction of area used to build the processor has been increased by almost two orders of magnitude to 11% with about 3% of the area in the function units.

The J-Machine bandwidth is also greatly increased compared to a conventional machine. The on-chip memory can be read or written every cycle and is accessed by 144-bit row. The peak memory bandwidth of a single node is 2.9Gbits/s. The communication controller manages six network ports each of which operates at 360Mbits/s (9 bits × 40MHz). The peak network port bandwidth of a single node is 2.2Gbits/s. A machine with the same total chip area of the SUN 3/110 would have 64 nodes and total peak memory and channel bandwidths of 184Gbits/s and 69Gbits/s. Channel bandwidth is half the port bandwidth since each channel requires two ports, one at either end. A fully populated 64K node machine would have bandwidths of 184Tbits/s and 69Tbits/s. The message bandwidth of these machines is the channel bandwidth divided by the average message distance.

Fine-grain concurrent computers have high memory and channel bandwidth because they exploit concurrency and locality. The memory bandwidth is high both because many memory references are being made simultaneously and because each reference is local, on chip, allowing a short access time and a wide path to memory. The channel bandwidth is high because many channels can transmit at once and because each channel is a short point-to-point link which can be operated much faster than a long multi-drop bus.

Fine-grain machines are area efficient. Area efficiency is given by $e_A = A_1 T_1 / A_N T_N$ (where A_i is the area of i processors, T_i is execution time on i processors and N is the number of processors). Many researchers have measured their machine's effectiveness in terms of node efficiency, $e_N =$

T_1/NT_N. Proponents of coarse-grain machines argue that a machine constructed from several thousand single-chip nodes would be inefficient because many of the processing nodes will be idle. N is large, hence e_N is small. A user, however, is not concerned with N, but rather with machine cost, A_N, and how long it takes to solve a problem, T. Fine-grain machines have a very high e_A because they are able to exploit more concurrency in a smaller area.

Fine-grain machines have tremendous peak performance. The challenge of fine-grain concurrent computing is to discover how to focus the power of thousands of processors on a single problem. Many machines have been built that combine a processor, memory and communications on each node. The InMOS Transputer is an example [14]. However, simply wiring together many conventional processors with small memories results in a machine that is difficult to program. A programmable machine must provide a set of mechanisms that efficiently support one or more parallel models of computation.

7.5   Most Models of Parallel Computation Can Share The Same Mechanisms

A model of computation is a set of abstractions that provides a programmer with a simplified view of a machine. A model typically provides abstractions for memory, operations and sequencing. For example, while the physical machine provides registers and memory locations, the model provides an abstract view of memory in terms of variables, objects and address spaces. Rather than deal with complex control sequences directly, the model provides abstractions for procedures and processes.

A machine provides a set of mechanisms to support one or more models of computation. For example, most sequential machines provide some mechanism for a push-down stack to support the last-in-first-out (LIFO) storage allocation required by many sequential models of computation. Most machines also provide some form of memory relocation and protection to allow several processes to coexist in memory at a single time without interference. The proper set of mechanisms can provide a significant improvement in performance over a brute-force interpretation of the models.

The most successful mechanisms are simple and *general purpose*. They require a minimum of hardware to implement, operate quickly and can be used by many different models of computation. The push-down stack is an example of a successful mechanism. Stacks are simple to implement and can be used by models as diverse as imperative programming, logic programming and functional programming. An example of an unsuccessful mechanism is a set of display registers as found on the Burroughs B6700 [19]. The registers were costly, could require a substantial amount of time to load on process switches, were used only to access nonlocal variables in lexically scoped programming languages, and were not significantly faster than software on a machine without display registers.

Over the past 40 years, sequential von Neumann processors have evolved a set of mechanisms appropriate for supporting most sequential models of computation. It is clear, however, from efforts to build concurrent machines by simply wiring together many sequential processors, that these highly-evolved sequential mechanisms are not appropriate for supporting parallel models of computation. In most concurrent models, for example, there is little LIFO storage allocation, and hence little need for a stack.

Is there a set of general purpose mechanisms appropriate for supporting parallel models of computation? The answer to this question is: yes. Most parallel models have abstractions that share the same basic requirements. They need efficient mechanisms for communication, synchronization and naming.

To see this, we will examine the requirements of four common models of parallel computation. The models are somewhat simplified as it is beyond the scope of this paper to present each model in detail. The simplified models accurately represent the mechanisms required by the full model.

Dataflow: In the dataflow model (Figure 7.5A) [21], each operation in the computation is independently placed and scheduled. Each operation is represented by an *actor*. Arcs between the actors denote data dependencies. Inputs are provided to an actor by *tokens* passed from other actors. When all of the input tokens have arrived at an actor, it fires and sends a token to each actor that requires its output. The model requires communication (to send tokens between actors), synchronization (to fire an actor after both inputs have arrived), and naming (to identify a particular input of a particular actor as the destination for a token).

Actors: The actor model (Figure 7.5B) [1] is a concurrent form of
object-oriented programming. The objects are called *actors*.
When a message is sent to an actor, it may respond by modifying
its state, sending messages to other actors, and/or creating new
actors. The actor graph can change dynamically as actors pass
references to one another in messages. The actor model requires
communication (to pass messages between actors), synchronization (to activate an actor when it receives a message), and naming
(to identify the actor that is the destination of a message).

Data Parallel: The data parallel model (Figure 7.5C) [13] is usually
associated with SIMD or vector machines. In this model, the
state is partitioned over a set of identical processes. The processes execute a program in lockstep synchronization—whereby
each process is executing the same instruction at the same time.
Processes may interact by reading and writing data from or into
each other's address spaces. While this model is significantly
different from the first two we have examined, the mechanisms
required are similar. It requires communication (to store data
into other processes' address spaces), synchronization (to keep
each process in lockstep with the others), and naming (to identify local and remote memory locations).

Shared Memory: The shared memory model (Figure 7.5D) is an out-
growth of the model used to program multiprocess sequential
computers. In this model, the program is partitioned into a set of
processes. The processes execute independently and need not be
identical. The processes interact by reading and writing shared
memory locations. As with the other models, the shared memory
model requires communication (to read and write shared memory locations), synchronization (for mutual exclusion and to await
the availability of data), and naming (to identify shared memory
locations).

The requirements of the four models are similar enough that a small
set of general purpose mechanisms supports all of them efficiently.

Communication: A communication mechanism is required that can
deliver a message to a named object and dispatch some action in

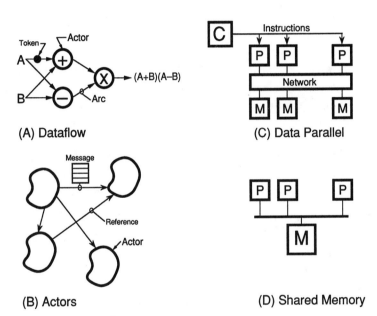

(A) Dataflow

(C) Data Parallel

(B) Actors

(D) Shared Memory

Figure 7.5
Some common parallel models of computation: (A) dataflow, (B) actors, (C) data parallel, and (D) shared memory.

response to the message. This mechanism can be used to deliver tokens in the dataflow model, messages in the actor model and to perform memory references in the data parallel and shared-memory models.

Synchronization: Three types of synchronization are required. First, a task must be awakened or created in response to a message arrival. This dispatch, already required as a communication mechanism, can be used to fire a dataflow actor when its final token arrives and to activate an object in the actor model when a message arrives. Second, a task must be suspended when data it requires is not present. This data presence synchronization can be used to synchronize data dependencies in the shared memory model. It has less obvious uses in the other models as well. Finally, a form of global or barrier synchronization is required. When a task arrives at the barrier, it must suspend until all other tasks arrive at the barrier. Barrier synchronization can be used to keep the data parallel processes in lockstep. Barrier synchronization can be implemented using the first two synchronization mechanisms and may not require special support.

Naming: A mechanism is required to name a memory location or object. This can be used to locate actors in the actor and dataflow models and to address memory locations in the data parallel and shared memory models.

One approach to building parallel machines is to directly implement a particular model of computation. Such single-model machines have been built for the dataflow [11], parallel logic programming [10], and shared memory models [3]. These machines start with the same primitive mechanisms described above. For example, at some level all nontrivial parallel machines have some mechanism to send a message.

Single-model machines are specialized in that they combine these primitive mechanisms into complex, specialized mechanisms by either microcoding specific sequences of operations or by pipelining multiple units. Neither approach significantly improves efficiency. With the microcoded approach, used in [10] and [3], performance is usually limited by memory and network references and similar performance can be achieved without microcode. The pipelined approach, used in [11], improves performance by at most the number of stages. However, many stages require memory and/or network bandwidth and thus cost as much as general purpose processing nodes. Also, because a task must propagate through all of the pipeline stages of such a machine before its result is available, the single-thread performance is no better than for an unpipelined machine.

Specialization does gain some efficiency. By hardwiring some data paths, specializing some registers, and hardwiring control sequences, much data movement and control overhead can be eliminated. Our expectation is that such gains are at most a factor of two or three. With a mature technology, this would be considered adequate reason to specialize. However, parallel programming is still very much a research area with models being refined and new models being proposed on a regular basis. In such a dynamic environment, specializing for a factor of two or three in efficiency is not justified.

Architects of sequential computers have discovered that eliminating complex, model-specific mechanisms (e.g., procedure call instructions) and providing a small, efficient set of primitive mechanisms can improve performance. Eliminating the overhead of complex mechanisms allows these reduced instruction set (RISC) computers [20] to operate faster. Breaking a complex mechanism into a sequence of primitive mechanisms also enables a number of compile time optimizations. These RISC principles apply equally well to concurrent computers.

To be successful, a set of mechanisms must be efficient. The overhead of a mechanism is a more important consideration than its conceptual elegance. In this section we have identified conceptually the mechanisms required to support four common models of parallel computation. In the next section, we will examine the overhead of a particular set of such mechanisms chosen for the J-Machine.

7.6 J-Machine Mechanisms

The J-Machine is a fine-grain concurrent computer that provides efficient, general purpose mechanisms for synchronization, communication and translation (naming) [5]. Communication mechanisms are provided that permit a node to send a message to any other node in the machine in $< 2\mu s$. On message arrival, a task is created and dispatched in $< 1\mu s$.

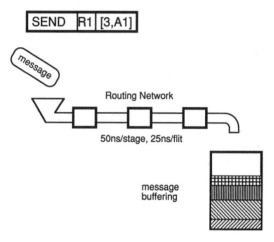

Figure 7.6
Communication involves (1) injecting a message into the network, (2) delivering the message to its destination node, (3) allocating storage to hold the arriving message, and (4) buffering the message into this storage.

All storage may be tagged to indicate that data is not present. A trap occurs if an attempt is made to access data before it is available. A translation mechanism supports a global virtual address space. This set of mechanisms efficiently supports the models of concurrent computation discussed above.

7.6.1   Communication Mechanisms

The J-Machine provides a fast message delivery mechanism that can be used to send dataflow tokens, actor messages, or perform remote memory references. As shown in Figure 7.6, communicating a message between two nodes involves four steps. First, the sending node *injects* the message into the network. The network then *delivers* the message to its destination. Delivery involves routing, choosing a path for the message, and flow control, allocating buffers and channels to the flits of the message as it progresses. When the message arrives, the destination node *allocates* storage for it and *buffers* (copies) the message into this storage.

```
SEND    R0          ; send net address
SEND2   R1,R2       ; send two message words from regs
SEND2E  R3,[3,A3]   ; send two more words, one from memory, and
                    ; end message
```

Figure 7.7
MDP assembly code to send a 4 word message uses three variants of the SEND instruction.

For message latency to be low, all four steps must be fast. A fast communication network is of little use if long delays are introduced allocating message buffers in software. To provide fast end-to-end communication, the J-Machine provides hardware support for each step.

Injection: The MDP injects messages into the network using a SEND instruction that transmits one or two words (at most one from memory) and optionally terminates the message. The first word of the message is interpreted by the network as an absolute node address (in x,y,z format) and is stripped off before delivery. The remainder of the message is transmitted without modification.

The SEND instruction is easy to implement because it applies the processor's existing operand fetch mechanism to message injection. It is convenient because the contents of a message can usually be accessed directly in a register or in memory using a simple addressing mode.

A typical message send is shown in Figure 7.7. The first instruction sends the absolute address of the destination node (contained in R0). The second instruction sends two words of data (from R1 and R2). The final instruction sends two additional words of data, one from R3, and one from memory. The use of the SEND2E instruction marks the end of the message and causes it to be transmitted into the network. This sequence executes in four clock cycles (200ns).

A first-in-first-out (FIFO) buffer is used to match the speed of message transmission to the network. In some cases, the MDP cannot send message words as fast as the network can transmit them. Without a buffer, *bubbles* (absence of words) would be injected into the network pipeline degrading performance. The SEND instruction loads one or two words into the buffer. When the message is complete or the buffer is full, the contents of the buffer are launched into the network.

Previous concurrent computers have used direct-memory access (DMA) or I/O channels to inject messages into the network. With this scheme, an instruction sequence composes a message in memory. DMA registers or channel command words are then set up to initiate sending. Finally, the DMA controller transfers the words from the memory into the network. This approach to message sending is too slow for two reasons. First, the entire message must be transferred across the memory interface twice, once to compose it in memory and a second time to transfer it into the network. Second, for very short messages, the time required to set up the DMA control registers or I/O channel command words often exceeds the time to simply send the message into the network.

Delivery: Message delivery is performed by the network consisting of the communication controllers on each node and the wires connecting them. As discussed in Section 7.4, the network has an average latency of 1μs. The design of the network is described in detail in [6].

Allocation and Buffering: When a message arrives at a node, a buffer is allocated and the message is copied into memory under hardware control. The MDP maintains two message/scheduling queues (one for each of two priority levels) in its on-chip memory. The queues are implemented as circular buffers. As messages arrive over the network, they are allocated space in the appropriate queue. When the task dispatched by the method completes, the space is reclaimed. Without this hardware buffer allocation, the software overhead of allocating message buffers would have been prohibitively expensive.

A message is copied from the network into memory by rows to improve bandwidth. Incoming message words are accumulated in a row buffer until the row buffer is filled or the message is complete. The row buffer is then written to memory. It is important that the queue have sufficient performance to accept words from the network at the same rate at which they arrive. Otherwise, messages would backup into the network causing congestion. The queue row buffers in combination with hardware update of queue pointers allow enqueuing to proceed using one memory cycle for each four words received. Thus a program can execute in parallel with message reception with little loss of memory bandwidth.

Providing hardware support for allocation of memory in a circular buffer on a multicomputer is analogous to the support provided for allocation of memory in push-down stacks on a uniprocessor. Each message stored in the MDP message queue represents a method activation much as each stack frame allocated on a push-down stack represents a procedure activation.

7.6.2   Synchronization Mechanisms

The MDP provides two synchronization mechanisms: dispatch and not-present tags. The dispatch mechanism creates and schedules a task (thread of control and addressing environment) to handle each arriving message. This mechanism eliminates the software overhead associated with creation and scheduling of tasks. Tags for *futures* [2] indicate when data is not present to synchronize tasks based on data dependencies.

Dispatch: When a message arrives at an MDP, a new task is created and scheduled to process it. Each message in the queues of an MDP represents a task that is ready to run. When the message becomes *active*, a task is created to handle the message. Messages become active either by arriving while the node is idle or is executing at a lower priority, or by being at the head of a queue when the preceding message *suspends* execution. At all times, the MDP is executing the task associated with the first message in the highest priority nonempty queue. If both queues are empty, the MDP is idle—that is, executing a background task. Sending a message implicitly schedules a task on the destination node. This simple two-priority scheduling mechanism removes the overhead associated with a software scheduler. More sophisticated scheduling policies may be implemented on top of this substrate.

Task creation, changing the thread of control and creating a new addressing environment are performed in one clock cycle as shown in Figure 7.8. Every message header contains a message *opcode* and the message *length*. The message opcode field contains the physical address of a message handler routine. This address is loaded into the *instruction pointer* (IP) to start execution of a new thread of control. The length field is used along with the queue head to create a message segment descriptor that represents the initial addressing environment for the task. The message handler may open additional segments by translating object IDs in the message into segment descriptors.

No state is saved when a task is created. If a task is pre-empting lower priority execution, it executes in a separate set of registers. If a task, A, becomes active when an earlier task, B, at the same priority suspends, B is responsible for saving its live state before suspending.

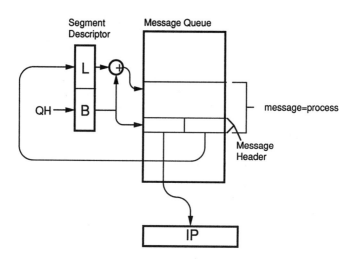

Figure 7.8
Message dispatch. In one clock cycle, a new task is created by (1) setting the IP
to change the thread of control and (2) creating a message segment to provide the
initial addressing environment.

The dispatch mechanism is used directly to process messages requiring
low latency, e.g., memory references and dataflow actor firing, by using a
handler that performs the desired function. Other messages, e.g., remote
procedure call, specify a handler that locates the required method (using
the translation mechanism described below) and then transfers control
to it.

Not-present Tags: The MDP uses tags for synchronization on data
availability in addition to their conventional uses for dynamic typing
and run time type checking. Every register and memory location in the
MDP includes a four-bit tag that indicates the type of data occupying
the location. Two tags are provided for synchronization: future, and
c-future. A future tag is used to identify a named placeholder for
data that is not yet available [2]. Applying a strict operator to a future
causes a fault. A future can, however, be copied without faulting. A
c-future tag identifies a cell awaiting data. Applying any operator to
a c-future causes a fault. As they are unnamed placeholders, they
cannot be copied.

The c-future tag is used to suspend a task if it attempts to access
data that has not yet arrived from a remote node. When a task sends a

message requesting a reply, e.g., a memory reference message, it marks
the cell that will hold the reply as a c-future. Any attempt to reference
the reply before it is available will fault and suspend the task. When
the reply arrives, it overwrites the c-future and resumes the task if it
was suspended.

The future tag is used to implement named futures as in Multilisp
[12]. Futures are more general than c-futures in that they can be
copied. However, they are much more expensive than c-futures. A
memory area and a name must be allocated for each future generated.

Barrier Synchronization: The J-Machine provides no direct support for global barrier synchronization, required by the data parallel
and shared memory models. These models, however, only need to synchronize on communication actions. Lockstep synchronization on every
instruction is not required. We expect that barrier synchronization at
this frequency can be efficiently implemented using the mechanisms described above. Another factor involved in the decision to omit a barrier
synchronization mechanism was the desire to keep all of the J-Machine
mechanisms other than message delivery local. A global mechanism
such as a wire- or synchronization line would have made multiprogramming (executing several independent programs simultaneously) on the
J-Machine difficult.

7.6.3 Translation

To allow different programming models to name different types of objects the MDP separates name translation from memory protection and
relocation. The name translation mechanism is exposed to the programmer with the ENTER and XLATE instructions. ENTER Ra,Rb associates the
contents of Ra (the key) with the contents of Rb (the data). The association is made on the full 36 bits of the key so that tags may be used
to distinguish different keys. XLATE Ra,Rb looks up the data associated
with the contents of Ra and stores this data in Rb. The instruction faults
if the lookup *misses*.

Most computers provide a set associative cache to accelerate translations. We have taken this mechanism and exposed it in a pair of instructions that a systems programmer can use for any translation. Providing
this general mechanism gives us the freedom to experiment with different address translation mechanisms and different uses of translation.

We pay very little for this flexibility since performance is limited by the number of memory accesses that must be performed.

Memory protection and relocation are provided by memory segmentation. A memory reference may be made via a segment register. The address is relocated using the segment base and bounds checked against the segment length.

Combined, name translation and segmented memory management provide a convenient means of naming memory objects such as tasks, records, arrays, or even individual memory locations. Separately, the translation mechanism can also be used to name nonmemory objects such as processing nodes and synchronization points.

7.7 Conclusion

Fine-grain concurrent computers with general purpose mechanisms make efficient use of VLSI technology and are easily programmed using many different models of computation. Reducing grain size improves efficiency by increasing the fraction of silicon area performing useful work. Fine-grain machines also make better use of their communication resources by providing a higher aggregate memory and network bandwidth. As VLSI technology continues to improve, more powerful concurrent computers can be built by adding more processing nodes. In contrast, it is becoming increasingly difficult to improve the performance of sequential computers.

A parallel machine with a few simple, general purpose mechanisms can support most proposed models of parallel computation. Using message communication, synchronization on message arrival and data presence, and general translation, the J-Machine can support actor, dataflow, data parallel and shared memory models of computation. It is not necessary to build a different machine for each model of computation, nor is a particular machine organization (e.g., SIMD) required for a particular model of programming (e.g., data parallelism).

A set of general purpose mechanisms for concurrency can serve as a standard interface to facilitate the development of portable parallel programming systems. Today, most parallel programming systems will run on a single machine or a small set of machines that provide similar mechanisms. Similarly, most machines support only a few programming systems. A machine that is specialized to data parallel programming will not in general run dataflow and actor programs. If machines were designed to support a standard set of mechanisms and programming systems were implemented using these mechanisms it would be relatively straightforward to move parallel programming systems, and thus programs, from machine to machine.

Fine-grain concurrent computers allow us to apply commodity or *jellybean* part technology to building supercomputers. These *jellybean machines* achieve both high performance and high efficiency (performance/cost). In contrast, conventional approaches to building supercomputers achieve performance at the expense of efficiency by using high cost, high speed, low density technology.

Many challenges remain in the development of fine-grain computing systems. The mechanisms described in Section 7.6 have not been shown to be optimum in any sense. As experience is gained with these machines, these mechanisms will evolve much as sequential mechanisms have evolved over the past 40 years. Much work remains to be done on building programming systems based on the models described in Section 7.5. As evidenced by the wide range of parallel applications already written [9], programming concurrent computers presents no insurmountable technical obstacles. Perhaps the largest obstacle limiting the use of parallel machines is the need to educate programmers in the art of parallel program design.

7.8   Acknowledgments

Support for this research was provided in part by the Defense Advanced Research Projects Agency of the Department of Defense, monitored under Office of Naval Research contracts N00014-88-K-0738, N00014-87-K-0825 and N00014-85-K-0124, and by a National Science Foundation Presidential Young Investigator Award with matching funds from General Electric Corporation and IBM Corporation.

Bibliography

[1] G.A. Agha. *Actors: A Model of Concurrent Computation in Distributed Systems.* MIT Press, Cambridge, MA, 1986.

[2] H. Baker and C.E. Hewitt. The incremental garbage collection of processes. *Proceedings of ACM Conference on AI and Programming Languages,* pages 55–59, Rochester, NY, August 1977.

[3] BBN Laboratories, Inc. *Butterfly Parallel Processor Overview.* BBN Report 6148, Cambridge, MA, 1986.

[4] W.J. Dally. Performance analysis of k-ary n-cube interconnection networks. To appear in *IEEE Transactions on Computers.*

[5] W.J. Dally. The J-machine: system support for actors. In C.E. Hewitt and G. Agha, editors, *Actors: Knowledge-based Concurrent Computing.* MIT Press, Cambridge, MA, 1989.

[6] W.J. Dally and P. Song. Design of a self-timed VLSI multicomputer communication controller. In *Proceedings of the International Conference on Computer Design, ICCD-87,* pages 230–234, October 1987.

[7] W.J. Dally, et al. Architecture of a message-driven processor. *Proceedings of the 14th ACM/IEEE Symposium on Computer Architecture,* pages 189–196, June 1987.

[8] W.J. Dally. Wire efficient VLSI multiprocessor communication networks. In *Proceedings of the Stanford Conference on Advanced Research in VLSI,* P. Losleben, editor, pages 391–415, MIT Press, Cambridge, MA, March 1987.

[9] G. Fox, et al. *Solving Problems on Concurrent Processors.* Prentice-Hall, Englewood Cliffs, NJ, 1988.

[10] A. Goto, et al. Overview of the parallel inference machine architecture. In *Proceedings of FGCS-88,* pages 208–229.

[11] J.R. Gurd, C.C. Kirkham, and I. Watson. The manchester prototype dataflow computer. *Communications of the ACM,* 28(1):34–52, January 1985.

[12] R.H. Halstead. Parallel symbolic computation. *IEEE Computer*, 19(8):35–43, August 1986.

[13] W.D. Hillis and G.L. Steele, Jr. Data parallel algorithms. *Communications of the ACM*, 29(12):1170–1183, December 1986.

[14] Inmos Limited, *IMS T424 Reference Manual*, Order No. 72 TRN 006 00, Bristol, UK, November 1984.

[15] T. Kilburn, et al. One-level storage system. *IRE Transactions*, EC-11(2):223–235, April 1962.

[16] L. Kohn and S-W. Fu. A 1,000,000 transistor microprocessor. *Proceedings of ISSCC '89*, pages 54–55, 1989.

[17] J.S. Liptay. Structural aspects of the system 360 model 85; part II—the cache. *IBM Systems Journal*, 7:15–21, 1968.

[18] W. Lonergan and P. King. Design of the B 5000 system. *Datamation*, 7(5):28–32, May 1961.

[19] E.I. Organick. *Computer System Organization, The B5700/6700 Series*. Academic Press, New York, 1973.

[20] D.A. Patterson. Reduced instruction set computers. *Communications of the ACM*, 28(1):8–21, January 1985.

[21] A.H. Veen. Dataflow machine architecture. *ACM Computing Surveys*, 18(4):365–396, December 1986.

II Policy and Education

8 Computers and Productivity

Michael L. Dertouzos

Director, Laboratory for Computer Science
Professor, Department of Electrical Engineering and Computer Science

Abstract

The first half century of the computer field has been largely
supply side driven by a wondrous new technology that is still
evolving and continues to fuel our imagination. As the field
now begins to mature and be driven by real needs and problems, we are confronted with a mission and a question. The
mission during the next half a century is to apply computer science and information technology across the entire front for the
purpose of increasing productivity. The question is to what
extent this mission can be successful. This paper addresses
the question by summarizing weaknesses of U.S. productivity
growth as identified by the work of the MIT Commission on
Industrial Productivity and by exploring how tomorrow's major computer technology developments might be harnessed to
increase productivity.

8.1 The Computer Productivity Paradox

The computer field has grown during the last three decades from essentially nothing to almost 10% of the U.S. Gross National Product [5].
The computer hardware, packaged software and custom software that
comprise this sector have already permeated nearly every type of human activity. The ubiquity and power of computers along with other
considerations have caused observers, including this author [2], to speculate that the information revolution will have a more profound effect
upon the world than the industrial revolution.

In the midst of this euphoria, a handful of analysts, based on scant data, are suggesting that computers may have either no impact or a negative impact on conventionally measured productivity!

In particular, Stephen Roach of Morgan Stanley concludes as follows [6]:

> We have in essence isolated America's productivity short-fall and shown it to be concentrated in that portion of the economy that is the largest employer of white collar workers and the most heavily endowed with high tech capital.

Roach goes on to estimate that compared to the average in the 1970's, the output per worker in 1986 has grown by 16.9% for production workers while it has dropped by 6.6% for office workers (and has risen by 3.6% for all workers).

These growth figures result from division of the overall value added to output by production and office worker inputs respectively. Thus they state, in effect, that office workers have increased in number (and cost), and this increase has not been accompanied by a comparable increase in overall firm output. Significantly, these figures do not attempt to gauge the direct consequences of office work or of computers upon productivity.

In another recent study [4], Gary Loveman of MIT concludes on the basis of a regression study conducted over 20 manufacturing companies, that the impact of information technology on the productivity of office workers in these firms is essentially nil to slightly negative.

Finally, Paul Strassman, of Strassman, Inc., reports [7] that the use of corporate computers bears no correlation whatsoever to conventional performance indices such as a firm's return on investment or its profitability.

The evidence presented by these three studies questions the effectiveness of computers at the very same time that the computer field is experiencing a spectacular growth. Indeed, from a broader perspective, we might ponder why the U.S., which has led the world in the production and use of information technology for the past two decades, has not experienced a corresponding surge in productivity during the same time.

Returning to the studies, several explanations may account for the paradox:

First, the computer's principal impact on office workers may be to induce structural changes rather than increase productivity. These changes in turn may involve previously nonexistent or radically different ways of doing business, such as the use of automated bank tellers, credit cards, automatic inventory systems, airline reservation systems, desktop publishing and spreadsheet analysis.

Second, the field may be so young and the learning yet to be done so extensive, that, according to this view, real productivity gains will come in due time.

There are other explanations as well. For example, computers are said to amplify management practices. Thus they help well managed companies to run more efficiently and they accentuate the inefficiencies of badly managed organizations, leaving the average unaffected.

For the purpose of this paper, it does not matter which, or even if any of these explanations turn out to be true. We use the computer productivity paradox as a stimulus that cannot be ignored to address several critical questions about the generation and use of computer technology.

The goal of this criticism, which falls primarily upon those of us who constitute the computer profession, is to raise our collective awareness about the productive use of computers, and to help us pursue constructive approaches that will make this extraordinary technology more productive.

8.2   The Supply Side of Computer Technology

During its four decades of existence, the computer field has been driven largely by the innovations that have caused its steep growth. Early machines had essentially no software, yet they were eagerly sought by users who were anxious to use this newest of technologies. Universities and research laboratories produced an avalanche of ideas, while manufacturers offered a bewildering and fast moving succession of computers, peripherals, systems software and, more recently, application software. This stream of ever newer computer artifacts was thirstily downed by a world intoxicated with the visible and promised capabilities of computers.

This is as it should have been. Few technologies are born in response to pent-up demand. Like lasers, transistors, radar and television, most technologies are somehow invented, often accidentally, and it is only after their dawn that the world scrambles to apply them. In all cases, though, there comes a time when technological supply begins to shift from that which is constructible to that which is needed.

The computer field is, I believe, at such a juncture today. This does not mean that it is finished as a source of innovation. Much remains to be discovered across its wide frontiers; probably more than what has been invented so far. What it does mean is that we have enough computer technology before us, and within close reach, to augment our predominantly supply side orientation with considerations of demand.

Toward this end, we begin (Figure 8.1) with an abbreviated sketch of the current and immediately forthcoming supply of information technology. This figure, representing the author's estimate, focuses on generic computer technologies. For example, databases and computer graphics are not included in the figure because they are likely to change, primarily as a result of changes in generic technologies like multiprocessor and learning systems.

Theory is the most unpredictable of all the supply categories. It has already yielded valuable results. For example, limits on what can be computed, algorithms for certain problem classes and a formal basis for designing complex systems such as compilers.

The VLSI **Tech Base** concerns the capabilities of solid state circuits. This supply category is widely expected to yield two to three order-of-magnitude improvements in performance/cost over the next two decades. Its significance for our purposes is that it will make microprocessors, custom VLSI circuits and solid state memories faster, less expensive and hence more abundant.

Software advances refer in this context primarily to ways of generating software more rapidly and more economically as well as making software easier to use. Regretfully, the processes of design, production and maintenance of software are inextricably bound and apparently still inseparable. No major advances are in sight, though surprises are always possible.

Both **multiprocessors** and **distributed systems** are aggregates that utilize many computers. Multiprocessors are fairly compact, a few meters long. They function mostly under centralized control and they tackle a single problem at a time, much like single processor machines. Distributed systems, on the other hand, involve networked computers,

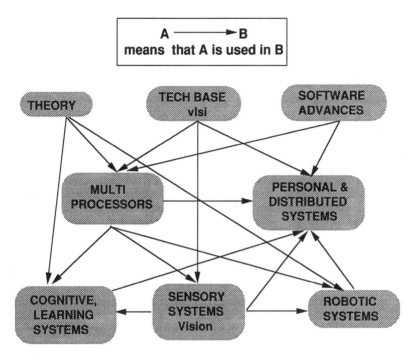

Figure 8.1
Technological Supply

which may span several kilometers and function generally under the autonomous and decentralized control of their users.

Major thrusts are expected in both areas. In particular, multiprocessors are expected to eventually replace single processor machines, because they are potentially more economical and because there is much parallelism in computer applications. Distributed systems will also grow considerably as users' appetites for sharing information increases. As a result of these two major trends, it is likely that tomorrow's computer systems will be networks of multiprocessors.

Sensory systems involve speech understanding and vision systems. In sensory systems these areas, progress will probably hinge largely on the growth of multiprocessors and, in particular on special purpose multiprocessors. Applications in specific domains with limited vocabularies (limited diversity of visual-scenes) are likely to appear in the period of interest. The significance of this supply category is that it will lower the barriers of communication between people and machines (including, beyond computers, entertainment electronics), thereby extending the utility of computers beyond the typing level.

Cognitive (learning) systems involve programs and machines that learn from practice rather than by being programmed. Here again, progress is hard to predict and is likely to be slow and tedious. Surprises, however, may happen, especially in the form of special purpose architectures that exploit a yet-to-be-discovered simple learning process.

Finally, **robotic systems** entail machines that can sense their environment and act upon it in order, for example, to assemble, move or process work. Their progress will largely depend on progress in sensory (particularly vision) systems.

This impressionistic and brief description of the supply side suffices for what we wish to do here. A more detailed analysis [5] of each of the categories portrayed in this figure has been prepared by the author and members of the U.S. National Research Council Board on Computer Science and Technology in order to articulate the computer field's most promising research thrusts.

8.3   Demand Generated by Productivity Weaknesses

It is natural to ask if computers, in which the U.S. still leads the world, can help increase U.S. industrial productivity which, at 1% per year, is growing slowly relative to the productivity growth of other nations today or of that of the U.S. 20 years ago. To tackle this question from the point of view of demand, it is essential that we begin with what needs to be corrected, that is with the weaknesses of U.S. industrial performance.

According to a recent account [3], the MIT Commission on Industrial Productivity has identified the following six broad weaknesses as the ones responsible for this problem.

1. **Outdated strategies**, including parochialism and clinging to an older system of mass production.

2. **Short time horizons:** Excessive preoccupation with short term profits.

3. **Technological weaknesses in development and production,** which include problems with product quality.

4. **Neglect of human resources**, which includes undereducation in schools and inadequate on-the-job training.

5. **Failures of cooperation** within and among companies, which often lead to delays in getting new products to the marketplace.

6. **Government and industry at cross purposes**, which implies that neither of these major players knows or cares about the other player's goals and aspirations.

Having identified the demand, we now ask which of the technologies in the supply basket of Figure 8.1 could be used (and in what way) to address these weaknesses. We ask this question realizing that many other factors [3] beyond computers, in particular changes in management practices and in the treatment of human resources, will be needed to correct these problems. We simply wish to examine here what computers can do toward this kind of demand.

While there are undoubtedly several possible answers to this question, we will focus on two approaches to illustrate demand-driven thinking:

First, **multiprocessors**, with their impressive power, could be used for design and simulation, which in turn could address at least three of the above weaknesses:

1. **Parochialism** could be reduced by computer-aided simulation of customer preferences. Many interconnected computers are used today to simulate complex physical phenomena like galaxy-to-galaxy interactions and chemical reactions. They could be used tomorrow to test how potential customers in different parts of the world might react to new products based, for example, on their income and past preferences for goods. Parochialism could also be reduced by special purpose, speech understanding multiprocessors that can translate among different languages.

2. The **quality** of products could be enhanced by extensive simulation and testing (torturing might be a better word) at the design stage. Assessing likely failure modes, best materials, tolerances,

product costs and other such factors *early* in the design of a product would help increase quality and accelerate the transition of products from conception to market.

3. **Neglect of human resources and, especially on-the-job training** could be improved through a new kind of simulation that would model business situations such as plant operation, interactions with customers, and the management of problematic situations. The simulators that come to mind here are similar to those used today to train airline pilots, who then go on to fly real planes based on that training. Only in this case, instead of honing a person's flying skills, the simulators would train and perfect the skills needed to operate sophisticated plant equipment, deal with customers or handle management problems.

For a second example, consider the use of another major supply item— **distributed systems technology** in response to the same demand. More specifically, suppose that the U.S. were to establish a large scale **national information network** that would easily link all the nation's computers, much like the telephone system links human voices today. Such a network could address at least four of the above weaknesses:

1. **Parochialism:** The National Information Network (N.I.N.) could help supply to companies information about world markets, best practices and consumer trends. Such knowledge would lower the barriers of parochial isolation.

2. Greater **quality** could be built into the design and development of new products by making it possible for designers, manufacturing specialists and marketing experts to work together, whether they are separated by a few floors of a building or by an entire continent. The N.I.N. could help bridge these distances, thereby addressing a need that is likely to increase as the world's businesses become progressively more international.

3. **Cooperation** could be enhanced and delays shortened by a N.I.N. that cuts through steep organizational hierarchies and brings people closer together, as has been the case with experimental networks like the ARPANET.

4. **Government and industry** could also be brought closer together
   by the N.I.N. over a wide spectrum of activities, from taxation and
   regulation to representation and policy formation.

Of course a National Information Network could go beyond what is
currently needed to address U.S. productivity weaknesses. It could, for
example, speed up business mail from days to seconds and give birth
to an entirely new way of handling the purchase and sale of goods and
services by creating an **information marketplace** [2] with important
consequences for business in the 21st century.

This supply-driven suggestion is included here to illustrate that a
demand-driven search such as the one we have been pursuing, does not
preclude supply-side concepts and approaches from emerging and growing in their own unpredictable but potentially useful ways.

Although these two examples could have arisen from the supply side
alone, they would have been undoubtedly interspersed with many other
examples of questionable or unknown usefulness to the nation's needs.

8.4 Demand in Office Worker Productivity

What might be the effect of a more productive use of computers by office
workers on the U.S. economy?

To answer this question we will begin with Figure 8.2, where the total
length of each bar shows the portion of the U.S. GNP contributed by
each of nine principal sectors of the U.S. economy. The solid portion of
each bar shows the **office worker leverage** on each of these sectors.
Leverage is defined here as the fraction of the office workers to total
workers in each sector multiplied by the total GNP contribution of that
sector.

We have defined leverage in this way, because it is the simplest conjecture of how improvements in the productivity of office workers in a sector
might affect the productivity of the overall sector. Unfortunately, office
worker leverage as defined here is guaranteed to be accurate only at its
two extremes—of no office workers and of all office workers, respectively.
At intermediate values, e.g., at 50% of all workers being office workers,
there is **no guarantee** that a unit improvement in the productivity of
the latter will result in a half-unit improvement in the productivity of
the whole sector. This is so, because the **actual** leverage of these office

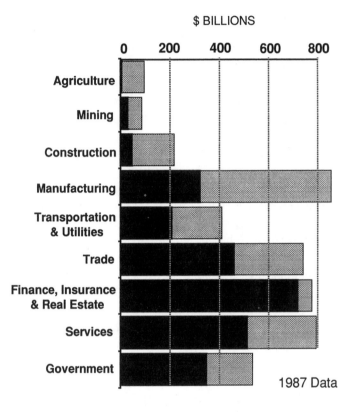

Figure 8.2
Office Worker Leverage

workers upon the sector's overall productivity may be greater or less than 50%.

After all, salesmen, accountants, secretaries and chief executives are all office workers. The ways in which they bring in new business, calculate spreadsheets or use the wordprocessor is likely to affect differently the overall productivity of a company. This lack of specific knowledge on exactly how office workers affect the productivity of their overall business is also at the root of any inaccuracies that may lurk behind the computer productivity paradoxes.

If computers are to be used more productively by office workers, a much better understanding will be needed on how office work affects business. **Let this, then, be a call to computer professionals, economists, and office specialists to develop theories and collect relevant data on the relationships between different types of office work and the overall business of firms.**

Returning to Figure 8.2, let us assume that the simple leverage that we have defined is an adequate measure of office worker impact upon a sector's overall productivity. This means that over the whole economy, the office worker leverage is nearly $2.7 trillion (out of a total 1987 GNP of $4.5 trillion). Thus, if computers could somehow increase office productivity by 3% per year, they would in turn cause the U.S. economy to grow by 2% more per year. The resultant figure would place annual U.S. productivity growth **above** that of Japan and Germany!,

Such is the power of computers ...if they could only increase office productivity by a mere 3%. We say "mere" because in some applications like drafting and computer-aided design, human productivity may rise by as much as 100% as a result of computer use. One is tempted to speculate that in processing office information, a productivity increase of 3% would not be such a formidable task.

8.5   Potential Demand Due to Underutilization of Computers

Where are computers **not** used today?

Assuming that the ubiquity of computers results in a more-or-less uniform distribution of these machines over the entire economy, we may probe in areas where computers are underutilized today in search of potential need.

Unfortunately, we can obtain only a rough measure of such underutilization. Figure 8.3 shows computer utilization over several categories of the U.S. economy for 1985 when the relevant data was available. Here, we have defined **per capita computer utilization** as the fraction of computer capital[1] in the sector divided by the fraction of the work force in the same sector. Thus a utilization of 1 means that the sector has the same share of the nation's computers as it has of the nation's workers.

---

[1] Actually, the allied entity of high tech capital, as defined by Roach.

NON - MANUFACTURING	
SECTOR	**UTILIZATION**
AGRICULTURE	0.00 ◄
MINING	0.15 ◄
CONSTRUCTION	0.11 ◄
TRANSPORTATION	0.31 ◄
Rail	0.38 ◄
Air	0.78
Trucking	0.00 ◄
Other	0.35 ◄
PUBLIC UTILITIES	**4.79**
TOTAL TRADE	0.56
Wholesale Trade	1.87
Retail Trade	0.13 ◄
FINANCE & INSURANCE	**3.01**
Banks	3.81
Credit Agencies	6.61
Securities Brokers	0.74
Insurance Carriers	1.43
Insurance Agents	0.47 ◄
Investment Holding Cos	3.94
REAL ESTATE	**11.13**
SERVICES	**0.66** ◄
Hotels & Lodging	0.19 ◄
Personal	0.47
Business	1.59 ◄
Auto Repair	0.34 ◄
Misc. Repair	0.00
Motion Pictures	3.58
Recreation	1.41 ◄
Other	

MANUFACTURING	
SECTOR	**UTILIZATION**
DURABLES	**1.09**
Primary Metals	1.84
Fabricated Metals	0.18 ◄
Nonelectrical Machinery	1.79
Electrical Machinery	1.91
Motor Vehicles & Parts	0.46 ◄
Other Transport. Equip.	0.74
Instruments	0.75
Stone, Clay And Glass	1.38
Lumber	0.00 ◄
Furniture	0.27 ◄
Misc. Manufacturing	0.35
NONDURABLES	**1.04**
Food	0.84
Tobacco	2.22
Textiles	0.19
Apparel	0.12 ◄
Paper	0.40 ◄
Printing	0.56 ◄
Chemicals	4.27
Petroleum	5.39

Computer Utilization, is the ratio of a sector's share of the nation's high-tech capital to its share of the nation's white-collar work force.

Thus, the average utilization over the whole econonmy is 1.

Under-utilized sectors (where utilization is less than 0.5) are marked.

Figure 8.3
Computer Utilization

Therefore, per capita computer utilization figures of $\frac{1}{2}$ (or 2) mean that the sector has half as much (twice as much) a share of the nation's high tech capital stock as it does of the nation's work force. Low utilization numbers therefore signal potential areas of demand.

We have excluded communications from Figure 8.3 because that sector contains an unusually high portion (37%) of the nation's high tech capital, and therefore skews the averages by making every other category seem undercapitalized. Thus the utilization percentages reported in Figure 8.2 are with respect to the nation's high tech capital excluding communications.

In Figure 8.2, areas where computer utilization is below $\frac{1}{2}$, have been marked with an arrow. They represent areas of computer underutilization, hence of potential demand. These categories include agriculture, mining, construction, rail and truck transportation, retail trade, insurance agents, hotels, personal services and repair. They also include the manufacture of fabricated metals, motor vehicles and parts, lumber, furniture, textiles, apparel, paper, rubber and leather.

Relatively low utilization, of course, does not imply an automatic need for computers. Some areas like agriculture or mining are likely to require, by their nature, fewer per capita computers than the rest of the economy. Other areas, however, like retail trade, are perhaps waiting for a class of sufficiently low cost machines that can be productive in handling the needs of the retail merchant. Designing machines for such a purpose would be another example of a demand-driven mindset.

Other suggestions stimulated by this list involve computers both on board and off board trucks to optimize loading and fuel utilization and perhaps computer controlled machines for customizing construction, furniture, automobiles and apparel.

8.6 Unproductive Uses of Computers—The Three Faults

There are at least three ways in which computers are misused, in terms of their effect on human productivity. These three **faults** are discussed in turn:

1. **Additive Fault:** This misuse happens when people carry out all (or most) of the computer work in addition to work that they

used to do before the arrival of computers. A typical example involves restaurant waiters who after jotting down an order on their note pad, they rush to a keyboard and key the order to the kitchen and presumably to the billing system. There are many other such examples. For instance, in the delivery of overnight packages, couriers may perform several manual entries, as before, along with automatic scans of the same information, so as to preserve reliability while providing convenience.

2. **Excessive Learning Fault:** This fault penalizes human learning in order to increase productive power. A typical example is the use of a six inch thick wordprocessing manual to instruct a human on how to place ink markings on paper. This process, which was at one time the sole province of pencils (for which the manuals are still thin) has admittedly become very powerful with the use of computers. Entire paragraphs and chapters can now be rapidly juggled, splintered and reassembled; glossaries and grammatical (even stylistic) correctors can be invoked. Even typography, which was once an art involving paper, ink and metal type, has been harnessed by the computer. Yet, if a good wordprocessor calls for 400 pages of manual, a good paint program for another 400 pages and a personal database for yet another 400 pages, we soon find ourselves immersed in learning entire encyclopedias in order to perform with more power what we used to do with pencil, color markers and 3 x 5 index cards! Do the automation gains justify these learning costs?

3. **Perfection Fault:** This fault involves excessive human input in order to use as effectively as possible the power of computers to perfect whatever work is in progress. Examples include wordprocessors, slide making programs and design programs, where the crafting of the final product reaches often ludicrous and time consuming extremes in the quest for visual perfection (here the author writes with firsthand experience).

There are undoubtedly other faults not captured by these three categories. We succumb to these faults because we are often so enthralled by what these machines can do, that we do not (yet) ask how much of our good labor they require to perform their miraculous tasks.

8.7 Measuring Computer Productivity

In all of this author's encounters with makers and users of computer systems, no one has ever been seen analyzing the tradeoff between the cost of a computer and the productivity gains expected through its use. No doubt, somewhere such calculations are being carried out ... perhaps secretly. In the majority of cases, computers are usually bought on faith or to relieve increasing demand without much, if any, analysis.

Yet, a productivity tradeoff analysis is in many cases simple to perform and can be quite useful. For example, assume that a worker, perhaps an office worker, has, prior to using computers, a **pre-computer productivity**, P_1, defined as

$$P_1 = \frac{O_1}{I + \alpha C_1}$$

where O_1 is the annual work output measured in any reasonable units, I is the annual work input measured as the cost of labor to produce O_1, C_1 is the (noncomputer) capital invested in the worker (e.g., furniture, phones, other machines and so forth) and a is a coefficient, for example, $1/5$ if C_1 is to be amortized over five years. Thus the denominator is the annual expenditure associated with labor and capital to produce O_1.

Now let us repeat this relation, using post-computer parameters

$$P_2 = \frac{O_2}{I + \alpha C_1 + \beta C_2}$$

where P_2 is the worker's **post-computer productivity**, O_2 is the worker's new output achieved by using the computer (in the same units as O_1), I is the same labor cost as before (we assume this without loss of generality), αC_1 is as before, the annual cost of pre-computer capital, C_2 is the computer capital (e.g., its total cost including training and lifetime maintenance), and b is the fraction of the computer cost that is amortized annually.

We are interested in the breakeven case

$$P_1 = P_2$$

where the pre-computer and post-computer productivities are equal. With the help of a little algebra, this happens when

$$C_2 = KG$$

where

$$G = \frac{O_2 - O_1}{O_1}$$

is the gain in output achieved through computer use, and the coefficient K is given by

$$K = \frac{I + \alpha C_1}{\beta}$$

This relationship is shown in Figure 8.4, where we have used the following numbers for illustration purposes:

$$I = \$40{,}000, \quad C_1 = \$10{,}000, \quad \alpha = 0.2, \quad \beta = 0.33,$$

hence $K = \$126{,}000$.

This breakeven between pre- and post-computer productivities is shown as a sloping line that separates two regions of productive (good) and unproductive (bad) uses of computers.

Thus a wordprocessing system that costs \$10,000 or less and improves the output of an office by some 30%, as is often the case with such systems, is within the productive region. The same holds for a drafting system costing in the \$40,000 range that usually doubles output. CAD systems of various kinds would also fall in the "good" region because they increase output dramatically.

Robots, on the other hand, that cost over \$100,000 and only improve output by 50%, as is the case on the average with such systems, are on the bad side of the tradeoff. Perhaps this explains, at least in part, why wordprocessing and CAD systems form large and successful markets, whereas robots still represent a very small fraction of their predicted potential. When their price comes into better balance with their productivity gains, perhaps they too will become a successful market.

Figure 8.4 suggests the need for new measures of computer productivity. Consider for example, the horsepower which was and still is an

exceedingly useful unit of **power**, a concept that can be easily applied
to gauge horse-drawn plows, automobiles, jet plane engines and nuclear
reactors—all on the same basis.

We have no such unit and no correspondingly useful concept of **computing power** in the computing field. The measures that we do have,
of memory (MBytes) and of processing speed (MIPS), do not have the
same ability as the horsepower to characterize and compare different
computer systems, each performing different applications. And the few
computing benchmarks that we often use to that end are restricted to
numerical uses of computers.

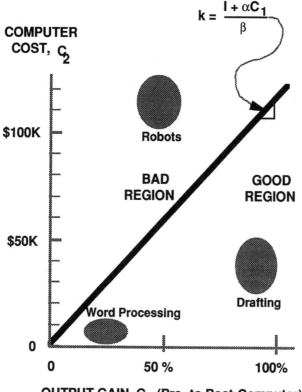

Figure 8.4
Pre- to Post-Computer Productivity Tradeoff

Let us then issue **the second call of this paper for the development of effective measures of computer productivity.** Such measures are sorely needed if we are going to assess, as we should, the utility of computers beyond the informal, qualitative and exclamatory levels. The computer profession and the users of computers must rise to the challenge of carrying out this task.

This is likely to be difficult, however, as we discuss next.

8.8 The Value of Information and of Information Processing

So far, we have discussed computer systems (hardware and software) that affect measurable human output. Wordprocessors, drafting systems and robots have this property, since they help produce letters, drawings and assembly operations that can be easily and conventionally measured as tangible goods.

What about computer uses that involve searching a database, compiling a program or developing a routing diagram for a VLSI circuit? How do we gauge the value of the output in such "intermediate" cases, where information, rather than a tangible good, is the output?

Today, we have no effective way of characterizing and measuring the value of information. Nor can we, therefore, characterize or measure the value of the processes that transforms one kind of information into another. Yet, we must tackle both if we are to begin seriously analyzing computer productivity.

In traditional economic theory, the value of information is defined [1] essentially as the value of a secret. This approach that draws on information theory is, unfortunately, not very useful for the purposes of measuring productivity since it ignores the **purpose** of information.

We need a new measure of the value of information that somehow captures **purpose.** Consider, for example, trying to sell encyclopedias by mail. The value of a mailing list (information) to be used for this purpose is related to the sales of encyclopedias that will result from its use. Let such a mailing list contain people in a geographical region who are above a certain income bracket, above a certain educational level, and who have young children of a certain age. Let us further assume that this list has value V, perhaps 0.2% of potential sales, as determined by prior use of such lists in other regions.

Suppose next, that this list is derived by a computer process that looks for the intersection of three much bigger lists—that tabulate wealth, educational level and parenthood of young children, respectively. Let these lists have values V_1, V_2, V_3, and let the information processing activity that gets the desired list from these bigger lists have cost C. These values are related by

$$V_1 + V_2 + V_3 + C \leq V$$

since if one had all three lists and used the above process, then one would have the desired list.

If these three lists had to be purchased from three different sources, a mailing list entrepreneur might pay as much as (d/3)(V-C) for each, assuming they are equally valuable, where d is a discount factor for the profit to be made and for the associated risk. If the three lists are already available at prices well below this figure, then the use of the computer process to combine the lists is certainly productive. If, however, (d/3)(V-C) is below the price of these lists, then proceeding with the enterprise would be certainly an unproductive use of this computer.

This example suggests the following **definition of the value of information:**

1. Information has economic value only if it can lead via a known way to the acquisition of economic goods or other economically valuable information.

2. The value of information is determined exclusively by the value of the good or information to which it leads through a backward process that discounts for risk, profits and other costs.

Information leading to a tip about a stock or a bargain sale has economic value because it may lead to the making of money or to the acquisition of products at exceptionally good prices. Information about the proper precedents in a legal case, involving a search of past precedents, has economic value because it is linked to the value of winning a trial. And the information about how components of an integrated circuit should be routed has value because it leads to that chip being manufactured and sold.

Thus information seems to differ from the conventional factors of production like labor, capital and land which, even though subject to the laws of supply and demand, have some inherent value independent of the purpose for which they are used. Information, on the other hand, acquires its value **solely** from the economic purpose that it makes possible. In short, no one is likely to pay for information that does not lead to some economic good.

Information can also have intangible value if it leads to the satisfaction of human wishes beyond economic ones—for example, knowing when a loved one will arrive, reading the weather forecast to see if it affects us, or getting educated to become famous.

Thus information could be classified as **terminal** if it leads directly to a desired economic good. Such information derives its value from the value of the good to which it leads. Information could be classified as **intermediate** if it leads to other information (intermediate or terminal) through some information processing process. Its value would then be derived recursively from the value of the information to which it leads, through some process that discounts for risk and other factors.

The above are presented here in part as suggestions and in part as **motivation for the third call of this paper—the development of theories that set a value on information and its processing, so that the productivity of computers may become tractable when they process one form of information into another.**

8.9   Conclusion

Stimulated by a few paradoxes on computer productivity, we have looked at the computer field and have found it to be largely driven by technological supply.

We first focused on demand and argued that computer professionals should **behave like architects** (of buildings) who become involved with and learn a great deal about the need for and the purpose of their creations. Architects, for example, never say (like computer professionals do), I will now work on **applications** of architecture. Instead, they think of themselves as building libraries, colleges, department stores, malls and the like. Perhaps we computer professionals can learn from this older profession that is so similar to ours, so that we may tackle the construction of information technology edifices by working together with users and learning much more about their purpose and intent, as an integral part of what we do.

In this paper, we have also tried to demonstrate a **demand-driven approach to the generation and use of computer technology** by focusing on three broad classes of demand—(1) rectifying the weaknesses of U.S. industrial performance, (2) increasing the productivity of office workers and (3) looking for potential utility in regions of the economy where computers are underutilized.

We have also argued that we should **behave like scientists.** Specifically, we have issued calls for (1) increasing our understanding of how office work affects the productivity of firms, (2) devising effective measures of computer productivity that are useful and equivalent across different applications and (3) developing an effective theory for the value of information and information processing.

We have argued too that we should **behave like engineers,** applying these and other measures, such as the tradeoff analysis that we have presented to the numerous projects that await the use of computers, in order to ensure that these machines will be productively used.

Finally, we have implied throughout this paper that we should seek **constructive** ways of designing new computer hardware and software, aimed at making the uses of these machines more productive than they are today.

The single-minded focus of this paper on computer productivity is not intended to suggest a displacement of other valuable driving forces like research. Our aim has been to sensitize our peers to the issues surrounding computer productivity and to cause at least a partial shift in our collective mindset from supply toward demand and from hope to measurement. Creativity can flourish in a demand-driven environment as well as it has in the supply-side approaches of the past. Maybe even better, for its fruits are then better linked to utility.

In conclusion, there is much to be done and much to be gained by developing the potential for productive use of this ubiquitous and wondrous technology. Enhancing human productivity through computer science and technology is a worthy and ambitious goal that could and should occupy a central place among the aspirations of computer professionals during the next few decades.

And taking this approach may even cause the computer productivity paradoxes of the 1980's to fade away!

8.10   Acknowledgments

The stimulus for this paper came from the work of the MIT Commission on Industrial Productivity, chaired by this author. The work of the Commission was sponsored by the Sloan Foundation, the Hewlett Foundation, and by MIT.

Bibliography

[1] K.J. Arrow. Information and economic behavior. Federation of Swedish Industries, Stockholm, 1973.

[2] M.L. Dertouzos. The information marketplace. *Electronic Mail and Message Systems, Technical and Policy Perspectives*, American Federation of Information Processing Societies, Inc., Arlington, VA, 1981.

[3] M.L. Dertouzos, R.K. Lester, R.M. Solow, and the MIT Commission on Industrial Productivity. *Made In America: Regaining the Productive Edge*. MIT Press, Cambridge, MA, 1989.

[4] G.W. Loveman. *An Assessment of the Productivity Impact of Information Technologies*. MIT Sloan School of Management, Technical Report, July 1988. Management in the 1990s working paper.

[5] National Research Council. *The National Challenge in Computer Science and Technology*. Prepared by The Computer Science and Technology Board, Commission on Physical Sciences, Mathematics, and Resources, 1988.

[6] S. Roach. *White Collar Productivity: A Glimmer of Hope?* Morgan Stanley and Co., Inc. Special economics study.

[7] P.A. Strassman. *Information Payoff: The Transformation of Work in the Electronic Age*. Free Press, New York, 1985.

9 Beyond the Desktop Metaphor

Nicholas Negroponte

Director, Media Laboratory
Professor, Department of Architecture

Abstract

This paper concludes that the desktop metaphor will be replaced with a theoretrical one, with actors to whom you delegate tasks. Speech is seen as the primary channel of communication, in a plural interface, characterized by extraordinary redundancy and concurrency. This picture of the future includes a gaggle of small, independent, but intercommunicating agents embedded in common objects.

9.1 Hospital Corners

When I learned to make my bed, I was artfully taught and dutifully learned to make hospital corners. This simple fold had both functional and esthetic advantages, and with practice, added no time to the tedium of bedmaking. Today, notwithstanding this skill, I cherish the opportunity of delegating the task and have little interest in the *direct manipulation* of my bedsheets.

Likewise, I feel no imperative to manage my computer files, route my telecommunications, or filter the onslaught of mail, messages, news and the like. I am fully prepared to delegate these tasks to agents I trust, as I tend to other matters (which could be as banal as getting dressed), while those other tasks are brought to a satisfactory conclusion. For the most part today, these agents are humans. Tomorrow they will be

An earlier version of this paper appeared as "An Iconoclastic View Beyond the Desktop Metaphor" in the *International Journal on Human–Computer Interaction*, 1(1), pages 109-113, 1989, and is reprinted with permission from Ablex Publishing Corporation, Norwood, NJ.

machines. But what cannot change in the equation, in the transition, is
trust.

9.2 Dynadots

Stalking the future is a curious game. More often than not we project our
current images, sometimes unwittingly, with mere technological changes
which, in the case of computers, include speed, memory and the exotica
of I/O. In the text which follows, I have a view of the future not generally
held, which enormously affects the human interface and is not a mere
technological advance, but a fundamental departure from commonly held
views.

The common assumption is that computers will move in the direction of paper and/or clipboard-like paraphernalia. Alan Kay's early
vision of the **dynabook** is now beginning to find implementations in
the back rooms of many corporate laboratories. The general portrait of
that future machine is: about the size of *Time Magazine*; maybe flexible; radio transmitting; high resolution, color and bright display; stylus
input; massive memory and lightning speed. When not in transport,
such a machine might be hung on the wall in front of a keyboard for
more traditional use. Anyway, that is the flavor of most people's view of
the future personal computers and is clearly embodied in John Sculley's
excellent videotape, "The Knowledge Navigator."

My view includes a slightly different mix of form factors and physical
embodiments of computers. Many or most will be small objects (hence
dynadots, to be in keeping with the jargon) that intercommunicate with
each other, serving special needs. I expect to carry much more computing power on my wrist tomorrow than is in my office today. Agents,
great and small, will be distributed all over the place.

The reason this dynadot view is important is twofold. For one, it leads
to a wider computer presence upon which truly personalized systems
will be built. Computers will go underground. My refrigerator will
know when it is out of milk, but take appropriate action only after a
conversation with my calendar or travel planning agent.[1] Yes, small,
highly interconnected objects which compute are a *society of objects*.

---

[1] "Some terminals of the future will be all knowing rooms without walls. Others
will be flat, thin, flexible touch sensitive displays. And others will be wrist watches
and cuff links with the right hand talking to the left by satellite." *−The Metaphysics*

The second consequence of this view of the future is that the form factor of such *dynadots* suggests that the dominant mode of computer interaction will be speech. We can speak to small things.

9.3   Speech Works in the Dark

Speech has other values too often overlooked. For example, it allows us to deal with computers out of arms' reach, it works around corners, it carries the richness and information content of tone and prosody, and it is frequently the free channel (like: while driving, dressing or reading).

Our tendency is to couple speech recognition with natural language understanding. While this is surely a proper long term view, it misleads us into believing that it is too far off to consider its current worth and usability.

The "space" of speech recognition is characterized by three axes:

- user-dependent versus user independent,

- small vocabularies versus large vocabularies, and

- discrete versus connected utterances.

In this volume, the hardest corner is clearly:

- user-independent, large vocabularies, connected speech.

Let's examine them one by one.

User-independent speech is a goal driven by two desires: not to require training the machine for each word, and not to be limited to a single user. One is obvious and one is suspect. It does not follow that user-dependent speech systems need to be trained word-for-word, versus evolve over time. And, it certainly does not follow that a system which can recognize anybody's speech is an asset. Sure, it should be able to cope with family, friends and our dog's bark. But, there is no real value in the ability to have such systems cope with random accents or strangers.[2]

---

of Television, N. Negroponte, Methodology of Interaction, North-Holland Publishing Company, Amsterdam, 1980.

[2]The telephone company might argue that such systems would allow for *anybody* to call American Airlines from *any* telephone and hold a discussion about flight plans. But, I can call my personal computer or talk to my wrist watch, instead, and have either of them deal with the airline in ASCII. No. Speaker independence only has niche applications, like vending machines and security systems.

Large vocabularies are also a myth. The secret is not size, but rapid downloading of speech subsets from a very large word space, call these: word windows. At any one moment, the total number of utterances required in a machine at any single moment might be as small as 500. Context is the trigger of what needs to be folded into the system from instant to instant. And remember, we are not talking about discussing Thomas Mann, but delegating, which more or less means issuing commands, asking questions and passing judgments; more like drill sergeant talk.

Figure 9.1

To complete the "problem space" of speech recognition, consider the matter of *connected speech*. Surely we have little interest in talking to a machine in broken language. Much of this in fact can be achieved with multiword utterance recognition. This is not the right way to do connected speech, but addresses the issue by widening the acoustic duration. Alas, sometimes we just might have to use more discrete talk.[3]

The real problem in speech recognition is spatial independence, so that one can speak to computers from a distance, in the presence of noise and the like. Many people think that speech is primarily to liberate you from the keyboard in the sense of not having to type (which some people can not do or feel it is beneath their station). I think it is indeed to liberate us from the keyboard, but in the different sense: of not having to be near it or to try to use it while our hands are tending to something else. Also, right now for personal computers there is a real **captive audience** of people. One cannot deal with them *en passant*.

9.4   "About So Big"

Speech does not stand alone. "So big" might be the small distance between two of your fingers, the space between your cupped hands, the volume embraced by your arms or the size of some huge mountain or building to which you are pointing in the distance. In short, the utterance is meaningless without the parallel channel of communication (in this case) of gesture.

Such plurality has another, and in my mind, greater significance: concurrence and redundancy. My classic (read: often used) story is that of dinner talk in a foreign country. If your hosts ask you, say in French, "Do you want some more wine?" or "Please pass the bread," you will understand them with and even without your high school French. Whereas, if they talk among themselves about politics, you will be totally at a loss unless your command of French is almost fluent.

Most people conclude that this is obvious because the first example is "baby talk," whereas a discussion about political matters engages all kinds of sophisticated metaphors, complex terms, grandiose concepts and oblique referents. These differences are true, but not the important

---

[3]This is the weakest argument I have. It is a near-term solution. Added with the rest, I suggest that user-dependent, small vocabulary, discrete speech systems could be used today, if people really were interested in a plural human interface.

ones by far. The important difference is that in the baby talk, table talk scenario all the objects and subjects of discourse are in the same **space and time** as you (and your hosts). This suggests that when somebody says "Please pass the water," his or her arm can be stretched out in the direction of the water pitcher, and his or her eyes can gaze upon the empty glass. What this means is that the message is enormously **redundant**, and you can pull the signal out of any of many **concurrent** channels. That's the real difference.

For this reason, when you know a foreign language to a limited degree, a most painful task is to use that language over the telephone. In such situations you are at the mercy of a single channel. But that is the way we use computers today, with single channels.[4]

9.5   Why Winking Works

At a recent dinner party I winked at my wife,[5] and she knew all the *paragraphs* of information it would have taken me (otherwise) to explain the same to some stranger. The reason is quite obvious. A vast amount of shared experiences and robust models of each other make the epitome of communication **be the lack of it**.

In an agent-model of computers, similar familiarity is required in order to preclude relentless explicitness that would destroy the value of agencies. In daily life, it can often be the case that it is easier to do something one's self than to explain it to somebody "new." No, the computer must be an old friend with as many shared experiences (facts, at least) as the future *computer presence* will allow. This is absolutely critical to a new metaphor, beyond the desktop.

---

[4]Note that when you talk on the telephone your face and body still emit expression, even though you know full well that the person at the other end can see none of it. This suggests that our human system of expression is quite tightly wired with the very same (somewhat uncontrollable) parallelism discussed above.

[5]In some perverted measure of information theory, this could be construed as one bit.

Figure 9.2

9.6   The Theatrical Metaphor

If you are prepared to accept the promise of **delegation** and the viability of speech, the desktop metaphor is subject to serious change, soon.[6]

My view of the future of desktop computing (versus dynadots in this case) is one where the bezel becomes a proscenium and agents are embodied to any degree of literalness you may desire. In the longer term, as holography prevails, little people will walk across your desk (if you have one) dispatched to do what they know how.

The picture is simple. The stage is set with characters of your own choice or creation whose scripts are drawn from the play of your life. Their expressiveness, character and propensity to speak out are driven by an event (external) and a style (yours). If you want your agents to wear bow ties, they will. If you prefer talking to parallelpipeds, fine.

---

[6]I have not addressed animation because I think it goes without saying that there will be a dramatic change in three dimensional engines and low cost, real time, high resolution animation will be as commonplace as *pull-down* menus.

This highly literal model of agents can be dismissed as a foolish scheme to replace serious **icons** with *Snow White and the Seven Dwarfs*. [7] But this begs the question about delegation and speech. In some form, we can expect surrogates who can execute complex functions, filter information and intercommunicate in our interest(s).

Figure 9.3

Direct manipulation has its place, and in many regards is part of the joys of life: sports, food, sex and, for some, driving. But, wouldn't you really prefer to run your home and office life with a gaggle of well trained butlers (to answer the telephone), maids (to make the hospital corners), secretaries (to filter the world), accountants or brokers (to manage your money)[8] and, on some occasions, cooks, gardeners and chauffeurs when there were too many guests, weeds or cars on the road?

---

[7]In 1977 I recall almost being laughed out of an auditorium when I suggested that a calculator icon would invoke that object on the screen and ease of use would naturally stem from familiarity.

[8]This one might make you nervous.

10 Computation as a Framework for Engineering Education

Harold Abelson

Associate Professor, Department of Electrical Engineering and
Computer Science
Co-Leader, AI/LCS Project on Mathematics and Computation

Abstract

Twenty-five years ago, when Project MAC was launched, MIT
located it not on campus, but rather in some rented office space
across Main Street. Even though everyone recognized computation to be an important technology, computation did not play
an important enough educational role to justify making room
for it on campus. Twenty-five years later, computer science at
MIT has grown substantially—but we are still located in the
same rented office space. In all fairness, it is still uncertain
whether computer science remains merely the study of an important technology, or whether it has a more central place in
MIT's educational mission.

In this paper, I want to hint at that second possibility: that
computer science can contribute something fundamental to our
educational perspective, not only in teaching about computers,
but in teaching about engineering more broadly, and perhaps in
teaching about other disciplines as well.

10.1   Formalizing Imperative Knowledge

To begin with, "computer science" is a terrible name for this pursuit.
It is not a science. Or at least it is not *yet* a science. It is also not
fundamentally about computers—in the same sense that chemistry is

The ideas and examples in this paper are drawn from the MIT Department of Electrical Engineering and Computer Science undergraduate subjects "Structure and
Interpretation of Computer Programs" and "Signals and Systems," both of whose
development is joint work with Gerald Sussman and William Siebert.

not fundamentally about test tubes, and that physics is not fundamentally about particle accelerators. Computer science is not fundamentally *computer* science in the same sense that geometry is not fundamentally *earth-measuring* science. Of course, when the ancient Egyptians invented geometry, as Herodotus relates, they viewed themselves as studying earth-measuring: $\gamma \epsilon \omega \mu \epsilon \tau \rho \grave{\iota} \alpha$. That is where our word "geometry" comes from. The reason we view computer science as the study of computers is the same reason that the ancient Egyptians viewed geometry as the use of surveying instruments. At the outset of a discipline, when people do not have clear ideas about what is fundamental and what is not, they tend to confuse the intellectual essence of the subject with the tools used in pursuing it.

In this discipline that we call computer science, we see the primitive, confused beginnings of something akin to the ancient Egyptians' geometry. Looking back after thousands of years, we recognize that, in their reasoning about earth measuring, the Egyptians were beginning to develop methods for formalizing *declarative knowledge*—methods for reasoning about what is true—methods that led eventually to geometry and the deductive method in mathematics and logic. Similarly, I think that when people look back after a long time at the beginnings of computer science, they will recognize that we confused people in the 20th century were indeed working with computers, but more significantly, that we were beginning to develop methods for formalizing *imperative knowledge*—methods for reasoning about how to do things.

To illustrate the difference between declarative and imperative knowledge, consider the following definition of a square root:

The square root of a number x is the number y, $y \geq 0$, such that $y^2 = x$.

This is declarative knowledge. It tells us something that is true about square roots. But it does not tell us how to find a square root. In contrast, consider the following ancient algorithm, attributed to Heron of Alexandria, for approximating square roots. To approximate the square root of a positive number x:

- Make a guess for the square root of x.

- Compute an improved guess as the average of the guess and x divided by the guess.

- Keep improving the guess until it is good enough.

Heron's method does not tell say anything about what square roots are, but it does say how to approximate them. It is a piece of imperative "how to" knowledge.

Computer science is in the business of formalizing imperative knowledge, i.e., developing formal notations and ways to reason and talk about *methodology*. Here is Heron's method formalized as a *procedure* in the notation of the Lisp computer language:

```
(define (sqrt x)
  (define (good-enough? guess)
    (< (abs (- (square guess) x)) tolerance))
  (define (improve guess)
    (average guess (/ x guess)))
  (define (try guess)
    (if (good-enough? guess)
        guess
        (try (improve guess))))
  (try 1))
```

The details of the notation are not important here, although it is worth pointing out that the program has distinct pieces that correspond to distinct pieces of Heron's method: how to try a guess for the square root, how to tell whether a guess is good enough, and how to improve a guess.

Of course, there are other methods for computing square roots. One way is to view $\sqrt{x}$ as a number y such that $y = x/y$. In other words, $\sqrt{x}$ is a *fixed point* of the function $y \mapsto x/y$. We can express this method for computing square roots with the aid of a general fixed-point procedure that takes a procedure P as argument and returns a fixed point of P:

```
(define (sqrt x)
  (fixed-point (lambda (y) (/ x y))))
```

Alternatively, we can view $\sqrt{x}$ as a solution of the equation $y^2 - x = 0$, and approximate it using a general equation-solving technique such as Newton's Method, which solves an equation $f(y) = 0$ by finding a fixed point of the function $y \mapsto y - f(y)/f'(y)$:

```
(define (sqrt x)
  (fixed-point (newton-iterate (lambda (y) (/ x y)))))
(define (newton-iterate f)
  (lambda (y) (- y (/ (f y) ((derivative f) y)))))
```

This example illustrates how, in formalizing even simple imperative knowledge, it is convenient to use a language in which procedures (methods) are *first class objects*, that is, a language in which procedures can accept procedures as arguments and return procedures as results. For instance, the procedure fixed-point accepts a procedure as argument. This allows us to express the idea that square roots are computed by applying a general fixed-point method to a particular function. The procedure newton-iterate (as well as derivative, whose definition is not shown) is a procedure whose argument is a procedure and which returns a procedure as its result. This allows us to express the idea that Newton's Method involves finding the fixed point of a function that is derived from another function according to a specified method.

Certainly, if the only things we ever computed were square roots, then computer science would not be of much interest. Similarly, if all one ever did in geometry was surveying, then geometry would not be of much interest. In each case, the importance of having a formalism is that it provides a framework for *controlling complexity*, a way to think about ideas that are too involved to think about all at once. The important techniques in computer science are the techniques for coping with methodological complexity.

In this paper, I will mention only two of these techniques. One is the method of defining languages that support abstractions that enable you to combine primitive pieces, and then stipulate that the combinations are entities that you can manipulate and reason about without looking at the individual pieces. The second technique is the method of establishing *conventional interfaces* that enable you to assemble programs from a library of components that can be mixed and matched.

10.2   Abstractions and Embedded Languages

Any design language provides primitive components and means by which these can be combined to build more complex things. In order not to be overwhelmed by complexity, we also require some way to abstract compound structures: to manipulate them as if they were primitive, so we can use them as components in creating more elaborate structures. A good technique for coping with design complexity is to use a language that supports appropriate abstractions—abstractions that emphasize relevant details and suppress other details—so that alternative designs can be conveniently explored.

This paradigm is beautifully illustrated by a simple graphics language, invented by Peter Henderson [3], that was inspired by M.C. Escher's woodcut "Square Limit" shown in Figure 10.1. Henderson's language makes it easy to describe designs like this, in which basic pieces are scaled and replicated. In this language, there is only one type of primitive element: a *picture*. A picture is a procedure that takes a rectangle as argument and draws an image, scaled to fit the rectangle. For instance, the three images shown in Figure 10.2 are all instances of the same picture, which we will call G, but drawn with respect to three different rectangles.

Figure 10.1
The woodcut "Square Limit" by M.C. Escher in the inspiration for Peter Henderson's graphics language. (Image copyright 1990 M.C. Escher Heirs/Cordon Art-Baarn-Holland.)

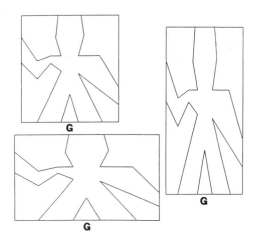

Figure 10.2
The primitive element in Henderson's language is called a *picture*. A picture is a procedure that draws an image, scaled to fit a specified rectangle. Th three images above are all instances of the same picture, drawn with respect to three different rectangles.

The means of combination in Henderson's language are geometric combinators that act on pictures, such as rotating a picture through 90 degrees, flipping a picture horizontally or vertically, or placing one picture above or beside another.

One way to make these combinators easy to implement is to represent pictures as procedures. The beside of two pictures A and B, for instance, is a procedure that takes a rectangle as argument and splits the rectangle horizontally into two subrectangles. It then passes the left-hand rectangle to picture A, which draws the A picture in that rectangle; and likewise passes the right-hand rectangle to picture B. The result is just what we require: a procedure that takes a rectangle as input and draws A beside B in that rectangle. Note that if we are to represent pictures as procedures, then our language must have first class procedures. Beside, for example, will be a procedure that takes two procedures (pictures) as arguments and returns a picture as result.

Observe how easy it is to build up complex pictures in only a few steps. The reason for this is that pictures are *closed* under the combination operations—the result of combining pictures is always another picture that can in turn be used as a primitive unit in forming more elaborate pictures. In general, we can attain considerable power in a design language by arranging matters so that the objects we manipulate are *closed* under the means of combination; that is, so that the results of combining objects can themselves be combined with the same combining operations. For instance, forming arrays in FORTRAN does not satisfy closure: although one can combine primitive elements by forming arrays, one cannot form arrays of arrays. This severely limits the flexibility of the FORTRAN array as a data structure.

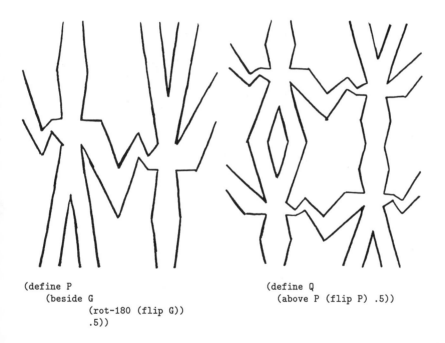

```
(define P                          (define Q
  (beside G                          (above P (flip P) .5))
    (rot-180 (flip G))
    .5))
```

Figure 10.3
Henderson's language includes geometric combinators that construct compound pictures. Here, we construct a picture *P* by placing *G* beside a rotated and flipped version of *G*, scaled so that the left-hand *G* is .5 as wide as the total picture *P*; and we construct *Q* by placing *P* above a flipped copy of *P*, scaled so that the top *P* is .5 the height of the total *Q*. It is easy to build up complex pictures in only a few steps, because pictures are closed under combination.

Another important point about Henderson's language is that it is *embedded* in a general programming language. The means of combination—beside, above, flip, and so on—are realized as ordinary procedures and thus are automatically enriched by all the general mechanisms available for dealing with procedures.

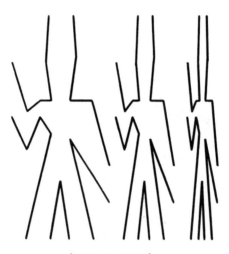

(right-push G 2)

```
(define (right-push pict n)
   (if (= n 0)
       pict
       (beside pict
               (right-push pict (- n 1))
               .75)))
```

Figure 10.4
The Right-push operation shown above is defined recursively in terms of the beside operation. Since beside and all other means of combination in Henderson's language are realized as ordinary procedures, they can be manipulated with all of the ordinary methods that Lisp provides for manipulating procedures, including recursion.

10.3   Streams and Standard Interfaces

A second important design strategy that arises in computer science is
the use of parts that have *conventional interfaces*. In general, we would
like to build structures that are *modular*—that can be constructed from
well understood pieces that can be designed and debugged separately.
This enables us to employ a library of interchangeable parts that fit
together in standard ways, so that designs can be made by mixing and
matching appropriate parts.

There are many examples of conventional interfaces in computer science. The one I will mention in this paper, called *stream processing*
adopts a signal processing metaphor. As an example, consider the following programming task. You are given a data structure—a tree, say—
whose elements are integers, and you are to find the sum of the squares
of the odd integers. A common way to accomplish this is with a program that walks through the tree, testing the parity of the integers and
accumulating the squares of the odd ones as it goes.

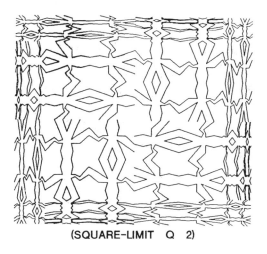

(SQUARE-LIMIT   Q   2)

Figure 10.5
Modifying the Right-push operation to recursively extend both beside and above
leads to a combinator that builds designs with the same plan as Escher's original
"Square Limit" figure. Here is the combinator applied to the picture Q of Figure 10.3.

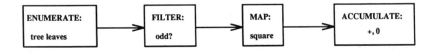

Figure 10.6
This block diagram "Signal processing" computation finds the sum of the squares of the odd-integer leaves of a tree. The data flowing between the blocks are realized streams.

Instead, let us structure the program as a cascade of "signal process-ing" modules. There is a "signal" consisting of integers, created by enumerating the leaves of the tree. This signal passes through a filter that retains only the odd integers. The result passes through a mapper that squares each integer, and the result of that goes into an accumu-lator that forms the sum. Figure 10.6 expresses this process using the block diagram notation of signal processing engineers. The correspond-ing program, structured analogously, is:

```
(accumulate sum
          (map square
               (filter odd?
                       (enumerate tree))))
```

Observe how the elements of the program—accumulate, map, filter, and enumerate—directly correspond to the modules in Figure 10.6. The value of organizing the program in this manner is that we can readily replace the modules with other modules that perform different opera-tions. For instance, we could enumerate a structure other than a tree, or apply a different kind of filter, or accumulate the results in some other way than by summing. This is the same technique that engineers use when designing real signal processing systems by combining standard components. The key to being able to decompose computations in this way is to have a data structure that represents the information flowing between modules. One way to do this is to represent the data as a (possibly infinite) sequence of elements called a *stream*. Here is a sample definition of a stream, the infinite stream of ones:

```
(define ones (cons-stream 1 ones))
```

The stream constructor cons-stream takes as its two arguments an item and a stream. It returns a new stream whose first element (the head of the stream) is the given item and the rest of whose elements (the tail of the stream) is the given stream. To see that all of the elements of this stream are 1 consider that the stream is equal to its tail. Thus the first element is equal to the second element, which is equal to the third element, and so on.

Here is another stream, the stream of consecutive integers beginning with 1:

```
(define integers
  (cons-stream
   1
    (add-streams ones integers)))
```

According to the definition, the head of integers is 1 and the tail is the result of elementwise adding (add-streams) ones to the stream integers. That is, the tail of the stream is the same as the original stream with each element incremented by 1.

Figure 10.7 shows a more complex stream definition. This is the stream of prime numbers, generated by an ancient method called the *sieve of Eratosthenes*: Begin by writing down all the integers starting with 2. Then cross out all multiples of 2, except for 2. The next integer remaining is 3, so further cross out all multiples of 3, except for 3. The next integer remaining is 5, and so on. At the end of this infinite process, what remains is the primes. The block diagram in Figure 10.7 describes this process as a signal processing system: a processing element called a sieve whose input is a stream—the stream of integers beginning with

2—and whose output is a stream—the stream of primes. The sieve splits off the head of the stream, which becomes the first element of the output. The rest of the output elements are obtained by filtering the tail of the input stream to remove all elements divisible by the head, and then (recursively) sieving the result. Thus sieve is a kind of filter, but it is an infinite filter because the sieve contains another identical sieve inside itself. An infinite recursive filter may be problematic from the perspective of building physical signal processing systems, but it is easy to imagine computationally. The program in Figure 10.7 shows the procedure that implements the recursive sieve. Observe how the structure of the program directly mirrors the structure of the block diagram.

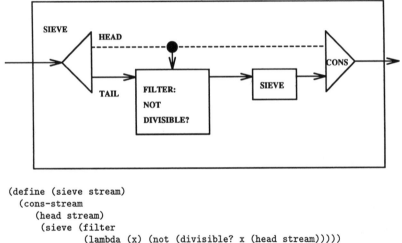

```
(define (sieve stream)
  (cons-stream
     (head stream)
     (sieve (filter
             (lambda (x) (not (divisible? x (head stream)))))
             (tail stream)))))
```

Figure 10.7
The sieve of Eratosthenes can be formulated as a stream processing block diagram. The sieve block takes in a stream of integers and puts out the sieved result. Inputting the stream of integers beginning with 2 generates the stream of primes. Sieve can be expressed as a computer program whose structure mimics that of the block diagram.

Stream processing illustrates how computer science can incorporate a system-design metaphor from another branch of engineering, and enrich it by combining it with other computational ideas such as recursion, and by applying it not only to physical systems but to abstract processes as well.

10.4 Computer Languages for Electrical Engineering Education

I have presented a view of computer science as a kind of engineering that formalizes methodology by constructing descriptive languages: defining primitive elements, combining and abstracting them, organizing libraries of mix-and-match design components. The question is: can this approach influence the way in which we teach engineering in general? I will present just two glimpses of that in some the material we are developing for a subject on "Signals and Systems" in the MIT Department of Electrical Engineering and Computer Science.

10.5 An Embedded Language for Electrical Networks

Let us begin with abstractions and embedded languages in teaching about electrical networks. There are many formalisms used in teaching students about networks. With most of them we draw a geometric picture or write down a set of equations that students analyze. But from the point of view of design, these descriptions are unstructured—they do not reflect a way of thinking about complex networks as combinations of simpler networks.

As an alternative formalism, think of a network as something that connects some number of *ports*, where each port has a voltage (with reference to some external ground) and a current (flowing into the network). The network is specified as a collection of constraints among the voltages and currents at the ports. We do not worry about what is "inside" the network—the network is completely characterized by the constraints on the ports.

The power of this network description is that it is *closed* under the operation of wiring networks together. If we combine two networks by

identifying a port of one with a port of the other then the constraints
for the combined network are the constraints for the two parts together
with two additional constraints—one saying that the voltages for the
two networks at the port must be equal, and one saying that the current
flowing into one network at the port must be the negative of the current
flowing into the other network.

A formalism that emphasizes combining networks encourages reasoning about networks in terms of the parts and how the parts combine.
For example, if we combine two networks all of whose constraints are
linear and time-invariant, then the constraints of the combination will
likewise be linear and time-invariant. Thus any network constructed
by connecting linear, time-invariant components will itself be linear and
time-invariant.

This approach to networks also forms the basis of a network simulation
program that follows the above framework, except that the node currents
are expressed implicitly, in terms of the voltages. A network, defined
with respect to some nodes and some parameters, is represented as a
procedure. For each node, the network can compute how much current
it draws at the node, producing an answer that is a symbolic expression
in the voltages. The network also dictates a set of constraints among the
voltages. The node currents and the constraints completely characterize
the network. If we connect a number of networks at a node, then the
current drawn at the node by the combined network is the sum of the
currents drawn at that node by the pieces. The constraints for the
combined network are the union of the constraints of the pieces. In
addition, if we stipulate that the connection node is to be *internal* to
the combination (no longer accessible for connections from outside the
network), then there is the extra constraint that the currents drawn at
that node by all the pieces (each current is an expression in the voltages)
must sum to zero.

For example, a `resistor` of resistance R is a primitive network with
two nodes n_a and n_b. The current drawn at each node is given by Ohm's
Law:

$$i_a = \frac{v_a - v_b}{R}$$

$$i_b = \frac{v_b - v_a}{R}$$

and there are no additional constraints. The *L-section* shown in Figure 10.8 is a network formed from two resistors of resistances $R1$ and $R2$, connected at a node n_2:

```
(define (L-section n1 n2 R1 R2)
  (combine-networks
    no-internal-nodes
    (resistor n1 n2 R1)
    (resistor n2 ground R2)))
```

Just as in the Henderson graphics language, the fact that the set of networks is closed under combination makes it straightforward to combine networks to produce more complex networks. For example, having defined an L-section, we can combine three L-sections to form a three-stage ladder network, also shown in Figure 10.8.

Additionally, as in the Henderson language, these descriptions are embedded in a general purpose programming language—both the elements (networks) and the means of combination (`combine-networks`) are represented as ordinary procedures, and thus inherit all the usual mechanisms for manipulating procedures. For instance, we could define a k-stage ladder recursively as an L-section connected to a $(k-1)$-stage ladder:

```
(define (ladder stages n1 n2)
  (if (= stages 1)                    ;if there is only 1 stage
      (L-section n1 n2)               ;then return an L-section
      (make-network                   ;otherwise connect
        (internal-nodes n)            ;at an internal node
        (ladder (- stages 1) n1 n)    ;a ladder
        (L-section n n2))))           ;and an L-section
```

For teaching about networks, the network language is a convenient formalism that emphasizes creating complex networks by combining simpler networks. Moreover, it is an operational network simulator. To solve a network, the system terminates all the noninternal nodes (makes the currents at these nodes sum to zero) and solves the set of constraint equations for the unknown node voltages. For instance, the *Sallen-Key circuit* [4] is a simple second-order filter that students can build in the lab and compare their measurements with the simulated results. Figure 10.9 shows this circuit, its network-language description, and a phase-magnitude plot of the frequency response produced by the simulator.[1]

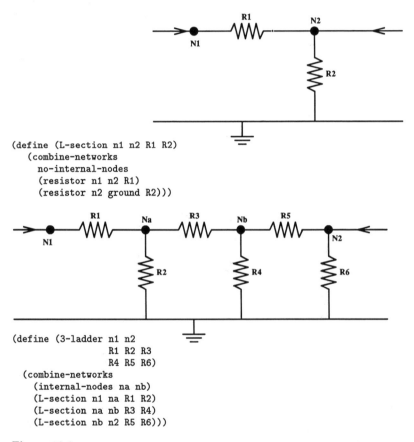

```
(define (L-section n1 n2 R1 R2)
  (combine-networks
    no-internal-nodes
    (resistor n1 n2 R1)
    (resistor n2 ground R2)))
```

```
(define (3-ladder n1 n2
                  R1 R2 R3
                  R4 R5 R6)
  (combine-networks
    (internal-nodes na nb)
    (L-section n1 na R1 R2)
    (L-section na nb R3 R4)
    (L-section nb n2 R5 R6)))
```

Figure 10.8
The network language emphasizes combining the networks to produce more complex networks. An L-section is formed by wiring together two resistors, and combining three L-sections produces a three-stage ladder. Observe that although the ladder has four nodes, it is a two-port network—na and nb are internal nodes that are not accessible for connections to other networks.

---

[1]In this circuit system, voltages and currents can be functions of a complex variable s, and the system can perform arithmetic with such functions. For example, a capacitor is just a resistor with "resistance" (impedance) $1/Cs$. In this way, the system can solve linear time-invariant networks in the frequency domain, producing voltage values that are functions of s. Plotting these functions of $j\omega$ produces frequency-response curves such as the one in Figure 10.9.

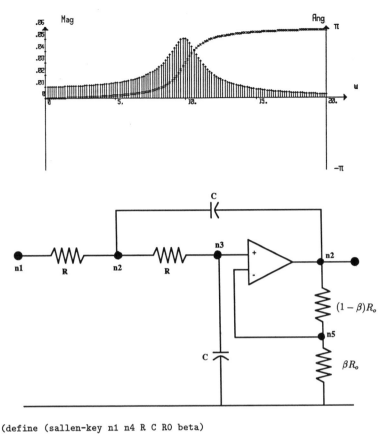

```
(define (sallen-key n1 n4 R C R0 beta)
  (combine-networks
    (internal-nodes n2 n3 n5)
    (op-amp n3 n5 n4)
    (resistor n1 n2 R)
    (resistor n2 n3 R)
    (capacitor n3 ground C)
    (capacitor n2 n4 C)
    (resistor n5 ground (* beta R0))
    (resistor n4 n5 (* (- 1 beta) R0))))
```

Figure 10.9
The Sallen-Key circuit can be constructed from resistors, capacitors, and an op-amp.
One the circuit definition has been entered, the network system can solve the circuit,
producing phase-magnitude frequency-response curves such as the one shown.

10.6   Streams and Discrete-time Systems

My second example builds upon stream processing. We saw above that
streams enable us to structure a computation in much the same way that
an engineer might structure a signal processing system. So it should
hardly be surprising that signal processing systems themselves can be
naturally described and simulated using streams.

Figure 10.10, for example, shows the block diagram for a simple discrete-time signal processing system that uses feedback. The output signal is scaled by 0.5, put through a unit delay and then fed back and added to the input signal. Using streams, we can represent this system in much the same way as we previously defined `integers` and `sieve`:

```
(define result
  (add-streams
     input
     (delay-stream (scale-stream 0.5 result))))
```

Since we can actually run stream procedures, students can simulate discrete-time block-diagram systems simply by writing down these descriptions. Moreover, the structure of each simulation program directly corresponds to the structure of the block diagram.

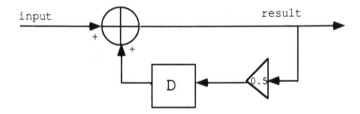

Figure 10.10
This simple feedback system can be represented as a simple recursive stream procedure.

One advantage of this is that we can go the other way—use insights from computation to help explain block-diagram systems. The system shown in Figure 10.11, for example, is a *canonical system of order n*. By picking the weights a_i and b_i appropriately, one can use this structure to realize any discrete-time linear-time-invariant system whose system function is the arbitrary rational function [4]:

$$\tilde{H}(z) = \frac{b_0 + b_1 z^{-1} + b_2 z^{-2} + \ldots + b_n z^{-n}}{a_0 + a_1 z^{-1} + a_2 z^{-2} + \ldots + a_n z^{-n}}$$

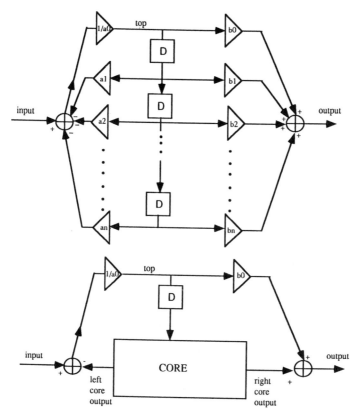

Figure 10.11
A canonical block diagram of order n (shown above) can be viewed hierarchically as
a system (shown below) with two adders, two gains, a delay, and a central core. The
stream simulation of the canonical system imitates this decomposition.

Figure 10.11 also shows how we can decompose the system into two
adders, two gain elements, a delay, and a core element with input a
signal at the top and output a pair of signals, one to the left and one to
the right. The following procedure implements this same decomposition.
Note that the feedback from the core output through the signal along
the top is reflected in the procedure by the mutually recursive definitions
of the streams core-outputs and top.

```
(define (DT-system a b)
  (lambda (input)
    (define core-outputs
      (core (delay-stream top) (rest a) (rest b)))
    (define top
      (scale-stream (/ 1 (first a))
                    (sub-streams input (left core-outputs))))
    (add-streams (scale-stream (first b) top)
                 (right core-outputs))))
```

The core element has a simple recursive structure, in which an order-n core extends an order-$(n-1)$ core as shown in Figure 10.12. This recursive structure is exhibited by the following stream procedure, which simulates the core:

```
(define (core top-in a b)
  (if (and (no-more? a) (no-more? b))
      (make-pair zeros zeros)
      (let ((internal-outputs
                (core (delay-stream top-in) (rest a) (rest b))))
        (make-pair (add-streams (left internal-outputs)
                                (scale-stream (first a) top-in))
                   (add-streams (right internal-outputs)
                                (scale-stream (first b) top-in))))))
```

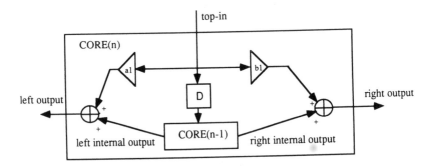

Figure 10.12
The central core of the order-n canonical system in Figure 10.11 can be defined recursively in terms of a central core of order $(n-1)$. The same recursive structure appears in the `make-central-core` procedure that simulates this system.

10.7   Computational Ideas or Just Computing Appliances?

In this paper, I have presented computer science as an activity that formalizes ideas about methodology by constructing appropriate languages. I have described two of these ideas, and I have shown how they support using computers in electrical engineering education—not just to obtain the results of calculations, but to gain insight through computational formalisms. The question is: are these merely isolated examples, or do they reflect a broadly useful approach to engineering education? Can activities like these form the basis for a new science, on the model of geometry, or will they remain a set of isolated technical tricks, like "earth measuring?"

Twenty-five years from now, when we return to celebrate the 50th anniversary of Project MAC, we will surely find students using computers. It may be that they use them merely as appliances—as useful pieces of technology, like typewriters and pencils and whatever. If that will be the case, then MIT will have as much business teaching computer science as it has teaching typewriter science or pencil science. Perhaps we will have learned by then how to exploit the power of computational formalisms. Perhaps we will find our science and engineering textbooks as permeated by the language of computation as they are now permeated by the language of geometry. Perhaps be we will find that computer science will be recognized as intellectually central to MIT as an academic institution. And who knows—perhaps we may even find a descendent of Project MAC that is located on campus.

10.8   Acknowledgments

Support for this research was provided in part by the Defense Advanced Research Projects Agency of the Department of Defense, monitored under Office of Naval Research contract number N00014-86-K-0180.

Bibliography

[1] H. Abelson and G. J. Sussman, with J. Sussman. *Structure and Interpretation of Computer Programs*. MIT Press, Cambridge, MA, 1985.

[2] H. Abelson and G.J. Sussman. Lisp: a language for stratified design. *Byte*, 207–218, February 1988.

[3] P. Henderson. Functional geometry. In *Proceedings of the Symposium on Lisp and Functional Programming*, 1982.

[4] W.M. Siebert. *Circuits, Signals, and Systems*. MIT Press, Cambridge, MA, 1986.

III   Theory

11 Theory of Learning: What's Hard and What's Easy to Learn

Ronald L. Rivest

Professor, Department of Electrical Engineering and Computer Science
Leader, LCS Theory of Computation Group

Abstract

Two recent developments in machine learning research are discussed in this paper. First, training even a very simple neural net is likely to be computationally intractable, i.e., NP-complete. Second, by using cleverly designed experiments, one can infer the structure of a large class of finite-state systems.

11.1 Introduction

"Our ultimate objective is to make programs that learn from their experience as effectively as humans do."

John McCarthy (1958)

The ability of machines to learn has been a central question since the creation of the field of artificial intelligence. After enjoying a flurry of activity in the 1960's, primarily associated with the study of perceptrons, machine learning was relatively quiescent during the 1970's as attention of AI researchers focused on issues of representation, search and planning. During the 1980's the field of "machine learning" has again undergone rapid development, drawing upon and blending together previous accomplishments in artificial intelligence, psychology, statistics, pattern recognition, algorithms, cryptography and complexity theory.

We shall illustrate recent developments on the theoretical side of machine learning research by highlighting two recent results obtained by the author and his students: that training even a very simple neural net is likely to be computationally intractable, i.e., NP-complete (Avrim

Blum) [4][5]; and that by using cleverly designed experiments one can infer the structure of a large class of finite-state systems (Rob Schapire) [12][13][15].

These results contrast with each other in several ways. First, Blum's result is a *negative* result, showing that effective learning by neural nets is likely to be computationally difficult, while Schapire's result is a *positive* result, giving an effective algorithm for learning finite-state systems.

Further, the problem is of learning a finite-state system is apparently the more difficult, since it involves learning a system that constantly changes state, whereas in the neural net problem there is an unchanging function to learn. Finally, the neural net learning problem examines *passive* learning from a given database of examples, whereas the finite-state learning algorithm *actively* experiments with the unknown finite-state system to learn its structure.

Both of these results can also be interpreted as emphasizing the importance of how learned knowledge is represented. The neural net result suggests that representing knowledge by neural nets may entail severe computational penalties. The finite-state system result is based around the design of a new representation for finite-state systems that is particularly suitable for learning.

11.2   Training Neural Nets

Neural networks and techniques for training neural networks, have again become active areas of research. During the 1960's there was much activity in this area; Minsky and Papert's book *Perceptrons* [11] reviews some of this work and analyzes the capabilities of very simple neural networks. The recent revival of interest in neural networks somewhat coincides with the publication of the "bible" *Parallel Distributed Processing* [14]. Many key articles, both old and new, have been reprinted in *Neurocomputing* [1].

A major reason for the recent surge in interest in neural networks is the development of the "back-propagation" algorithm for training neural networks [14]. The ability to train large multi-layer neural networks is essential for utilizing neural networks in practice, and the back-propagation algorithm promises just that. In practice, however, the back-propagation algorithm runs very slowly. The question naturally arises as to whether there are necessarily intrinsic computational difficulties associated with training neural networks, or whether better training algorithms might exist. We provide here additional support for the position that training neural networks is intrinsically difficult.

A common method of demonstrating a problem to be intrinsically difficult is to show the problem to be "NP-complete." The theory of NP-complete problems is well understood [6] and many notorious problems—such as the traveling salesman problem—are now known to be NP-complete. While NP-completeness does not render a problem totally inapproachable in practice, it usually implies that only small instances of the problem can be solved exactly and that large instances can at best only be solved approximately, even with large amounts of computer time.

Our work is inspired by Judd [10] who shows the following problem to be NP-complete:

> "Given a neural network and a set of training examples, does there exist a set of edge weights for the network so that the network produces the correct output for all the training examples?"

Judd also shows that the problem remains NP-complete even if it is only required to produce the correct output for two thirds of the training examples, so that even approximately training a neural network is intrinsically difficult.

The networks in Judd's results have a number of hidden nodes that grow with the number of inputs, and they also have a rather irregular connection pattern. We extend his result by showing that it is NP-complete to train a very simple network, having only two hidden nodes and a very regular interconnection pattern.

Our results, like Judd's, are described in terms of "batch" style learning algorithms that are given all the training examples at once. It is worth noting that training is at least as hard with an "incremental" algorithm (such as back-propagation) that sees the examples one at a time. Thus the NP-completeness result given here also implies that incremental training algorithms are likely to run slowly.

We consider a very simple network; a multilayer network having n binary inputs and three nodes: N_1, N_2 and N_3. All the inputs are connected to nodes N_1 and N_2. The outputs of nodes N_1 and N_2 are connected to node N_3 that produces the output of the network. (See Figure 11.1.)

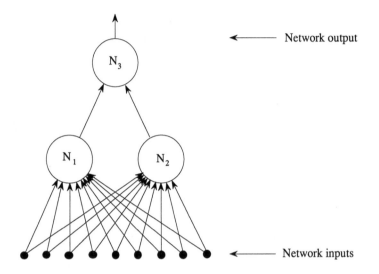

Network output

Network inputs

Figure 11.1
A three-neuron neural network where nodes N_1 and N_2 are "hidden" nodes that compute threshold functions of the inputs. The outputs of N_1 and N_2 are input to node N_3, that produces the output of the network.

Each node N_i computes a linear threshold function f_i of its inputs. More precisely, if N_i has input $x = (x_1, x_2, \ldots, x_n)$, then for some constants $a_0, a_1, \ldots, a_n$

$$f(x) = \begin{cases} +1 & \text{if } a_1 x_1 + a_2 x_2 + \cdots + a_n x_n > a_0 \\ -1 & \text{otherwise.} \end{cases}$$

The a_i's $(i \geq 1)$ are typically viewed as *weights* on the incoming edges and a_0 as the *threshold*. We note that the network uses "sharp" threshold functions rather than the "smooth" approximations provided by sigmoid or logistic functions [14]; we conjecture that our results can be extended to handle smooth threshold functions as well. (For example, Judd [10] was able to extend his results to handle smooth threshold functions.)

The network studied is about as simple as one can have without degenerating into the "trivial" (perceptron) case of a single threshold node. It is interesting to see that training even such a simple network is NP-complete.

To *train* such a network means to find a set of weights and thresholds so that the input-output behavior of the network agrees with a given set of *labeled training examples*. Each labeled training example consists of a length-n binary input vector and a label that is either "+1" (for *positive* examples) or "−1" (for *negative* examples).

We show the following problem to be NP-complete. Note that we have stated it as a decision problem (determining if the weights exist), as is standard for NP-complete problems, but that the search problem (actually finding the weights) is at least as hard.

TRAINING A 3-NODE NEURAL NETWORK:

Given: A training set consisting of $O(n)$ labeled training examples on n binary inputs.

Question: Do there exist linear threshold functions f_1, f_2, f_3 for nodes N_1, N_2, N_3 such that the network of Figure 11.1 produces outputs consistent with the training set?

Theorem 1 Training a 3-node neural network is NP-complete [4][5].

The proof of this theorem is omitted here; it is based on a reduction from the "Set-splitting" problem.

What are the implications of this result? We offer the following thoughts.

First, we observe that the result is about the *problem* of training neural nets; it is not a statement about any particular training procedure. Looking for different training procedures does not avoid the NP-completeness of the problem.

Second, training algorithms that find an "optimal" set of weights for a given network are likely to be prohibitively expensive from a computational point of view. If we wish to use networks in practice, we must either restrict ourselves to very small networks (with few inputs and few nodes), or be content with training heuristics that attempt to find good, but only approximately optimal, weight settings. Even so, very large networks, with millions of weights, may be effectively untrainable. (We remark that we have only proven that training simple networks is NP-complete, and that extrapolating this result to larger networks, while natural, is a matter of conjecture.)

Third, we should search for alternative ways to represent the desired input-output relationships, ways that are as expressive as ordinary neural networks but that are easier to train. The moral here may be that the computational difficulty is not intrinsic to the learning problem itself, but that it is a consequence of trying to force the learned knowledge to fit into a procrustean bed of a set of weights and thresholds. A different way of representing the patterns to be learned may allow very rapid optimal training algorithms.

Fourth, we might re-examine whether there is any unused prior information or unused capabilities that might make a particular learning task easier. For example, prior knowledge about the true form of the unknown function might enable one to circumvent the computational difficulties by restricting attention to a simpler class of functions, such as perceptrons. Or, the ability to ask questions about the unknown function, instead of merely using a given set of training examples, may make the learning problem easier. The next section of the paper gives an example of the latter

11.3 Learning the Structure of Finite Automata

We consider the problem of inferring a description of a deterministic finite-state automaton from its input-output behavior. Our motivation is the artificial intelligence problem of identifying an environment by experimentation. We imagine a robot wandering around in an unknown environment, whose characteristics must be discovered. Such an environment need not be deterministic, or even finite-state, so the approach suggested here is only a beginning on the more general problem. In line with our motivation, our inference procedure experiments with the automaton to gather information.

The problem of inferring a finite-state automaton from its input-output behavior has a long history.

The problem of "passively" learning an automaton is known to be NP-complete. More precisely, Angluin [3] and Gold [7] have shown that finding an automaton of n states or less agreeing with a given training set of input-output pairs is NP-complete. In passive learning, the input-output pairs are given and the learner is not able to experiment with the unknown automaton.

Gold [8] studies the problem of "black box identification," assuming that the learner may experiment with the unknown black box. At each time step, the learner supplies the black box with an input symbol and the black box produces an output symbol calculated as a function of all the input symbols provided so far. Gold shows that if the black box is a finite automaton, then it can be identified "in the limit." (Gold did not address the time complexity of his procedures.)

In a later paper [9], Gold re-examines the problem of inferring a black box finite automaton, assuming that the experimenter may at any time reset the automaton to a "start state." He describes how the automaton can be identified in a finite amount of time if the experimenter is told beforehand the number of states of the automaton.

Angluin [2] elaborates Gold's algorithm. In her model, the learner may experiment with and reset the automaton. Occasionally, the learner may stop and produce a conjecture as to the structure of the unknown automaton. Angluin assumes the existence of a "helpful teacher" who, when the learner makes an incorrect conjecture, gives the learner a "counterexample" demonstrating some incorrect behavior by the conjectured automaton. It can be shown that such a teacher is required for efficient identification, since otherwise the learner may never see some hard-to-reach states of the automaton. Although the existence of such a helpful teacher may seem problematic, in practice the learner can usually replace the helpful teacher with some random experimentation, since an incorrect conjecture often makes rather frequent prediction errors and a prediction error yields a counterexample. Angluin's algorithm correctly identifies the unknown automaton in time polynomial in the number of states of the automaton and in the length of the longest counterexample.

A major goal of our research is to extend Angluin's procedure so that it is not dependent on the existence of a "reset" operation that puts the unknown automaton into a fixed "start state." The motivation for this goal follows from our target application: in "real life," a robot cannot arbitrarily reset the world to some prior state; it must learn about its environment in one continuous experiment.

A second major goal of our research is to greatly extend the class of finite-state systems that can be effectively inferred. The standard representation of such systems, based on explicitly enumerating all of the global states of the system, is not an efficient representation when the global state can be effectively represented by a collection of local state variables. Learning of systems that can be effectively represented using local state variables is another goal of our research. This task is particularly challenging when the number of such state variables and their modes of interaction are not directly observable.

We have discovered a universal representation for finite-state systems, called a "diversity-based" representation, that can be effectively inferred by experimentation without the need for a reset operation. An example of such a representation is given in Figure 11.2.

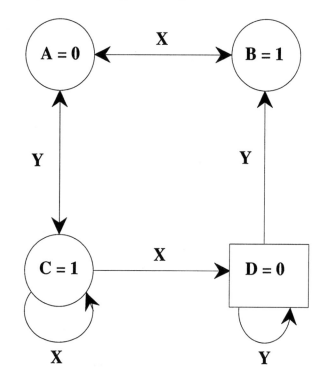

Figure 11.2
An example of a diversity-based representation of a finite-state system.

This figure shows an automaton with four local state variables: A, B, C and D. We say that the "diversity" of this automaton is 4 because it has 4 state variables. In this example, the local state variables are binary; the current value of each variable is indicated ($A = 0$, $B = 1$,

$C = 1$, $D = 0$). There are thus $2^4 = 16$ possible global states, where a global state specifies a value for each local state variable.

Some of the local variables may be "hidden," while others may be "visible" (observable). In the figure, the hidden state variables (A, B and C) are drawn as circles while the visible variables (D) are drawn as squares. The learner can only see the visible variables; the existence of, values of, and connections between the hidden variables are not directly observable. The invention by the learner of the necessary hidden state variables to explain the observed changes in the visible variables is philosophically rather intriguing, but we will not delve into such philosophy here.

In this example, there are two input symbols: X and Y. Providing one of these two input symbols causes the system to change state. Note that each local state variable has exactly one arrow labeled X directed into it, and one arrow labeled Y directed into it. If state R has an arrow directed into it labeled X from state S, then on input X the variable R is assigned the old value of state variable S. All of the state variables are updated simultaneously. For example, on input Y the automaton depicted in Figure 11.2 would change to the state $A = 1$, $B = 0$, $C = 0$, $D = 0$. Note that in this case from the learner's point of view nothing has changed, since the visible variable (D) is still 0.

It can be shown that such a "diversity-based" representation is universal in that it can represent any deterministic finite-state automaton. It can also be shown that such a representation can be exponentially smaller than the standard representation. (Although it need not be; sometimes it is even larger than the standard representation.)

Theorem 2 A finite-state system can be inferred (from experimentation and counterexamples, but without reset) in time polynomial in the diversity of the finite-state system and the length of the counterexamples, with arbitrarily high reliability [12][13][15].

Since the inference procedure contains some randomized statistical testing subprocedures, it is not guaranteed to produce the correct result, but only to produce the correct result with probability at least $1 - \delta$, where $\delta > 0$ can be arbitrarily small. The running time increases as a function of $\log(1/\delta)$, so very small δ's can be used with only a small penalty.

The most efficient version of our inference procedure [13] is based on the notion of a "homing sequence": a sequence of inputs whose corresponding outputs suffice to "orient" the learner (tell him what state he has ended up in). The inference procedure proceeds in a rather "scientific" manner, building up hypotheses, testing them and discarding those that do not work until a correct one is found. Because the overall structure can be built out of subhypotheses that can be separately tested, the overall running time is only polynomial in the complexity of the inferred automaton (measured in terms of its diversity). We omit the details of the inference procedure in this paper.

We see that we have achieved the desired goal: an arbitrary finite-state system can be efficiently inferred without the use of a reset. Furthermore, the new representation is often much more compact than the standard one, since it allows the representation of a global state to be decomposed into a collection of local state variables. The invention by the learner of "hidden" state variables to explain the changes in the visible variables is rather pleasing from a philosophical point of view.

11.4 Conclusions

The results described here emphasize the importance of the following:

- **Computational complexity:** We can measure the ease of learning by determining the amount of computation required.

- **Representation:** How the learned knowledge is represented can have a dramatic effect on the ease of learning.

- **Active versus passive learning:** Learning by actively experimenting, rather than working with a passively obtained set of training examples, can make learning much easier.

The results given here are meant to illustrate the characteristics and richness of research in machine learning today. There remains much exciting research to do to close the gap between theory and practice, and to learn how to integrate systems that learn with conventional computer systems.

11.5   Acknowledgments

Support for this research was provided in part by the National Science Foundation under grant number DCR-8607494, ARO under grant number DAAL03-86K0171, and a grant from Siemens Corporation.

Bibliography

[1] J. A. Anderson and E. Rosenfeld, editors. *Neurocomputing: Foundations of Research*. MIT Press, Cambridge, MA, 1988.

[2] D. Angluin. Learning regular sets from queries and counterexamples. *Information and Computation*, 75:87–106, November 1987.

[3] D. Angluin. On the complexity of minimum inference of regular sets. *Information and Control*, 39:337–350, 1978.

[4] A. Blum. *On the Computational Complexity of Training Simple Neural Networks*. Master's thesis, MIT Department of Electrical Engineering and Computer Science, May 1989. Also MIT Laboratory for Computer Science, Technical Report 445, May 1989.

[5] A. Blum and R.L. Rivest. Training a 3-node neural net is NP-Complete. In D.S. Touretzky, editor, *Advances in Neural Information Processing Systems I*, pages 494–501, Morgan Kaufmann, 1989.

[6] M. Garey and D. Johnson. *Computers and Intractability: A Guide to the Theory of NP-Completeness*. W. H. Freeman, San Francisco, CA, 1979.

[7] E. M. Gold. Complexity of automaton identification from given data. *Information and Control*, 37:302–320, 1978.

[8] E. M. Gold. Language identification in the limit. *Information and Control*, 10:447–474, 1967.

[9] E. M. Gold. System identification via state characterization. *Automatica*, 8:621–636, 1972.

[10] J. S. Judd. *Complexity of Connectionist Learning with Various Node Functions*. University of Massachusetts at Amherst, Department of Computer and Information Science, Technical Report 87-60, July 1987. Also presented at the First IEEE International Conference on Neural Networks, San Diego, CA, June 1987.

[11] M. Minsky and S. Papert. *Perceptrons: An Introduction to Computational Geometry*. MIT Press, Cambridge, MA, 1969.

[12] R. L. Rivest and R. E. Schapire. Diversity-based inference of finite automata. In *Proceeding of the 28th Annual Symposium on Foundations of Computer Science*, pages 78–87, Los Angeles, CA, October 1987.

[13] R. L. Rivest and R. E. Schapire. Inference of finite automata using homing sequences. In *Proceedings of the 21st Annual ACM Symposium on Theory of Computing*, pages 411–420, Seattle, WA, May 1989.

[14] D. E. Rumelhart and J. L. McClelland, editors. *Parallel Distributed Processing (Volume I: Foundations)*. MIT Press, Cambridge, MA, 1986.

[15] R. E. Schapire. *Diversity-Based Inference of Finite Automata*. Master's thesis, MIT Department of Electrical Engineering and Computer Science, May 1988. Also MIT Laboratory for Computer Technical Report 413, May 1988.

12 The Limits of Computation

Michael Sipser

Professor, Department of Mathematics
Member, LCS Theory of Computation Group

Abstract

In the past quarter century, the field of computational complexity theory has grown into a rich and vibrant area of investigation. The goals of this theory are 1) the development of a scheme for classifying problems according to computational difficulty and 2) the placement of familiar problems within this scheme. This has given rise to a number of exciting, unsolved questions concerning the fundamental nature of computation.

12.1 Introduction

Hand in hand with the development of computer technology has grown a new area of scientific investigation: the classification of problems according to computational difficulty. For many of the problems that we would like to solve by computer, researchers have designed algorithms having a fast running time. For other problems we know slower, but still acceptably efficient algorithms. Still other problems seem to be solvable only by very slow algorithms. In our classification scheme, our goal is to assign to each problem its inherent computational complexity, telling the amount of computation that would be required for solution.

In most cases, we have not been able to attain this attractive goal. In general, it is very difficult to determine the complexity of a given problem. Indeed, there have been several well publicized cases where the discovery of a new, cleverer algorithm has shown that a problem can be solved much more quickly than previously thought possible. Perhaps most other problems today thought to be computationally impractical will in the future yield to clever fast algorithms in the same way.

However, for a certain class of problems, most researchers believe that we will never find practical algorithms. This belief is largely founded on the great deal of fruitless effort that has been expended on the search for such algorithms. This state of affairs poses a challenge for the theoretical investigator: show a way to design such algorithms or give a mathematical proof that none exist. We cannot say that we understand the nature of computation in a deep way until these questions of such a fundamental nature are resolved.

In this paper, we will survey the background and current research in this area. We will describe a number of simply stated problems whose computational complexity is not known. We will present the theoretical notions that have been devised to formulate this as a precise mathematical question and show some of the progress that has been made.

12.2   Computational Problems

Let us begin our discussion by presenting some problems which appear suitable for solution by computer. We first examine two problems which, though appearing superficially to be quite similar, seem to have quite different complexities. The *matching problem* is an example of one for which a relatively fast algorithm has been discovered. The *clique problem* on the other hand seems to require enormous time.

The Matching Problem: Suppose there is a collection of n people to be paired off for some reason, say to assign them to double rooms in a dormitory. Some pairs of people may be compatible while others are not. The goal is to find the largest collection of compatible pairs. This is an example of the famous *matching problem* which in abstract form is given a graph of n points find a maximal collection of edges no two of which have a point in common.

How difficult is this problem to solve computationally? About 25 years ago, Jack Edmonds proposed an algorithm to solve this problem with reasonable efficiency. His algorithm, with subsequent refinements, is practical for input sizes where n is in the thousands or tens of thousands.

The Clique Problem: Let us now slightly change the above situation. Instead of trying to find the largest collection of pairs of compatible people, we now wish to find the largest group of mutually compatible people, say for the purposes of throwing a party. This is an example of the *clique problem*: given a graph of n points, find a maximum collection of nodes all of which are connected together.

One algorithm for solving this problem is to examine every possible collection of people, keeping track of the largest mutually compatible collection that has been found so far. This procedure, called the *brute force algorithm*, works in principle but it becomes very slow when n reaches even a modest size. There are so many of possible subsets of n people that for n equal to 200 the time required by this algorithm would exceed the lifetime of the universe.

Of course, the brute force algorithm is a very simple minded approach. It operates by searching for a solution over a very large space. This is why it takes so long. The algorithm for the matching problem is much more clever. It works by gathering more and more information and constructing the solution rather than searching for it.

Is there a better method for the clique problem that the brute force algorithm? This is one of the most fundamental unsolved questions in theoretical computer science today. Most researchers believe that the answer to this question is no; the brute force algorithm is essentially the best possible. This belief primarily rests upon experience. A great deal of effort has been spent in the hope of finding a clever algorithm. None has been found.

We would like to find a definitive answer to this question. That is, either give an efficient algorithm, or a proof that the clique problem is inherently complex and that no such algorithm can exist. The means for proving that there is no clever, efficient way to solve a problem is at present very limited. One of the most exciting challenges to contemporary mathematics is to develop a theory which can give us a way to prove such things.

12.2.1   Other Examples

Reading the above, one might wonder why the clique problem has attained such a central position. There are a large variety of other problems which are currently best solved by a brute force algorithm and for which better algorithms are sought. One remarkable advance in understanding the complexity of these problems has been the realization that many of them are actually disguised variants of the same problem. These problems are all equivalent to each other in the sense that if an efficient algorithm is ever found for any of them, it may be transformed into efficient algorithms for all of them. Thousands of such equivalent problems have been discovered. To get a sense of the extent of this class of problems we give a few examples. Later on we will try to give some idea of how we show they are equivalent.

Traveling Salesman Problem: Suppose one is given a collection of cities and a list of distances between cities. The traveling salesman wishes to plan a trip that visits each city. He wishes to do this in the shortest possible way. How should one find this optimal tour? The naive brute force algorithm is simply to try every possible tour and see which is the shortest. Though somewhat more efficient algorithms have been devised which eliminate some of the possibilities, these too must contend with enormous searches when the number of cities grows.

Scheduling Problem: One is given a list of students who desire to take certain classes and a list of professors who will teach these classes. The University wishes to come up with a schedule that minimizes the number of conflicts. Again one could try all possible schedules, but this would be very slow.

Finding Mathematical Proofs: One of the main tasks of a mathematician is to find proofs of mathematical statements. Even when the proof is quite short, requiring a page or a few pages of description, it may be very difficult to discover it. One might hope to automate this process. There are algorithms for finding proofs of mathematical statements but they proceed by essentially trying all possible proofs until the desired one is found. This is too inefficient to be useful, but no better general algorithm is known.

In addition to problems of the above kind, there are also problems which are semi-equivalent to the clique problem. This means that an efficient algorithm for one of them is transformable to an efficient algorithm for the clique problems or that the reverse is true, but that both directions do not necessarily hold. Examples of this type of problem follow.

Game Strategies: Computer programs for many familiar games such as chess, checkers and Go have been written. Some of these programs play rather well, even rivalling the strength of the best human players. In principle, an algorithm could play perfectly, by examining the entire tree of possibilities. For most positions, this exhaustive search would take an astronomical amount of time. This problem of optimum play in each of the above three games, suitably generalized to $n \times n$

boards, is at least as difficult as the clique problem. Any efficient algorithm which solves it can be transformed to a clique algorithm.

Integer Factoring Problem: A composite number is one which can be divided evenly by some factor other than 1 and itself. The problem of factoring, i.e., finding the factors of a number, is another one that seems to require enormous search. Even though some improvement over the most simple-minded approach of trying all possible divisors has been made, 200 digit numbers take impossibly long to factor on the most powerful present-day computer.

Cryptographic Codes: For our last example of an apparently difficult computational problem we consider the breaking of cryptographic codes. In order to do this one must find the secret password or *key* which allows one to convert the encrypted message into the original message text. This is one case where no one (except the spy!) wants to find an efficient solution. Here, and in the preceding example, an efficient clique algorithm could be transformed into efficient code breaking and factoring algorithms.

12.3   Complexity Classes

In order to give some idea of how we can show the equivalence or semi-equivalence of these problems, we will introduce a few concepts from complexity theory.

12.3.1   Polynomial Time: The Class P

The preceding discussion treated the notion of efficient computation in an informal way. Computer theorists have come up with a formalization of this concept. If we think of representing the input to a computer algorithm as a string of characters, then we can see how the running time depends upon the length of the input. In other words, we can see how the number of steps the algorithm uses is affected by the input size. Typically brute force algorithms require a number of steps that is an exponential, say 2^n, in the length of the input. Exponential functions grow very rapidly and thus the running times become excessive even when the input is not very large. Polynomial functions, like n^2, grow at a much more modest rate. When we say that we seek an efficient algorithm we mean that we are trying to find an algorithm whose running time is, at most, polynomial in the input length.

Besides the aforementioned algorithm for the matching problem, polynomial time algorithms have been discovered for many other problems. These include the *sorting problem*, given a list of keys to arrange them in increasing order; the *shortest path problem*, finding the best way to get from one point to another through a network, graph or city streets; and the *linear programming problem*, to find the best way to adjust a variety of parameters to achieve a certain goal. All of the problems solvable in polynomial time are collectively called the class of polynomial time solvable problems, designated as the class P.

The choice of polynomial time as the definition of efficient is arguable. On the one hand, an algorithm requiring n^{100} steps can hardly be said to run efficiently, and even an n^2 time algorithm is often too slow to be useful. On the other hand, as a precise mathematical property which captures many of the features of efficient computation, it as an attractive definition. It does roughly correspond with practical considerations of efficiency. Furthermore it is mathematically robust in that it does not depend upon the model of computation that is selected. Whereas the exact number of steps taken by an algorithm might be sensitive to the language or machine of implementation, the polynomial or nonpolynomial growth of running time is not.

12.3.2   Nondeterministic Polynomial Time: The Class NP

Even though the we do know of a fast algorithm for the clique problem it does have the following important *verifiability* property. Someone can easily convince you that a clique of a certain size is present in the graph by merely exhibiting the clique. Once the location of the clique is known, checking to see that it is really there is straightforward and quick. This verifiability property is also enjoyed by many of the other problems on our list. For example, it is easy to demonstrate that there is a schedule with, at most, some number of conflicts simply by exhibiting this schedule.

In contrast, note that the problem of verifying that one has the *largest* clique or the schedule with the *fewest* number of conflicts is not so easy. It seems that one still has to examine all possible solutions to determine that one has the best one. So, we modify the examples above to be decision problems where one tests whether there is a solution that satisfies a certain criterion of success, rather than optimization problems which require the optimal solution, in order to obtain problems which are obviously verifiable.

There are certain problems which do not appear to have the verifiability property even though they are already decision problems. Determining who has a winning strategy in a chess game position is one such problem. Even after expending the effort to search the entire game tree to determine the answer, the only way known to convince someone that the answer is correct is essentially to take them through the tree again. There does not appear to be any way to prove succinctly that one side can win against all possible opponents.

Even though a problem is not known to have an efficient solution, if we can show that it has the verifiability property they we have said something positive about its complexity. The class of all problems with this property is called the class of nondeterministic polynomial time solvable problems, nicknamed NP. Thus P consists of those problems where one can *find* the solution quickly and NP consists of those problems where one can *verify* the solution quickly.

12.3.3   The P versus NP Question

We have just described two complexity classes, P and NP. What is their relationship? Obviously P is contained within NP since in any problem where one can find the solution quickly one can check the solution quickly, too. In fact, it seems that NP should properly contain P, that is, it should contain even more problems. Surprisingly it is not known if this is true. Conceivably P equals NP, meaning that if one could quickly verify that a solution is correct then one could also find the solution quickly. The clique problem, traveling salesman problem and scheduling problem are all in the class NP. So, if P equals NP, then there would be efficient algorithms for solving all these problems. The same holds for the problems of integer factoring and cryptographic codes.

Most researchers believe that P does not equal NP. This is because many thousands of man years have been spent searching for efficient solutions to these problems, without success. Of course, there may be some algorithmic idea which has been eluding everyone all this time. We will not be sure of the answer until someone either finds this idea or provides a mathematical proof that it does not exist, namely, that some of these problems really are *intractable,* intrinsically hard to solve by computer. A good deal of effort has already been put into finding such a proof, but it too remains elusive. To do it one must show that there is no clever way of solving some NP problem. No one yet has a clue of how to do this.

12.4 Evidence for Intractability

Even though we do not know how to prove that these problems are intractable, we do have a way of giving evidence for their intractability. There is a special subclass of NP called the *NP-complete problems*. They enjoy the property that if *any* problem in NP is intractable then so are they. Since it is considered likely that *some* problem in NP is intractable, the same holds for the NP-complete problems. Thus showing that a problem is NP-complete is taken to be evidence of its intractability, though not a proof of it.

Conversely, if any NP-complete problem is found to have an efficient algorithm for its solution then so do all problems in NP. Consequently, all NP-complete problems are seen to be computationally equivalent in the sense that they are either all easy or all hard to solve.

There are now many known NP-complete problems. Among the problems mentioned here so far, the clique, traveling salesman, scheduling and mathematical proof finding problems are in this class.

These problems are computationally equivalent because an instance of any one of them may be efficiently converted into an instance of any other. For example, if one had a particular case of the traveling salesman problem to solve it would be possible to convert it into a graph where finding a clique of a certain size would give the low-cost tour through all of the cities. This notion of efficient conversion, called *polynomial time reducibility* is the key to showing that the NP-complete problems are in a sense all variations of the same underlying problem.

The P versus NP question is thus the same as the question of determining the difficulty of solving any one of these NP-complete problems. In essence, it is the following question: when looking for any object in a large space, does one have to search occasionally the entire space, or is there always a much quicker way of homing in on the solution?

12.5   Progress on the P versus NP Question

The P versus NP question had gained widespread attention in recent
years. It is fundamental, related to the foundations of mathematics,
and gives a new perspective on classical mathematical subjects such as
number theory, algebra, geometry, and logic. Equally important, it is
a question about computer algorithms, with practical consequences. Its
naturalness and concreteness have drawn the attention of the international mathematics community over the past two decades.

As stated earlier, it is generally believed that P is different from NP,
i.e., that there are no fast algorithms for certain NP problems such as
the clique and traveling salesman problems. Solving the P versus NP
question in this way would entail showing that there is no fast, clever
algorithm for any of these problems. A number of research directions towards proving this are being pursued. One active approach is to consider
limiting the class of allowable algorithms. Within this restricted class, it
has been possible to prove that certain problems have high complexity.

12.5.1   Circuit Complexity

The notion of digital circuitry has long been familiar to electrical engineers. Claude Shannon in 1948 also introduced them as objects of
theoretical study. By a *Boolean circuit* we mean a network of *gates* computing simple functions such as AND, OR and NOT linked together by
wires from the outputs of certain gates to the inputs of others. Additionally, there are wires coming from input variables. Finally, there is a
specially designated gate whose output is taken to be the value of the
entire circuit on these inputs. Shannon asked: given a function, how
many gates are needed to represent it with a Boolean circuit?

It turns out that this question is closely connected to the P versus NP
question. It is not hard to show that any problem which may be solved
with a polynomial time algorithm can also be computed with circuits
which have a number of gates that is polynomial in the size on the input
to the circuit. This is true for the simple reason that one can design
circuitry to simulate the algorithm. So, one way to show that a problem
does not have a polynomial time algorithm would be to show that its
circuits must be large.

Unfortunately, research on proving that circuits require many gates
to compute specific functions has also reached an impasse. Circuits are

complex objects that are very hard to analyze. We have had no more luck proving that functions have high complexity with respect to circuits than we have had proving high complexity with respect to algorithms.

12.5.2 Progress on Restricted Circuit Models

In the past decade researchers have changed their strategy, since the direct approach to these questions has not been fruitful. Instead of looking at the standard model of computation and trying to show that algorithms to solve these apparently complicated problems must take a long time, research has proceeded on restricted, or *handicapped* models of computation. In this way we have been able to show that certain problems have more than polynomial complexity for a limited class of algorithms. We will sketch some of the principal results that have been obtained in this direction. For a fuller treatment see the survey paper by Boppana and Sipser (1989).

Bounded Depth Circuits: This first significant result of this kind was obtained by Furst, Saxe and Sipser (1981) and Ajtai (1981) who showed that certain simple functions such as the parity function require more than a polynomial number of gates for circuits whose depth, i.e., distance from the inputs to the output, is held constant. Subsequently, Yao (1985) and Hastad (1988) strengthened the bounds on this theorem. These results are proved using the method of *restriction* where some of the input variables are preset to 0 or 1. This allows the circuit to be simplified because some of the gates near the inputs become determined. The special property of the parity function is that it does not become simpler under this operation. Hence, if the initial circuit is small, it simplifies to a trivial circuit computing a nontrivial function, yielding a contradiction. The tricky part is how to choose the restriction so that it has the desired properties. The technique introduced by Furst, Saxe and Sipser is to select it at random, using nonconstructive methods.

Monotone Circuits: Another way of handicapping circuits is to restrict the kinds of gates they may have. Monotone circuits are those which do not have any NOT gates. In a recent paper, Razborov (1985) showed that monotone circuits computing the clique function must have more than a polynomial number of gates. Andreev (1985) established stronger bounds on the size of monotone circuits for a different function and Alon and Boppana (1987) gave stronger bounds for the clique function. The technique of these papers is to show how one may approximate a certain function computed by a monotone circuit. The quality of the approximation is determined by the size of the circuit: the smaller the better. Separately, one shows that the clique function has the special property that it cannot be well approximated in this way. Hence, any monotone circuit computing it must be large.

12.6 Other Complexity Classes

Since the introduction of the complexity classes P and NP by Cook in 1971, a rich collection of other complexity classes has been proposed and investigated. These are based on other measures of computational complexity besides the time measure. We may wish to consider how much storage space is necessary to solve a problem or whether it is amenable to fast solution by a highly parallel computer. Possibly a problem can be solved more quickly if one gives the algorithm access to a source of randomness and permits a small probability of error.

Space Complexity: An interesting class of problems are those which can be solved by a machine using an amount of storage that is logarithmic in the size of the input. For this class of problems it is helpful to think of input sizes which are very large, for example a database with millions of entries. Logarithmic storage is exactly the amount necessary to store a fixed number of pointers into the input, so one way to visualize this model of computation is picture the very large input written down over a large area, say the state of Massachusetts. Then the pointers may be thought of as a small collection of people who are at various locations in the state, with the ability to move around and communicate with each other, but only able to look at the portion of the input directly under the place where they are standing. Together they must solve some problem concerning this input.

For example, the input might represent some very large collection of cities and the distances between them. The problem is to determine whether it is possible to travel from one designated city to some other designated city without going too many miles. Note that this differs from the traveling salesman problem in that there is no requirement to visit all of the other cities along the way. This *connectivity problem* is known to be solvable on polynomial time, though it is not known if it can be solved using only logarithmic space. Interestingly, this problem is in *nondeterministic* logarithmic space in that one can *verify* the distance between cities if the people representing the pointers know the best route to get from one city to the other. As in the case for time complexity, it is not known if the class of problems solvable in logarithmic space coincides with the class of problems solvable in nondeterministic logarithmic space.

Parallel Computation: Designing computers with many processors is one way to bring more power to bear on a problem and hopefully solve it more quickly. Certain problems, however, seem to be composed of many small parts, where each part must be completed before tackling the next part. In these cases, it is not obvious that parallelization will allow for a speedup in the solution time. Again, it is an open question whether more cleverness will yield algorithms which can take advantage of parallelism for these problems or whether they are inherently sequential.

Randomized Computation: A surprising way to enhance the power of many computational models is to provide a source of randomness. It is surprising because a random input appears to contain no structured information, so it hard to see how it might be useful. Consider instead the case where one is trying to conduct an opinion poll among a large number of people. Asking each person for his opinion would be prohibitively expensive. An alternative is to select a random sample of the people and ask only them for their opinions and use this data to extrapolate the opinions of the rest. Of course this way introduces the possibility of error, but it certainly is cheaper, and it illustrates how randomness can be useful. In fact, this way of randomly sampling a large space to get some idea of its contents lies at the heart of many randomized algorithms. One example is the primality testing algorithm. This algorithm uses randomness to test whether a number is prime much more quickly than one could do so without randomness.

12.7   Conclusion

Complexity theory has grown to a rich and exciting branch of computer science since its inception a quarter century ago. As the technology has advanced, so has its theoretical counterpart. An extensive body of algorithms has been designed and much progress in understanding the nature of complexity has occurred. Some of the most basic questions concerning complexity turn out to be of striking mathematical difficulty. We are optimistic that the attention that these questions have been getting in the scientific community will lead to answers in the coming years. This field is still in its infancy. The most important work lies ahead.

12.8 Acknowledgments

Support for this research was provided in part by the National Science Foundation under grant number CLR-8912586.

Bibliography

[1] N. Alon and R.B. Boppana. The monotone circuit complexity of boolean functions. *Combinatorica*, 7(1):1–22, 1987.

[2] M. Ajtai. $\sum_1^1$-formulae on finite structures. *Annals of Pure and Applied Logic*, 24:1–48, 1983.

[3] A.E. Andreev. On a method for obtaining lower bounds for the complexity of individual monotone functions. *Doklady Akademii Nauk SSSR*, 282(5):1033–1037, 1985. In Russian. English translation in *Soviet Mathematics Doklady*, 31(3):530–534.

[4] R.B. Boppana and M. Sipser. The complexity of finite functions. To appear in *The Handbook of Theoretical Computer Science*, 1989.

[5] J. Edmonds. Paths, trees and flowers. *Canadian Journal of Mathematics*, 17:449–467, 1965.

[6] M. Furst, J. Saxe, and M. Sipser. Parity, circuits and the polynomial time hierarchy. *Mathematical Systems Theory*, 17:13–27, 1984.

[7] J. Hastad. *Advances in Computer Research*. Volume 5 of *Randomness and Computation*. Chapter in *Almost Optimal Lower Bounds for Small Depth Circuits*. JAI Press, 1989. Also in *Computational Limitations for Small Depth Circuits*, MIT Press, Cambridge, MA, 1986.

[8] A.A. Razborov. Lower bounds on the monotone complexity of some boolean functions. *Doklady Akademii Nauk SSSR*, 281(4):798–801, 1985.

[9] C.E. Shannon. The synthesis of two-terminal switching circuits. *Bell Systems Technical Journal*, 28(1):59–98, 1949.

[10] M. Sipser. Borel sets and circuit complexity. In *Proceedings of 15th Annual ACM Symposium on Theory of Computing*, pages 61–69, 1983.

[11] A.C. Yao. Separating the polynomial-time hierarchy by oracles. In *Proceedings of 26th Annual IEEE Symposium on Foundations of Computer Science*, pages 1–10, 1985.

IV Artificial Intelligence

13 Intelligence Without Representation

Rodney A. Brooks

Associate Professor, Department of Electrical Engineering and
Computer Science
Member, Artificial Intelligence Laboratory

Abstract

Artificial Intelligence research has foundered on the issue of representation. When intelligence is approached in an incremental manner, with strict reliance on interfacing to the real world through perception and action, reliance on representation disappears. In this paper, we outline our approach to incrementally building complete intelligent Creatures. The fundamental decomposition of the intelligent system is not into independent information processing units which must interface with each other via representations. Instead, the intelligent system is decomposed into independent and parallel activity producers which all interface directly to the world through perception and action, rather than interface to each other. The notions of central and peripheral systems evaporate—everything is both central and peripheral. Based on these principles we have built a very successful series of mobile robots which operate without supervision as Creatures in standard office environments.

13.1   Introduction

Artificial intelligence started as a field whose goal was to replicate human level intelligence in a machine.

Early hopes diminished as the magnitude and difficulty of that goal was appreciated. Slow progress was made over the next 25 years in

This paper appeared in the *AI Journal* 47(1), 1991 and is reprinted with permission from Elsevier Science Publishers B.V., North Holland.

demonstrating isolated aspects of intelligence. Recent work has tended to concentrate on commercializable aspects of "intelligent assistants" for human workers.

No one talks about replicating the full gamut of human intelligence anymore. Instead we see a retreat into specialized subproblems, such as ways to represent knowledge, natural language understanding, vision or even more specialized areas such as truth maintenance systems or plan verification. All the work in these subareas is benchmarked against the sorts of tasks humans do within those areas. Amongst the dreamers still in the field of AI, (those not dreaming about dollars, that is) there is a feeling that one day all these pieces will fall into place and we will see "truly" intelligent systems emerge.

However, I and others believe that human level intelligence is too complex and little understood to be correctly decomposed into the right subpieces at the moment and that, even if we knew the subpieces, we still would not know the right interfaces between them. Furthermore, we will never understand how to decompose human level intelligence until we have had a lot of practice with simpler level intelligences.

In this paper I therefore argue for a different approach to creating artificial intelligence:

- We must incrementally build up the capabilities of intelligent systems, having complete systems at each step of the way and thus automatically ensure that the pieces and their interfaces are valid.

- At each step, we should build complete intelligent systems that we let loose in the real world with real sensing and real action. Anything less provides a candidate with which we can delude ourselves.

We have been following this approach and have built a series of autonomous mobile robots. We have reached an unexpected conclusion (C) and have a rather radical hypothesis (H).

C: When we examine very simple level intelligence, we find that explicit representations and models of the world simply get in the way. It turns out to be better to use the world as its own model.

H: Representation is the wrong unit of abstraction in building the bulkiest parts of intelligent systems.

Representation has been the central issue in artificial intelligence work over the last 15 years only because it has provided an interface between otherwise isolated modules and conference papers.

13.2   The Evolution of Intelligence

We already have an existence proof of the possibility of intelligent entities—human beings. Additionally, many animals are intelligent to some degree. (This is a subject of intense debate, much of which really centers on a definition of intelligence.) They have evolved over the 4.6 billion year history of the earth.

It is instructive to reflect on the way in which earth-based biological evolution spent its time. Single cell entities arose out of the primordial soup roughly 3.5 billion years ago. A billion years passed before photosynthetic plants appeared. After almost another billion and a half years, around 550 million years ago, the first fish and vertebrates arrived, and then insects 450 million years ago. Then things started moving fast. Reptiles arrived 370 million years ago, followed by dinosaurs at 330 and mammals at 250 million years ago. The first primates appeared 120 million years ago and the immediate predecessors to the great apes a mere 18 million years ago. Man arrived in roughly his present form 2.5 million years ago. He invented agriculture a mere 19,000 years ago, writing less than 5000 years ago and "expert" knowledge only over the last few hundred years.

This suggests that problem solving behavior, language, expert knowledge and application, and reason, are all pretty simple once the essence of being and reacting is available. That essence is the ability to move around in a dynamic environment, sensing the surroundings to a degree sufficient to achieve the necessary maintenance of life and reproduction. This part of intelligence is where evolution has concentrated its time—it is much harder.

I believe that mobility, acute vision and the ability to carry out survival-related tasks in a dynamic environment provide a necessary basis for the development of true intelligence. [15] argues this case rather eloquently.

Human level intelligence has provided us with an existence proof but we must be careful about what the lessons are to be gained from it.

13.2.1 A Story

Suppose it is the 1890's. Artificial flight (AF) is the glamour subject in science, engineering and venture capital circles. A crew of AF researchers are miraculously transported by a time machine to the 1980's for a few hours. They spend the whole time in the passenger cabin of a commercial passenger Boeing 747 on a medium duration flight.

Returned to the 1890's they feel invigorated, knowing that AF is possible on a grand scale. They immediately set to work duplicating what they have seen. They make great progress in designing pitched seats, double pane windows, and know that if only they can figure out those weird 'plastics' they will have their grail within their grasp. (A few connectionists amongst them caught a glimpse of an engine with its cover off and they are preoccupied with inspirations from that experience.)

13.3 Abstraction as a Dangerous Weapon

Artificial intelligence researchers are fond of pointing out that AI is often denied its rightful successes. The popular story goes that when nobody has any good idea of how to solve a particular sort of problem (e.g., playing chess) it is known as an AI problem. When an algorithm developed by AI researchers successfully tackles such a problem, however, AI detractors claim that since the problem was solvable by an algorithm, it was not really an AI problem after all.

Thus AI never has any successes.

But have you ever heard of an AI failure?

I claim that AI researchers are guilty of the same (self) deception. They partition the problems they work on into two components. The AI component, which they solve, and the non-AI component which they do not solve. Typically AI "succeeds" by defining the parts of the problem that are unsolved as not AI. The principal mechanism for this partitioning is abstraction. Its application is usually considered part of good science, not, as it is in fact used in AI, as a mechanism for self delusion. In AI, abstraction is usually used to factor out all aspects of perception and motor skills. I argue below that these are the hard problems solved by intelligent systems, and further that the shape of solutions to these problems greatly constrains the correct solutions of the small pieces of intelligence which remain.

Early work in AI concentrated in games, geometrical problems, symbolic algebra, theorem proving, and other formal systems, e.g., [6][9]. In each case, the semantics of the domains were fairly simple.

In the late sixties and early seventies, the blocks world became a popular domain for AI research. It had a uniform and simple semantics. The key to success was to represent the state of the world completely and explicitly. Search techniques could then be used for planning within this well understood world. Learning could also be done within the blocks world. There were only a few simple concepts worth learning and they could be captured by enumerating the set of subexpressions which must be contained in any formal description of a world including an instance of the concept. The blocks world was even used for vision research and mobile robotics, as it provided strong constraints on the perceptual processing necessary, e.g., [11].

Eventually, criticism surfaced that the blocks world was a "toy world" and that within it there were simple special purpose solutions to what should be considered more general problems. At the same time, there was a funding crisis within AI (both in the U.S. and the U.K., the two most active places for AI research at the time). AI researchers found themselves forced to become relevant. They moved into more complex domains, such as trip planning, going to a restaurant, medical diagnosis, etc.

Soon there was a new slogan: **"Good representation is the key to AI,"** e.g., *conceptually efficient programs* in [2]. The idea was that by explicitly representing only the pertinent facts, the semantics of a world (which on the surface was quite complex) were reduced to a simple closed system once again. Abstraction to only the relevant details thus simplified the problems.

Consider a chair for example. While the following two characterizations are true:

(CAN (SIT-ON PERSON CHAIR))
(CAN (STAND-ON PERSON CHAIR))

there is much more to the concept of a chair. Chairs have some flat (maybe) sitting place, with perhaps a back support. They have a range of possible sizes, requirements on strength and a range of possibilities in shape. They often have some sort of covering material, unless they are made of wood, metal or plastic. They sometimes are soft in particular places. They can come from a range of possible styles. In particular the concept of what is a chair is hard to characterize simply. There is certainly no AI vision program which can find arbitrary chairs in arbitrary images; they can at best find one particular type of chair in carefully selected images.

This characterization, however, is perhaps the correct AI representation of solving certain problems, e.g., a person sitting on a chair in a room is hungry and can see a banana hanging from the ceiling just out of reach. Such problems are never posed to AI systems by showing them a photo of the scene. A person (even a young child) can make the right interpretation of the photo and suggest a plan of action. For AI planning systems however, the experimenter is required to abstract away most of the details to form a simple description in terms of atomic concepts such as PERSON, CHAIR and BANANAS.

This abstraction is the essence of intelligence and the hard part of the problems being solved. Under the current scheme, the abstraction is done by the researchers leaving little for the AI programs to do but search. A truly intelligent program would study the photograph, perform the abstraction and solve the problem.

The only input to most AI programs is a restricted set of simple assertions deduced from the real data by humans. The problems of recognition, spatial understanding, dealing with sensor noise, partial models, etc. are all ignored. These problems are relegated to the realm of input black boxes. Psychophysical evidence suggests they are all intimately tied up with the representation of the world used by an intelligent system.

There is no clean division between perception (abstraction) and reasoning in the real world. The brittleness of current AI systems attests to this fact. For example, MYCIN [12] is an expert at diagnosing human bacterial infections, but it really has no model of what a human (or any living creature) is or how they work, or what are plausible things to happen to a human. If told that the aorta is ruptured and the patient is losing blood at the rate of a pint every minute, MYCIN will try to find a bacterial cause of the problem.

Thus, because we still perform all the abstractions for our programs, most AI work is still done in the blocks world. Now the blocks are slightly different shapes and colors, but their underlying semantics have not changed greatly.

It could be argued that performing this abstraction (perception) for AI programs is merely the normal reductionist use of abstraction common in all good science. The abstraction reduces the input data so that the program experiences the same perceptual world (*Merkwelt* in [14]) as humans. Other (vision) researchers will independently fill in the details at some other time and place. I object to this on two grounds. First, as Uexküll and others have pointed out, each animal species, and clearly each robot species with their own distinctly nonhuman sensor suites, will have their own different *Merkwelt*. Second, the *Merkwelt* we humans provide to our programs is based on our own introspection. It is by no means clear that such a *Merkwelt* is anything like what we actually use internally—it could just as easily be an output coding for communication purposes (e.g., most humans go through life never realizing they have a large blind spot almost in the center of their visual fields).

The first objection warns of the danger that reasoning strategies developed for the human-assumed *Merkwelt* may not be valid when real sensors and perception processing are used. The second objection says that even with human sensors and perception, the *Merkwelt* may not be anything like that used by humans. In fact, it may be the case that our introspective descriptions of our internal representations are completely misleading and quite different from what we really use.

13.3.1 A Continuing Story

Meanwhile our friends in the 1890's are busy at work on their AF machine. They have come to agree that the project is too big to be worked on as a single entity and that they will need to become specialists in different areas. After all, they had asked questions of fellow passengers on their flight and discovered that the Boeing Company employed over 6000 people to build such an airplane.

Everyone is busy but there is not much communication between the groups. The people making the passenger seats used the finest solid steel available as the framework. There was some muttering that perhaps they should use tubular steel to save weight, but the consensus was that if such an obviously big and heavy airplane could fly then clearly there was no problem with weight.

On their observation flight none of the original group managed a glimpse of the driver's seat, but they have done some hard thinking and think they have established the major constraints on what should be there and how it should work. The pilot, as he will be called, sits in a seat above a glass floor so that he can see the ground below so he will know where to land. There are some side mirrors so he can watch behind for other approaching airplanes. His controls consist of a foot pedal to control speed (just as in these new fangled automobiles that are starting to appear), and a steering wheel to turn left and right. In addition, the wheel stem can be pushed forward and back to make the airplane go up and down. A clever arrangement of pipes measures airspeed of the airplane and displays it on a dial. What more could one want? Oh yes. There is a rather nice setup of louvers in the windows so that the driver can get fresh air without getting the full blast of the wind in his face.

An interesting sidelight is that all the researchers have by now abandoned the study of aerodynamics. Some of them had intensely questioned their fellow passengers on this subject and not one of the modern flyers had known a thing about it. Clearly the AF researchers had previously been wasting their time in its pursuit.

13.4   Incremental Intelligence

I wish to build completely autonomous mobile agents that coexist in the world with humans, and are seen by those humans as intelligent beings in their own right. I will call such agents *Creatures*. This is my intellectual motivation. I have no particular interest in demonstrating how human beings work, although humans like other animals are interesting objects of study in this endeavor as they are successful autonomous agents. I have no particular interest in applications; it seems clear to me that if my goals can be met then the range of applications for such Creatures will be limited only by our (or their) imagination. I have no particular interest in the philosophical implications of Creatures, although clearly there will be significant implications.

Given the caveats of the previous two sections, and considering the parable of the AF researchers, I am convinced that I must tread carefully in this endeavor to avoid some nasty pitfalls.

For the moment then, consider the problem of building Creatures as an engineering problem. We will develop an *engineering methodology* for building Creatures.

First, let us consider some of the requirements for our Creatures.

- A Creature must cope appropriately and in a timely fashion with changes in its dynamic environment.

- A Creature should be robust with respect to its environment. Minor changes in the properties of the world should not lead to total collapse of the Creature's behavior; rather one should expect only a gradual change in capabilities of the Creature as the environment changes more and more.

- A Creature should be able to maintain multiple goals and, depending on the circumstances it finds itself in, change which particular goals it is actively pursuing; thus it can both adapt to surroundings and capitalize on fortuitous circumstances.

- A Creature should do *something* in the world; it should have some purpose in being.

Now, let us consider some of the valid engineering approaches to achieving these requirements. As in all engineering endeavors it is necessary to decompose a complex system into parts, build the parts then interface them into a complete system.

13.4.1 Decomposition by Function

Perhaps the strongest traditional notion of intelligent systems (at least implicitly among AI workers) has been of a central system, with perceptual modules as inputs and action modules as outputs. The perceptual modules deliver a symbolic description of the world, and the action modules take a symbolic description of desired actions and make sure they happen in the world. The central system then is a symbolic information processor.

Traditionally, work in perception (and vision is the most commonly studied form of perception) and work in central systems has been done by different researchers and even totally different research laboratories. Vision workers are not immune to earlier criticisms of AI workers. Most

vision research is presented as a transformation from one image representation (e.g., a raw gray scale image) to another registered image (e.g.,
an edge image). Each group, AI and vision, makes assumptions about
the shape of the symbolic interfaces. Hardly anyone has ever connected
a vision system to an intelligent central system. Thus the assumptions
that independent researchers make are not forced to be realistic. There
is a real danger from pressures to neatly circumscribe the particular
piece of research being done.

The central system must also be decomposed into smaller pieces. We
see subfields of artificial intelligence such as "knowledge representation,"
"learning," "planning," "qualitative reasoning," etc. The interfaces between these modules are also subject to intellectual abuse.

When researchers working on a particular module get to choose both
the inputs and the outputs that specify the module requirements, I believe there is little chance the work they do will fit into a complete
intelligent system.

This bug in the functional decomposition approach is hard to fix. One
needs a long chain of modules to connect perception to action. In order
to test any of them, they all must first be built. But, until realistic
modules are built, it is highly unlikely that we can predict exactly what
modules will be needed or what interfaces they will need.

13.4.2   Decomposition by Activity

An alternative decomposition makes no distinction between peripheral
systems, such as vision, and central systems. Rather, the fundamental
slicing up of an intelligent system is in the orthogonal direction dividing it into *activity*-producing subsystems. Each activity, or behavior-
producing system individually connects sensing to action. We refer to
an activity-producing system as a *layer*. An activity is a pattern of interactions with the world. Another name for our activities might well
be *skill*, emphasizing that each activity can at least *post facto* be ratio-
nalized as pursuing some purpose. We have chosen the word activity
because our layers must decide when to act for themselves, not be some
subroutine to be invoked at the beck and call of some other layer.

The advantage of this approach is that it gives an incremental path
from very simple systems to complex autonomous intelligent systems.
At each step of the way it is only necessary to build one small piece, and
interface it to an existing, working, complete intelligence.

The idea is to first build a very simple complete autonomous system, and **test it in the real world**. Our favorite example of such a system is a Creature, actually a mobile robot, which avoids hitting things. It senses objects in its immediate vicinity and moves away from them, halting if it senses something in its path. It is still necessary to build this system by decomposing it into parts, but there need be no clear distinction between a "perception subsystem," a "central system" and an "action system." In fact, there may well be two independent channels connecting sensing to action (one for initiating motion and one for emergency halts), so there is no single place where "perception" delivers a representation of the world in the traditional sense.

Next, we build an incremental layer of intelligence which operates in parallel to the first system. It is pasted on to the existing debugged system and tested again in the real world. This new layer might directly access the sensors and run a different algorithm on the delivered data. The first level autonomous system continues to run in parallel, and unaware of the existence of the second level. For example, in [3] we reported on building a first layer of control which let the Creature avoid objects and then adding a layer which instilled an activity of trying to visit distant visible places. The second layer injected commands to the motor control part of the first layer directing the robot towards the goal, but independently the first layer would cause the robot to veer away from previously unseen obstacles. The second layer monitored the progress of the Creature and sent updated motor commands, thus achieving its goal without being explicitly aware of obstacles which had been handled by the lower level of control.

13.5   Who Has the Representations?

With multiple layers, the notion of perception delivering a description of the world gets blurred even more as the part of the system doing perception is spread out over many pieces which are not particularly connected by data paths or related by function. Certainly there is no identifiable place where the "output" of perception can be found. Furthermore, totally different sorts of processing of the sensor data proceed independently and in parallel, each affecting the overall system activity through quite different channels of control.

In fact, not by design, but rather by observation we note that a common theme in the ways in which our layered and distributed approach helps our Creatures meet our goals is that there is no central representation.

- Low level simple activities can instill the Creature with reactions to dangerous or important changes in its environment. Without complex representations and the need to maintain those representations and reason about them, these reactions can easily be made quick enough to serve their purpose. The key idea is to sense the environment often, and so have an up-to-date idea of what is happening in the world.

- By having multiple parallel activities and by removing the idea of a central representation, there is less chance that any given change in the class of properties enjoyed by the world can cause total collapse of the system. Rather, one might expect that a given change will at most incapacitate some but not all of the levels of control. Gradually, as a more alien world is entered (alien in the sense that the properties it holds are different from the properties of the world in which the individual layers were debugged), the performance of the Creature might continue to degrade. By not trying to have an analogous model of the world centrally located in the system, we are less likely to have built in a dependence on that model being completely accurate. Rather, individual layers extract only those *aspects* [1] of the world which they find relevant—projections of a representation into a simple subspace, if you like. Changes in the fundamental structure of the world have less chance of being reflected in every one of those projections than they would have of showing up as a difficulty in matching some query to a central single world model.

- Each layer of control can be thought of as having its own implicit purpose (or goal if you insist). Since they are *active* layers, running in parallel and with access to sensors, they can monitor the environment and decide on the appropriateness of their goals. Sometimes goals can be abandoned when circumstances seem unpromising, and other times fortuitous circumstances can be taken advantage of. The key idea here is to be using the world as its own model and to continuously match the preconditions of each goal against the real world. Because there is separate hardware for each layer, we can match as many goals as can exist in parallel and do not pay any price for higher numbers of goals as we would if we tried to add more and more sophistication to a single processor, or even some multiprocessor with a capacity-bounded network.

- The purpose of the Creature is implicit in its higher level purposes, goals or layers. There need be no explicit representation of goals that some central (or distributed) process selects from to decide what is most appropriate for the Creature to do next.

13.5.1   No Representation versus No Central Representation

Just as there is no central representation, there is not even a central system. Each activity-producing layer connects perception to action directly. It is only the observer of the Creature who imputes a central representation or central control. The Creature itself has none; it is a collection of competing behaviors. Out of the local chaos of their interactions there emerges, in the eye of an observer, a coherent pattern of behavior. There is no central purposeful locus of control. [10] gives a similar account of how human behavior is generated.

Note carefully that we are not claiming that chaos is a necessary ingredient of intelligent behavior. Indeed, we advocate careful engineering of all the interactions within the system (evolution had the luxury of incredibly long time scales and enormous numbers of individual experiments and thus perhaps was able to do without this careful engineering).

We do claim that there need be no explicit representation of either the world or the intentions of the system to generate intelligent behaviors for a Creature. Without such explicit representations, and when viewed locally, the interactions may indeed seem chaotic and without purpose.

I claim there is more than this, however. Even at a local level we do not have traditional AI representations. We never use tokens which have any semantics that can be attached to them. The best that can be said in our implementation is that one number is passed from one process to another. But it is only by looking at the state of both the first and second processes that that number can be given any interpretation at all. An extremist might say that we really do have representations, but that they are just implicit. With an appropriate mapping of the complete system and its state to another domain, we could define a representation that these numbers and topological connections between processes somehow encode.

However, we are not happy with calling such things a representation. They differ from standard representations in too many ways.

There are no variables (e.g., see [1] for a more thorough treatment of this) that need instantiation in reasoning processes. There are no rules which need to be selected through pattern matching. There are no choices to be made. To a large extent, the state of the world determines the action of the Creature. Herb Simon noted [13] that the complexity of the behavior of a system was not necessarily inherent in the complexity of the Creature, but perhaps in the complexity of the environment. He made this analysis in his description of an ant wandering the beach, but ignored its implications in the next paragraph when he talked about humans. We hypothesize (following Agre and Chapman) that much of even human level activity is similarly a reflection of the world through very simple mechanisms without detailed representations.

13.6   The Methodology in Practice

In order to build systems based on an activity decomposition so that they are truly robust, we must rigorously follow a careful methodology.

13.6.1   Methodological Maxims

First, it is vitally important to test the Creatures we build in the real world, i.e., in the same world that we humans inhabit. It is disastrous to fall into the temptation of testing them in a simplified world first, even with the best intentions of later transferring activity to an unsimplified world. With a simplified world (matte painted walls, rectangular vertices everywhere, colored blocks as the only obstacles) it is very easy to accidentally build a submodule of the system which happens to rely on some of those simplified properties. This reliance can then easily be reflected in the requirements on the interfaces between that submodule and others. The disease spreads and the complete system depends in a subtle way on the simplified world. When it comes time to move to the unsimplified world, we gradually and painfully realize that every piece of the system must be rebuilt. Worse than that, we may need to rethink the total design as the issues may change completely. We are not so concerned that it might be dangerous to first test simplified Creatures and later add more sophisticated layers of control, because evolution has been successful using this approach.

Second, as each layer is built it must be tested extensively in the real world. The system must interact with the real world over extended periods. Its behavior must be observed and be carefully and thoroughly debugged. When a second layer is added to an existing layer there are three potential sources of bugs: the first layer, the second layer or the interaction of the two layers. Eliminating the first of these sources of bugs as a possibility makes finding bugs much easier. Furthermore, there is only one thing possible to vary in order to fix the bugs—the second layer.

13.6.2 An Instantiation of the Methodology

We have built a series of four robots based on the methodology of task decomposition. They all operate in an unconstrained dynamic world (laboratory and office areas in the MIT Artificial Intelligence Laboratory). They successfully operate with people walking by, people deliberately trying to confuse them and people just standing by watching them. All four robots are Creatures in the sense that on power-up, they exist in the world and interact with it, pursuing multiple goals determined by their control layers implementing different activities. This is in contrast to other mobile robots that are given programs or plans to follow for a specific mission.

The four robots are shown in Figure 13.1. Two are identical, so there are really three designs. One uses an offboard Lisp Machine for most of its computations, two use onboard combinational networks and one uses a custom onboard parallel processor. All the robots implement the same abstract architecture, called *subsumption architecture*, which embodies the fundamental ideas of decomposition into layers of task achieving behaviors, and incremental composition through debugging in the real world. Details of these implementations can be found in [4].

Each layer in the subsumption architecture is composed of a fixed-topology network of simple finite-state machines. Each finite-state machine has a handful of states, one or two internal registers, one or two internal timers, and access to simple computational machines which can

Figure 13.1
The Four MIT AI Laboratory Robots. Left most is the first built Allen, which relies on an offboard Lisp Machine for computation support. The right most one is Herbert, shown with a 24 node CMOS parallel processor surrounding its girth. New sensors and fast early vision processors are still to be built and installed. In the middle are Tom and Jerry, based on a commercial toy chassis, with single PALs (Programmable Array of Logic) as their controllers.

compute things such as vector sums. The finite-state machines run asynchronously, sending and receiving fixed length messages (1 bit messages on the two small robots, and 24 bit messages on the larger ones) over *wires*. On our first robot these were virtual wires; on our later robots we have used physical wires to connect computational components.

There is no central locus of control. Rather, the finite-state machines are data-driven by the messages they receive. The arrival of messages or the expiration of designated time periods causes the finite-state machines to change state. The finite-state machines have access to the contents of the messages and might output them, test them with a predicate and conditionally branch to a different state, or pass them to simple computation elements. There is no possibility of access to global data, nor of dynamically established communications links. There is thus no possibility of global control. All finite-state machines are equal, yet at the same time they are prisoners of their fixed topology connections.

Layers are combined through mechanisms we call *suppression* (whence the name subsumption architecture) and *inhibition*. In both cases as a new layer is added, one of the new wires is side-tapped into an existing wire. A predefined time constant is associated with each side-tap. In the case of suppression, the side tapping occurs on the input side of a finite-state machine. If a message arrives on the new wire it is directed to the input port of the finite-state machine as though it had arrived on the existing wire. Additionally, any new messages on the existing wire are suppressed (i.e., rejected) for the specified time period. For inhibition, the side tapping occurs on the output side of a finite-state machine. A message on the new wire simply inhibits messages being emitted on the existing wire for the specified time period. Unlike suppression, the new message is not delivered in their place.

As an example, consider the three layers of Figure 13.2. These are three layers of control that we have run on our first mobile robot for well over a year. The robot has a ring of 12 ultrasonic sonars as its primary sensors. Every second these sonars are run to give 12 radial depth measurements. Sonar is extremely noisy due to many objects being mirrors to sonar. There are thus problems with specular reflection and return paths following multiple reflections due to surface skimming with low angles of incidence (less than 30 degrees).

In more detail, the three layers work as follows:

1. The lowest level layer implements a behavior which makes the robot (the physical embodiment of the Creature) avoid hitting objects. It avoids both static objects and moving objects, even those that are actively attacking it. The finite-state machine labeled *sonar* simply runs the sonar devices and every second emits an instantaneous map with the readings converted to polar coordinates. This map is passed on to the *collide* and *feelforce* finite-state machine. The first of these simply watches to see of there is anything dead ahead, and if so sends a *halt* message to the finite-state machine in charge of running the robot forwards—if that finite-state machine is not in the correct state, the message may well be ignored. Simultaneously, the other finite-state machine computes a repulsive force on the robot, based on an inverse square law, where each sonar return is considered to indicate the presence of a repulsive object. The contributions from each sonar are added to produce an overall force acting on the robot. The output is passed to the *runaway* machine which thresholds it and passes it

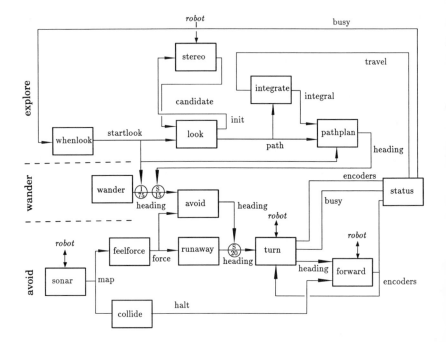

Figure 13.2
We wire finite-state machines together into layers of control. Each layer is built on top of existing layers. Lower level layers never rely on the existence of higher level layers.

on to the *turn* machine which orients the robot directly away from the summed repulsive force. Finally, the *forward* machine drives the robot forward. Whenever this machine receives a halt message while the robot is driving forward, it commands the robot to halt.

This network of finite-state machines generates behaviors which let the robot avoid objects. If it starts in the middle of an empty room it simply sits there. If someone walks up to it, the robot moves away. If it moves in the direction of other obstacles, it halts. Overall, it manages to exist in a dynamic environment without hitting or being hit by objects.

2. The next layer makes the robot wander about, when it is not busy avoiding objects. The *wander* finite-state machine generates a random heading for the robot every ten seconds or so. The *avoid* machine treats that heading as an attractive force and sums it with the repulsive force computed from the sonars. It uses the result to suppress the lower level behavior, forcing the robot to in a direction close to what *wander* decided, but at the same time avoiding any obstacles. Note that if the *turn* or *forward* finite-state machines are busy running the robot, the new impulse to wander will be ignored.

3. The third layer makes the robot try to explore. It looks for distant places, then tries to reach them. This layer suppresses the wander layer, and observes how the bottom layer diverts the robot due to obstacles (perhaps dynamic). It corrects for any divergences and the robot achieves the goal.

   The *whenlook* finite-state machine notices when the robot is not busy moving, and starts up the free space finder (labeled *stereo* in the diagram) finite-state machine. At the same time, it inhibits wandering behavior so that the observation will remain valid. When a path is observed it is sent to the *pathplan* finite-state machine, which injects a commanded direction to the *avoid* finite-state machine. In this way, lower level obstacle avoidance continues to function. This may cause the robot to go in a direction different from that desired by *pathplan*. For that reason, the actual path of the robot is monitored by the *integrate* finite-state machine, which sends updated estimates to the *pathplan* machine. This machine then acts as a difference engine forcing the robot in the desired direction and compensating for the actual path of the robot as it avoids obstacles.

These particular layers were implemented on our first robot. See [3] for more details. [5] reports on another three layers implemented on that particular robot.

13.7   What This Is Not

The subsumption architecture with its network of simple machines is reminiscent, at the surface level at least, with a number of mechanistic approaches to intelligence, such as connectionism and neural networks. But it is different in many respects from these endeavors, and also quite different from many other post-Dartmouth traditions in artificial intelligence. We briefly explain those differences in the following paragraphs.

It Isn't Connectionism: Connectionists try to make networks of simple processors. In that regard, the things they build (in simulation only—no connectionist has ever driven a real robot in a real environment, no matter how simple) are similar to the subsumption networks we build. However, their processing nodes tend to be uniform and they are looking (as their name suggests) for revelations from understanding how to connect them correctly (which is usually assumed to mean richly at least). Our nodes are all unique finite-state machines and the density of connections is much lower, certainly not uniform, and very low indeed between layers. Additionally, connectionists seem to be looking for explicit distributed representations to arise spontaneously from their networks. We harbor no such hopes because we believe representations are not necessary and appear only in the eye or mind of the observer.

It Isn't Neural Networks: Neural networks is the parent discipline of which connectionism is a recent incarnation. Workers in neural networks claim that there is some biological significance to their network nodes, as models of neurons. Most of the models seem wildly implausible given the paucity of modeled connections relative to the thousands found in real neurons. We claim no biological significance in our choice of finite-state machines as network nodes.

It Isn't Production Rules: Each individual activity-producing layer of our architecture could be viewed as in implementation of a production rule. When the right conditions are met in the environment, a certain action will be performed. We feel that analogy is a little like saying that any FORTRAN program with IF statements is implementing a production rule system. A standard production system really is more—it has a rule base, from which a rule is selected based on matching preconditions of all the rules to some database. The preconditions may include variables which must be matched to individuals in the database. Our layers run in parallel and have no variables or need for matching.

Instead, aspects of the world are extracted and these directly trigger or modify certain behaviors of the layer.

It Isn't a Blackboard: If one really wanted, one could make an analogy of our networks to a blackboard control architecture. Some of the finite-state machines would be localized knowledge sources. Others would be processes acting on these knowledge sources by finding them on the blackboard. There is a simplifying point in our architecture however: all the processes know exactly where to look on the blackboard as they are hardwired to the correct place. I think this forced analogy indicates its own weakness. There is no flexibility at all on where a process can gather appropriate knowledge. Most advanced blackboard architectures make heavy use of the general sharing and availability of almost all knowledge. Furthermore, in spirit at least, blackboard systems tend to hide from a consumer of knowledge who the particular producer was. This is the primary means of abstraction in blackboard systems. In our system we make such connections explicit and permanent.

It Isn't German Philosophy: In some circles, much credence is given to Heidegger as one who understood the dynamics of existence. Our approach has certain similarities to work inspired by this German philosopher, e.g., [1] but our work was not so inspired. It is based purely on engineering considerations. That does not preclude it from being used in philosophical debate as an example on any side of any fence, however.

13.8   Limits to Growth

Since our approach is a performance-based one, it is the performance of the systems we build which must be used to measure its usefulness and to point to its limitations.

We claim that as of mid-1987 our robots, using the subsumption architecture to implement complete Creatures, are the most reactive real time mobile robots in existence. Most other mobile robots are still at the stage of individual "experimental runs" in static environments, or at best in completely mapped static environments. Ours, on the other hand, operate completely autonomously in complex dynamic environments at the flick of their on switches, and continue until their batteries are drained. We believe they operate at a level closer to simple insect level intelligence than to bacteria level intelligence. Our goal (worth nothing if we do not deliver) is simple insect level intelligence within two years. Evolution took three billion years to get from single cells to insects, and only another 500 million years from there to humans. This statement is not intended as a prediction of our future performance, rather to indicate the nontrivial nature of insect level intelligence.

Despite this good performance to date, there are a number of serious questions about our approach. We have beliefs and hope about how these questions will be resolved, but under our criteria, only performance truly counts. Experiments and building more complex systems take time, so with the caveat that the experiments described below have not yet been performed, we outline how we currently see our endeavor progressing. Our intent in discussing this is to indicate that there is at least a plausible path forward to more intelligent machines from our current situation.

Our belief is that the sorts of activity-producing layers of control that we are developing (mobility, vision and survival related tasks) are necessary prerequisites for higher level intelligence in the style we attribute to human beings.

The most natural and serious questions concerning limits of our approach are:

- How many layers can be built in the subsumption architecture before the interactions between layers become too complex to continue?

- How complex can the behaviors be that are developed without the aid of central representations?

- Can higher level functions such as learning occur in these fixed topology networks of simple finite-state machines?

We outline our current thoughts on these questions.

13.8.1   How Many Layers?

The most layers we have run on a physical robot is three. In simulation we have run six parallel layers. The technique of completely debugging the robot on all existing activity-producing layers before designing and adding a new one seems to have been practical at least until now.

13.8.2   How Complex?

We are currently working towards a complex behavior pattern on our fourth robot which will require approximately 14 individual activity-producing layers.

The robot has infrared proximity sensors for local obstacle avoidance. It has an onboard manipulator which can grasp objects at ground and tabletop levels, and also determine their rough weight. The hand has depth sensors mounted on it so that homing in on a target object in order to grasp it can be controlled directly. We are currently working on a structured light laser scanner to determine rough depth maps in the forward looking direction from the robot.

The high level behavior we are trying to instill in this Creature is to wander around the office areas of our laboratory, find open office doors, enter, retrieve empty soda cans from cluttered desks in crowded offices and return them to a central repository.

In order to achieve this overall behavior, a number of simpler task achieving behaviors are necessary. They include avoiding objects, following walls, recognizing doorways and going through them, aligning on learned landmarks, heading in a homeward direction, learning homeward bearings at landmarks and following them, locating table-like objects, approaching such objects, scanning table tops for cylindrical objects of roughly the height of a soda can, serving the manipulator arm, moving the hand above sensed objects, using the hand sensor to look for objects of soda can size sticking up from a background, grasping objects if they are light enough, and depositing objects.

The individual tasks need not be coordinated by any central controller. Instead, they can index off the state of the world. For instance, the grasp behavior can cause the manipulator to grasp any object of the appropriate size seen by the hand sensors. The robot will not randomly grasp just any object however, because it will only be when other layers or behaviors have noticed an object of roughly the right shape on top of a table-like object that the grasping behavior will find itself in a position where its sensing of the world tells it to react. If from above the object no longer looks like a soda can, the grasp reflex will not happen and other lower level behaviors will cause the robot to look elsewhere for new candidates.

13.8.3   Is Learning and Such Possible?

Some insects demonstrate a simple type of learning that has been dubbed "learning by instinct" [7]. It is hypothesized that honey bees for example are pre-wired to learn how to distinguish certain classes of flowers, and to learn routes to and from a home hive and sources of nectar. Butterflies have been shown to be able to learn to distinguish flowers but in an information-limited way [8]. If they are forced to learn about a second sort of flower, they forget what they already knew about the first in a manner that suggests the total amount of information which they know remains constant.

We have found a way to build fixed-topology networks of our finite-state machines which can perform learning as an isolated subsystem at levels comparable to these examples. At the moment, of course, we are in the very position we lambasted most AI workers for earlier in this paper. We have an isolated module of a system working, and the inputs and outputs have been left dangling.

We are working to remedy this situation, but experimental work with physical Creatures is a nontrivial and time consuming activity. We find that most predesigned equipment or software has so many built-in preconceptions of how it is to be used, that it is not flexible enough to be a part of our complete systems. Thus, as of mid-1987, our work in learning is held up by the need to build a new sort of video camera and a high speed, low power processing box to run specially developed vision algorithms at ten frames per second. Each of these steps is a significant engineering endeavor which we are undertaking as fast as resources permit.

Of course, talk is cheap.

13.8.4   The Future

Only experiments with real Creatures in real worlds can answer the natural doubts about our approach. Time will tell.

13.9   Acknowledgments

Phil Agre, David Chapman, Peter Cudhea, Anita Flynn, David Kirsh and Thomas Marill made many helpful comments on earlier drafts of this paper.

Support for this research was provided in part by an IBM Faculty Development Award, a grant from the System Development Foundation, the University Research Initiative under the Office of Naval Research contract number N00014-86K-0685, and by the Defense Advanced Research Projects Agency of the Department of Defense, monitored under Office of Naval Research contract number N00015-85-K-0124.

Bibliography

[1] P. Agre and D. Chapman. MIT Artificial Intelligence Laboratory, Unpublished Memo, 1986.

[2] R.J. Bobrow and J.S. Brown. Representation and understanding. Chapter in *Systematic Understanding: Synthesis, Analysis, and Contingent Knowledge in Specialized Understanding Systems*, Bobrow and Collins, editors, pages 103–129, Academic Press, New York, 1975.

[3] R.A. Brooks. A robust layered control system for a mobile robot. *IEEE Journal of Robotics and Automation*, RA-2:14–23, April 1986.

[4] R.A. Brooks. A hardware retargetable distributed layered architecture for mobile robot control. In *Proceedings of IEEE Robotics and Automation*, pages 106–110, Raleigh, NC, April 1987.

[5] R.A. Brooks and J.H. Connell. Asynchronous distributed control system for a mobile robot. In *Proceedings of SPIE*, pages 77–84, Cambridge, MA, 1986.

[6] E.A. Feigenbaum and J. Feldman, editors. *Computers and Thought*. McGraw-Hill, San Francisco, CA, 1963.

[7] J.L. Gould and P. Marler. Learning by instinct. *Scientific American*, 74–85, December 1986.

[8] A.C. Lewis. Memory constraints and flower choice in pieris rapae. *Science*, 232:863–865, May 1986.

[9] M.L. Minsky, editor. *Semantic Information Processing*. MIT Press, Cambridge, MA, 1968.

[10] M.L. Minsky. *Society of Mind*. Simon and Schuster, New York, 1986.

[11] N.J. Nilsson. Shakey the robot. SRI Technical Note 323, Artificial Intelligence Center, April 1984.

[12] E.H. Shortliffe. *Mycin: Computer-based Medical Consultations*. Elsevier, New York, 1976.

[13] H.A. Simon. *The Sciences of the Artificial.* MIT Press, Cambridge, MA, 1969.

[14] J.Von Uexküll. Ummwelt und innerwelt der tiere. 1921.

[15] H.P. Voravec. Robotics research 1. Chapter in *Locomotion, Vision and Intelligence*, Brady and Paul, editors, pages 215–224, MIT Press, Cambridge, MA, 1984.

14 Parallel Networks for Machine Vision

Berthold K.P. Horn

Professor, Department of Electrical Engineering and Computer Science
Member, Artificial Intelligence Laboratory

Abstract

The amount of computation required to solve many early vision problems is prodigious, and so it has long been thought that systems that operate in a reasonable amount of time will only become feasible when locally interconnected systems become available. Such systems now exist in digital form, but most are large and expensive. These machines constitute an invaluable testbed for the development of new algorithms, but they cannot be scaled down rapidly in both physical size and cost, despite continued advances in semiconductor technology and machine architecture.

Simple analog networks can perform interesting computations, as has been known for a long time. We have reached the point where it is feasible to experiment with implementation of these idea in VLSI form, particularly if we focus on networks composed of locally interconnected passive elements, linear amplifiers, and simple nonlinear components. While there have been excursions into the development of ideas in this area since the very beginnings of work on machine vision, much work remains to be done. Progress will depend on careful attention to matching of the capabilities of simple networks to the needs of early vision.

This paper is not intended to be a review of the field, merely a collection of interesting ideas. The focus is on eikonic computations, that is, computations that occur in parallel at all picture cells.

An earlier version of this paper, with a more extended technical development, appeared in *Artificial Intelligence at MIT: Expanding Frontiers* edited by P.H. Winston and S.A. Shellard, MIT Press, Cambridge, MA, 1990.

14.1   Introduction

The purpose of *early vision* is to analyze one or more images and to derive a description of the world being viewed in a form suitable for a given task. In some sense, early vision has to invert the imaging process in order to recover information about a three dimensional world from mere two dimensional images. This is not an easy thing to do, as hinted at by the large fraction of our cortex that is devoted to this operation. This is not the place, however, to discuss in detail what is known about this problem, or to review progress in this field over the quarter century since its inception. The curious reader may wish to consult the text *Robot Vision* [14]. We address here just a few of the many problems raised by work on early vision without relating them in detail to actual applications of machine vision.

The term "parallel networks" in the title of this paper may appear to be redundant, since the computations at different nodes of an analog network naturally proceed in parallel. In several of the examples explored here, however, a number of different interacting networks are used, and these do indeed operate "in parallel." We have to try and understand the kinds of computations that simple networks can perform and then use them as components in more complex systems designed to solve early vision problems.

Some of the ideas presented here were first developed in continuous form, where one deals, for example, with resistive sheets instead of a regular grid of resistors. This is because the analysis of the continuous version is often simpler, and lends itself to well known mathematical techniques. Some thought must, of course, be given to what happens when we approximate this continuous world with a discrete one. This typically involves mathematical questions about accuracy and convergence, but also requires that the network be laid out on a two dimensional plane, since today's implementations allow only very limited stacking in the third dimension. This can be a problem when the network is inherently three dimensional or layered, or where several networks are used cooperatively. There are four major systems addressed here:

1. A Gaussian convolver for smoothing that operates continuously in time.

2. Coupled resistive networks for interpolation of image-derived data.

3. Moment calculation methods for determining position and orientation.

4. Systems for recovering motion and shape from time varying images.

In the process, we will touch on several important subtopics, including:

- Use of the two dimensional version of Green's theorem to move computations from the interior of a regular network to its boundary.

- An equivalence between two apparently quite different uses of a resistive network, one of which requires much less auxiliary circuitry.

- Interlaced arrangements of the cells of the layers of a three dimensional multi-resolution network on a two dimensional surface.

- Laying out time as an extra spatial dimension so as to build a system in which information flows continuously.

- Tradeoffs between closed form solutions favored on serial computers and feedback methods more suited for analog networks.

- Methods for solving constrained optimization problems using gradient projection, normalization and penalty functions.

Note, by the way, that the four remaining sections of this paper are essentially independent and not arranged in any particular order.

The focus here is on what may be called *eikonic* computations—that is, computations that occur in parallel at all picture cells, producing results that remain in the image domain. Computations that rapidly move to the symbolic domain do not lend themselves as easily to implementation in analog networks. This is a condensed version of a more technical paper—for further details and references see [15].

14.2 A Nonclocked Gaussian Convolver for Smoothing

A number of early vision operations require smoothing of the image, typically either to reduce the noise component or to suppress higher spatial frequency components of the image. Gaussian convolution is a useful smoothing operation, often used in early vision, particularly in conjunction with discrete operators that estimate derivatives. There exist several digital hardware implementations, including one that exploits the separability of the two dimensional Gaussian operator into the convolution of two one dimensional Gaussian operators. Analog implementations have also been proposed that use the fact that the solution of the heat equation at a certain time is the convolution of a Gaussian kernel with the initial temperature distribution [30].

One novel feature of the scheme described here is that data flows through continuously, with output available at any time. Essentially the time dimension in the heat equation is mapped into a third spatial dimension. Another interesting feature is an elegant way of interlacing the nodes of layers representing the image at several resolutions. First a brief review of why one might want to use Gaussian convolution.

14.2.1 Edge Detection

An important early vision task is the segmentation of the image into regions that appear to correspond to different surfaces in the scene. One approach to segmentation starts with the recovery of edges between regions that have different brightnesses. The detection of step-edge transitions in image brightness requires numerical estimation of derivatives. Image brightness measurements are quite noisy, with typically signal-to-noise ratios of less than a hundred to one. Hence all but the earliest efforts employed a certain degree of smoothing to suppress the noise before or after application of finite difference operators. Equivalently, these algorithms use computational molecules of large support. While most of the early work focused on the image brightness gradient, that is, the first partial derivatives of image brightness, there where some suggestion that second-order partial derivatives might be useful. Rotationally symmetric derivative operators appeared particularly appealing and it was noted that the Laplacian is the lowest order linear operator that allows recovery of the image information from the result.

It was also clear early on that smoothing filters should be weighted so as to put less emphasis on points further away than those nearby. The Gaussian was popular for smoothing because of a number of its mathematical properties, including the fact that the two dimensional Gaussian can be viewed as the convolution of two one dimensional Gaussians.

This gave rise to the hope that it might be computed with reasonable efficiency, an important matter when one is dealing with an image containing hundreds of thousands of picture cells. Note that the Gaussian is the only function that is both rotationally symmetric and separable in this fashion.

14.2.2 Multi-resolution Techniques

There are other reasons for smoothing a discretized image, including suppression of higher spatial frequency components before subsampling. Subsampling of an image produces an image of lower resolution, one that contains fewer picture cells. Ideally, one would hope that this lower resolution image retains all of the information in the original higher resolution image, but of course, in general this is not possible. The original image can be reconstructed only if does not contain spatial frequency components that are too high to be represented in the subsampled version. This suggests suppressing higher frequency components before subsampling in order to avoid *aliasing* phenomena. An ideal low pass filter should be used for this purpose. While the Gaussian filter is a poor approximation to a low pass filter, it has the advantage that it does not have any over- or undershoot in either the spatial or the frequency domain. Consequently, the Gaussian smoothing operator has been used in several multi-scale schemes.

The difference of two spatially displaced Gaussians was used quite early on in edge detection. The idea of working at multiple scales occurred around about this time. Based on this, an elegant theory of edge detection using zero-crossings of the Laplacian of the Gaussian at multiple scales was developed by Marr and Hildreth [13][25].

Since then, it has been shown that the rotationally symmetric operators do have some drawbacks, including greater inaccuracy in edge location when the edge is not straight, as well as higher sensitivity to noise than directional operators (see for example [14]). Operators for estimating the second derivative in the direction of the largest first derivative (the so-called *second directional derivative*) have been proposed. Canny developed an operator that is optimal (in a sense he defines) in a one dimensional version of the edge detection problem [3]. His operator is similar, but not equal to, the first derivative of a Gaussian. A straightforward (although *ad hoc*) extension of this operator to two dimensions has recently become popular.

If we view the problem as one of estimating the derivatives of a noisy signal, we can apply Wiener's optimal filtering methods. Additive white noise is uncorrelated and so has a flat spectrum, while images typically have spectra that decrease as some power of frequency, starting from a low frequency plateau. The magnitude of the optimal filter response ends up being linear in frequency at low frequencies, then peaks and drops off as some power of frequency at higher frequencies. Under somewhat specialized assumptions about the spectra of the ensemble of images being considered, this response may be considered to roughly match the transform of the derivative of a Gaussian.

The above suggests that while there is nothing really magical about the Gaussian smoothing filter, it has been widely used and has several desirable mathematical properties. It is thus of interest to find out whether convolutions with Gaussian kernels can be computed directly by simple analog networks.

14.2.3 Binomial Filters

In practice, we usually have to discretize and truncate the signal, as well as the filters we apply to it. If we sample and truncate a Gaussian, it loses virtually all of the interesting mathematical properties mentioned above. In particular, truncation introduces discontinuities that assure that the transform of the filter will fall off only as the inverse of frequency at high frequencies, not nearly as fast as the transform of the Gaussian itself. Furthermore, while the transfer function of a suitable scaled Gaussian lies between zero and one for all frequencies, the transfer function of a truncated version will lie outside this range for some frequencies. These effects are small only when we truncate at a distance that is large compared to the spatial scale of the Gaussian.

In addition, when we sample, we introduce aliasing effects, since the Gaussian is not a low pass waveform. The aliasing effects are small only when we sample frequently in relation to the spatial scale of the Gaussian. It makes little sense then to talk about convolution with a "discrete Gaussian" obtained by sampling with spacing comparable to the spatial scale, and by truncating at a distance comparable to the spatial scale of the underlying Gaussian. The resulting filter weights could have been obtained by sampling and truncating many other functions and so it is not reasonable to ascribe any of the interesting qualities of the Gaussian to such a set of weights.

Instead, we note that the appropriate discrete analog of the Gaussian is the binomial filter, obtained by dividing the binomial coefficients of order n by 2^n so that they conveniently sum to one [14]. Convolution of the binomial filter of order n with the binomial filter of order m yields the binomial filter of order $(n + m)$, as can be seen by noting that multiplication of polynomials corresponds to convolution of their coefficients. The simplest binomial smoothing filter has the weights:

$$\left\{ \frac{1}{2}, \frac{1}{2} \right\}.$$

Higher order filters can be obtained by repeated convolution of this filter with itself. So, for example,

$$\left\{ \frac{1}{4}, \frac{2}{4}, \frac{1}{4} \right\} \otimes \left\{ \frac{1}{2}, \frac{1}{2} \right\} = \left\{ \frac{1}{8}, \frac{3}{8}, \frac{3}{8}, \frac{1}{8} \right\}.$$

The transform of the binomial filter of order n is simply $\cos^n \omega/2$, since the transform of the simple filter with two weights is just $\cos \omega/2$. This shows that the magnitude of the transform is never larger than one for any frequency, a property shared with a properly scaled Gaussian. Such a filter cannot amplify any frequency components, it can only attenuate them.

14.2.4   Analog Implementation of Binomial Filters

Binomial filters can be conveniently constructed using charge coupled device technology. It is also possible to use potential dividers to perform the required averaging. Consider, for example, a uniform one dimensional chain of resistors with inputs applied as potentials on even nodes and results read out as potentials on odd nodes. The potentials on the odd nodes clearly are just averages of the potentials at neighboring even nodes. The outputs in this case are offset by one half of the pixel spacing from the inputs, but this is not really a problem. In particular, an even number of such filtering stages produces results that are aligned with the original data.

One such resistive chain can be used to perform convolution with the simple two-weight binomial filter shown above. To obtain convolution with higher order binomial filters, we can reuse the same network, with inputs and outputs interchanged, provided that we have clocked sample-and-hold circuits attached to each node. At any particular time, one half of the sample-and-hold circuits are presenting their potentials to the nodes they are attached to, while the other half are sampling the potentials on the remaining nodes.

But we may be more interested in nonclocked circuits, where outputs are available continuously. The outputs of one resistive chain can be applied as input to another, provided that buffer amplifiers are interposed to prevent the second chain from loading the first one. We can cascade many such resistive chain devices to obtain convolutions with binomial filters of arbitrary order.

It is possible to extend this idea to two dimensions. Consider nodes on a square grid, with each node connected to its four edge-adjacent neighbors by a resistor. Imagine coloring the nodes red and black, like the squares on a checkerboard. Then the red nodes may be considered the inputs where potentials are applied, while the black nodes are the outputs where potentials are read out. Each output potential is the average of four input potentials, and each input potential contributes to four outputs.

Unfortunately, the spatial scale of the binomial filter grows only with the square root of the number of stages used. Thus, while a lot of smoothing happens in the first few stages, it takes many more stages later in the sequence to obtain significant additional smoothing. Now the smoothed data has lost some of its high frequency content and so can perhaps be represented by fewer samples. These considerations suggest a multi-scale approach, where the number of nodes decreases from layer to layer. Averaging of neighbors in a later layer involves connections between nodes corresponding to points that are far apart in the original layer. Thus the smoothing that results in one of the later layers is over a larger spatial scale. We will still have to discuss how to efficiently interlace the nodes of several such layers of different resolution on a two dimensional surface.

The kind of network we are discussing here can also be approached in a different way, starting from the properties of continuous resistive sheets, and analog methods for solving the heat equation. Successive layers here correspond to successive time steps in a discrete approximation of the heat equation. This illustrates the idea of laying out time as an extra spatial dimension so as to build a system in which information flows continuously. For details of this approach see [15].

14.2.5   Multiple Scales

The information is smoothed out more and more as it flows through the layers of this system. Consequently, we do not need to preserve full resolution in layers further from the input—the information is low pass filtered and so fewer samples are required to represent it. This suggests that successive sheets could contain fewer and fewer nodes.

Note also that it would be very difficult indeed to superimpose, in two dimensions, multiple layers of the three dimensional network described above, if each of them contained the same (large) number of nodes. Now if, instead, a particular layer contains only $1/k$ times as many nodes as the previous layer then the total number of nodes is less than

$$\frac{k}{k-1}$$

times the number of nodes in the first layer, as can be seen by summing the appropriate geometric series. If, for example, we reduce the number of nodes to a quarter each time, then the whole network has less than $4/3$ times as many as the first layer. If we reduce the number of nodes by one half each time, then a network containing a finite number of layers still has less than twice the number of nodes that the first layer requires.

14.2.6   Growth of Standard Deviation with Number of Layers

If we define the *width* of the binomial filter as the standard deviation from its center position, while the *support* is the number of nonzero weights, then it turns out that width grows only as the square root of the support. So one argument for subsampling is that, if all the layers and the interconnections are the same, then the width of the binomial filter grows only with the square root of the number of layers. One way to obtain more rapid growth of the width of the smoothing filter is to arrange for successive layers to contain fewer nodes. This can be exploited to attain exponential growth of the effective width of the smoothing filter with the number of layers.

In the case of a square grid of nodes, a simple scheme would involve connecting only one cell out of four in a given layer to the next layer. This corresponds to a simple direct subsampling scheme. Sampling, however, should always be preceded by low pass filtering (or at least some sort of smoothing) to limit aliasing, as mentioned above. A better approach therefore involves first computing the average of four nodes in a given 2×2 pattern in order to obtain a smoothed result for the next layer. Each cell in the earlier layer contributes to only one of the averages being computed in this scheme.

The average could be computed directly using four resistors, but these would load down the network. The average can be computed instead using resistors connected to buffer amplifiers. Each cell in the earlier layer feeds a buffer amplifier and the output of the amplifier is applied to one end of a resistor. The other ends are tied together in group of four and connected to the nodes in the next layer. Note that the nodes of the latter sheet should be thought of as corresponding to offset image locations *between* those of the earlier sheet, rather than lying on top of a subset of these earlier nodes. But this subtlety does not present any real problems—particularly if there is an even number of layers overall.

14.2.7   Layout of Interlaced Nodes

A four-to-one reduction in number of nodes is easy to visualize and leads to rapid reduction in the number of nodes in successive layers, but it does not yield a very satisfactory subsampling operation. Aliasing effects can be curtailed if the number of nodes is reduced only by a factor of two instead. Note that in this case the total number of nodes in any finite number of layers is still less than twice the number of nodes in the first layer. An elegant way of achieving the reduction using a square grid of nodes is to think of successive layers as scaled spatially by a factor of $\sqrt{2}$ and also rotated $45°$ with respect to one another, as explained later. Once again, each of the new nodes is fed a current proportional to the difference between the average potential on four nodes in the earlier layer and the potential of the node itself. This time, however, each of the earlier nodes contributes to two of these averages rather than just one, as in the simple scheme described in the previous section. A node receives contributions from four nodes that are neighbors of its ancestor node in the earlier layer, but it receives no contribution directly from that ancestor.

An elegant partitioning of a square tessellation into subfields may be used in the implementation of this scheme in order to develop a satisfactory physical layout of the interlaced nodes of successive layers of this network (Robert Floyd drew my attention to this partitioning in the context of parallel schemes for producing pseudo grey-level displays

```
0 1 3 1 5 1 3 1 7 1 3 1 5 1 3 1 9
1 2 1 2 1 2 1 2 1 2 1 2 1 2 1 2 1
3 1 4 1 3 1 4 1 3 1 4 1 3 1 4 1 3
1 2 1 2 1 2 1 2 1 2 1 2 1 2 1 2 1
5 1 3 1 6 1 3 1 5 1 3 1 6 1 3 1 5
1 2 1 2 1 2 1 2 1 2 1 2 1 2 1 2 1
3 1 4 1 3 1 4 1 3 1 4 1 3 1 4 1 3
1 2 1 2 1 2 1 2 1 2 1 2 1 2 1 2 1
7 1 3 1 5 1 3 1 8 1 3 1 5 1 3 1 7
1 2 1 2 1 2 1 2 1 2 1 2 1 2 1 2 1
3 1 4 1 3 1 4 1 3 1 4 1 3 1 4 1 3
1 2 1 2 1 2 1 2 1 2 1 2 1 2 1 2 1
5 1 3 1 6 1 3 1 5 1 3 1 6 1 3 1 5
1 2 1 2 1 2 1 2 1 2 1 2 1 2 1 2 1
3 1 4 1 3 1 4 1 3 1 4 1 3 1 4 1 3
1 2 1 2 1 2 1 2 1 2 1 2 1 2 1 2 1
9 1 3 1 5 1 3 1 7 1 3 1 5 1 3 1 6
```

Figure 14.1
A way to interlace nodes of several layers of a multi-scale network so they can be laid out on a two dimensional surface. The network containing nodes labeled $(n + 1)$ has half as many nodes as the network whose nodes are labeled n. The total number of nodes is less than twice the number of nodes in the finest layer.

on binary image output devices). This leads to the interlaced pattern shown in Figure 14.1, where each cell is labeled with a number indicating which layer it belongs to.

In this scheme the nodes of the first layer may be thought of as the black cells in a checkerboard. The remaining cells are red and form a diagonal pattern with $\sqrt{2}$ times the spacing of the underlying grid. We can now consider this new grid as a checkerboard, turned 45° with respect to the first. If we color the cells in this checkerboard black and red, then the black cells belong to the second layer. The remaining red cells form a square grid aligned with the underlying grid but with twice the spacing between nodes. Considering this as a checkerboard in turn, we let the black cells be the nodes of the third layer, an so on ...

Note that one half of the cells are labeled 1, one quarter are labeled 2, one eight are labeled 3 and so on. The top left node, labeled 0, does not belong to any of the partitions. If we consider the nodes labeled with their row number i and there column number j, both starting at zero at the top left node, we find that a node belongs to layer k if the binary representation of $(i^2 + j^2)$ has $(k - 1)$ trailing zeros!

14.3 Coupled Poisson's Equation for Interpolation

Often properties of a scene can only be recovered on a sparse set of locations in the image, but are needed on a dense set. Feature-based binocular stereo, for example, provides depth information only where there are edges in the image, yet recognition algorithms typically require information about the whole of an object's surface [9]. In this situation, image properties, such as distance from the camera, need to be interpolated.

Now resistive networks can be used for several things other than smoothing. Uniform resistive sheets can, for example, solve Poisson's and Laplace's equations. One application of this property is in interpolation. Many modern interpolation methods are based on physical models of deformation of elastic sheets or thin plates; so these will be briefly reviewed here.

14.3.1 Mathematical Physics of Elastic Membranes

An elastic membrane takes on a shape that minimizes the stored elastic energy. In two dimensions the stored energy is proportional to the change in area of the membrane from its undisturbed shape, which we assume here is flat. The area is, of course, just given by the integral

$$\iint_D \sqrt{1 + z_x^2 + z_y^2}\, dx\, dy$$

where $z(x, y)$ is the height of the membrane above some reference plane. It can be shown that the membrane minimizes

$$\iint_D (z_x^2 + z_y^2)\, dx\, dy$$

provided that the partial derivatives z_x and z_y are small. A unique minimum exists if the sheet is constrained to pass through a simple closed curve ∂D on which the height is specified. The Euler equation for this calculus of variations problem yields

$$z_{xx} + z_{yy} = 0 \quad \text{or} \quad \Delta z = 0$$

except on the boundary where the height $z(x,y)$ is specified [4].

14.3.2   Interpolation by Means of a Thin Plate

The above equation has been proposed as a means of interpolating from sparse data specified along smooth curves, not necessarily simple closed contours. We explored the use of this idea, for example, in generating digital terrain models from contour maps in our work on automated hill-shading as well as in remote sensing. Recently, a 48×48 cell analog chip has been built to do this kind of interpolation [24].

The result of elastic membrane interpolation is not smooth, however, since, while height in the result is a continuous function of the independent variables, slope is not. Slope discontinuities occur all along contour lines, and the tops of hills and the bottoms of pits are flat.

This is why we decided to use thin plates for interpolation from contour data instead. The potential energy of a deformed plate can be approximated by a multiple of

$$\iint_D \left((z_{xx} + z_{yy})^2 - 2(1 - \mu)(z_{xx} z_{yy} - z_{xy}^2) \right) \, dx \, dy,$$

provided again that the slope components z_x and z_y are small. If the material constant μ happens to equal one, this simplifies to the integral of the square of the Laplacian. The Euler equations for this variational problem lead to the bi-harmonic equation

$$\Delta(\Delta z) = 0$$

except where the plate is constrained [4]. This fourth-order partial differential equation has a unique solution when the height $z(x,y)$, as well as the normal derivative of $z(x,y)$ are specified on a simple closed boundary ∂D.

Solutions of the bi-harmonic equation, while involving considerably more work than solutions of Laplace's equation, yield excellent results in interpolation from contours. Simple iterative methods for solving these equations are available, although some obvious implementations are not stable, particularly when updates are executed in parallel. The problem is that computational molecules or stencils with negative weights are needed, and these can amplify errors with components at some spatial frequencies, rather than attenuating them. This issue is not pursued any further here.

The same methods have been used for interpolation of surface depth from stereo data along brightness edges [9]. Grimson observed that the null-space of the quadratic variation $(z_{xx}^2 + 2z_{xy}^2 + z_{yy}^2)$ is smaller than that of the squared Laplacian $(\Delta z)^2$, and so decided to use the quadratic variation as the basis for his binocular stereo interpolation scheme. This corresponds to choosing $\mu = 0$. It turns out that this affects only the treatment of the boundary; one still solves the bi-harmonic equation inside the boundary.

The methods discussed here rapidly get rid of high spatial frequency components of the error, but take many iterations to reduce the low frequency components. The number of iterations required grows *quadratically* with the width of the largest gap between contours on which data is available. Efficient multi-resolution algorithms were developed to speed up the iterative computation of a solution. This approach has also been applied to variational problems other than interpolation [29].

14.3.3   Resistive Networks for the Bi-harmonic Equation

From the above, it should be clear that methods for solving the bi-harmonic equations are important in early vision. Unfortunately, simple locally connected networks of positive resistors can not be constructed to solve discrete approximations of this equation. Computational molecules or stencils [14] for the bi-harmonic operator involve negative weights and connections to nodes two steps away.

It is of interest then to discover ways of using methods for solving Poisson's equation $\Delta z(x, y) = f(x, y)$ in the solution of the bi-harmonic equation, since simple resistive networks can be constructed to solve Poisson's equation.

Harris recently developed a scheme that involves a functional in which both z and the slope components $p = z_x$ and $q = z_y$ are represented [10]. In his scheme, three coupled Poisson's equations are used, each of which can be solved using coupled resistive networks. Constraints on both $z(x, y)$ as well as z_x and z_y can be easily incorporated.

Harris's scheme is an extension of a scheme developed by the author for recovering depth $z(x, y)$, given dense estimates of the components p

and q of the gradient of the surface (as described in [18]). There one minimizes

$$\iint_D (z_x - p)^2 + (z_y - q)^2 \, dx \, dy$$

for which the Euler equation yields

$$\Delta z = p_x + q_y,$$

where p and q are here the given estimates of the components of the surface gradient. In Harris's scheme we do not have estimates of p and q at all points, instead we are given z at some points, and some linear combination of p and q at some other points. What is exciting about his method is that it leads to three coupled networks containing only positive resistors, and that these resistors connect only immediately neighboring nodes. See [11] for details of the analog implementations of the thin plate interpolation method.

The above ideas can be extended to help solve the *image irradiance equation* that occurs in the *shape from shading* problem [17][19].

14.4   Moment Calculations for Position and Orientation

The size, position and orientation of simple two dimensional image patterns can be determined using so-called *moment calculations*. In simple cases, knowledge of the two dimensional image position allows one to plan an action such as picking a part off a conveyor belt using an industrial manipulator. Moments are sums of products of various powers of image coordinates and functions of the picture cell grey-levels. These moments can be easily calculated using many different architectures, including bit-sliced, pipelined, analog networks, and by means of charge coupled devices. Such methods have recently been shown to have several other applications. A new technique for directly estimating motion of the camera from first derivatives of image brightness, for example, depends on the calculation of such moments (as discussed in the next section).

Binary images have "grey-levels" that can be only zero or one, often indicating the presence of absence of an object at a point in the image. Common operations in binary image processing are the computation of the zeroth, first and second moments of the regions of the image considered to be the image of one object. Presently, most commercially available machine vision systems have only rudimentary mechanisms for dealing with grey-level images and are aimed mainly at binary images. These systems typically have digital means for computing the moments. While such systems are restricted in their application, they are widely available and well understood. They can be used, for example, to determine the position and orientation of an isolated, contrasting workpiece lying flat on a uniform surface (see, for example, Chapter 3 in [14]). Also, a device that finds the centroid of a spot of light in the image can be used as a high resolution light-pen and a means of tracking a light source, such as a light bulb or light emitting diode (LED) attached to an industrial robot arm.

A variety of methods are available for efficiently computing the first-order moments, including methods that work with projections of the image, or even run-length encoded versions of the image. Less appears to be known about how to easily compute second and higher order moments, except that iterated summation can be used to avoid the implied multiplications. Such ideas are used in special purpose digital chips that have been built for finding moments [12]. We explore analog networks for this task, despite the existence of special purpose digital circuitry, partly to see whether they may have advantages over existing implementations, and partly because they constitute a stepping stone on the way to some types of networks used in the recovery of motion from time varying images, as discussed in the next section. Analog circuitry for motion vision tasks share many of the features of the simple moment generating circuits, but are more complex.

In this section a few different methods are explored for computing moments using analog networks. It will become clear that elegant methods exist for determining these moments using networks with relatively few components.

14.4.1   Use of First Moments for Position

Suppose that we have a characteristic function that indicates places in the image where the object region is thought to be. That is,

$$b(x, y) = \begin{cases} 1, & \text{if } (x, y) \text{ is in the region;} \\ 0, & \text{otherwise.} \end{cases}$$

Under favorable circumstances, such a characteristic function can be obtained by simply thresholding a grey-level image. The area of the object is obviously just the "zeroth-order" moment

$$A = \iint_D b(x, y) \, dx \, dy$$

where the integral is over the whole image.

The position of the object can be considered to be the location $(\bar{x}, \bar{y})$ of its center of area, defined in terms of the two first-order moments as follows:

$$A\bar{x} = \iint_D x \, b(x, y) \, dx \, dy \quad \text{and} \quad A\bar{y} = \iint_D y \, b(x, y) \, dx \, dy.$$

Note that the position of the center of area, relative to the object region in the image, is independent of the choice of coordinate system.

14.4.2 Use of Second Moments for Orientation

There are three second-order moments (integrals of products with x^2, xy, and y^2), and these can be used to define the orientation of the object as well as a shape factor. The orientation of the object may be taken to be specified by the direction of the axis of least inertia, which is independent of the choice of coordinate system.

It is easy to show that the axis of least inertia passes through the center of area, so it is convenient to compute the second-order moments with respect to the center of area. The axis of least inertia can be found if the integral of xy and the integral of $(x^2 - y^2)$ times the characteristic function can be computed. These are two particular combinations of the three second-order moments (see, for example, Chapter 3 in [14]). For a variety of other methods for computing moments see [14][15].

14.4.3 Resistive Networks for Moment Calculation

If area and center of area are all we are computing, then a very simple scheme can be used. Let us study this problem first in one dimension. Consider a regular chain of N resistors each with resistance R. We can use such a simple resistive chain to generate potentials at each node linearly related to the position. This potential can then be used in further calculation—to generate a current injected into a global bus for example—which may require a multiplier at each node [15].

Now consider a different way of using the very same chain. Suppose that the chain is grounded at the left and right ends, and that we can measure the currents I_l and I_r flowing into the ground at these points. There are k resistors to the left and $(N - k)$ to the right of the k-th node. Suppose a potential V develops at the k-th node when we inject a current I there. The two parallel parts of the chain can be thought of as a current divider. Clearly

$$I_l = \frac{V}{kR} \quad \text{and} \quad I_r = \frac{V}{(N - k)R}$$

while the total current is

$$I = I_l + I_r = \frac{N}{k(N - k)} \frac{V}{R}$$

so that

$$\frac{I_l}{I} = \frac{N - k}{N} \quad \text{and} \quad \frac{I_r}{I} = \frac{k}{N}.$$

We can compute the "centroid" of these two currents:

$$\bar{x} = x_l \frac{I_l}{I} + x_r \frac{I_r}{I} = x_l + \frac{k}{N}(x_r - x_l),$$

which is the x coordinate of the place where the current was injected. If we inject currents at several nodes, we can show, using superposition, that the computation above yields the centroid of the injected currents in one dimension.

Now imagine a regular two dimensional resistive grid grounded on the boundary. Current is injected at each picture cell where $b(x, y) = 1$. The currents to ground on the boundary from the network are measured. The total current obviously is proportional to the area, that is, the number of picture cells where $b(x, y) = 1$. More importantly, and somewhat surprisingly, the center of area of the current distribution on the boundary yields the center of area of the injected current distribution [15]!

The computation of the second moments is more complex. Fortunately, the two dimensional version of Green's formula

$$\iint_D (u\Delta v - v\Delta u)\, dA = \int_{\partial D} \left(u\frac{\partial v}{\partial n} - v\frac{\partial u}{\partial n} \right) ds$$

allows one to compute integrals of products with harmonic functions (functions whose Laplacian is zero) from the currents on the boundary, provided the boundary is grounded. This gives one easy access to two of the $(n + 1)$ n-th order moments [15].

To obtain the combinations of moments required here, we have to integrate the product of the boundary current with

$$1, \quad x, \quad y, \quad (x^2 - y^2) \quad \text{and} \quad 2xy.$$

The first is just the total current flowing out of the resistive network. The computation of the rest will be affected somewhat by the shape chosen for the resistive network. In the case of a circular image region, for example, we multiply the currents by weights that vary as

$$1, \quad \cos\theta, \quad \sin\theta, \quad \cos 2\theta \quad \text{and} \quad \sin 2\theta,$$

where θ is the angle measured from the center of the image. Note that these weights are fixed for each point on the boundary. The computation may be somewhat simplified by using a square boundary, but at the cost of loss of rotational symmetry.

There has been considerable work on finding moments using digital means. Special purpose systems have been developed for tracking objects using such schemes [8]. Also, a number of special purpose digital signal processing systems have been built to compute moments. Some of these systems have much of the required circuitry on a single digital chip [12]. Furthermore, a discrete analog chip has been built that determines the centroid using a gradient descent method [5]. With considerable increase in circuit complexity, this could perhaps be extended to also determine orientation using the approach described in the first part of this section.

There even exists a continuous analog light-spot position sensor that uses a method similar to the one described above (Selspot Systems). It consists of a single, large, square photo-diode and some electronics. Electrodes are attached along almost the full length of each of the four edges of the "lateral effect" photo-diode and four operational amplifiers are used to measure the short circuit current out of each of the four edges. The total current is just the integral of the signal. The ratio of the difference to the sum of the currents on opposite edges gives the position of the centroid in one direction. The currents in the other two edges give the other component of the centroid.

Apparently the possibility of computing combinations of higher moments from the boundary currents, and thus determining orientation, has not been previously noted.

14.4.4   A Network Equivalence Theorem

In the above we have discussed two apparently quite different ways of using a simple resistive network:

- Apply a given potential distribution along the edge of the network and use the open circuit potentials at interiors nodes in further calculation.

- Inject currents at interior nodes and use the measured short circuit currents on the edge in further calculation.

There is an intimate relationship between these two ways of using a resistive network. In some cases one of the two schemes leads to much simpler implementation than the other, so it is important to understand the equivalence. This will now be explored in more detail for arbitrary networks of resistors.

Consider a resistive network with external nodes segregated into two sets A and B of size N and M respectively. Now perform two experiments:

1. Connect the nodes in group A to voltage sources with potentials V_n for $n = 1, 2, \ldots, N$ and measure the resulting open circuit potentials on the nodes in group B. Let these be called v_m, for $m = 1, 2, \ldots, M$.

2. Connect the nodes in group B to current sources with currents i_m, for $m = 1, 2, \ldots, M$, and measure the short circuit currents in the nodes of group A. Let these be called I_n for $n = 1, 2, \ldots, N$.

Then

$$\sum_{n=1}^{N} I_n V_n = \sum_{m=1}^{M} i_m v_m.$$

We do not prove this result here, but note that it can be obtained using only the reciprocity of the circuit components [15].

14.4.5   Application

One application of this theorem is in the simplification of circuits for the analog computation of some weighted average. Suppose that we have a resistive network that is used to compute some quantities v_m (for example, a potential representing the x position in an image) from some fixed inputs V_n (for example, potentials representing x on the edge of the resistive network). These potentials are then used to compute a weighted average such as

$$\overline{v} = \frac{\sum_{m=1}^{M} i_m \, v_m}{\sum_{m=1}^{M} i_m},$$

where the quantities i_m are the weights (for example, image brightness).

Then an equivalent way of obtaining the same result is to inject currents proportional to i_m into the resistive network, now grounded in the places where inputs where applied earlier. Let the currents at the places where the network is grounded be I_n. Then the same weighted average can be obtained by computing instead

$$\overline{V} = \frac{\sum_{n=1}^{N} I_n V_n}{\sum_{n=1}^{N} I_n}.$$

Which of the two schemes is simpler depends on details of the implementation, including the relative sizes of N and M. For computing moments, the second scheme has a clear advantage, since the first scheme requires an analog multiplier at every node of the network.

It should be clear that the method described earlier for computing centroids is a particular application of this more general result. The computation of the required combinations of the second-order moments depends on the same equivalence result.

14.5   Short-range Motion Vision Methods

Time varying imagery can be used to recover the motion of the camera with respect to the environment. In addition, distances to points in the scene, and hence the shapes of objects, can be estimated since the image motion varies inversely with distance. Obvious applications of such capabilities include collision avoidance, spacecraft docking, object recognition and cross-country navigation.

Attacks on the motion vision problem can be categorized in a number of ways. First of all, there is the question of how large a change between successive images the method is meant to deal with. Feature-based methods appear to be best suited for the so-called *long range* motion vision problem, where there is a relatively large change between images. Conversely, these methods generally are not good at estimating motions with subpixel accuracy. Feature-based methods essentially solve the correspondence problem, which is the central problem in binocular stereo. Unfortunately, the problem in motion vision is even harder than the corresponding binocular stereo problem, because the search for a match is not confined to an epipolar line [14].

Gradient-based methods are better suited to situations where the motion between successive images is fairly small, that is, the *short range* motion vision problem. Correlation methods appear to fall somewhere in between, since they cannot deal with significant changes in foreshortening or photometric changes, yet are not able to easily produce displacement estimates with subpixel accuracy.

There are several different approaches to the short range motion vision problem. Here we briefly list some based directly on brightness derivatives rather than matching of isolated features or correlation. We first discuss several methods for recovering optical flow and then go on to methods for recovering rigid body motion directly, without using optical flow as an intermediate result.

All methods for recovering motion implicitly make some assumptions about how images change when the viewer moves with respect to the scene. Simple correlation methods, for example, assume that changes in foreshortening can be ignored and that the image moves as a two dimensional pattern without changes in brightness. This is not a good assumption in wide-baseline binocular stereo—as used in constructing topographic maps from aerial photographs—nor in some long range motion vision applications. Feature-based methods and correlation methods also assume that the brightness pattern does not change drastically with viewpoint. Fortunately, the brightness of many real surfaces does not depend significantly on the viewing direction for fixed illumination geometry.

Methods based on brightness gradients implicitly assume that the variations in brightness at a particular point in the image due to motion are much larger than the brightness fluctuations induced by changes in viewpoint. This is a reasonable assumption unless the surface lacks markings and is illuminated by rapidly moving light sources. Almost all methods will be "fooled" by the motion of virtual images resulting from specular or glossy reflections of point light sources.

14.5.1 Recovering Optical Flow from Brightness Derivatives

The *motion field* is the projection in the image of velocities of points in the environment with respect to the observer. Observer motion and object shapes can be estimated from the motion field. The *optical flow*, on the other hand, is a vector field in the image that indicates how brightness patterns move with time. The optical flow field is not unique, since the matching of points along an isophote in one image with an isophote of the same brightness in the other image is not unique. Additional constraints have to be introduced in order to select a particular "optical flow." Under favorable circumstances the optical flow so computed is a good estimate of the motion field. There are several algorithms of different complexity and robustness for estimating optical flow. At one end of the spectrum we have algorithms that assume the flow is constant over the image, at the other, there are algorithms that can deal with depth discontinuities. Many of the interesting variations are listed here in order of increasing complexity:

1. **Constant Optical Flow:** Here the flow velocity, (u, v), is assumed to be constant over the image patch. This may be a good approximation for a small field of view. Several cameras aimed in different directions (spider head) could then yield flow vectors that provide the information necessary to solve for the observer motion. Alternatively, this computation may be applied to (possibly overlapping and weighted) patches of one image. A basic least squares analysis leads to a simple algorithm. All that is required is: (a) estimation of the brightness derivatives E_x, E_y, and E_t, (b) accumulation of the sums of the products E_x^2, $E_x E_y$, E_y^2, $E_x E_t$, and $E_y E_t$, and, (c) solution of two linear equations in the two unknowns u and v. This last step could be done off-chip, if the required totals are accumulated on-chip. Alternatively, the computation can be done in a feedback mode on chip (as it is in [28]). The bandwidth going off-chip is very low in either case.

If the computation is done for many (possibly overlapping and weighted) image windows, then an optical flow vector field results (at resolution less than the full image resolution). Such a vector field can then be processed off-chip to yield camera motion and scene structure using a least-squares method.

2. **Basic Optical Flow** [21]: Here the velocity field is allowed to vary from place to place in the image, but is assumed to vary smoothly. Depth discontinuities are not treated, but elastic deformations, fluid flows and rigid body motions yield reasonable results. The calculus of variations problem here leads to a coupled pair of Poisson's equations for $u(x, y)$ and $v(x, y)$, the components of the optical flow. The right-hand sides of these equations (that is, parts not involving u and v) are computed from the brightness derivatives. One needs to be able to compute terms such as $(\alpha^2 + E_x^2 + E_y^2)$ (or approximations thereto). The partial differential equations themselves, of course, can be conveniently solved on two interlaced resistive networks. The inputs may be currents injected at nodes, while the outputs are the potentials there. The boundaries have to be treated carefully. The algorithm is robust with respect to small random errors in the resistive network. As is commonly the case in machine vision, there is some small advantage to working on a hexagonal grid.

3. **Optical Flow with Multiplier**: The basic optical flow algorithm is based on the assumption that the brightness of a small patch of the surface does not change as it moves. In practice, there are small brightness changes, since the shading on the surface may change slowly as a patch moves into areas that are illuminated differently. When the surface is highly textured, brightness variations at a point in the image resulting from motion are much larger than those due to changes in shading and illumination, and so these can be safely ignored. If there is no strong texture on the surface, somewhat better results can be obtained if one takes account of these small changes in shading. One can do this using a simple multiplier model. Here the brightness of a patch in a frame of an image sequence is assumed to be a multiple of the brightness of the same patch in the previous frame. The multiplier (assumed to be near unity) is allowed to vary from point to point in the image,

but is assumed to vary slowly with position. The resulting calculus of variations problem leads to three coupled partial differential equations. The new algorithm is not much more complex (about 50% more work) than the basic one, yet yields better results.

4. **Optical Flow with Discontinuities**: The notion of a *line process* for dealing with discontinuities in images originated with [7]. This idea was later applied to discontinuities in optical flow [23]. To deal with discontinuities in the optical flow, which typically occur at object boundaries, one introduces line processes that cut the solution and prevent smoothing over discontinuities. The resulting penalty function to be minimized is no longer convex and the solution involves more than simply solving a set of coupled partial differential equations. It seemed at first that this approach was doomed to failure, since methods like simulated annealing for solving such nonlinear problems are hopelessly inefficient. However, a reasonably efficient method results if one gives up the demand for the absolute global minimum and instead is satisfied with a good solution, with cost close to the absolute minimum cost [2]. It helps to base the decision about whether to introduce a line process at a particular place only on the local change in the cost of the solution. Further improvements in performance can be had if line processes are allowed only very near to discontinuities in brightness, that is, edges [6]. This suggests integrating some edge finding algorithm on the same chip. The approach here leads to an analog network that interacts with some logic circuits implementing the line-process decision making (see Figure 5 in [23]).

Often there is a concern about the rate of convergence of simple methods for solving Poisson's equation. Multi-grid methods are suggested as a means of speeding up the process. This is fortunately not so much of a concern here since:

- It is rare to have no inputs (zero right-hand side) over large patches (that is, large patches of uniform brightness are rare).

- The analog networks ought to settle fairly rapidly, even when there are many nodes, since the time-constant should be small.

- Excellent starting values are available from the solution for the previous frame.

Because it is difficult to get good estimates of optical flow from noisy image data, there has been a trend recently to go directly to the ultimately desired information, namely observer motion and object shape. Instead of computing these from a flow field, they are derived directly from image brightness and the partial derivatives of brightness. These methods too lend themselves to implementation in a parallel network (see next section). They do, however, assume rigid body motion. Thus these methods are of little use when we are dealing with elastic deformations and fluid flow. Consequently there is still strong interest in finding rapid, robust methods for estimating the optical flow.

14.5.2   Direct Recovery of Rigid Body Motion

It is possible to derive observer motion and object shape directly from brightness gradients using something like a least-squares approach. These methods are not as mature as those for estimating the optical flow, but may ultimately be of more interest. A number of special cases have been solved so far:

1. **Pure Rotation** [22]: In the case of pure rotation, the motion field is particularly simple since it does not depend on the distances of the observer from the objects in the scene. In this case, a simple least-squares analysis leads to a set of three linear equations in the three unknown components of the angular velocity vector $\omega = (A, B, C)^T$. The coefficients of these equations are once again sums over the whole image of products of brightness derivatives and image coordinates. The algorithm is remarkably robust with respect to noise in the brightness derivatives, since the problem is so highly overdetermined (three unknowns and hundreds of thousands of measurements).

2. **Pure Translation** [22]: In the case of pure translation, the task is to recover the direction of the translation vector. The *focus of expansion* is the intersection of this vector with the image plane, that is, it is the image of the point towards which the observer is moving. Once the focus of expansion has been located, relative distances of selected points in the scene (where the brightness

gradient is large enough in the direction towards the focus of expansion) can be estimated—one simply divides the rate of change of brightness in the direction towards the focus of expansion by the time rate of change of brightness. There are several methods for recovering the direction of translation. The most promising at this point requires eigenvector-eigenvalue decomposition of a 3 × 3 matrix constructed using sums of products of brightness derivatives and image coordinates. These sums could be computed on-chip, with the final analysis being done off-chip. This algorithm is not nearly as robust as the one for pure rotation, since there are now an enormous number of additional "unknowns," namely the distances to the scene at each picture cell. For the same reason this algorithm is much more interesting since it allows us to recover depth and thus obtain surface shape information.

3. **Planar Surface** [20]: If the scene consists of a single planar surface (perhaps an airport viewed from a landing aircraft), it is possible to compute the direction of translation, the orientation of the plane, the rotational velocity of the observer, as well as the time to impact, directly from certain sums accumulated over the whole image. There is a two-way ambiguity in the result that can be resolved using other sensory information or by waiting for new solutions based on subsequent frames. The sums required are "moments," products of the partial derivatives of brightness (E_x, E_y, and E_z) and the image coordinates x, and y. The final calculation involves eigenvector-eigenvalue decomposition of a 3 × 3 matrix constructed using these sums, but this can be done off-chip. Both closed form and iterative solutions are known. There are quite a large number of different sums needed, but each is relatively simple to compute.

4. **Fixation**: If one fixates on a point in the moving environment, a constraint is introduced between the instantaneous rotational and translational velocities of the observer relative to the environment. This allows one to simplify the motion constraint equation and reduces the problem to something similar to that of pure translation.

The general case (arbitrary surface, both translation and rotation) has not been solved yet. Also, the pure translation solutions are not very robust, suggesting that to one needs to continue the solution in time in order to get stable results (all of the methods discussed above work "instantaneously" using two image frames, and do not make direct use of information in earlier frames).

In the case of pure translation, depth is recovered only in places where the local brightness gradient is strong enough in the direction towards the focus of expansion. This suggests the need for a smooth interpolation process that fills in the rest. It might take the form of the solution of Poisson's equation or the bi-harmonic equation. A simple passive network will do for Poisson's equation, of course. If the higher order approach is taken, negative resistances and more connections are required. It is possible, however, as we saw earlier, to decompose the bi-harmonic equation into three coupled Poisson's equations [10]. The latter can then be solved using coupled resistive network.

Finally, to deal with depth-discontinuities, one can introduce line-processes once again. Naturally, we are now talking about a pretty complex system! We now discuss the above in more detail.

14.5.3   Constant Flow Velocity

The method that assumes that optical flow is constant in a patch will be considered first, as a simple illustration of the kind of approach taken. First we review the brightness change constraint equation. Image brightness $E(x, y, t)$ is a function of three variables. If the brightness of a small patch does not change as it moves, we can write

$$\frac{dE}{dt} = 0$$

which can be expanded, using the chain rule, to yield

$$\frac{\partial E}{\partial x}\frac{dx}{dt} + \frac{\partial E}{\partial y}\frac{dy}{dt} + \frac{\partial E}{\partial t} = 0$$

or

$$uE_x + vE_y + E_t = 0,$$

where E_x, E_y are the components of the brightness gradient, while E_t is the time rate of change of brightness. This so-called *brightness change constraint equation* provides only one constraint on the two components of image flow, u and v. Thus image flow cannot be recovered locally without further information.

Suppose now that the image flow components u and v are constant over a patch in the image. Then we can recover them using a least squares approach: We minimize the total error

$$I = \iint_D (uE_x + vE_y + E_t)^2 \, dx\, dy.$$

Differentiation with respect to u and v, and setting the results equal to zero, leads to a pair of linear equations in u and v, which can, of course, be solved in closed form [15]. The required coefficients are easily calculated in parallel, if so desired.

While this closed form solution is very appealing in a sequential digital implementation, it involves division and other operations that are not particularly easily carried out in analog circuitry. In this case, a feedback strategy may be favored. Using a gradient descent approach, we arrive at

$$\frac{du}{dt} = -\alpha \iint_D (uE_x + vE_y + E_t)\, E_x \, dx\, dy,$$

$$\frac{dv}{dt} = -\alpha \iint_D (uE_x + vE_y + E_t)\, E_y \, dx\, dy.$$

At each picture cell, we have to estimate the derivatives of brightness, and compute the error in the brightness change constraint equation

$$e = (uE_x + vE_y + E_t)$$

using global buses whose potentials represent u and v. Currents proportional to $-e\, E_x$ and $-e\, E_y$ are then injected into the buses for u and v respectively. The potential on the distributed capacitance of each global bus settles to a value that represents the optical flow components u and v. This is essentially how the constant flow velocity chip of Tanner and Mead works [28].

If we allow u and v to vary from place to place in the image, but require that they do so smoothly, we obtain a problem in the calculus of variations [21]. This was in fact the first vision problem where the calculus of variations was used to introduce a preference for solutions satisfying prior selection criteria.

14.5.4 Special Purpose Direct Motion Vision Systems

We have seen that in short range motion vision one need not solve the correspondence problem. One can instead use derivatives of image brightness directly to estimate the motion of the camera. The time rate of change of image brightness at a particular picture cell can be predicted if the brightness gradient and the motion of the pattern in the image is known. This two dimensional motion of patterns in the image can be predicted if the three dimensional motion of the camera is given. Given these facts, it should be apparent that the motion of the camera can be found by finding the motion that best predicts the time rate of change of brightness (the t-derivative) at all picture cells, given the observed brightness gradients (the x- and y-derivatives). Once the instantaneous rotational and translational motion of the camera have been found, one can determine the depth at points where the brightness gradient is large enough and oriented appropriately.

We will next describe in detail a method for the solution of the pure rotation case and a method for the solution of the pure translation case. We saw earlier that if the brightness of a patch does not change as it moves, we obtain the brightness change constraint equation

$$uE_x + vE_y + E_t = 0$$

where E_x, E_y are the components of the brightness gradient, while E_t is the time rate of change of brightness. This equation provides one constraint on the two image flow components u and v. Thus image flow cannot be recovered locally without additional constraint.

We are now dealing, however, with rigid body motion, where image flow is heavily constrained—there are only six unknown degrees of freedom of motion. The image flow components u and v dependent on the instantaneous translational and rotational velocities of the camera, denoted $\mathbf{t} = (U, V, W)^T$ and $\omega = (A, B, C)^T$ respectively. It can be shown by differentiating the equation for perspective projection, that

$$u = \frac{-U + xW}{Z} + A\,xy - B(1 + x^2) + C\,y,$$

$$v = \frac{-V + yW}{Z} + A(1 + y^2) - B\,xy - C\,x,$$

where Z is the depth (distance along the optical axis) at the image point (x, y). Combining this with the brightness change constraint equation, we obtain [22]

$$E_t + \mathbf{v} \cdot \omega + \frac{1}{Z}\mathbf{s} \cdot \mathbf{t} = 0$$

where

$$\mathbf{v} = \begin{pmatrix} +E_y + y(xE_x + yE_y) \\ -E_x - x(xE_x + yE_y) \\ yE_x - xE_y \end{pmatrix}, \quad \text{and} \quad \mathbf{s} = \begin{pmatrix} -E_x \\ -E_y \\ xE_x + yE_y \end{pmatrix}.$$

This is called the *rigid body brightness change constraint equation*.

14.5.5 Feedback Computation of Instantaneous Rotational Velocity

Horn & Weldon [1988] rediscovered a method apparently first invented by Alomoinos & Brown [1985] for direct motion vision in the case of pure rotation. This method uses integrals of products of first partial derivatives of image brightness and image coordinates and involves the solution of a system of three linear equations in three unknowns. When there is no translational motion, the brightness change constraint equation becomes just

$$E_t + \mathbf{v} \cdot \boldsymbol{\omega} = 0.$$

This suggests a least-squares approach, where we minimize

$$I = \iint_D (E_t + \mathbf{v} \cdot \boldsymbol{\omega})^2 \, dx \, dy$$

by suitable choice of the instantaneous rotational velocity $\boldsymbol{\omega}$. The system of linear equations obtained by differentiation with respect to $\boldsymbol{\omega}$ and setting the result equal to zero, can be solved explicitly, but this involves division by the determinant of the coefficient matrix. When considering analog implementation, it is better to use a resistive network to solve the equations. Yet another attractive alternative is to use a feedback scheme (not unlike the one used to solve for the optical flow velocity components in the case when they are assumed to be constant over the image patch being considered).

The solution can be obtained by "walking" down the gradient of the total error. The derivative with respect to $\boldsymbol{\omega}$ of the sum of squares of errors is just

$$\frac{dI}{d\boldsymbol{\omega}} = 2 \iint_D (E_t + \mathbf{v} \cdot \boldsymbol{\omega})\mathbf{v} \, dx \, dy.$$

This suggests a simple feedback scheme described by the equation

$$\frac{d\boldsymbol{\omega}}{dt} = -\alpha \iint_D (E_t + \mathbf{v} \cdot \boldsymbol{\omega})\mathbf{v} \, dx \, dy.$$

A simple implementation design involves a bus, with potential on three wires proportional to the present estimates of the components A, B and C of the instantaneous angular velocity ω. Estimates of the partial derivatives of image brightness (the components of the brightness gradient and the time rate of change of brightness) are computed at each picture cell. From them, and the position (x, y) of the cell, one can compute $\mathbf{v}$. The coordinates x and y can be made available to each cell using resistive chains that are connected to fixed potentials on the sides of the chip. It may be useful also to directly supply xy, $(1 + x^2)$ and $(1 + y^2)$, since these are coefficients in the expression for $\mathbf{v}$.

Next, one computes the error term $e = E_t + \mathbf{v} \cdot \omega$, which, in the absence of noise, is zero when the correct solution has been found. Currents are fed into the bus proportional to $-e\mathbf{v} = -(E_t + \mathbf{v} \cdot \omega)\mathbf{v}$. Each of the three bus wires is terminated in a capacitance. We now have a system that obeys the equation given above for $d\omega/dt$, the steady state solution of which is

$$\iint_D (E_t + \mathbf{v} \cdot \omega)\mathbf{v} \, dx \, dy = \mathbf{0},$$

that is, where the derivative of the expression we are trying to minimize is equal to zero. The feedback scheme involves considerably less computation than the closed form solution (for example, we do not have to compute the 3×3 matrix $\mathbf{vv}^T$). Also, the feedback scheme can be shown to be stable (as long as the integral of $\mathbf{vv}^T$ is not singular, that is, as long as there is sufficient contrast in the image texture and the field of view is large enough).

The elementary components needed are the photo sensors, differential buffer amplifiers that estimate spatial derivatives, approximate time delays for estimating the temporal derivative, four-quadrant analog multipliers, and current sources. There also will be resistive chains to supply values of x and y at each image location.

14.5.6 Computation of Instantaneous Translational Velocity

While the scheme described above for recovering the rotational velocity is very robust, as shown both by sensitivity analysis and experimentation on computers with both synthetic and real images, it does not allow one to recover depth. This is because there is no dependence of the brightness derivatives on depth when there is no translational motion.

We now consider the other extreme, when there is only translational motion.

When there is no rotational motion, the brightness change constraint equation becomes just

$$E_t + (\mathbf{s} \cdot \mathbf{t})\frac{1}{Z} = 0.$$

Note that multiplying both Z and $\mathbf{t}$ by a constant does not perturb the equality. This tells us right away that there will be a scale factor ambiguity in recovering motion and depth. We take care of this by attempting only to recover the direction of motion. That is, we will treat $\mathbf{t}$ as a unit vector.

If we solve the constraint equation above for the depth Z in terms of the unknown motion parameters, we obtain

$$Z = -\frac{\mathbf{s} \cdot \mathbf{t}}{E_t}.$$

If our estimate of the instantaneous translational motion $\mathbf{t}$ is incorrect, we will obviously obtain incorrect values for the depth from this equation. Some of these values may be negative (which correspond to points behind the camera), while others will be unexpectedly large. Some methods have been explored that find a direction of translational motion that yields the smallest number of negative depth values when applied to the image brightness gradients [22]. Although these methods work, they have yet to show promise in terms of computational expediency. We consider another approach next.

In many cases, particularly in industrial robotics, the depth range is bounded and the occurrence of very large depth values is not normally anticipated. One method for estimating the instantaneous translation velocity takes advantage of this observation. Essentially, we look for a translational velocity $\mathbf{t}$ that keeps Z within a finite range at most points in the image. Suppose, for example, that we find the translational velocity that minimizes

$$I = \iint_D Z^2 \, dx \, dy = \iint_D \frac{(\mathbf{s} \cdot \mathbf{t})^2}{E_t^2} \, dx \, dy,$$

subject to the constraint that $\mathbf{t}$ be a unit vector. We cannot measure brightness exactly, so there will be some error in our estimate of E_t. To avoid problems due to noise in places where E_t is almost zero, we may introduce an offset in the denominator as follows:

$$I = \iint_D w(E_t) \, (\mathbf{s} \cdot \mathbf{t})^2 \, dx \, dy$$

where $w(E_t) = 1/(E_t^2 + \epsilon^2)$. This integral can be rewritten in the form

$$I = \mathbf{t}^T \left(\iint_D w(E_t) \, \mathbf{s}\mathbf{s}^T \, dx \, dy \right) \mathbf{t} = \mathbf{t}^T S \, \mathbf{t}$$

where S is a 3×3 matrix. The expression for I is clearly a quadratic form in $\mathbf{t}$. Given the constraint that $\mathbf{t}$ be a unit vector, such a quadratic form attains its minimum when $\mathbf{t}$ is the eigenvector of the matrix S corresponding to the smallest eigenvalue. Analog circuits can be devised to compute these eigenvectors [15].

It is also possible to deal with a situation where motion can be arbitrary (that is, both rotation and translation), but the surface shape is constrained. While such problems have closed-form solutions [20], it turns out to be much easier to use gradient descent. The circuitry for this is considerably more complex than that for the pure rotation case, with several four-quadrant multipliers needed at each picture cell [15].

In general, gradient descent methods are very appealing when one is thinking about analog implementation. Fortunately it is possible to deal with *constrained* minimization as well as unconstrained minimization using either gradient projection [15] or a reversal of the gradient component corresponding to the Lagrangian multiplier, combined with additional penalty functions [27].

14.6   Summary and Conclusions

A number of problems in early vision have been explored here and shown to lead to interesting analog networks. The focus was on implementations involving resistive networks, perhaps with capacitors and analog multipliers, as well as simple buffer amplifiers. In several cases, feedback schemes where shown to be considerably simpler to implement than circuits based on the closed-form solutions usually sought after in digital implementations. Simple feedback networks with local connections can invert local operations [16]. This is of interest since the inverses of local operations typically are global, and direct implementation of these inverses would require unimplementably high wiring densities.

A theorem giving an equivalence between two apparently quite different ways of using the same resistive network sometimes allows one to find a way of implementing a particular computation that is much simpler than the obvious direct implementation. Gradient projection provides a way of solving constrained minimization problems, although in several cases it is possible to avoid this added complication through judicious normalization of the terms to be minimized and addition of a penalty term [15].

Also described here is a novel way of interlacing the nodes of a three dimensional multi-resolution network in a two dimensional tessellation. The number of nodes decreases from layer to layer by subsampling after approximate low pass filtering. Each layer contains half the number of nodes in its predecessor.

Use of a spatial dimension to represent time in a partial differential equation was shown to lead to new ways of implementing certain convolutional algorithms that would otherwise require a clocked architecture [15]. In this alternate scheme, image data flows in continuously on one end, while processed information flows continuously out the other end.

It is clear that many early vision problems lend themselves to implementation in parallel analog networks. This applies particularly to so-called *direct* methods, as opposed to *feature-based* methods, since the direct methods deal mostly with quantities connected to measurements at individual picture cells as well as their relationship to values at neighboring picture cells. We call algorithms that remain in the image domain as long as possible *eikonic*.

Work on analog methods for early vision started more than 20 years ago, but so far has not been widely appreciated. It has now received a strong new impetus from the more general availability of facilities for integrated circuit design and fabrication. This renewed interest is reflected in the pioneering work at Caltech in Carver Mead's group [26]. But no one should think that the methods explored there, or the ideas collected here, comprise anything more than a very sparse sampling of what is yet to come!

14.7   Acknowledgments

The author wishes to acknowledge helpful discussions with Robert Floyd, John Harris, Christof Koch, Jim Little, Carver Mead, Tomaso Poggio, David Standley and John Wyatt.

Support for this research was provided in part by National Science Foundation grant number MIP-8814612, and by DuPont Corporation.

Bibliography

[1] Y. Alomoinos and C. Brown. Direct processing of curvilinear motion from sequence of perspective images. In *Proceedings of the Workshop on Computer Vision Representation and Control*, Annapolis, MD, 1985.

[2] A. Blake and A. Zisserman. *Visual Reconstruction*. MIT Press, Cambridge, MA, 1988.

[3] J. Canny. *Finding Edges and Lines in Images*. MIT Artificial Intelligence Laboratory Technical Report 720, July 1983.

[4] R. Courant and D. Hilbert. *Methods of Mathematical Physics I*, John Wiley & Sons, New York, 1953.

[5] S.P. DeWeerth and C.A. Mead. A two-dimensional visual tracking array. In *Proceedings of the 1988 MIT Conference on Very Large Scale Integration*, pages 259–275, MIT Press, Cambridge, MA, 1988.

[6] E. Gamble and T.A. Poggio. *Visual Integration and Detection of Discontinuities: The Key Role of Intensity Edges*. MIT Artificial Intelligence Laboratory Memo 970, October 1987.

[7] S. Geman and D. Geman. Stochastic relaxation, gibbs' distributions, and the bayesian restoration of images. *IEEE Transactions on Pattern Analysis and Machine Intelligence*, 6(6):721–741, November 1984.

[8] A.L. Gilbert. Video data conversion and real-time tracking. *IEEE Computer*, 50–56, 1981.

[9] W.E.L. Grimson. *From Images to Surfaces—A Computational Study of the Human Early Visual System*. MIT Press, Cambridge, MA, 1981.

[10] J.G. Harris. *The Coupled Depth/Slope Approach to Surface Reconstruction*. MIT Artificial Intelligence Laboratory Technical Report 908, June 1986. Also in *Proceedings of the IEEE International Conference on Computer Vision*, pages 277–283, London, England, June 1986.

[11] J.G. Harris. An analog VLSI chip for thin-plate surface interpolation. In *Proceedings of IEEE Neural Information Processing Systems Conference*, Denver, CO, November/December 1989.

[12] M. Hatamian. A fast moment generating chip. In *Proceedings of the International Conference on Digital Signal Processing*, pages 230–234, Florence, Italy, September 1987.

[13] E. Hildreth. The detection of intensity changes by computer and biological vision systems. *Computer Vision, Graphics and Image Processing*, 22(1):1–27, April 1983.

[14] B.K.P. Horn. *Robot Vision*. MIT Press, Cambridge, MA and McGraw-Hill, New York, 1986

[15] B.K.P. Horn. Parallel networks for machine vision. Chapter 3 in *Artificial Intelligence at MIT: Expanding Frontiers*, volume 2. P.H. Winston and S.A. Shellard, editors, pages 530–573, 1990.

[16] B.K.P. Horn. Determining lightness from an image. *Computer Graphics and Image Processing*, 3(1):277–299, December 1974.

[17] B.K.P. Horn. Height and gradient from shading. To appear in *International Journal of Computer Vision*, 1991.

[18] B.K.P. Horn and M.J. Brooks. The variational approach to shape from shading. *Computer Vision, Graphics and Image Processing*, 33(2):174–208, February 1986. Also MIT Artificial Intelligence Laboratory Memo 813, March 1985.

[19] B.K.P. Horn and M.J. Brooks. *Shape from Shading*. MIT Press, Cambridge, MA, 1989.

[20] B.K.P. Horn and S. Negahdaripour. Direct passive navigation: analytical solution for planes. *IEEE Transactions on Pattern Analysis and Machine Intelligence*, 9(1):168–176, January 1987.

[21] B.K.P. Horn and B.G. Schunck. Determining optical flow. *Artificial Intelligence*, 16(1-3):185–203, August 1981.

[22] B.K.P. Horn and E.J. Weldon, Jr. Direct methods for recovering motion. *International Journal of Computer Vision*, 2(1):51–76, June 1988.

[23] C. Koch, J. Marroquin, and A. Yuille. Analog 'neuronal' networks in early vision. In *Proceedings National Academy of Sciences, USA* (Biophysics), 83, pages 4263–4267, June 1983. Also MIT Artificial Intelligence Laboratory Memo 751, June 1985.

[24] J. Luo, C. Koch, and C. Mead. An experimental subthreshold, analog CMOS two-dimensional surface interpolation circuit. In *Proceedings of IEEE Neural Information Processing Systems Conference*, Denver, CO, November 1988.

[25] D. Marr and E. Hildreth. Theory of edge detection. In *Proceedings of the Royal Society*, B, 207, pages 187–217.

[26] C.A. Mead. *Analog VLSI and Neural Systems*, Addison-Wesley, Reading, MA, 1989.

[27] J.C. Platt and A.H. Barr. *Constrained Differential Optimization for Neural Networks*. California Institute of Technology, Computer Science Department Technical Report TR-88-17, 1988. Also in *Proceedings of IEEE Neural Information Processing Systems Conference*, 1987.

[28] J.E. Tanner and C.A. Mead An integrated optical motion sensor. In *VLSI Signal Processing II, (Proceedings of the ASSP Conference on VLSI Signal Processing)*, pages 59–76, Los Angeles, CA, November 1987.

[29] D. Terzopoulos. Efficient multi-resolution algorithms for computing lightness, shape from shading, and optical flow. In *Proceedings of the International Joint Conference on Artificial Intelligence*, pages 314–317, Austin, TX, August 1984.

[30] T. Knight. *Design of an Integrated Optical Sensor with On-chip Preprocessing*. PhD thesis, MIT Department of Electrical Engineering and Computer Science, 1983.

[31] T.A. Poggio and V. Torre. *Ill-posed Problems and Regularization Analysis in Early Vision*. MIT Artificial Intelligence Laboratory Memo 773, October 1984.

15 Knowledge-based Systems

Peter Szolovits

Associate Professor, Department of Electrical Engineering and
Computer Science
Leader, LCS Clinical Decision Making Group

Abstract

Embedding knowledge is a popular and effective means of
increasing the power of sophisticated computer applications.
While the intellectual roots of this method go back to the late
1960's, the ideas were first codified, systematized and simplified in the 1970's and have led to a large and successful expert
systems industry in the 1980's. Despite these successes, most
types of expertise are still extremely difficult to capture and
many fundamental scientific and engineering challenges remain
to this field.

This paper will briefly review the origins and motivations for
the field, indicate the considerable successes it has achieved,
outline the many remaining difficulties and highlight a few individual research results that point the way to its future development.

15.1 Expertise

What is expertise? We can turn to one of the great experts in English
literature, Sherlock Holmes:

> "It is simplicity itself," said he; "my eyes tell me that on
> the inside of your left shoe, just where the fire-light strikes it,
> the leather is scored by six almost parallel cuts. Obviously
> they have been caused by someone who has very carelessly
> scraped round the edges of the sole in order to remove crusted
> mud from it. Hence, you see, my double deduction that you

had been out in vile weather, and that you had a particularly
malignant boot-slitting specimen of the London slavey."

— A. Conan Doyle, *Sherlock Holmes*, A Scandal in Bohemia

What is it that can account for Holmes' outstanding analytical ability?
Certainly, he is capable of brilliant, long, perhaps convoluted logical
chains of inference. In this simple case, parallel cuts in Watson's shoe
may be explained by scraping, which implies that they were muddy, thus
Dr. Watson must have been about in bad weather. Probably more important to Holmes' capacity is his wealth of knowledge about the world.
He must be able to make accurate and detailed observations, or else the
informative slits in the leather would escape his notice. He must be able
to interpret these signs and symptoms appropriately, within a context of
immense knowledge about what is likely and what implausible. He must
understand customary actions and behavior, habits and social relations.
In short, his mind is alive with a vivid and crowded model of the world
he seeks to understand.

It is the ability to represent and use such vast and complex interre-
lationships of real-world knowledge that is the goal of knowledge-based
systems, and that sets them apart from other computer programs. In
this paper, we begin by making an argument, first recognized in the
1960's, that encoding a great deal of this real-world knowledge is essential to enable computer programs to behave intelligently. We then
describe a few simple architectures for programs that can exploit large
bodies of knowledge encoded in stylized forms, and point out the success
that such programs have had in the commercial marketplace. Next, we
turn to a number of nagging problems that indicate a need for deeper
analysis, and illustrate some of the promising directions of work by showing some current experimental systems that use novel methods to encode
or use knowledge. Finally, we comment on the practice of "knowledge
engineering" and the further commercial prospects of expert systems.

15.2   The Case for Knowledge

How would a robot respond in the morning to hearing its alarm clock
ring?[1]   Conventional artificial intelligence (AI) approaches to such a

---

[1]This example was first suggested to me in a conversation with Joel Moses in the
late 1970's.

problem would suggest that the robot should first make a plan: for example, first roll out of bed, then walk to the clock, and hit the "off" button. Such plans are ordinarily made by a process of search through a vast space of possible alternative plans. Figure 15.1 illustrates a typical view of a search-based problem solving process. We start in the initial situation, I, and have available to us a set of possible operations, O_i, each of which leads to a new possible situation, from which we have various further possible operations available. In addition, there is a goal predicate G that tells us whether a given situation in fact satisfies our goal. In the alarm clock example, the initial situation is the robot lying in bed, with the alarm clock ringing, and various other possibly-relevant facts about the scene (e.g., the locations of the bed, clock, intervening obstacles, whether the bed is on the floor or a bunk, ...). Operators include those needed to implement the above plan: getting out of bed, walking, pushing buttons on the alarm clock. Typically, they also include others with possible relevance to the current task, such as throwing light objects, avoiding disturbing noises by covering the ears, etc., as well as those with no obvious relevance, such as making a phone call, eating a meal, etc. Our goal would be that the alarm clock no longer be disturbing the robot.

A particularly simple planner might, for example, begin with our initial scene and consider those situations that would result from taking each possible action (operation) from that scene. Because none of them leads directly to the achievement of the goal, it could then consider further situations resulting from new operators applied to those situations, and so on, until a goal state was reached. If at each step there are k available operations, there will be k^n n-step plans to consider, which is quite impractical for even modest values of k and (especially) n.

Unfortunately, this simple planning-oriented view of problem solving can degrade even further as we consider more details in a problem. For example, our hypothetical plan begins with the intent to roll out of bed. But in fact, how are we to accomplish this? We may have to consider numerous means of getting off the bed. Having selected a possible method, don't we in fact have to worry about whether we are capable of implementing that method in detail? For example, are our robot's muscles strong enough? Is it possible that our robot's side will be crushed by its weight as it begins to roll? Thus when we solve problems by ex-

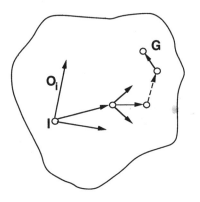

Figure 15.1
Search space for a robot planning system. I represents the initial state from which
search begins, arcs outward from any node indicate possible operations, O_i, that may
be done there, leading to the state at the end of the arc, and G is a predicate that
tells whether a given state is acceptable as the goal of search.

plicit planning, we are in the counterintuitive situation where apparently
adding more knowledge about the domain makes reasoning harder.

Human thinkers fail to be paralyzed by such possibilities by having
built up a large repertoire of physical and mental actions that they
apply seemingly without thinking—unless some feature of the problem
tips them off to a special need for care. Note that this use of *heuristics*
is far from guaranteed. Indeed, the floor may have given way and I
might fall through by blithely striding toward the clock, my muscles
may in fact have atrophied during the night from a yet undiscovered,
rapidly progressive degenerative disease, or a vagrant satellite may be
about to rip a swath through my house and destroy the alarm clock,
leaving no need for my intervention. Thus any aspect of the problem
is subject to changes that are sufficiently drastic that only a careful re-
evaluation of my situation, capabilities and goals will lead to reasonable
behavior. Nevertheless, in the vast majority of cases, we act without
such re-evaluation.

Fortunately, though virtually nothing of what we "know" is certain,
much of it is fairly reliable. Furthermore, as argued above, we cannot afford the alternative—to figure out everything from first principles.

(D36) $(3x^2 + 2)\sin^3 x + 3(x^3 + 2x + 1)\cos x \sin^2 x$

(C37)   INTEGRATE(%,X);

(D37) $3\left(-\dfrac{(9x^3 - 6x)\sin 3x + (9x^2 - 2)\cos 3x}{108}\right.$

$+\dfrac{(162x - 27x^3)\sin x + (162 - 81x^2)\cos x}{108}$

$\left.-\dfrac{3x\sin 3x + \cos 3x - 9x\sin x - 9\cos x}{18} + \dfrac{\sin^3 x}{3}\right)$

$-\dfrac{6x\sin 3x + (2 - 9x^2)\cos 3x - 162x\sin x + (81x^2 - 162)\cos x}{36}$

$+2(\dfrac{\cos^3 x}{3} - \cos x)$

$\ldots$

(C40)   TRIGSIMP(%);

(D40) $(x^3 + 2x + 1)\sin^3 x$

Figure 15.2
Example of an interaction with MACSYMA. Command C37 says to integrate the formula D36, and command C40 says (after two steps not shown here) to use trigonometric identities to simplify the result, yielding D40 as the integral of D36.

Indeed, an intelligent agent that always questions its own mental operations is likely to be in deep trouble, and we identify such a disturbance as psychosis. Thus a wealth of routine knowledge and the faith to apply it (mostly) uncritically is necessary for everyday life.

Large stocks of knowledge are essential in technical fields as well as in routine life. This is because creativity is actually relatively rare and difficult. Therefore, knowing how to do something is far better than being able to figure it out. Most of what we know in science, engineering, business, medicine, law, architecture, etc., does not derive from personal invention but from being taught and shown.

15.3 Early Expert Systems

Two research groups, both facing difficult real-world technical problems, independently recognized the need to incorporate large amounts of

knowledge into programs in the mid- to late 1960's. The Mathlab Group
at Project MAC, whose principal leaders at that time were Bill Martin,
Joel Moses and Carl Engleman, began the development of a powerful,
comprehensive system for symbolic mathematical manipulation, which
became MACSYMA. Unlike most of its predecessors, which tended to
focus on one part or another of the symbolic manipulation task, MAC-
SYMA provides a broad range of capabilities, including integration, power
series, various forms of simplification, and support for manipulating matrices, tensors, etc. Figure 15.2 shows a simple example of an interaction
with the system. As is the case with much of the best "expert systems"
work to follow, these researchers were less concerned with fitting their
efforts into a neat AI paradigm than with taking a credible cut at their
problem. Moses, in his doctoral dissertation describing the symbolic
integration program SIN, states their manifesto:

> "We ... intended no ... study of specific problem solv-
> ing mechanisms, but mainly desired a powerful integration
> program which behaved closely to our conception of expert
> human integrators."

> "Our emphasis in SIN is on the analysis of the problem
> domain. ... When SIN is solving ... difficult problems, [most
> notable is] how quickly SIN usually manages to decide which
> plan to follow and the straightforward manner with which it
> obtains the solution thereafter."

SIN followed a three-stage strategy, derived from a careful analysis
of the problem of symbolic integration. First was a powerful single
method, an elaboration of integration by parts, that solved most common problems directly. Second, and most importantly, SIN tried a set
of 11 highly-specific methods that attempted to recognize troublesome
features of the problem that prevented the first method from working,
and then tried to fix those features locally. For example, failure might
have been caused by a complex term under a radical; in this case, SIN
would try applying a specific method to transform that term into a form
amenable to further processing. Third, and finally, SIN would resort to
a general purpose problem solver—one that searched a set of possible
solution paths. This last stage only rarely came into play, and when
it did, only rarely helped; if the special "tricks" failed, it was unusual
for the general purpose methods to succeed. Thus perhaps half of SIN's

power came from analyzing the problem of integration and determining that the first method was very frequently adequate, and most of the other half came from the second stage tricks, which reworked problems that had (perhaps temporarily) escaped solution by the first.

SIN became part of MACSYMA [8] and continues to play an important role in that system. Later progress in symbolic integration led to the development of the Risch algorithm, which integrates any integrable function in a broad class, and much of this capability is now included in MACSYMA. Nevertheless, the SIN-like first and second stage strategies remain because if they work, they generate more compact solutions. The system as a whole has grown more and more comprehensive, as a user community of thousands of researchers has developed and itself contributed to its significant, sometimes idiosyncratic, but highly useful expansion. The 1986 MACSYMA Reference Manual, for example, defines the function

bdvac(): generates the covariant components of the vacuum field equations of the Brans-Dicke gravitational theory ...

which is clearly of use to researchers in a rather narrow domain.

In a retrospective analysis of MACSYMA's success, Bill Martin suggested [17] that building a knowledge-based system consists of identifying and integrating four categories of contributions:

1. *Powerful ideas:* Any system will have, at its core, a small number (perhaps less than ten) of outstanding ideas. These are usually rather general, such as the notion of *recursion* or, indeed, the *analyze/treat special cases* architecture of SIN.

2. *Great Tricks or Facts of Nature:* What makes a system "expert" is the ability to exploit some techniques of power within its domain. There may be a few tens of such "tricks." The Risch algorithm and Euclid's algorithm would certainly qualify.

3. *Unavoidable Engineering Decisions:* Typically, there will be one or two hundred significant engineering decisions that must all be made with a reasonable degree of harmony in order to make the system elegant, uniform and usable. An example might be the choice in a symbolic manipulation system whether to treat unary minus as a special case or whether always to represent expressions

of the form $-x$ as if they were $0 - x$. Such decisions may not, in themselves, seem very critical, but they have far-ranging consequences for many other aspects of the system. The unary/binary choice for negation, for instance, can have a big impact on the design of the simplifier.

4. *Avoidable Engineering Decisions:* Martin might well have called these *postponable* rather than avoidable, but they are the myriad detailed decisions made in the course of fleshing out the capabilities of a large system. MACSYMA at around its 10th anniversary contained over three thousand individual Lisp procedures, each embodying several detailed design decisions.

Of course it is important to pour in the knowledge roughly in the order of categories given above. The powerful ideas and great tricks define the overall approach to a problem domain and what a program can hope to accomplish, and engineering decisions—whether unavoidable or postponable—make sense only within those confines. Unfortunately, this lesson has often been lost in later systems that emphasize the value of uniformity over careful analysis and organization; this is a topic we take up again later.

The other major early expert system came from the collaborative efforts of a Stanford University group headed by Joshua Lederberg and Ed Feigenbaum. DENDRAL's task was to determine the three dimensional structure (isomer) of a chemical compound from its chemical formula, a mass spectrum, and perhaps other information such as nuclear magnetic resonance (NMR) data. Figure 15.3 shows a schematic mass spectrometer. At the left, the unknown is fragmented, and the fragments are ionized and injected into a magnetic field. The more massive any fragment, the less its trajectory is curved, therefore the further it travels before registering in an array of detectors at the bottom. The number of fragments detected at each mass yields the mass spectrum of the compound.[2]

The naive approach to this task might be to catalog all known mass-spectra and then attempt to match each observed spectrum to all the known ones. Unfortunately, the required degree of accurate and selective matching is probably impossible to achieve, and even if it were, this

---

[2]This is a rather naive description of mass spectrometry. For more details on this technique and on DENDRAL itself, see the retrospective volume on that project [15].

method would fail for any compound not in the program's library. Furthermore, the relationship between structures and mass spectra is not arbitrary, but is largely predictable from an analysis of how chemical compounds fragment in a mass spectrometer. Merely listing empirical associations between structures and spectra fails to exploit this source of regularity in the domain, and thus makes such a naive program much weaker than necessary.

Mass Spectrometer

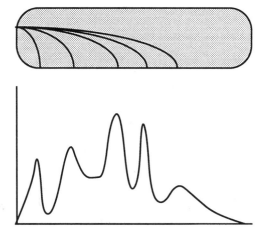

Mass Spectrum

Figure 15.3
A Mass Spectrometer and the Mass Spectrum input to DENDRAL. The mass spectrometer fragments a chemical compound into constituent parts, accelerates them, and deflects them in proportion to their mass. The result is a mass spectrum, a graph showing for each mass value how many fragments with that mass were detected.

A significant improvement to this scheme formed the initial starting-point for the DENDRAL team. They observed that if one knows the empirical formula for an unknown, one can enumerate all the possible three dimensional structures into which that collection of atoms could possibly be organized.[3] Next, by modeling the fragmentation process

---

[3]Incidentally, one of the major contributions to chemistry from this project was the development of this generator, called CONGEN, or *constrained generator*. Its main

in the mass spectrometer, it is possible to predict which bonds in any such structure are likely to break, and thus to predict the sizes of the fragments that should be seen in the spectrum. Therefore the problem of identifying the structure of an unknown with a given formula reduces "merely" to generating all possible structures for that formula, simulating the effects of the mass spectrometer on each such structure, and comparing the predicted mass spectrum to the one observed for the unknown. It is as if the program were generating a custom library for each unknown. Note that this is far more flexible than the original scheme. Unfortunately, it is also computationally quite intractable, because the number of distinct structures possible for an unknown compound may run into the millions.

Nevertheless, human experts working at this task were able to identify unknown compounds, clearly without examining a myriad possible structures. Studying their methods, it seemed that rather than beginning by enumerating possible structures, the human expert started by looking in the observed spectrum for evidence that certain substructures were present in the unknown. The expert would then consider only those overall structures that included these observed substructures. Similarly, the program was designed [5] to:

> "use whatever specialized knowledge and processes and whatever auxiliary data are available to infer pieces ... of the solution. ... For the remaining atoms, ... use the general structure-generating machinery."

The program thus contained a large number of *specialists*—small program fragments that examined the mass spectrum for relevant clues and proposed various substructures. These then contained much of the expert knowledge of the system and led to performance dramatically faster than that of the naive approach. An example of a specialist for

---

advances were that it could generate all of the often vast number of isomers without repeating any, and that it could take constraints into account. Thus, if the user is willing to posit a given structure for some portion(s) of the molecule, CONGEN will only generate those complete structures that include the posited portions. Significantly, this is done intelligently: it does not simply generate all possibilities and cast out those that do not include the known portions. Instead, it actually uses those known portions as the starting point for generating the possible total structures. This strategy made CONGEN quite efficient. Not only did this represent an advance in theoretical chemistry, but it also provided a computational tool of great value quite independent of the DENDRAL system.

Look for two peaks at x_1 and x_2 such that

1. $x_1 + x_2 = M + 28$

2. $x_1 - 28$ $(= x_1')$ is a high peak

3. $x_2 - 28$ $(= x_2')$ is a high peak

4. at least one of x_1 or x_2 is high.

$$\underbrace{x_1' - \overset{\displaystyle O}{\overset{\displaystyle \|}{C}} - x_2'}_{x_2}$$
$$\underbrace{}_{x_1}$$

Figure 15.4
A DENDRAL *specialist* for recognizing a ketone. The conditions correspond to fragmentation of the chain on either side of the $C = O$ structure.

detecting a ketone is shown in Figure 15.4. Because the chain is likely to break at either side of the carbon double-bonded to the oxygen, we expect to see peaks corresponding to the CO being attached to either half of the broken chain and other peaks corresponding to those halves without the CO. Though presumably such evidence could be mimicked by an alternative, more complicated explanation, expert chemists, like Sherlock Holmes, are willing to take the chance of being misled by such outstanding and valuable clues. So is DENDRAL.

Compound	No. of isomers	Mass spec.	NMR
Di-iso-pentyl ether	989	18	7
Di-n-hexyl ether	6,045	125	2
Bis-2-ethylhexyl ether	151,375	780	21
Di-n-decyl ether	11,428,365	22,366	1

Table 15.1
Number of isomers generated using no data, mass spectrometer data only, and mass spectra plus NMR data, (excerpted from [5]).

The specialists and the architecture that exploits their observations make an enormous difference. Table 15.1 (from [5]) summarizes a few of the delightful results of this technique, showing the number of total possible isomers, the number consistent with constraints suggested only by mass spectrum specialists, and the number consistent with constraints from both mass spectrum and NMR specialists. In the most dramatic demonstration of the value of this technique, note the eleven-

million-fold reduction of search for the case of Di-n-decyl ether. Even
when search cannot be eliminated, its reduction by orders of magnitude
makes possible a simulate-and-match solution to the reduced problem.

15.4 Expert Systems Architectures

The success of these early expert systems suggested that one should be
able to build other such systems for other domains based on the same
fundamental ideas. Neither MACSYMA nor DENDRAL was built in a way
that was easy to generalize, however, and it quickly became obvious that
if expert system construction were to be made a more routine activity,
we would have to invent standard ways of capturing and combining
knowledge. The goal was to provide the expert system builder with a
fixed architecture and to require only that the appropriate knowledge
be added. Over the course of a half-dozen years of experimentation
with particular systems, mostly in the medical decision making domain,
researchers identified a few apparently useful such general architectures:

- Working backward from a goal to its prerequisites by chaining of
  simple production rules.

- Matching a pattern of observables to predictions of alternative
  (clusters of) models.

- Responding to the time-course of a changing system.

15.4.1 Rule-based Systems

Probably the most influential of these early systems was MYCIN, whose
task was the diagnosis and prescription of drugs for bacterial infections
of the blood (bacteremia), and later for meningitis as well. Mycin's organization rested on the use of a collection of modular if-then rules, the
uniform use of backward chaining to trace back from goals to supporting
arguments, and a model of probabilistic inference called *certainty factors* [24] inspired by Carnap, and later shown to be a variant of Bayesian
inference with a particularly strong independence assumption [12]. Figure 15.5 shows a rule typical of MYCIN's knowledge base. This rule is
particularly simple in that it requires only knowledge of various characteristics of the organism under consideration to derive another of its
characteristics, identity.

```
IF the organism
   1) stains grampos
   2) has coccus shape
   3) grows in chains
THEN
   There is suggestive evidence (.7) that the identity
   of the organism is streptococcus.
```

Figure 15.5
A MYCIN rule relating characteristics of an organism to its identity.

```
IF
   1) The site of the culture is throat, and
   2) The identity of the organism is streptococcus
THEN
   There is strongly suggestive evidence (.8) that the subtype
   of the organism is not group-D.
```

Figure 15.6
A MYCIN rule requiring contexts for its proper interpretation. Context must assure
that the organism and the culture mentioned in the rule are in fact related; i.e., that
the organism grew out of that culture.

Figure 15.6 requires a somewhat more complex method of interpretation because it refers to not just a single entity but also to a
culture. In general, there may be many cultures and many organisms being considered, but it only makes sense to apply a rule to
those cultures and organisms where the organism was grown out of
that particular culture. MYCIN therefore introduces a *context mechanism*, depicted in Figure 15.7, that helps control the matching of
rules only with appropriate bindings of related variables. It assures
that another rule, which might mention a culture, an organism and
a drug being used to treat it, can be applied to only the three sets
of related entities: {culture-2, organism-2, drug-1}, {culture-2,
organism-2, drug-2} and {culture-3, organism-4, drug-3}.

The beginning of a typical MYCIN consultation is shown in Figure 15.8.
After collecting initial data about the patient, including name, age and
sex, the program sets as its goal to determine whether there are any significant infections present in this patient that require treatment. Then
it hands control over to its general backward-chaining mechanism. In
this case, that will seek rules in the knowledge base that can conclude

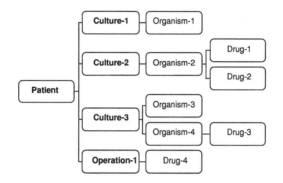

Figure 15.7
A typical MYCIN context, showing the relationships between the patient, cultures, organisms and drugs.

whether there is a significant infection present. Among the premises of such a rule might be attributes of the culture from which an organism was drawn, as well as attributes of the organism, the patient, any currently-active therapies the patient is receiving, etc. In seeking any of these additional data, the program can initiate further backward chaining, tracing through the rules capable of confirming or denying each of these subsidiary questions in turn.

In general, backward chaining follows a highly recursive pattern:

- To find out a fact:

  - If there are rules that can conclude it, try them.

  - After the rules (if any) have been tried and the fact is still not known, ask the user.

- To "try" a rule:

  - Try to find out if the facts in the premises are true.

  - If they all are, then assert the conclusion(s), with a suitable certainty.

```
--------PATIENT-1--------
```
1) Patient's name: **FRED SMITH**
2) Sex: **MALE**
3) Age: **55**
4) Have you been able to obtain positive cultures from
   a site at which Fred Smith has an infection? **YES**
```
--------INFECTION-1--------
```
5) What is the infection? **PRIMARY-BACTEREMIA**
6) Please give the date when signs of INFECTION-1
appeared. **5/5/75**
The most recent positive culture associated with the
primary-bacteremia will be referred to as:
```
--------CULTURE-1--------
```
7) From what site was the specimen for CULTURE-1
taken? **BLOOD**
8) Please give the date when this culture was
obtained. **5/9/75**
The first significant organism from this blood culture will be
called:
```
--------ORGANISM-1--------
```
9) Enter the identity of ORGANISM-1. **UNKNOWN**
10) Is ORGANISM-1 a rod or coccus (etc.)? **ROD**
11) The gram stain of ORGANISM-1: **GRAMNEG**
   ...

Figure 15.8
Beginning of a MYCIN consultation. After determining the patient's name, sex and
age, MYCIN begins to identify the relevant objects for its investigation, and to ask
questions by chaining backward via its rules from the fundamental goal: determine
if there are any significant organisms requiring treatment present in this patient.

```
INFECTION-1 is PRIMARY-BACTEREMIA
The identity of ORGANISM-1 may be
   <1> PSEUDOMONAS-AERUGINOSA
   <2> KLEBSIELLA-PNEUMONIAE
   <3> E. COLI
   <4> BACTEROIDES-FRAGILIS
   <5> ENTEROBACTER
   <6> PROTEUS-NON-MIRABILIS
. . .
[Rec 1] My preferred therapy recommendation is as follows:
   In order to cover for items <1 2 3 5 6>:
      Give GENTAMYCIN
      Dose: 119 mg (1.7 mg/kg) q8h IV [or IM] for 10 days
      Comments: Modify dose in renal failure
   In order to cover for item <4>
      Give CLINDAMYCIN
      Dose: 595 mg (8.5 mg/kg) q6h IV [or IM] for 14 days
      Comments: If diarrhea or other GI symptoms develop, patient
         should be evaluated for possible pseudomembranous colitis.
```

Figure 15.9
MYCIN's therapy recommendation. Recommendations with the fewest number of drugs that nevertheless cover for all the suspected organism identities are preferred, but other, lower-ranking recommendations may also be displayed.

In addition, the context mechanism will cause MYCIN to ask about the presence of additional cultures, organisms or drugs if premises of a rule refer to such an object that does not yet exist in the context.

After reaching a diagnostic conclusion, MYCIN turns to making a therapeutic prescription (Figure 15.9) based on trying to minimize the number of antimicrobial agents needed to do a good job of knocking out the most likely and most dangerous suspected infecting organisms.

Operation of this general scheme with MYCIN's stock of 400-800 rules[4] led to behavior that was arguably indistinguishable from that of expert physicians and that was often clearly superior to that of lesser-trained physicians [33]. In addition, by keeping track of what rules were run in which situations, the program can generate moderately sophisticated explanations of its reasoning. Figure 15.10, for example, shows a trace of how one particular rule, RULE163, was used but turned out not to

---

[4]The knowledge base grew with time, as the domain was extended to include meningitis.

** Did you use RULE 163 to find out anything about ORGANISM-1?

RULE163 was tried in the context of ORGANISM-1, but it failed
because it is not true that the patient has had a genito-urinary
tract manipulative procedure (clause 3).

** Why didn't you consider streptococcus as a possibility?

The following rule could have been used to determine that the
identity of ORGANISM-1 was streptococcus: RULE033

But clause 2 (the morphology of the organism is coccus) was
already known to be false for ORGANISM-1, so the rule was never
tried.

Figure 15.10
Explanation from a MYCIN consultation. The first question investigates how a particular rule was (or, in this case was not) applicable to a case. The second explores why MYCIN did not reach a particular conclusion.

be relevant, and why the system did not reach a conclusion that the
questioner might have considered plausible. Our intuition has always
been strong that such abilities of programs to explain and justify their
behavior would turn out to be critical to their acceptance [1][27], and
more recent surveys of physicians' attitudes support this intuition [30].

15.4.2   Frame Matching

For diagnostic reasoning, the simplest heuristic is: "it is what it looks
like." Figure 15.11 suggests what happens when a description of the
facts about a case are overlaid onto a description of a hypothesis. If the
hypothesis is appropriate, there will be a reasonably good fit, though
typically some predictions made by the hypothesis will not be found in
the patient data, and those data may contain features not explained
by the hypothesis. These discrepancies can be used as a good source
of guidance to help collect needed additional information to reach the
correct diagnostic conclusions efficiently.

The Present Illness Program (PIP), built by our group in the early
1970's [22], embodied this view:

1. From the patient's initial complaints, *guess* a suitable hypothesis.

2. Use the current active hypotheses to guide questioning.

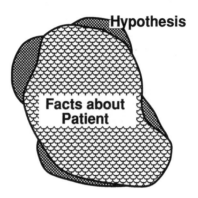

Figure 15.11
Pattern matching as a basis for diagnostic reasoning. In the absence of a perfect overlap between a case and a hypothesis, differences may be used to drive information acquisition.

3. Failure to satisfy expectations is the strongest clue to a better hypothesis. Concentrate on the traditional notion of *differential diagnosis*, a means of rapidly shifting attention from an incorrect hypothesis to a better, related one when discrepant information arises.

4. Hypotheses are *activated, de-activated, confirmed* or *rejected* based on (a) logical criteria and (b) probabilities resulting from the presence or absence of findings local to a hypothesis and causal relations to other hypotheses.

Figure 15.12 shows the information flows centered on hypotheses in PIP. *Triggers,* or strongly evocative findings, implement the guessing strategy. Thus an important and specific fact that arises early in the consultation can immediately focus the program's attention to the right problem. Once a hypothesis is active, it can suggest others of its expected manifestations as reasonable foci for the program to question the user about. Further confirmation for a hypothesis can also come from the program's coordinated beliefs in the presence of related hypotheses. PIP made its decisions to accept or reject a hypothesis either on the basis of logical criteria—the most effective method, when available—or by

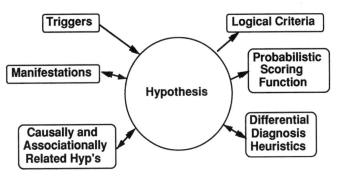

Figure 15.12
PIP's components and information flows. The knowledge base is organized around
hypotheses. Triggers and other manifestations may evoke hypotheses, which may, in
turn, suggest asking about other manifestations. Logical criteria and a scoring function help determine whether a hypothesis should be accepted or rejected, and how
strongly it should be pursued. Links to other hypotheses include a set of causal relations and also specific heuristics for how to change the program's focus of attention
when it believes it has been misled by earlier evidence.

a complicated probabilistic scoring function that rewarded for the presence of expected findings and expected related hypotheses and penalized
for their absence.

Because PIP's underlying focus of attention was strongly influenced
by the guesses it made based on triggering from features of the input,[5]
it was important for the program to have a graceful way of recovering
from an incorrect guess. Our studies of expert human problem solving
in medicine [13] suggested that simple backtracking is not what expert
physicians do in this case. Instead, they appear to have "compiled" a
set of recovery routines that say "Ah, if I've been misled into pursuing
hypothesis x and the following discrepancies arise, this means I should
be pursuing y instead." It may well be that learning these recovery
heuristics is an important key to the difference between the expert and
novice decision maker. Having them at hand allows the expert to make
more rapid guesses, possibly solving a problem very efficiently, because
he or she knows that if the guess turns out to be problematic, there
are probably good ways to recover from it. The novice, by contrast,

---

[5]This is somewhat reminiscent of DENDRAL.

```
NEPHROTIC SYNDROME, a clinical state
FINDINGS:
  *1. Low serum albumin concentration
   2. Heavy proteinuria
  *3. >5 gm/day proteinuria
  *4. Massive symmetrical edema that is painless and not red
  *5. Facial or peri-orbital symmetric edema
   6. High serum cholesterol
   7. Urine lipids present
IS-SUFFICIENT:  Massive pedal edema & >5 gm/day proteinuria
MUST-NOT-HAVE: Proteinuria absent
SCORING ...
MAY-BE-CAUSED-BY:  AGN, CGN, nephrotoxic drugs, insect bite,
   idiopathic nephrotic syndrome, lupus, diabetes mellitus
MAY-BE-COMPLICATED-BY:  hypovolemia, cellulitis
MAY-BE-CAUSE-OF:  sodium retention
DIFFERENTIAL DIAGNOSIS:
   neck veins elevated -> constrictive pericarditis
   ascites present -> cirrhosis
   gross hematuria -> renal vein thrombosis
```

Figure 15.13
PIP's frame for nephrotic syndrome. Among the findings, an asterisk marks triggers.
The scoring clause has been suppressed to save space.

must explore hypotheses more thoroughly and systematically, for fear of getting stuck at a bad hypothesis and having nowhere to turn except to start over from the beginning.

Figure 15.13 shows PIP's model of nephrotic syndrome. Note the differential diagnosis clues at the bottom. For example, if this hypothesis is being considered and evidence arises for ascites (fluid accumulation in the abdomen), then cirrhosis should be considered as an alternative.

PIP was the first expert system to break into the medical literature [22], and demonstrated reasonable performance and interactive style in its narrow domain of specialty. The INTERNIST-I program [19] developed at the University of Pittsburgh at around the same time used similar techniques, though with more of an emphasis on the systematic sorting of findings and their relations to competing and complementary hypotheses rather than the guess/correct scheme of PIP. The knowledge of INTERNIST-I, which has been developed extensively through the massive efforts of Dr. Jack Myers and his associates, is now also used in a

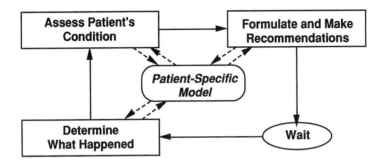

Figure 15.14
Feedback loop in therapy in the Digitalis Therapy Advisor. Solid arrows represent the flow of control, cycling clockwise around the therapy loop. Dashed arrows represent data flow to and from the patient-specific model.

medical educational program called QMR (Quick Medical Reference) [18]. Unlike PIP and INTERNIST-I, both of which guide the interaction to help elicit data that seems most useful to confirm or deny hypotheses under consideration, QMR takes a nondirective approach. It helps to interpret the significance of data reported to it, to compare various hypotheses, and to examine its large knowledge base. Control of the interaction, however, rests completely with the user.

15.4.3 Feedback in Therapy

Another general model suggested itself in our work on a program for advising physicians on the appropriate use of the heart drug digitalis, given to patients with certain cardiac arrhythmias and heart failure [7]. The early diagnostic programs (like MYCIN, PIP and INTERNIST-I) all considered their task to be a one-shot consultation. For therapy, the most important ability is not to make the right one-time suggestion but to analyze what is happening to the patient over a longer period and to adjust therapy to best meet the treatment's goals. Figure 15.14 shows a schematic diagram of this feedback loop. We begin with an initial description of the patient's situation, recorded in the *patient-specific model* (PSM). This model is used repeatedly as the source of information about the important factors to consider at any point, what has actually happened to the patient, the program's interpretation of those events, and the program's plans and current concerns. The model is repeatedly updated as therapy proceeds, both when new facts are determined and when new conclusions are reached. This record is intended to parallel the *problem-oriented medical record*, suggested by Weed [31] as the appropriate organization for keeping hospital medical records in general.

Control flows clockwise around the loop. Each treatment cycle begins by assessing the patient's condition (as represented by the PSM). That assessment is stored in the PSM and forms the basis for the program's next step, to formulate and issue its treatment recommendations. These recommendations and the program's expectations of what will happen in the course of therapy are also recorded in the PSM, for later comparison against what actually takes place. Of course no user is obliged to follow these recommendations, so after an appropriate time has passed (based either on the program's estimate of when some event of interest should have happened or the autonomous request of the user for a further evaluation) the program determines what actions were actually taken and what consequences followed. By comparing what happened against the expectations stored in its model, the program can quickly assess whether therapy is proceeding appropriately or needs to be significantly modified or abandoned. This program combined a knowledge of the pharmacokinetics of the various preparations of digitalis with a set of expert-provided heuristics about how to balance the effectiveness versus the risk of side effects of therapy. It reproduced quite well the treatment style of the expert on which it was patterned, and although its conservative style was somewhat controversial with other experts, there were indications that it was less liable than human physicians to make life-threatening decisions by overlooking important factors in the therapy plan [29].

15.5   State of the Art in the Late 1980's

The good news is that today the application of 1970's technology—made far more attractive by 1980's additions of graphics, smart user interfaces and ubiquitous availability on personal computers—is good enough to solve many interesting, worthwhile problems.

Ed Feigenbaum and his colleagues, in their recent book *The Rise of the Expert Company* [6], report that there are now on the order of 1500 expert system applications in actual use, with a few thousand more in prototype or field testing. These systems are being used for a number of distinct reasons, including assuring that consistent and thorough consideration is given to all relevant factors in decision making, capturing and distributing rare or vanishing expertise, and enabling more customized products and services to be assembled in response to the needs of customers. Despite the wide variety of reasons for using expert systems and the broad range of their application, a small number of central tasks come up over and over again:

Diagnosis: Much as in the early systems described above, the problem is to determine an appropriate explanation for some (abnormal) constellation of observables. The topic is often computing a short term response to abnormal or dangerous conditions, for example in a chemical plant or power station, in quality control monitoring, etc.

Selection: Often the central task is to select an appropriate part, the right regulation to apply, the most apt form letter. Usually there are many possibilities that satisfy some set of requirements. First one must weed out the ones that do not, then apply some optimizing (or alternatively, *satisficing*, in Simon's terminology) criterion to choose one. Often, such systems are a means of formalizing corporate rules and regulations, to get consistent and explainable behavior across the organization. Examples include insurance, credit authorization, personnel, etc.

Configuration and planning: Configuration tasks are ones in which either a partial design must be completed in routine ways or a complete design checked and adjusted to meet certain constraints. A well-known example is the XCON system of Digital Equipment Corporation, which is used to check the configuration of all orders for Digital computers. Complexity in such tasks arises principally from interactions among the various interdependent choices that must be made. Scheduling, which is in a sense the configuration of a set of time-dependent activities, has a similar character.

Feigenbaum points out that, perhaps contrary to initial expectations, if we classify projects as elephants, buffaloes or rabbits, depending on their size and scope, there are very few elephants, a small number of buffaloes and a large preponderance of rabbits. Thus in fact, it is often the simplest of the system-building ideas from the research lab that have been packaged into convenient tools for the end-user and are now being used to create quite small applications that automate, check on or augment the capabilities of the worker who developed the system for himself. Though the continuing investment in Digital's XCON is of the order of several million dollars per year and the estimated saving resulting from it is tens of millions per year, most systems that have been built require an investment of no more than a few tens of thousands of dollars (a few man-months of effort) and yield returns that pay back that investment in well under a year. It seems that universally, when a project succeeds at all, its benefit is at least an order of magnitude greater than its cost.

What remains to be done, then? Why haven't we simply declared the field a success, turned it over to commercial interests and moved on?

15.5.1 Fragility of Encoded Knowledge

To illustrate some of the remaining problems, let me cite an anecdote from the late 1970's, in which one of my students decided to impress Marvin Minsky with a developmental version of PIP. Marvin, being somewhat of a joker, responded to the program's request for an initial complaint by typing the word "sick." Much to everyone's surprise, the program's immediate comeback was "Has he had his teeth cleaned lately?" The student's puzzlement only grew when he used the program's explanation capabilities to trace back through its logic to see what strange and unlikely path it followed to lead it to this unexpected question.

Alas, though this is a program about the diagnosis of kidney disease, it has no knowledge of the word "sick." Provided with a spelling checker to help ease problems of users mistyping medical terms, the program happily accepted the word "sick" and turned it into "sigmoidoscopy," apparently its best match at correcting the misspelled word. Sigmoidoscopy happens to be an unpleasant procedure in which a tube is inserted from the bottom up in your intestinal tract to see if there are abnormalities indicating possible disease. The program's "logic" then proceeded roughly as follows:

1. Sigmoidoscopy can introduce bacteria into the blood stream (if the tube scrapes the lining of the intestine) and might thus lead to bacteremia.

2. Bacteremia having been suggested as a hypothesis worthy of pursuit, the program then tried to find other evidence that it may be present.

3. Dental cleaning in the recent past is commonly observed in patients with bacteremia. In fact, it is another way of introducing bacteria into the blood stream. The program, knowing very little of interest about the patient at this point, wondered if it could thus find evidence to help confirm the only hypothesis it had been able to generate.

Of course its reaction is inappropriate and there were a number of technical corrections that we could impose to eliminate this particular unanticipated bad behavior. For example, the direction of causality needed to be clearly marked in associations such as those between dental cleaning and bacteremia. Though in general seeking additional consequences of a condition is a good way to help establish its presence, seeking additional possible causes of a condition for which a good possible cause is already established is not reasonable. Minsky's conclusion from this episode, which can hardly be dismissed, is that the real problem is that the program has no *common sense*. According to his view, independent of its particular expert medical knowledge, it should be able to determine that the above behavior violates some common understanding that all people, not only physicians, share.

In a similar vein, Clancey discovered that although the knowledge base of MYCIN was adequate to lead to good diagnostic performance, trying to use its knowledge to help teach medicine illuminated many pitfalls. Consider, for example, the rule in Figure 15.15. Among the five premises, there appear at least the following component bits of knowledge:

1. Bacterial meningitis in an alcoholic is often caused by diplococcus-pneumoniae.

2. Do not rely on this if you know better.

3. Assume that children are not alcoholics (or at least have not been
long enough for the purpose of the first relationship to hold).

The existing rule is perfectly adequate to cause MYCIN to behave as if it
understood these distinct facts. In reality, however, it does not. When
trying to build a teaching program from such jumbled knowledge, we
can easily be misled into the sorts of common-sense-violating behavior
we encountered above. For example, one possible reading of the rule is
that being young somehow protects you from the observed association
that alcoholism makes diplococcus-pneumoniae meningitis more likely.

Some, such as Minsky, have argued that problems of this sort are
endemic to the enterprise of trying to build expert systems, and that
only a set of fundamental advances in our ability to understand and
model common-sense reasoning has any hope of overcoming such difficulties [20]. In short, this argument holds that one cannot build a
robust expert without first having built a robust generalist. Thus what
prevents human doctors (for example) from making silly mistakes of the
sort illustrated here is not great expertise, but much common experience
acquired more through childhood and adolescence than through post-
graduate training. Others believe that a more conventional engineering
approach will yield significant advances. According to this view, what
we think of as common sense is really just the accumulation of a vast
stock of knowledge, orders of magnitude greater than what has thus far
been encoded in any expert system [14]. Thus, if only we could catalog
and encode such a body of knowledge, one could build new programs not
"from scratch" but from that substantial base. The task of collecting

```
IF  1) the infection is meningitis
    2) the subtype of meningitis is bacterial
    3) only circumstantial evidence is available
    4) the patient is at least 17 years old
    5) the patient is an alcoholic
THEN
    There is suggestive evidence (.7) that diplococcus-pneumoniae
        is an organism causing the meningitis.
```

Figure 15.15
A MYCIN rule that confounds several distinct issues, including diagnostic strategy,
default reasoning, and social conventions about whether to ask if children are alcoholics.

this knowledge base is daunting. It involves not only the identification of an encyclopedic volume of information but also the development of an appropriate formalism to encode it. Nevertheless, such ambitious tasks are now underway in at least two groups [4][14].

15.5.2   Complexity in the Real World

A second, and at least as serious, difficulty with the current state of the art is that many of the methods we can now apply work very well on relatively straightforward problems but fail on more complex ones. Consider the problem of medical diagnosis as we increase its complexity in the following scenarios:

1. Suppose we could guarantee that any patient was either healthy or had exactly one disease. In this ideal world (for the diagnostician), the process of diagnosis is relatively easy. Every observation may revise our relative degree of belief in every hypothesis but eventually a single hypothesis must explain all the known data.

2. In a slightly more complex world, suppose a patient could have more than one disease, but we know that no two diseases ever effect each other or ever share common symptoms. In this case, the bookkeeping required for diagnosis becomes more complex and we can no longer use arguments against one disease as arguments for another.

3. In the real world, patients may have not only multiple disorders but also those disorders may interact strongly. This raises serious problems of how to allocate "credit" for an observation to any of a set of diseases that may cause it, how to deal with issues of "partial credit," where no disease by itself may explain an observation but any of a number of sets of diseases may combine to do so. Therapeutic interventions often share the character of such interacting diseases—after all, the therapy is intended to affect the manifestations of the disease against which it is targeted, and so the patient's actual condition will be some net result of the effects of the disease and effects of the therapy.

Clearly, the complexity of the diagnostic task increases greatly as we loosen the constraining assumptions about the world. Among the early diagnostic programs described above, MYCIN and PIP do not deal well with any situation more complex than scenario 1. INTERNIST-I provides the additional machinery to tackle some of the complexity of scenario 2.

Sometimes the specific goals of a project help ameliorate deficiencies in its techniques. For example, MYCIN had difficulty differentiating between the case of a single infection by an organism whose identity was in doubt and a multiple infection in which each of two or more infecting organisms are simultaneously present. Fortunately, in dealing with bacterial infections, the risks of therapy are normally much smaller than the risks posed by an untreated organism. As a result, it happens that the appropriate response to either of these situations is to treat for all of the possible identities of all suspected organisms. If it turns out that only a single infection is present, treating for all will surely cover the right one, whereas if there are multiple infections, treating for all will also cover all the right ones. Thus, by a fortunate truth about the domain, this potential weakness in the program does not matter. Alas, such strokes of good luck do not generalize well. For example, if one of the possible infecting agents requires treatment with a drug with possible serious morbidities, then a human expert would put a much greater emphasis on distinguishing the two situations posed here.

Among the generalizable models of expert reasoning that are understood thoroughly enough to have reached the commercial marketplace, very few provide facilities that go beyond the single-problem scenario we have outlined. And virtually none help with problems of rampant interaction suggested in the third scenario. This one is truly difficult, as we have come to realize in some of our work on the diagnosis and therapy of acid/base and electrolyte imbalances. Consider the following medical facts:

- Diarrhea causes bicarbonate (alkali) loss (*lowered pH*).

- Vomiting causes acid loss (*increased pH*).

As a result, a patient who has diarrhea and is vomiting may in fact exhibit a *normal* pH. To capture this in a MYCIN-like system, we would need some equivalent of

```
IF    the patient has a normal pH
THEN  There is suggestive evidence that the patient is suffering
        from diarrhea and from vomiting.
```

which is, on the face of it, an absurd interpretation of medical knowledge. Because virtually any abnormality may be canceled out by another under appropriate circumstances, this path leads to saying that every normal finding suggests a vast number of these canceling combinations of diseases.

Clearly, something more fundamentally sound is needed.

15.5.3   Sources of Better Models

An expert physician knows a broad range of material. He or she has learned the "basic science" of medicine, including college and then medical school courses in biochemistry, physiology, etc. Medical school teaches the specifics of medicine: pathophysiology, pathology, genetics, etc. The expert has also learned through a process of clerkships, internship and residency the field's state of the art or practice: the available tests, treatments and procedures. In addition, experience teaches much of value: how to apply one's knowledge most effectively, what occurs commonly (learning not to guess "zebra" when hearing hoofbeats, in the parlance of the field), local wisdom as distilled by colleagues about the preferred ways of approaching various problems, etc.

Someone embarking on research in the field of medical decision making might in fact be tempted to approach its problems from the traditional scientific front: build appropriate models of what is known, then apply that knowledge to the individual patient to answer any questions. For example, decades of research have led to fairly specific models of some aspects of human physiology, such as the control machinery of the circulatory system [9]. Why not plan therapy for heart disease, then, by adjusting such a model to the patient at hand and simply predicting the model's response to all therapies under consideration? Alas, the typical physiologic model contains hundreds of parameters, and determining their values for an individual requires much more data than could be reasonably collected. In fact, collecting those required data might not only be tedious but could well require challenging the patient's system in ways that are unacceptably risky. Yet in the previous section we have argued that ignoring true models that underlie our experiences leave us with too little knowledge to handle tough cases.

For most domains, not just for medicine, we really do not yet know how to capture the desired breadth and depth of knowledge in a computer, or how to develop programs that effectively call forth just the right parts to produce expert behavior. The following sections present short descriptions of a number of interesting ideas that have evolved and been explored in the past few years. The first batch will be drawn from medical reasoning, whose difficulties make it the area that has demanded the most of evolving AI methods. The second batch will illustrate that similar needs and opportunities exist as well in other areas of knowledge-based systems. Each project has exploited some insight about its domain and task to make possible the use of a representation and a reasoning method that is intermediate between the simple early systems we have seen and the demanding formal models of scientific investigation. The common thread seems to be finding the right level of detail and precision and ignoring just those factors that can be omitted from the analysis while still getting significant value from it.

15.6   Sophistication in Medical Reasoning

We examine a handful of research projects that appear to point in appropriate directions for progress in AI applied to medical reasoning. The first addresses the problem we pointed out earlier: how to deal with disease hypotheses that interact strongly. The second concerns the use of qualitative versions of physiological models to derive results that are useful clinically without having to resort to massive data collection. The third introduces a fundamental advance in thinking about probabilistic relationships.

Unfortunately, each of these projects exists in isolation of the others and it is a difficult but important research goal to formulate ways of achieving simultaneously in a single system the advances of each.

15.6.1   Multi-level Models in Acid/Base Diagnosis

In critiquing the inadequacies of first-generation expert systems, we mentioned the need for diagnostic programs to deal effectively with interactions among disorders, even ones that might effectively cancel out some of their abnormal effects. Ramesh Patil, in his MIT doctoral thesis [21], introduced several important notions that combine effectively. First is that, at least in domains in which some of the knowledge and observations are quantitative, the program must be able to deal explicitly with not only the presence or absence, but the severity of any abnormalities. For acid/base disorders, where at least some of the models are well-known and quite precise, one may even make quantitative calculations to assure consistency in the model. For example, in a hospitalized patient with severe diarrhea, the quantity and composition of the fluid lost may have been measured and recorded, allowing an accurate assessment of the body's losses of fluid, bicarbonate, potassium, etc. Even if the quantities are not known with precision, requirements of material balance and similar simple notions can help point out unsuspected but important components of a complex disease state. For example, if the degree of observed acidemia is inconsistent with the known sources of bicarbonate loss, the program can legitimately speculate about offsetting factors. In the patient with diarrhea, to return to our earlier example, the absence of a low serum pH would suggest some other mechanism of bicarbonate gain or hydrogen ion loss. Thus the program might investigate whether the patient has also suffered from vomiting to a sufficient extent that the loss of the expected additional hydrogen ion can be explained.[6] In this way, a normal pH can indeed serve as supporting evidence for the diarrhea-and-vomiting scenario, but without the need to encode that and all other such offsetting pairs in the program's associational database.

The second major contribution of this work was to introduce the notion of multi-level models. As suggested in Figure 15.16, it is often very useful to be able to consider a case at a number of interrelated levels of detail, ranging from the experiential clinical associations represented by the top level to the pathophysiological details represented at the lowest. The vertical connections, which ultimately tie the clinical relationships to the physiological mechanisms that account for them (if known) allow information to flow in both directions. Upward, the clinical significance of laboratory data can be assessed. Downward, clinical impressions can constrain the interpretations that may be derived by the detailed models. In principle, this sort of organization also allows drawing the relationships between possibly related observations at the most appropriate level where knowledge of those relationships exists. In this particular program, however, we were unable to exploit this capability, because the program always tended to try to elaborate every model as deeply as possible. As a result, even straightforward cases in which

---

[6]The fluid lost in vomiting is normally rich in acid.

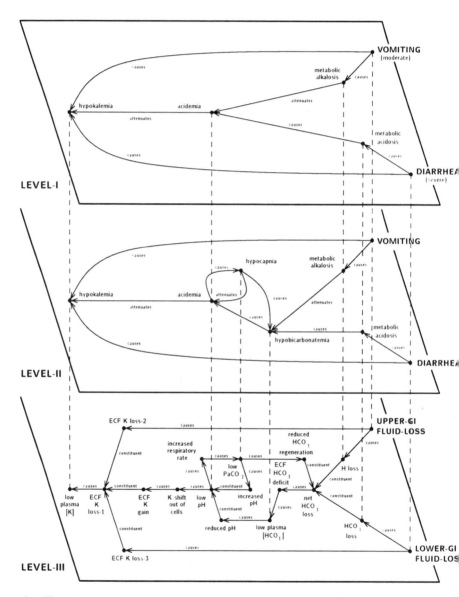

Figure 15.16

ÁBEL's multi-level model of a case with diarrhea and vomiting. Level I depicts clinical associations, level II an intermediate level of detail, and level III the physiological mechanisms involved in the case.

the associations were perfectly adequate to arrive at the correct answer would become subject to a deep, detailed and slow analysis.

The combination of its abilities to deal with models at multiple levels of detail and to investigate components of abnormal values gave ABEL a powerful basis, not only for reaching sophisticated diagnostic conclusions, but also for planning an effective strategy of diagnostic testing and for producing good graphical and English-language explanations of its reasoning. Its principal limitations resided in the rather special nature of its domain—one of the best in medicine for having available deep quantitative models—and in the complexity of the program and data that made it difficult to extend even to related fields, much less to ones from other domains.

15.6.2 Qualitative Physiological Models

Often, to understand the behavior of a complex system one must abstract away from the particular details to a more qualitative view. The same observation underlies the enormous preference of traditional scientists and engineers for closed-form solutions to complex systems. After all, it is much easier to think about what a system does given a description of that behavior in a simple equation than to pore over dozens or hundreds of simulation runs trying to comprehend it. Unfortunately, very few systems of real-world complexity and interest have classical closed-form solutions, so the name of the game is to find the right approximations that allow compact descriptions of the system that are nevertheless reasonably accurate, at least to the degree required for the task.

AI researchers have introduced a large number of related ideas and systems, going under names such as qualitative physics, qualitative simulation, qualitative process theory, etc. Despite important variations, each of these represents quantities of interest, including levels, rates of change (and sometimes higher derivatives) not by numbers but by more abstract quantities. In some cases, these can specify only whether a value is positive, zero or negative. Other variants allow for a small number of "landmark" values that partition the space of quantities into equivalence classes. Given these, any value may be described as belonging to one of the intervals between landmarks (and usually ∞ and $-\infty$ are considered landmarks).

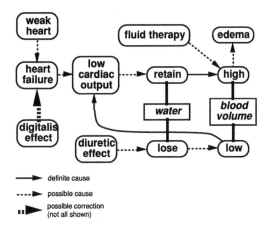

Figure 15.17
Heart-Failure Program's simplified model of fluid balance, indicating the effects of
a weak heart, use of the drug digitalis, fluid therapy and diuretics on blood volume
and edema (swelling in the tissues caused by an accumulation of fluid). Each arc is
also associated with a typical delay, which is not shown here.

William Long, of MIT/LCS, developed an interesting model of this
general character to help reconstruct a scenario of past events in order
to explain the current presence of an apparently contradictory situation [16]. Consider a heart failure patient with low blood volume and
edema (an accumulation of fluids in the tissues). This situation, on the
face of it, appears contradictory because low blood volume suggests an
overall loss of fluid from the body, whereas edema suggests its gain. Such
a situation is in fact an implausible steady state, but can arise at times
transiently because some of the body's responses are virtually instantaneous, whereas others are manifested only over long periods of time.
To resolve this apparent contradiction, we need a system that can recognize and exploit the different speeds with which various physiological
mechanisms react.

To understand this case and similar ones, we need a qualitative model
of how the underlying disease, its effects and possible therapies interact
and of the typical time course of these effects. Figure 15.17 shows a
highly simplified model of the consequences of heart failure. With each

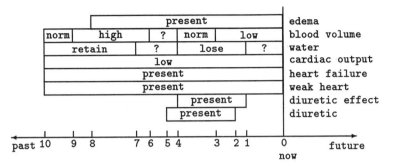

Figure 15.18
Postdiction for a case of heart failure with edema and low blood volume. The time line stretching back into the past shows significant events as numbered times. The specific time of these is not known, only their relative order. Each line in the diagram represents the state of a variable of interest at times in the past. The history of states shown is consistent with a case in which (at the present time) the patient has edema in the face of a low blood volume.

causal relationship there is also an indication of the typical time over which it acts. From this information it is possible for us (and for the program) to reconstruct a plausible history of how the patient arrived at the current state. In Figure 15.18, we can trace the following chain of events back from the present, relying on the model of Figure 15.17 to justify each intermediate conclusion:

1. According to the model, the only way to reach a low blood volume is to have been losing water for some time in the past, shown here in the time interval from points 4 to 1. We do not know if water loss is continuing now. (Note that these time points are ordinal, but have no specific durations implied.)

2. The only way to lose water, in this model, is to be acted on by a diuretic. Because diuretics act with a small time delay, we conclude that the diuretic effect was present between times 5 and 2, which precede the beginning and end points of the period of water loss, respectively.

3. Because volumes can change only continuously, blood volume must have been normal before it became low, with the transition occur-

ring at some time 3, which must fall during the period of water loss.

4. According to the model, the only way to have edema is to have had a high blood volume for some time in the past, here shown in the interval 9 to 6.

5. The only way to develop a high blood volume, according to the model, is to retain water, here shown in the interval 10 to 7.

   . . .

In this way, we can reconstruct a plausible history. The process, which might be called *postdiction*, is essentially the dual of qualitative simulation, or prediction, where we try to describe possible future states of a system from knowing its present and its laws. In the case of postdiction, we also benefit from strong constraints imposed by any real facts we know about the actual past. For example, knowing the time of diuretic administration gives a fix on time points 2 and 5, and thereby constrains all the others.

The power of methods such as this is great. Note that it permits a conceptual shift in what we mean by the notion of diagnosis. We no longer ask for the name of a disease, but for a temporally and causally-connected historical reconstruction. If combined with the ability to reason about the quantitative aggregation of effects, as suggested above, this can form the basis for a very strong diagnostic reasoner.

15.6.3   Qualitative Probabilistic Modeling

We noted in our introductory discussion of expertise that virtually nothing of human knowledge is truly certain. Then we argued that despite this uncertainty, we often act as if we believed things with certainty, perhaps buttressing our reasoning with special mechanisms to help get out of trouble when the inevitable false assumption actually leads to a blunder.

Though this approach appears quite workable for many areas of human competence, there are others in which a far more explicit devotion to the study of probabilistic relationships is required. For example, there are many areas of medicine in which the theoretical underpinnings are so weak that most real decisions have to be made based on the carefully aggregated experience of past cases. In trying to assess the risks posed by various drugs or environmental conditions, in attempting to optimize the empirical treatment of cancer by an ever-growing pharmacopoeia of noxious agents, we may understand relatively little of just how or why an agent works. We can nevertheless extrapolate from past experiences by treating them as a statistical sample, and assume that a new patient is drawn from the same population and therefore can look forward to (statistically) the same range of outcomes.

AI research has traditionally eschewed the straightforward application of these ideas because of a sense that statistics tend to sweep the interesting differences under the rug rather than exposing them to explicit scrutiny. Thus when a failure is noted in a statistically-based decision making program, e.g., a diagnostician misdiagnoses a known case—the statistical approach may be content to dismiss this error as the rare but expectable error case; it is, after all, expected that only 95% or so of the cases will fall exactly within the model. By contrast, the AI approach would be to try to examine in detail what led to the wrong conclusion and to learn from it some distinguishing feature that might help avoid this error in the future. In brief, AI researchers often act as if they believed that noise is not random but is simply the result of a deeper, yet discoverable process.

The other major argument against probabilistic reasoning in AI has been the observation that such reasoners tend to treat probabilistic relationships in very uniform ways, either imposing unrealistically strong assumptions such as conditional independence across the board, or requiring the collection of huge databases to provide adequate data to assess all the dependencies. Recent advances in the methods for analyzing probabilistic networks of dependencies [23] have dramatically improved our abilities to take true probabilistic models into account in AI reasoning programs. Nevertheless, many researchers sense that such models are highly sensitive to the particular distributions of probabilities that stock their models. Indeed, a probabilistic decision model tuned to work very well at deciding which patients are suffering from appendicitis at one institution falters when moved to a different setting, and regains its acumen only when retrained on a large volume of locally-gathered data [2].

Just as we noted in the case of qualitative models of physical or physiological systems, there is a strong argument to be made for developing qualitative models of probabilistic relationships. An example of such a

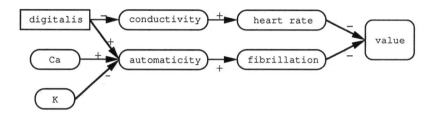

Figure 15.19
Effects of digitalis and serum calcium and potassium on the heart and the patient.
Digitalis has a beneficial effect, indicated by the top path to *value*: by decreasing
conductivity, it leads to a lower heart rate, which is beneficial for the patients under consideration. The bottom path shows a possibly-fatal mechanism of toxicity:
increasing digitalis increases automaticity, which in turn increases the risk of ventricular fibrillation, which is very highly undesirable. High levels of calcium (Ca) and
low levels of potassium (K) in the blood also contribute to increased automaticity.

qualitative statement is that the presence of the heart drug digitalis in a
patient's blood increases the automaticity of the heart (the tendency of
muscle fibers to fire spontaneously). Though we are uncommitted about
the degree to which we will find this increase, the general statement can
be interpreted to mean that the higher the level of the drug, the more
likely is the spontaneous firing. At this level of generality, the relation is
virtually a corollary of cardiac physiology and is likely to be very robust
to changes in the subject population. Thus, though the strength of this
relationship may vary from one group of patients to another, the sign of
the relation is almost sure to remain the same.

Figure 15.19 shows part of Michael Wellman's model of the interactions of digitalis, serum calcium and serum potassium on the control
of the heart [32]. Digitalis is a drug often used to treat (among other
disorders) tachycardia, a high heart rate. The benefits of treatment are
summarized in the top path in the graph: digitalis tends to decrease
the conductivity of the heart. Increased conductivity leads to an increased heart rate, therefore a decrease in conductivity tends to lower
the heart rate. Because, in this instance, a higher heart rate is bad
for the patient (leads to decreased value), the lower heart rate expected
from decreased conductivity is beneficial. The lower path in the figure
shows that increased digitalis, increased serum calcium and decreased
serum potassium all increase automaticity, which increases the risk of

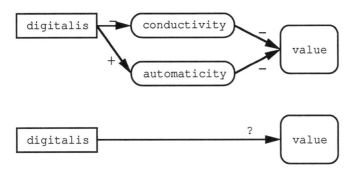

Figure 15.20
In this model, there is not enough information to tell the aggregate effect of giving digitalis. The qualitative graph-reduction operations defined in [32] lead to an ambiguous result, showing that there is not enough information, in general, to tell whether the benefits or risks of the drug are greater.

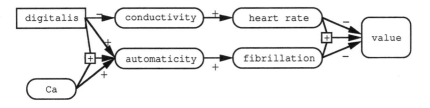

Figure 15.21
Introducing synergy into the model. Positive synergy between *dig* and *Ca* on *automaticity* indicates that the likelihood of digitalis causing automaticity is greater in the presence of higher levels of serum calcium. Positive synergy between the negative effects of heart rate and ventricular fibrillation serves to model indifference to heart rate when ventricular fibrillation is present.

ventricular fibrillation, an often-fatal condition that clearly decreases value.

In the description given so far, we have said nothing about the magnitudes of the expected effects, only their directions. It is not surprising, therefore, that when we aggregate this information (in Figure 15.20) to ask "Is giving digitalis a good idea?" the system is unable to tell because it cannot determine whether the beneficial or harmful effects of the drug will predominate.

However, it is possible to get useful information out of such a model without knowing quantitative relations if we add more qualitative knowledge about the joint effects of drugs and existing conditions. For exam-

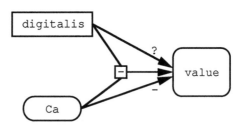

Figure 15.22
Though the effect of giving digitalis is still uncertain, synergy in the model implies
that the optimal digitalis dose must be a decreasing function of serum calcium.

ple, there is a synergistic interaction between the effects of digitalis and
calcium on automaticity, as shown in Figure 15.21. This means that a
given change in digitalis has a greater effect on automaticity when serum
calcium is high than when it is low. Applying Wellman's calculus for
drawing implications from such qualitative models, we arrive at the diagram of Figure 15.22: though we still cannot tell whether giving more
digitalis is a good idea or not, we can tell that the optimum dose of digitalis is a decreasing function of serum calcium. This is in fact a result
we had explicitly encoded from experience in the digitalis advisor, but
the new qualitative probabilistic reasoning methods allow us to derive
it from very general and robust principles.

15.7   Model-based Reasoning

The above examples have been chosen from medical applications, which
have indeed often inspired the development of the relevant ideas.
Medicine is by no means the only field, however, that requires reasoning
more deeply about systems. In cases where simple experiential knowledge turns out to be inadequate, we need to build suitably abstract
models of the domain and then reason about those models to help answer difficult questions.

The fundamental notion of a model, in expert systems as in traditional
fields like bridge design, is a smaller, simpler entity than the actual
system that nevertheless exhibits many of the properties of interest in
the real system. If the model is well-designed, simple reasoning about
the model may be able to answer difficult questions of genuine interest

about the actual system. AI systems often emphasize the desire to model explicitly only the structural components of a system and then automatically to derive the behavior of the system. When the behaviors and interactions of the component parts are understood well enough, this is a very powerful method because it means that any system consisting of such parts can be successfully modeled merely by writing down the parts and their connections, and the remainder of the analysis of the system can take place automatically. In practice, issues such as lack of precise knowledge and the combinatorics of modeling interesting systems with a very large number of parts conspire against this simple view and force on the model creator a demand for careful thought about just what to include in and exclude from the model.

In this section, we examine briefly two recent theses in model-based reasoning from Randy Davis' group in the AI Lab, one concerning geological reasoning, the other reasoning about the behavior of complex electrical circuits.

15.7.1   Using Models for Geological Interpretation

Reid Simmons' chosen problem was to give a geological account for an observed cross-section through the earth, such as that shown in Figure 15.23. A plausible interpretation of this picture corresponds to the following tale. Shale was deposited on the site. Granite then intruded under it. After the region was uplifted, the fault toward the left of the diagram occurred. Then a maficigneous rock intruded across the right, and finally erosion leveled the top. The GORDIUS PROGRAM generates just such interpretations [25].

In a sense, the problem here is analogous to Long's attempt to reconstruct the history of a complex medical process. In geology, added complexity derives from the geometric complexity of the diagram, the very large number of (combinations of) mechanisms that could have accounted for almost any part of the diagram, and the fact that we almost never have real data about what was actually true in the past (as might be the case in a carefully-tracked medical case).

GORDIUS' approach is summarized as a sequence of three steps, the first two of which are analogous to the strategy developed for DENDRAL. First, features of the diagram are used to generate hypotheses, which are constrained by relations in the diagram to fit together only in a few acceptable ways. Second, a qualitative simulation checks whether the

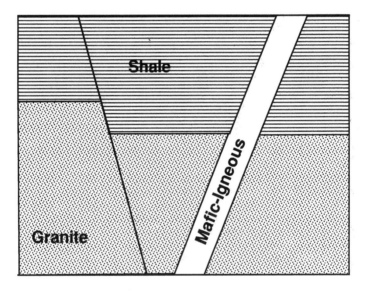

Interpretation:

1. Deposition1(Rock1,Shale)
2. Batholithic-Intrusion2(Rock2, Granite)
3. Uplift3(Uamount1)
4. Faulting(Fault1)
5. Dike-Intrusion5(Ign1, Mafic-Igneous)
6. Erosion6(Elevel1)

Figure 15.23
GORDIUS' diagram of a geological cross-section, and its interpretation. The diagram shows a cross-section at the present time, and the interpretation gives a plausible course of events that could have resulted in the given cross-section.

hypothesis could in fact generate the currently observed diagram. Finally, a debugging process is used to adjust the hypothesis to eliminate discrepancies pointed out by the simulator. A hypothesis is repeatedly simulated and debugged until its consequences are consistent with observations.

15.7.2 Temporal Abstraction for Reasoning about Complex Circuits

To drive home the importance of choosing the correct abstractions for reasoning about complex systems, consider the (cramped) portion of the circuit diagram of a Symbolics 3600 video controller board shown in Figure 15.24. In the natural representation of digital circuits, where we may view each logic element at any time as being either on or off, almost any small part of this circuit is sufficiently complex that it exceeds the reach of our meager analytical tools. To make matters worse, many circuit parts have internal states and a number of the wires in this diagram are in fact buses carrying multiple, interrelated signals. Simply simulating the behavior of such a circuit, given complete knowledge of the behavioral rules of its parts and its initial state, is a complex and time-consuming task. Trying to figure out what is wrong with it by postulating defects and then simulating until the observed abnormalities are reproduced seems hopeless—at least at the detailed bit-by-bit circuit level.[7]

Walter Hamscher actually spent a summer repairing faulty versions of this board and learning how technicians approached the problem. He discovered [11] that they use a rich language of temporal abstractions to describe behavior, including concepts such as: stay-same, change, duration, count, sequence, cycle, frequency, sampling, etc.; and their compositions. Once the circuit and its parts are understood in such abstract terms, relatively simple diagnostic rules suffice to help direct suspicion to the right candidates. For example, a *very* simple diagnostic rule might be:

A circuit component that is supposed to be a clock, but whose output is not changing, must be faulty.

---

[7]Notice that the argument here is very much the one we made against physiological simulation to diagnose human disease. Randy Davis and I sometimes joke in fact that our two domains—medicine and circuits—are not so different. The main differences are that in his, he can at least assume a circuit diagram that God has not chosen to publish for people; whereas in mine, I only have to deal with one basic model.

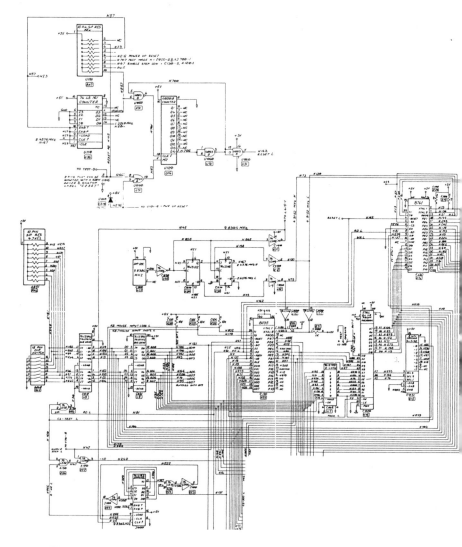

Figure 15.24
Part of the circuit diagram of a Symbolics 3600 video controller.

Here we are not speaking of individual gate transitions, but rather of much more appropriate aggregate behavior. The notion of a clock embodies a sequence of regular transitions, with a certain frequency. "Not changing" is a simple, easily tested aggregate behavior. When described and approached in such terms, even the apparent complexity of Figure 15.24 seems approachable.

15.8 Software Methodology

The successful exploitation even of the somewhat limited means at our current disposal has some interesting lessons for the field of software methodology. In contrast to the rather formal specification-implementation-verification-based methods advocated by many (including John Guttag in this volume), the expert systems field places a great emphasis on the incremental interweaving of specification, design, implementation and testing [26]. The fundamental driving force for this radically different orientation is that, in building expert systems, it is quite typical that the developers do not fully understand what their system is really supposed to do until they have worked seriously with experts from the domain, implemented various preliminary ideas, revised their goals based on test cases, etc. How could one specify a priori what it means to build a system for providing therapeutic management assistance to doctors treating patients with heart failure? What is the "correct" specification of a geological interpretation system? Initially neither the expert nor the system builder may have a clear idea. Further, such a clear idea may not be able to emerge until the developers have had a chance to assess just what is technically feasible (within the time and resource constraints of the project) or how useful it actually is to get the sort of interpretation or advice that was initially the goal. It is mostly through such experience that new task requirements or new modes of use are worked out.

The fact that in a very real sense expert system developers "don't know what they're doing" means that the greatest emphasis must be placed on high quality development environments. Such environments include support for rapid prototyping, incremental debugging, and the ability to postpone commitments. This often means systems that provide both compilation and interpretation, generic operators, "object-oriented" programming, all in the interest of simplifying the process of changing one's mind. These environments may also take the form of shells or toolkits that pre-package simple, routine methods for solving various problems or problem components. In light of the observation that many of the systems being built are small, often built by the domain expert, these environments must also support the illusion that anyone, even "nonprogrammers," can program.

What is new to software engineering in the tools that currently support practical system development? Primary is the adoption of a "very high level language" viewpoint—direct support for problem solving abstractions that are not present in conventional programming languages. Also important is support for the characteristics of expert systems (listed below), primarily the explicit representation of knowledge and built-in facilities for explanation and the examination and updating of the system's knowledge.

The final advance brought to software engineering is mainly an interesting and important matter of perception. Many expert system languages and tools appeal to the end user to program his or her ideas directly. We have suggested some of the technical reasons why this will strike many as more plausible than a similar appeal for end-users to take up COBOL or C directly. In addition, however, it appears that there is a component akin to Dumbo's magic feather[8] in these appeals. Interestingly, the motivated end-user discovers that he or she can, indeed, fly!

15.9   Conclusion

We have argued that the embedding of large quantities of knowledge in computer programs is an excellent technique for enabling us to build sophisticated applications, called expert systems. We examined the roots of this idea, looked at some of the simplified ways in which it has reached commercial application, considered some of the problems remaining in our basic conception of how to build such systems, and looked at a hand-

---

[8]For those without small children, in the Walt Disney classic animated film, Dumbo discovers that he can fly with the aid of a "magic" feather. Upon accidentally losing the feather, his fast-talking mouse assistant has a hard time convincing him that he really can fly, feather or no.

ful of interesting efforts recently emerged from the research laboratories that point toward dramatically improved future capabilities.

In conclusion, I want to take a retrospective look at what characterizes knowledge-based, or expert, systems and to reflect on the difficulties that lie ahead in adapting today's exciting research ideas to practical use.

Having looked at a number of expert systems, can we now say just what they are? After all, any system is in a sense an expert at whatever it was designed to do, and saying that knowledge-based systems embody knowledge can not really distinguish them from other programs. After all, how many programs are there that do not in some sense contain knowledge? What do we mean, then? Perhaps the following list of characteristics is a useful guide:

1. Expert systems typically operate in domains in which there are many possible answers to most problems. Therefore, the naive approach to problem solving, as suggested in our robot and alarm clock example, will involve search. The prime responsibility of the expert system is to apply its knowledge to eliminate or significantly reduce the magnitude of the search. Thus expertise yields the ability to get an adequate answer without systematically exploring nearly all the possibilities.

2. Expert systems, like most AI systems, use predominantly symbolic rather than numerical computing methods. Thus the data structures are often composed of complex interlinked structures.

3. Explicit representations of the universe of discourse typically play a causal role in the reasoning of the system. Thus the system works by manipulating an explicit encoding of its knowledge, which is thought to be an abstraction and decomposition of the most important aspects of the real world. A corollary is that the system typically has some form of self-knowledge: it can explain what it knows explicitly, and trace out the reasoning steps that led from its observations to its conclusions.

4. The problem solving methods are often deliberately human-like, patterned on the observed behavior of human experts. Sometimes this is because no other theories of the domain are available. In other circumstances, it is motivated by the desire to make details

of the program's operation meaningful to human experts who may have to evaluate it or work with it.

5. Finally, expert systems often contain an explicit representation of their own goals. They can therefore participate in the choice of the most appropriate problem solving methods for addressing the task at hand.

15.9.1 Difficult Challenges

In the late 1980's, there appear to be only a few principal challenges standing in the way of our ability to create much more sophisticated expert systems.

First is the need to conjoin the clever insights and techniques exemplified by some of the research projects above. Though each program achieves an impressive demonstration of needed capabilities, we have little idea how to combine these coherently. Thus a program that reasons about a multi-level causal hierarchy of hypotheses, while at the same time including appropriate temporal abstractions and postdiction machinery, while at the same time allowing the expression of quantitative and qualitative probabilistic relationships, is not currently in sight. A few years ago, our intuition was that progress in knowledge representation research would slowly lay the groundwork to achieve just this sort of integration, if not at one stroke, at least by providing powerful representation languages that would allow us to express all the relevant knowledge in a single language [28]. Given that start, we could then evolve toward systems with multiple abilities to handle all aspects of very complex domains and problems. Alas, this intuition has at least temporarily foundered on harsh experience [3][10]—the current languages just are not up to the task.

The second difficulty is the sheer size of the knowledge base needed for a program to have a comprehensive understanding of a field. In 1976 our colleagues [22] arrived at "an upper bound of approximately one million facts as the core body of information in general internal medicine." Even to encode such a vast body of knowledge once is a daunting task. Lacking an agreed-upon universal representation language (at least one that is easier for computers to manipulate than English) means that this task may need to be undertaken repeatedly, as new ways of using it are discovered.[9] One consequence is that research in the field is slow. Between the need to develop interesting new ideas, to implement these as complex and large computer programs, and to describe a respectable chunk of knowledge in a form appropriate for the new program, five years passes easily in the life of a researcher (read "graduate student").

The problem of acquiring the required knowledge is being attacked by two routes. The frontal assault simply treats the difficulty as a very large engineering problem. Thus such projects as Lenat's CYC [14] plan to build a very large encyclopedic knowledge base by incrementally resolving representation problems, inventing conventions as needed, and steadily accumulating a valuable collection of descriptions of aspects of the world. Similarly, though in a more limited domain, the UMLS (Unified Medical Language Systems) project attempts to develop translation methods to allow the interchange and integration of knowledge among various existing representation and indexing schemes [4]. The flanking maneuver assumes that the best way to gather the required knowledge is by developing techniques for the computer to learn it directly from interactions with human experts, direct investigation and experimentation under autonomous program control, or experience as described in large databases. Learning is currently a vibrant topic of AI research, but just as with advanced expert systems techniques themselves, the results are more promising than achieved.

15.9.2   The Future

Ultimately, it seems impossible to separate the long term advance of expert systems from AI research in general. Rather simple tools available today, based on ten-year-old ideas, empower users to build valuable applications. As we succeed in integrating and simplifying today's research ideas, new generations of expert system technology will enable tomorrow's users to build much more sophisticated programs. Eventually, every interesting advance at the roots of AI research feeds directly into better experimental expert systems, and finally into applications.

---

[9]In addition, in many rapidly-evolving domains such as medicine, the knowledge itself changes with dramatic speed. This means that quite aside from the technical reasons for re-encoding knowledge, portions of it may need to be continually re-encoded just to keep up to date.

15.10   Acknowledgments

My early views on knowledge-based systems were very much influenced by the late William A. Martin. The presentation here was greatly helped by discussions with my colleagues Ramesh S. Patil, Randall Davis and Howard E. Shrobe.

Support for this research was provided in part by the National Institutes of Health grant number 5 R01 LM 04493 from the National Library of Medicine.

Bibliography

[1] W. J. Clancey. From GUIDON to NEOMYCIN to HERACLES in twenty short lessons. *AI Magazine*, 7(3):40–60, 1986.

[2] F. T. de Dombal, J. R. Staniland, and S. E. Clamp. Geographical variation in disease presentation. *Medical Decision Making*, 1:59–69, 1981.

[3] J. Doyle and R.S. Patil. Two dogmas of knowledge representation: language restrictions, taxonomic classifications, and the utility of representation services. TM 387b, MIT Laboratory for Computer Science, Cambridge, MA, September 1989.

[4] D. A. Evans and R. A. Miller. Final task report (task 2)—unified medical language system (UMLS) project: Initial phase in developing representations for mapping medical knowledge: INTERNIST-I/QMR, HELP, and MeSH. Technical Report CMU-LCL-87-1, Laboratory for Computational Linguistics, Carnegie Mellon University, Pittsburgh, PA, 1987.

[5] E. A. Feigenbaum, B. G. Buchanan, and J. Lederberg. On generality and problem solving: A case study using the dendral program. In B. Meltzer and D. Michie, editors, *Machine Intelligence 6*, pages 165–190. American Elsevier, New York, 1971.

[6] E. Feigenbaum, P. McCorduck, and H. Penny Nii. *The Rise of the Expert Company*. Times Books, 1988.

[7] G. A. Gorry, H. Silverman, and S. G. Pauker. Capturing clinical expertise: A computer program that considers clinical responses to digitalis. *American Journal of Medicine*, 64:452–460, March 1978.

[8] Computer-Aided Mathematics Group. *Macsyma Reference Manual*. Symbolics, Inc., Cambridge, MA, version 12 edition, June 1986.

[9] A. Guyton, C. Jones, and T. Coleman. *Circulatory Physiology: Cardiac Output and its Regulation*. W.B. Saunders Company, Philadelphia, PA, 1973.

[10] I. J. Haimowitz, R. S. Patil, and P. Szolovits. Representing medical knowledge in a terminological language is difficult. In *Symposium on Computer Applications in Medical Care*, pages 101–105, 1988.

[11] W. C. Hamscher. *Model-Based Troubleshooting of Digital Systems*. PhD thesis, MIT Department of Electrical Engineering and Computer Science, August 1988.

[12] D. Heckerman. Probabilistic interpretations for MYCIN's certainty factors. In Laveen N. Kanal and John F. Lemmer, editors, *Uncertainty in Artificial Intelligence*. North-Holland, 1986.

[13] J. P. Kassirer and G. A. Gorry. Clinical problem solving: A behavioral analysis. *Annals of Internal Medicine*, 89:245–255, 1978.

[14] Doug Lenat, Mayank Prakash, and Mary Shepherd. CYC: Using common sense knowledge to overcome brittleness and knowledge acquisition bottlenecks. *AI Magazine*, 6(4):65–85, 1986.

[15] R. K. Lindsay, B. G. Buchanan, E. A. Feigenbaum, and J. Lederberg. *Applications of Artificial Intelligence for Organic Chemistry: The DENDRAL Project*. McGraw-Hill, 1980.

[16] W. J. Long. Reasoning about state from causation and time in a medical domain. In *Proceedings of the National Conference on Artificial Intelligence*, pages 251–254, 1983.

[17] W. A. Martin. Interactive systems—theories of implementation. Course notes for Knowledge-Based Application Systems, 1977.

[18] R. A. Miller, M. A. McNeil, S. M. Challinor, F. E. Masari, Jr., and J. D. Myers. The Internist-1/Quick Medical Reference project— status report. *Western Journal of Medicine*, 145:816–822, 1986.

[19] R. A. Miller, H. E. Pople, Jr., and J. D. Myers. Internist-1, an experimental computer-based diagnostic consultant for general internal medicine. *New England Journal of Medicine*, 307:468–476, 1982.

[20] M. Minsky. Why people think computers can't. *AI Magazine*, pages 3–15, 1982.

[21] R. S. Patil. Causal representation of patient illness for electrolyte and acid-base diagnosis. Technical Report MIT/LCS/TR 267, MIT Laboratory for Computer Science, Cambridge, MA, October 1981.

[22] S. G. Pauker, G. A. Gorry, J. P. Kassirer, and W. B. Schwartz. Towards the simulation of clinical cognition: Taking a present illness by computer. *American Journal of Medicine*, 60:981–996, 1976.

[23] J. Pearl. *Probabilistic Reasoning in Intelligent Systems: Networks of Plausible Inference*. Morgan Kaufmann, 1988.

[24] E. H. Shortliffe and B. G. Buchanan. A model of inexact reasoning in medicine. *Mathematical Biosciences*, 23:351–379, 1975.

[25] R. G. Simmons. *Generate, Test, and Debug: A Paradigm for Solving Interpretation and Planning Problems*. PhD thesis, MIT Department of Electrical Engineering and Computer Science, 1988.

[26] W. Swartout and R. Balzer. On the inevitable intertwining of specification and implementation. *Communications of the ACM*, 25(7):438–440, 1982.

[27] W. R. Swartout. XPLAIN: A system for creating and explaining expert consulting programs. *Artificial Intelligence*, 21:285–325, 1983.

[28] P. Szolovits, J. P. Kassirer, W. J. Long, A. J. Moskowitz, S. G. Pauker, R. S. Patil, and M. P. Wellman. An artificial intelligence approach to clinical decision making. Technical Memo MIT/LCS/TM 310, MIT Laboratory Computer Science, Cambridge, MA, September 1986.

[29] P. Szolovits and W. J. Long. The development of clinical expertise in the computer. In Peter Szolovits, editor, *Artificial Intelligence in Medicine*, volume 51 of *AAAS Selected Symposium Series*, pages 79–117. Westview Press, Boulder, Colorado, 1982.

[30] R. L. Teach and E. H. Shortliffe. An analysis of physician attitudes regarding computer-based clinical consultation systems. *Computers and Biomedical Research*, 14:542–548, 1981.

[31] L. L. Weed. *Medical Records, Medical Education and Patient Care*. Case University Press, Cleveland, OH, 1969.

[32] M. P. Wellman. Formulation of tradeoffs in planning under uncertainty. Technical Report MIT/LCS/TR 427, MIT Laboratory for Computer Science, Cambridge, MA, August 1988. Revised version of a Ph.D. dissertation, July 1988.

[33] V. L. Yu, B. G. Buchanan, E. H. Shortliffe, S. M. Wraith, R. Davis, A. C. Scott, and S. N. Cohen. An evaluation of the performance of a computer-based consultant. *Computer Programs in Biomedicine*, 9:95–102, 1979.

16 Legged Robots

Marc H. Raibert

Professor, Department of Electrical Engineering and Computer Science
Member, Artificial Intelligence Laboratory

Abstract

The construction of useful legged vehicles depends on progress in several areas of engineering and science. Legged vehicles will need systems that control joint motions, sequence the use of legs, monitor and manipulate balance, generate motions to use known footholds, sense the terrain to find good footholds and calculate negotiable foothold sequences. As yet, most of these tasks are not well understood, but research is underway. If this research is successful, it will lead to the development of legged vehicles that travel efficiently and quickly in terrain where softness, grade or obstacles make existing vehicles ineffective. Such vehicles may be useful in industrial, agricultural and military applications. This paper reviews these issues as well as a history of research on active balance, running and legged robot development.

16.1 Why Study Legged Machines?

Aside from the sheer thrill of creating machines that actually run, there are two serious reasons for exploring legged machines. One reason is mobility: there is a need for vehicles that can travel in difficult terrain, where existing vehicles cannot go. Wheels excel on prepared surfaces such as rails and roads, but perform poorly where the terrain is soft or uneven. Because of these limitations only about half the earth's landmass is accessible to existing wheeled and tracked vehicles, whereas a much greater area can be reached by animals on foot. It should be

This paper is excerpted from *Legged Robots that Balance* by M.H. Raibert, MIT Press, Cambridge, MA, 1986.

possible to build legged vehicles that can go to the places that animals can now reach.

One reason legs provide better mobility in rough terrain is that they can use isolated footholds that optimize support and traction, whereas a wheel requires a continuous path of support. As a consequence, a legged system is free to choose among the best footholds in the reachable terrain whereas a wheel is forced to negotiate the worst terrain. A ladder illustrates this point: rungs provide footholds that enable legged systems to climb, but the spaces between the rungs prevent the wheeled system from making progress.

Another advantage of legs is that they provide an active suspension that decouples the path of the body from the paths of the feet. The payload is free to travel smoothly despite pronounced variations in the terrain. A legged system can also step over obstacles. The performance of legged vehicles can, to a great extent, be independent of the detailed roughness of the ground.

The construction of useful legged vehicles depends on progress in several areas of engineering and science. Legged vehicles will need systems that control joint motions, sequence the use of legs, monitor and manipulate balance, generate motions to use known footholds, sense the terrain to find good footholds and calculate negotiable foothold sequences. As yet, most of these tasks are not well understood, but research is underway. If this research is successful, it will lead to the development of legged vehicles that travel efficiently and quickly in terrain where softness, grade or obstacles make existing vehicles ineffective. Such vehicles may be useful in industrial, agricultural and military applications.

A second reason for exploring legged machines is to understand how humans and animals use their legs for locomotion. A few instant replays on television will reveal the large variety and complexity of ways athletes can carry, swing, toss, glide and otherwise propel their bodies through space, maintaining orientation, balance and speed as they go. Such performance is not limited to professional athletes; behavior at the local playground is equally impressive from a mechanical engineering, sensory-motor integration or computational point of view. Animals also demonstrate great mobility and agility. They use their legs to move quickly and reliably through forest, swamp, marsh and jungle, and from tree to tree. They move with great speed and efficiency.

Despite the skill we apply in using our own legs for locomotion, we are still at a primitive stage in understanding the principles that underlie walking and running. What control mechanisms do animals use? The development of legged machines will lead to new ideas about animal locomotion. To the extent that an animal and a machine perform similar locomotion tasks, their control systems and mechanical structures must solve similar problems. Of course, results in biology will also help us to make progress with legged robots. This sort of interdisciplinary approach is already becoming effective in other areas where biology and robotics have a common ground, such as vision, speech and manipulation.

16.2   Research on Legged Machines

The scientific study of legged locomotion began just over a century ago when Leland Stanford, then Governor of California, commissioned Eadweard Muybridge to find out whether or not a trotting horse left the ground with all four feet at the same time. Stanford had wagered that it never did. After, Muybridge proved him wrong with a set of stop-motion photographs that appeared in *Scientific American* in 1878. Muybridge went on to document the walking and running behavior of over 40 mammals, including humans [15] [16]. Even after 100 years, his photographic data are of considerable value and beauty, and survive as a landmark in locomotion research.

The study of machines that walk also had its origin in Muybridge's time. An early walking model appeared in about 1870 [8]. It used a linkage to move the body along a straight horizontal path while the feet moved up and down to exchange support during stepping (see Figure 16.1). The linkage was originally designed by the famous Russian mathematician Chebyshev some years earlier. During the 80 or 90 years that followed, workers viewed the task of building walking machines as the task of designing linkages that would generate suitable stepping motions when driven by a source of power. Many designs were proposed (see Figure 16.2), but the performance of such machines was limited by their fixed patterns of motion, since they could not adjust to variations in the terrain by placing the feet on the best footholds. By the late

1850	Chebyshev	Designs linkage used in early walking mechanism [8].
1872	Muybridge	Uses stop-motion photography to document running animals.
1893	Rygg	Patents human powered mechanical horse.
1945	Wallace	Patents hopping tank with reaction wheels that provide stability.
1961	Space General	Eight legged kinematic machine walks on outdoor terrain.
1963	Cannon, Higdon and Schaefer	Control system balances single, double, and limber inverted pendulums.
1968	Frank and McGhee	Simple digital logic controls walking of Phony Pony.
	Mosher	GE quadruped truck climbs railroad ties under control of human driver.
1969	Bucyrus-Erie Co.	Big Muskie, a 15,000 ton walking dragline is used for strip mining. It moves in soft terrain at a speed of 900 ft/hr.
1977	McGhee	Digital computer coordinates leg motions of hexapod walking machine at OSU.
	Gurfinkel	Hybrid computer controls hexapod walker in USSR.
	McMahon and Greene	Human runners set new speed records on Harvard *tuned track*. Its compliance is adjusted to mechanics of human leg.
1980	Hirose and Umetani	Quadruped machine climbs stairs and over obstacles using simple sensors. Ingenious leg mechanism simplifies control.
	Kato	Hydraulic biped walks with quasi-dynamic gait.
	Matsuoka	Mechanism balances in the plane while hopping on one leg.
1981	Miura and Shimoyama	Walking biped balances actively in 3D space.
1983	Sutherland	Hexapod walks with human rider. Computer, hydraulics, and human share computing task.
	Odetics	Self-contained hexapod lifts and carries back end of pickup truck.
1987	OSU	Three ton self-contained hexapod carrying human driver travels at 5 mph and climbs over obstacle.
1988	SFU	McGeer demonstrates passive dynamic walking.

Table 16.1
Milestones in the Development of Legged Robots

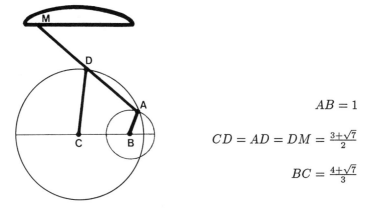

$$AB = 1$$

$$CD = AD = DM = \frac{3+\sqrt{7}}{2}$$

$$BC = \frac{4+\sqrt{7}}{3}$$

Figure 16.1
Linkage used in an early walking machine. When the input crank AB rotates, the output point M moves along a straight path during part of the cycle and an arched path during the other part of the cycle. Two identical linkages are arranged to operate out of phase so at least one provides a straight motion at all times. The body is always supported by the feet connected to the straight moving linkage (after [8]).

1950's it had become clear that linkages providing fixed motion would not do the trick and that useful walking machines would need *control*.

One way to control a walking machine is to harness a human. Ralph Mosher used this approach in building a four-legged walking truck at General Electric in the mid-1960's [7]. The project was part of a large program to develop advanced teleoperators capable of providing better dexterity through high fidelity force feedback. The walking machine Mosher built stood 11 feet tall, weighed 3000 pounds, and was powered hydraulically. It is shown in Figure 16.3. Each of the driver's limbs was connected to a handle or pedal that controlled one of the truck's four legs. Whenever the driver caused a truck leg to push against an obstacle, force feedback let the driver feel the obstacle as though it were his or her own arm or leg doing the pushing.

After about 20 hours of training, Mosher was able to handle the machine with surprising agility. Films of the machine operating under his control show it ambling along at about 5 mph, climbing a stack of railroad ties, pushing a foundered jeep out of the mud and maneuvering a large drum onto some hooks. Despite its dependence on a well trained

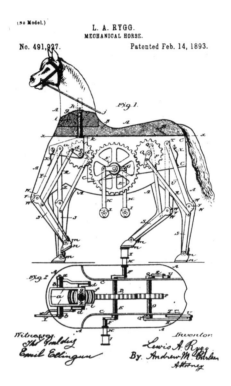

Figure 16.2
Mechanical horse patented by Lewis A. Rygg in 1893. The stirrups double as pedals so the rider can power the stepping motions. The reins move the head and forelegs from side to side for steering. Apparently the machine was never built.

human for control, the GE Walking Truck was a milestone in legged technology.

An alternative to human control became feasible in the 1970's when minicomputers became available to every laboratory. Robert McGhee's group at the Ohio State University was the first to use a digital computer to control a walking machine successfully [12]. In 1977 they built an insect-like hexapod that would walk with a number of gaits, turn, walk sideways and negotiate simple obstacles. The computer's primary task was to solve kinematic equations in order to coordinate the eighteen electric motors driving the legs. This coordination ensured that the

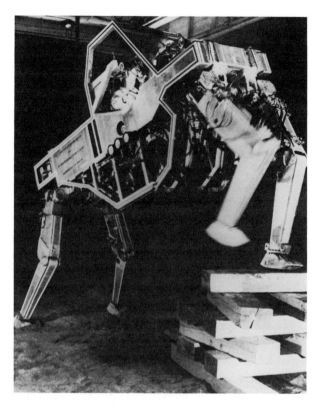

Figure 16.3
Walking truck developed by Ralph Mosher at General Electric in about 1968. The human driver controlled the machine with four handles and pedals that were connected to the four legs hydraulically. (Photograph courtesy of General Electric Research and Development Center.)

machine's center of mass stayed over the polygon of support provided by the feet while allowing the legs to sequence through a gait (see Figure 16.4). The machine traveled quite slowly, covering several meters per minute. Force and visual sensing provided a measure of terrain accommodation in later developments. The hexapod provided McGhee with an experimental means of pursuing his earlier theoretical findings on the combinatorics and selection of gait [11].

Gurfinkel and his coworkers in the USSR built a machine with characteristics and performance quite similar to McGhee's at about the same

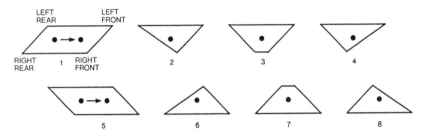

Figure 16.4
Statically stable gait. The diagram shows the sequence of support patterns provided
by the feet of a quadruped walking with a crawling gait. The body and legs move
to keep the projection of the center of mass within the polygon defined by the feet.
A supporting foot is located at each vertex. The dot indicates the projection of the
center of mass. (Adapted from McGhee and Frank, 1968.)

time [1]. They used a mixture of analog and digital computers for control, with analog computation doing the kinematic calculations.

The group at Ohio State recently built a much larger hexapod (see
Figure 16.5) designed for self-contained operation on rough terrain [24].
It carries a gasoline engine for power, several computers and a human
operator for control, and a laser range sensor for terrain sensing. This
machine has walked at about 5 mph, negotiated a muddy cornfield and
walked over railroad ties.

Shigeo Hirose of the Tokyo Institute of Technology realized that mechanical linkage and computer were not mutually exclusive with respect
to control. His experience with clever and unusual mechanisms—he
built seven kinds of mechanical snakes—led to a special leg that simplified the control of locomotion and could improve efficiency [2]. The leg
was a three dimensional pantograph that translated the motion of each
actuator into a pure Cartesian translation of the foot. With the ability to generate x, y and z translations of each foot by merely choosing
an actuator, the control computer was freed from the arduous task of
performing kinematic solutions. The mechanical linkage was helping to
perform the calculations needed for locomotion. The linkage was effi-

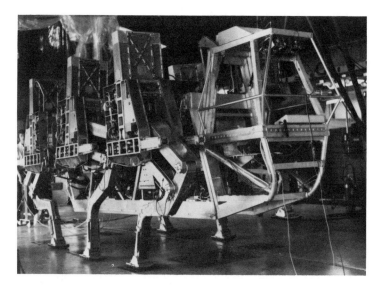

Figure 16.5
The hexapod walking machine developed at Ohio State University. It stands about 10 feet tall, 15 feet long, and weighs 3 tons. A 90 horsepower motorcycle engine provides power to 18 variable displacement hydraulic pumps that drive the joints. The legs use pantographs linkages to improve energy efficiency. The operator normally provides steering and speed commands while computers control the stepping motions of the legs. (Photograph courtesy of Prof. K. Waldron, OSU.)

cient because the actuators performed only positive work in moving the body forward.

Hirose used the pantograph leg design to build a small quadruped, about one meter long. It was equipped with touch sensors on each foot and an oil-damped pendulum attached to the body. Simple algorithms used the sensors to control the actions of the feet. For instance, if a touch sensor indicated contact while the foot was moving forward, the leg would move backward a little bit, move upward a little bit, then resume its forward motion. If the foot had not yet cleared the obstacle, the cycle would repeat. The use of several simple algorithms like this one permitted Hirose's machine to climb up and down stairs and to negotiate other obstacles without human intervention.

These three walking machines, McGhee's, Gurfinkel's and Hirose's, represent a class called *static crawlers*. Each differs in the details of construction and in the computing technology used for control, but they share a common approach to balance and stability. They all keep enough feet on the ground to guarantee a broad base of support at all times, and the body and legs move to keep the center of mass over this broad support base. The forward velocity is kept low enough so that stored kinetic energy can be ignored in the stability calculation. Each of these machines has been used to study rough terrain locomotion in the laboratory through experiments on terrain sensing, gait selection and selection of foothold sequences. Several other machines that fall into this class have been studied in the intervening years.

16.3   Dynamics and Balance Improve Mobility

We now consider the study of dynamic legged systems that balance actively. These systems operate in a regime where the velocities and kinetic energies of the masses are important to the behavior. Geometry and configuration taken alone are not adequate to model a system that moves with substantial speed or has large mass. In order to predict and influence the behavior of a dynamic system, we must consider the energy stored in each mass and spring, as well as the geometric structure and configuration of the mechanism. Consider, for example, a fast moving vehicle that would tip over if it stopped suddenly with its center of mass too close to the front feet.

The exchange of energy among its various forms is also important in dynamic legged locomotion. For example, there is a cycle of activity in running that changes the form of the stored energy several times: the body's potential energy of elevation changes into kinetic energy during falling, then into strain energy when parts of the leg deform elastically during rebound with the ground, then into kinetic energy again as the body accelerates upward, and finally back into potential energy of elevation. This sort of dynamic exchange is central to an understanding of legged locomotion.

Dynamics also plays a role in giving legged systems the ability to balance actively. A statically balanced system avoids tipping and the ensuing horizontal accelerations by keeping its center of mass over the polygon of support formed by the feet. Animals sometimes use this sort of balance when they move slowly, but usually they balance actively.

A legged system that balances actively can tolerate departures from static equilibrium, tipping and accelerating for short periods of time. The control system manipulates body and leg motions to ensure that each tipping interval is brief and that each tipping motion in one direction is compensated by a tipping motion in the opposite direction.

Thus an effective base of support is maintained over time. A system that balances actively can also tolerate vertical acceleration, such as the ballistic flight and bouncing that occur during running.

The ability of an actively balanced system to depart from static equilibrium relaxes the rules governing how legs can be used for support, which in turn leads to improved mobility. For example, if a legged system can tolerate tipping, then it can position its feet far from the center of mass in order to use footholds that are widely separated or erratically placed. If it can remain upright with a small base of support, then it can travel where there are closely spaced obstructions or where there is a narrow path of firm support. The ability to tolerate intermittent support also contributes to mobility. Intermittent support allows a system to move all its legs to new footholds at one time, to jump onto or over obstacles, and to use short periods of ballistic flight for increased speed. These abilities to use narrow base and intermittent support generally increase the types of terrain a legged system can negotiate. Animals routinely exploit active balance to travel quickly on difficult terrain; legged vehicles will have to balance actively, too, if they are to move with animal like mobility and speed.

16.4   Research on Active Balance

The first machines that balanced actively were automatically controlled inverted pendulums. Everyone knows that a human can balance a broom on his finger with relative ease. Why not use automatic control to build a broom that can balance itself? Claude Shannon was probably the first to do so when, in 1951, he used the parts from an erector set to build a machine that balanced an inverted pendulum atop a small powered truck. The truck drove back and forth in response to the tipping movements of the pendulum, as sensed by a pair of switches at its base. In order to move from one place to another, the truck first had to drive away from the destination to unbalance the pendulum, then proceed toward the destination. In order to balance again at the destination, the truck moved past the destination until the pendulum was again upright with no forward velocity, then moved back to the destination.

At Shannon's urging, Robert Cannon and two of his students at Stanford University set about demonstrating controllers that could balance two inverted pendulums at once. In one case, the pendulums were mounted side by side on the cart. In the other, they were mounted one on top of the other (see Figure 16.6). Cannon's group was interested in the single input, multiple output problem and in the limitations of achievable balance: how could they use the single force that drove the cart's motion to control the angles of two pendulums as well as the position of the cart? How far from balance could the system deviate before it was impossible to return to equilibrium, given such parameters of the mechanical system as the cart motor's strength and the pendula lengths?

Using analysis based on normal coordinates and optimal switching curves, Cannon's group expressed regions of controllability as explicit functions of the physical parameters of the system. Once these regions were found, their boundaries were used to find switching functions that provided control. Later, they extended these techniques to provide balance for a flexible inverted pendulum [21]. These studies of balance for inverted pendulums were important precursors to later work on locomotion and the inverted pendulum model for walking would become the primary tool for studying balance in legged systems (e.g., [5][13][23].) It is unfortunate that no one has yet extended Cannon's elegant analytical results to the more complicated legged case.

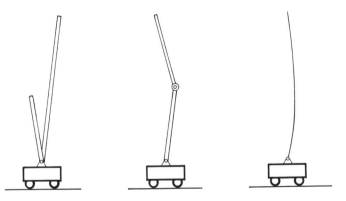

Figure 16.6
Cannon and his students built machines that balanced inverted pendulums on a moving cart. They balanced two pendulums side by side, one pendulum on top of another, and a long limber inverted pendulum. Only one input, the force driving the cart horizontally, was available for control. (Adapted from [21].)

The importance of active balance in legged locomotion had been recognized for some years, but progress in building physical legged systems that employ such principles was held back by the perceived difficulty of the task. It was not until the late 1970's that experimental work on balance in legged systems got underway.

Kato and his coworkers built a biped that walked with a *quasi-dynamic* gait [5]. The machine had ten hydraulically powered degrees of freedom and two large feet. This machine was usually a static crawler, moving along a preplanned trajectory to keep the center of mass over the base of support provided by the large supporting foot. Once during each step, however, the machine temporarily destabilized itself to tip forward so that support would be transferred quickly from one foot to the other. Before the transfer took place on each step, the *catching* foot was positioned to return the machine to equilibrium passively. No active response was required. A modified inverted pendulum model was used to plan the tipping motion. In 1984, this machine walked with a quasi-dynamic gait, taking about a dozen 0.5 m steps per minute. The use of a dynamic transfer phase makes an important point: a legged system can exhibit complicated dynamic behavior without requiring a very complicated control system.

Miura and Shimoyama built the first walking machine that balanced itself actively [13]. Their *stilt biped* was patterned after a human walking on stilts. Each foot provided only a point of support and the machine had three actuators: one for each leg that moved the leg sideways, and a third that separated the legs fore and aft. Because the legs did not change length, the hips were used to pick up the feet. This gave the machine a pronounced shuffling gait reminiscent of Charlie Chaplin's stiff-kneed walk.

Control for the stilt biped relied, once again, on the inverted pendulum model of its behavior. Each time a foot was placed on the floor, its position was chosen according to the tipping behavior expected from an inverted pendulum. Actually, the problem was broken down as though there were two planar pendulums, one in the pitching plane and one in the rolling plane. The choice of foot position along each axis took the current and desired state of the system into account. The control system used tabulated descriptions of planned leg motions together with linear feedback to perform the necessary calculations. Unlike Kato's machine, which came to static equilibrium before and after each dynamic transfer, the stilt biped tipped all the time.

Dynamic bipeds that balance are now being studied in several laboratories around the world. Miura has edited a videotape that reports recent work, including new machines by Kato, Arimoto, Masubuchi and Furusho.

An interesting recent development is Tad McGeer's work on passive dynamic walking [10]. McGeer analyzed and constructed a planar mechanism that walks downhill with almost no actuation. Each leg is a tuned pendulum that swings forward passively and is propelled backward with respect to its hip by forward motion of the body. The only actuators in the system are used to shorten each leg so the foot clears the ground during the swing phase. The system is tuned so that the amplitude of the passive swing of each leg compensates for variations in forward motion of the body.

16.5 Running Machines

Running is a form of legged locomotion that uses ballistic flight phases to obtain high speed. Matsuoka [9] was the first to build a machine that ran, where running is defined by periods when all feet are off the ground at one time. Matsuoka's goal was to model repetitive hopping in humans. He formulated a model with a body and one massless leg, and he simplified the problem by assuming that the duration of the support phase was short compared with the ballistic flight phase. This extreme form of running, in which nearly the entire cycle is spent in flight, minimizes the influence of tipping during support. This model permitted Matsuoka to derive a time-optimal state feedback controller that provided stability for hopping in place and for low speed translations.

To test his method for control, Matsuoka built a planar one-legged hopping machine. The machine operated by rolling on ball bearings on a table, inclined 10 degrees from the horizontal in an effective gravity field of 0.17 g. An electric solenoid provided a rapid thrust at the foot, hence the support period was short. The machine hopped in place at about one hop per second and traveled back and forth on the table.

To study running, my coworkers and I have explored a variety of legged systems including one-, two, and four-legged systems. Our first machine ran on just one leg. It hopped like a kangaroo, using a series of leaps. A machine with one leg allowed us to concentrate on active balance and dynamics while avoiding the difficult task of coordinating many legs. We wanted to know if there were algorithms for walking and running that are independent of gait and that work correctly for any number of legs. Perhaps a machine with just one gait could suggest answers to this question.

The first machine we built to study these problems had two main parts: a body and a leg. The body carried the actuators and instrumentation needed for the machine's operation. The leg could telescope to change length and could pivot with respect to the body at a simple hip. The leg was springy along the telescoping axis. Sensors measured the pitch angle of the body, the angle of the hip, the length of the leg, the tension in the leg spring and contact with the ground. This first machine was constrained to operate in a plane, so it could move only up and down, fore and aft, and rotate in the plane. An umbilical cable connected the machine to power and a control computer.

The running cycle has two phases. During one phase, called *stance* or *support*, the leg supports the weight of the body and the foot stays in a fixed location on the ground. During stance, the system tips like an inverted pendulum. During the other phase, called *flight*, the center of mass moves ballistically, with the leg unloaded and free to move.

16.5.1 Control of Running Was Decomposed into Three Parts

We found that a simple set of algorithms can control the planar one-legged hopping machine, allowing it run without tipping over. Our approach was to separately consider the hopping motion, forward travel and posture of the body. This decomposition lead to a control system with three parts:

- *Hopping.* One part of the control system excites the cyclic hopping motion that underlies running and regulates the height to which the machine hops. The hopping motion is an oscillation governed by the mass of the body, the springiness of the leg and gravity. During support, the body bounces on the springy leg and, during flight, the system travels a ballistic trajectory. The control system delivers a vertical thrust with the leg during each support period to sustain the oscillation and to regulate its amplitude. Some of

1982	Planar one-legged machine hops in place, travels at a specified rate, keeps its balance when disturbed, and jumps over small obstacles.
1983	Three dimensional one-legged machine runs and balances on an open floor. Simulations reveal passively stabilized bounding gait for quadruped-like model.
1984	Quadruped runs with trotting gait using generalization of one-leg algorithms. Data from cat and human found to exhibit symmetries like those used to control running machines.
1985	Planar biped runs with one- and two-legged gaits and changes between gaits.
1986	Planar biped does flips, aerials, and runs at 11.5 mph. Monopod uses new leg design with rotary joint and leaf-spring foot.
1987	Quadruped runs with pacing and bounding gaits.
1988	Planar biped uses selected footholds and climbs short stairway. Quadruped switches between gaits while running. Reentrant trajectories found for simulated passive dynamic running.
1989	Planar biped jumps through hoop and runs with top speed of 13.1 mph, and gallops in simulation. Hoof added to monopod improves performance of leafspring foot. Three dimensional biped does simple running.

Table 16.2
Summary of Research in the Leg Laboratory. (The Leg Laboratory was located at Carnegie-Mellon University from 1981—1986 and at the MIT Artificial Intelligence Laboratory from 1987—present.)

the energy needed for each hop is recovered by the leg spring from the previous hop.

- *Forward Speed.* A second part of the control system regulates the forward running speed. This is done by moving the leg to a specified forward position with respect to the body during the flight portion of each cycle. The position of the foot with respect to the body when landing has a strong influence on tipping and acceleration behavior during the support period that follows. The body will either continue to travel with the same forward speed, accelerate to go faster or slow down, depending on where the control system places the foot. To calculate a suitable forward position for the foot, the control system takes account of the actual forward speed, the desired speed and a simple model of the system's dynamics. The algorithm works correctly when the machine is hopping in place, accelerating to a run, running at a constant speed and slowing to a stationary hop.

  The rule for placing the positioning the foot is based on a kind of symmetry found in running. In order to run at constant forward speed, the instantaneous forward accelerations that occur during a stride must integrate to zero. One way to satisfy this requirement is to shape the running motion so that forward acceleration has an odd symmetry throughout each stride—functions with odd symmetry integrate to zero over symmetric limits. A symmetric motion is produced by choosing an appropriate forward position for the foot on each step. In principle, symmetry of this sort can be used to simplify locomotion in systems with any number of legs and for a wide range of gaits.

- *Posture.* The third part of the control system stabilizes the pitch angle of the body to keep the body upright. Torques exerted between the body and leg about the hip accelerate the body about its pitch axis, provided that there is good traction between the foot and the ground. During the support period there is traction because the leg supports the load of the body. Linear feedback control operates on the hip actuator during each support period to restore the body to an upright posture.

Breaking down running into the control of these three functions simplifies locomotion. Each part of the control system acts as though it influences just one component of the behavior and the interactions that result from imperfect decoupling are treated as disturbances. The algorithms implemented to perform each part of the control task are themselves quite simple. Using the three part control system, the planar one-legged machine hops in place, travels at a specified rate, maintains balance when disturbed and jumps over small obstacles. Top running speed was about 2.6 mph.

16.5.2   Locomotion in Three Dimensions

The one-legged machine just described was mechanically constrained to operate in the plane, but useful legged systems must balance themselves in three dimensional space. Can the control algorithms used for hopping in the plane be generalized for hopping in three dimensions? A key to answering this question was the recognition that animal locomotion is primarily a planar activity, even though animals are three dimensional systems. Films of a kangaroo hopping on a treadmill first suggested this point. The legs sweep fore and aft through large angles, the tail sweeps in counter-oscillation to the legs, and the body bounces up and down. These motions all occur in the sagittal plane, with little or no motion normal to the plane.

Sesh Murthy realized that the plane in which all this activity occurs can generally be defined by the forward velocity vector and the gravity vector. He called this the *plane of motion* [14]. For a legged system without a preferred direction of travel, the plane of motion might vary from stride to stride, but it would be defined in the same way. We found that the three part decomposition could be used to control activity within the plane of motion.

We also found that the mechanisms needed to control the remaining *extraplanar* degrees of freedom could be cast into the original three part framework. For instance, the algorithm for placing the foot to control forward speed became a vector calculation. One component of foot placement determined forward speed in the plane of motion, whereas the other component caused the plane to rotate about a vertical axis, permitting the control system to steer. A similar extension applied to body posture. The result was a three dimensional, three part control system that was derived directly from the one used for the planar case.

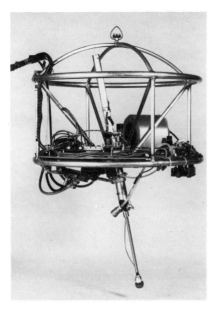

Figure 16.7
Three dimensional one-legged hopping machine used for experiments. The control system operated to regulate hopping height, forward velocity and body posture. Top recorded running speed was about 2.2 m/s (4.8 mph).

To explore these ideas, we built a second hopping machine which is shown in Figure 16.7. This machine has an additional joint at the hip to permit the leg to move sideways as well as fore and aft. This machine travels on an open floor without mechanical support. It balances itself as it hops along simple paths in the laboratory, traveling at a top speed of 4.8 mph.

16.5.3 Running on Several Legs

Experiments on machines with one leg were not motivated by an interest in one-legged vehicles. Although such vehicles might very well turn out to have merit,[1] our interest was in getting at the fundamentals of active balance and dynamics in the context of a simplified locomotion problem. In principle, results from machines with one leg could have value for understanding all sorts of legged systems, perhaps with any number of legs.

Our study of locomotion on several legs progressed in two stages. For a biped that runs like a human, with strictly alternating periods of support

---

[1]Wallace and Seifert saw merit in vehicles with one leg. Wallace patented a one-legged hopping tank that was supposed to be hard to hit because of its erratic movements. Seifert proposed the *Lunar Pogo* as a means of efficient travel on the moon.

and flight, the one-leg control algorithms apply directly. Because the legs are used in alternation, only one leg is active at a time. One leg is placed on the ground at a time, one leg thrusts on the ground at a time and one leg exerts a torque on the body at a time. We call this sort of running a *one-foot gait*. Assuming the behavior of the other leg does not interfere, the one-leg algorithms for hopping, forward travel and posture can each be used to control the active leg. Of course, to make this workable, some bookkeeping is required to keep track of which leg is active and which leg is idle, and it is required to keep the idle leg "out of the way."

Jessica Hodgins and Jeff Koechling demonstrated the effectiveness of this approach by using the one-leg algorithms to control each leg of a planar biped. The machine can run with an alternating gait, run by hopping on one leg, switch back and forth between gaits, and it can run fast. Top recorded speed is 13.1 mph. The planar biped also climbed a short flight of stairs, jumped through a hoop, and did a forward flip as shown in Figure 16.8 [3][4][6]. More recently, we demonstrated control of a three dimensional biped machine using the same approach.

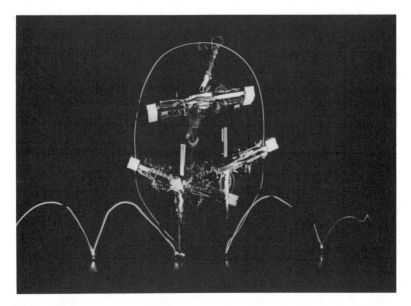

Figure 16.8
Planar biped doing a flip. The three images were made at the touchdown before the flip, the peak altitude of the flip, and the lift-off after the flip.

In principle, this approach could be used to control running on any number of legs, so long as just one leg touches the ground at a time. Unfortunately, when there are several legs, this approach runs into difficulties. There is a conflict between the need to provide balance and the need to move the legs without collisions. For the legs to provide balance, the feet must be positioned so as to sweep under the center of mass during support. This argues for attaching all the legs to the body directly at or below the center of mass. However, the legs must be able to swing without colliding with one another, suggesting separation between the hips (shoulders). In principle, it is possible for a quadruped to run using this approach, however they rarely do (Hildebrand, private communication).

An alternative is to use the legs in pairs. Suppose we introduce a new control mechanism that coordinates the legs of a pair to act like a single equivalent leg—what Ivan Sutherland called a *virtual leg*. Such coordination requires that: the two legs of a pair exert equal forces on the ground, they exert equal torques on the body, and the position of each leg's foot with respect to its hip be the same. To control locomotion, the three part control algorithms described previously specify the behavior of each virtual leg while the control system ensures that the physical legs move so as to obey the rules required for virtual leg behavior.

Using this approach there are three quadruped gaits to consider: the *trot* which uses diagonal legs in a pair, the *pace* which uses lateral legs in a pair, and the *bound* which uses the front legs as a pair and the rear legs as a pair.

We argue that the quadruped is like a virtual biped, that a biped is like a one-legged machine, and we already know how to control one-legged machines. A control system for quadruped running consists of a controller that coordinates each pair of legs to act like one virtual leg, a three part control system that acts on the virtual legs, and a bookkeeping mechanism that keeps track. Figure 16.9 shows a four-legged machine that trots, paces and bounds, and switches between gaits using this approach to control.

State	Trigger Event	Action
1 LOADING A	A touches ground	Zero hip torque A
		Shorten B
		Don't move hip B
2 COMPRESSION A	A air spring shortened	Erect body with hip A
		Shorten B
		Position B for landing
3 THRUST A	A air springs lengthening	Extend A
		Erect body with hip A
		Keep B short
		Position B for landing
4 UNLOADING A	A air spring near full length	Shorten A
		Zero hip torque A
		Keep B short
		Position B for landing
5 FLIGHT A	A not touching ground	Shorten A
		Don't move hip A
		Lengthen B for landing
		Position B for landing

States 6–10 repeat states 1–5, with A and B interchanged.

Table 16.3
Details of State Machine for Biped and Quadruped. The state shown in the left column is entered when the event listed in the center column occurs. During normal running states advance sequentially. During states 1–5, leg A is in support and leg B is in recovery. During states 6–10, these roles are reversed. For biped running A refers to leg 1 and B refers to leg 2. For quadruped trotting each letter designates a pair of physical legs.

Figure 16.9
Quadruped machine that runs by trotting, pacing, and bounding. The control algorithms are based on those used for one-leg running. Pairs of physical legs are treated
like single *virtual legs*, making quadruped running like biped running. The machine
has some ability to switch between gaits.

16.5.4   Computer Programs for Running

The behavior of the running machines just described was controlled by
a set of computer programs that ran on our laboratory computer. These
computer programs performed several functions including:

- sampling and filtering data from the sensors,

- transforming kinematic data between coordinate systems,

- executing the three part locomotion algorithms for hopping, forward speed and body attitude,

- controlling the actuators,

- reading operator instructions from the console, and

- recording running behavior.

The control computer was a VAX 11/785 running the UNIX operating
system. In order to provide real time service with short latency and high

bandwidth feedback, the real time control programs were implemented
as a device driver that resided within the UNIX kernel. The device
driver responded with short latency to a hardware clock that interrupted
through the UNIBUS every eight milliseconds. All sensors and actuators
were also accessed through interfaces connected to the UNIBUS. Each
time the clock ticked, the running machine driver programs sampled
and scaled data from the sensors, estimated joint and body velocities
to determine the state of the running machine, executed the three part
locomotion algorithms, and calculated a new output for each actuator.

The control programs were synchronized to the behavior of the running machine by a software finite-state machine. The state machine
made transitions from one state to another when sensory data from the
running machine satisfied the specified conditions. For instance, the
state machine made a transition from COMPRESSION to THRUST
when the derivative of the support leg's length changed from negative
to positive. Figure 16.10 and Table II give some detail for the state
machine that was used for the biped and quadruped running machines.
We found that using a state machine along with properly designed transition conditions aided the interpretation of sensory data by providing
noise immunity and hysteresis.

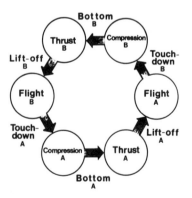

Figure 16.10
Simplified diagram of state machine that synchronizes the control programs to the
behavior of the running machine. This state machine is for the biped and quadruped
machines, but the one-legged state machines are similar. State transitions are determined by sensory events related to the hopping motion. A different set of control
actions are put into effect in each state, as indicated in Table 16.3.

Whereas sensory data determine when the state machine makes transitions, the resulting states determine which control algorithms operate to provide control. For instance, when the biped is in the THRUST A state, the control programs extend leg A, exert torque on hip A, shorten leg B and position foot B.

In addition to the real time programs that control the running machines, a top level program was used to control the real time programs. The top level program permitted the user to initiate a running experiment, select among control modes, examine or modify the variables and parameters used by the control programs, specify sensor calibration data, mark variables for recording, and save recorded real time data for later analysis and debugging. Each of these functions was accomplished by one or more system calls to the driver. The top level program had no particular time constraints, so it was implemented as a timesharing job that was scheduled by the normal UNIX scheduler.

16.6   The Development Of Useful Legged Robots

The running machines described in the previous section are not useful vehicles nor even prototypes for such vehicles. They are experimental apparatus used in the laboratory to explore ideas about legged locomotion. Each was designed to isolate and examine a specific locomotion problem, while postponing or ignoring many other problems. Let us now step back and ask what problems remain to be solved before legged robots can become practical machines that do useful work.

Terrain Sensing: Perhaps the deepest problem limiting current walking machines as well as other forms of autonomous vehicle, is their inability to perceive the shape and structure of their immediate surroundings. Humans and animals use their eyes to locate good footholds, avoid obstacles, measure their own rate and direction of progress, and navigate with respect to visible landmarks. The problem of giving machines the ability to see has received intensive and consistent attention for the past 25 or 30 years. There has been steady progress during that period. Current machines can see well enough to operate in well structured and partially structured environments, but it is difficult to predict when machines will be able to see well enough to operate autonomously in rough outdoor terrain. I do not expect to see such autonomous machine behavior for at least ten years.

Sensors simpler than vision may be able to provide solutions to certain parts of the problem under certain circumstances. For instance, sonar and laser range data may be used to detect and avoid nearby obstacles. Motion data may be used for measuring speed and direction of travel with techniques that are substantially simpler than those needed to perceive shape in three dimensions.

16.6.1   Travel on Rough Terrain

Complete knowledge of the geometry of the terrain, as might be supplied by vision or these other senses would not in itself solve the problem of walking or running on rough terrain. A system traveling over rough terrain needs to know or figure out what terrain shapes provide good footholds, which sequence of footholds would permit traversal of the terrain, and how to move so as to place the feet on the available footholds. It will be necessary to coordinate the dynamics of the vehicle with the dynamics of the terrain.

There are several ways that terrain becomes rough and therefore difficult to negotiate:

- not level;

- limited traction (slippery);

- areas of poor or nonexistent support (holes);

- vertical variations:

  - minor vertical variations in available footholds (less than about one half the of leg length), and

  - major vertical variations in available footholds (footholds separated vertically by distances comparable to the dimensions of the whole leg),

- large obstacles between footholds (poles); and

- intricate footholds, e.g., rungs of a ladder.

The techniques that will allow legged systems to operate in these sorts of terrain will involve the mechanics of locomotion, kinematics, dynamics, geometric representation, spatial reasoning and planning. Although course- and medium-grain knowledge of the terrain will be important, I expect techniques that make legged systems inherently insensitive to fine-grain terrain variations to play an important role too. Ignoring the hard sensing issues mentioned earlier, I believe the perception and control mechanisms required for legged systems to travel on rough terrain will require a substantial research effort, but the important problems can be solved within the next ten years if they are pursued vigorously.

16.6.2 Mechanical Design and System Integration

When the sensing and control problems are solved, it will remain to develop mechanical designs that function with efficiency and reliability. Useful vehicles must carry their own power, control computers and a payload. A host of interesting problems present themselves including such matters as energy efficiency, structural design, strength and weight of materials, and efficient control. For instance, the development of materials and structures for efficient storage and recovery of elastic energy will be particularly important for legged vehicles. I expect that early useful legged vehicles can be built with existing mechanical and aerospace technique, but performance will improve rapidly as designs are refined, embellished and improved.

16.7   Experiments in Animal Locomotion

Earlier in this paper I said that studying legged machines could help us to understand more about locomotion in animals. Detailed knowledge of concrete locomotion algorithms with well understood behavior might help us formulate experiments that elucidate the mechanisms used by humans and animals for locomotion. For instance, one might ask if animals control their forward speed, as each of the running machines do, by choosing a forward position for the leg during each flight phase with no adjustments during stance. Is there any decomposition of control? There are several questions like these that I am studying in collaboration with Thomas McMahon of Harvard University. The questions we would

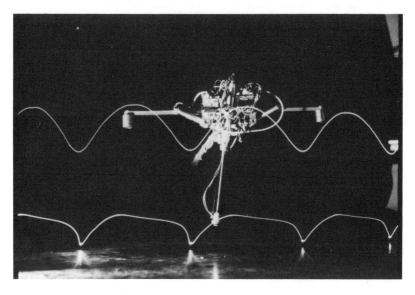

Figure 16.11
Planar hopping machine traveling at about 0.8 m/s (1.75 mph) from right to left. Lines made by light sources attached to the machine indicate paths of the foot and the hip.

like to answer are summarized in the following list. Each is based on observations or ideas that arose in the course of studying legged machines.

16.7.1 Animal Experiments Motivated by Robot Experiments

Algorithms for Balance. The legged machines and computer simulations we have studied all use a specific algorithm for determining the landing position of the foot with respect to the body's center of mass. The foot is advanced a distance based on the expected symmetric tipping behavior of an inverted pendulum.

Do animals use this algorithm to position their feet? To find out, one must measure small changes in the forward running speed, in the angular momentum of the body during the flight phase and in the placement of the feet. Rather than look at average behavior across many steps, as is done in studies of energetics and neural control, we must look at error terms within each step.

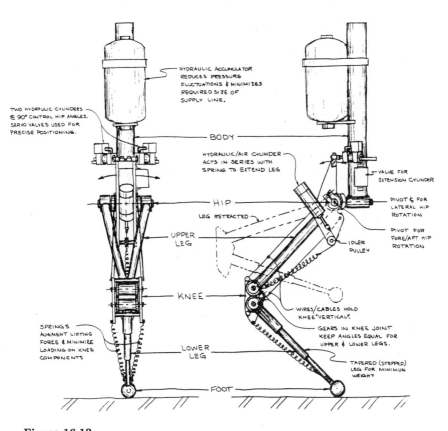

Figure 16.12
Ben Brown and I had this early concept for a one-legged hopping machine that was
to operate in three dimensions. This version never left the drawing board.

Symmetry in balance. Symmetry plays a central role in simplifying the
control of the dynamic legged robots described earlier. The symmetry
of interest specifies that motion of the body in space, and of the feet
with respect to the body, are even and odd functions of time during each
support period. See Figure 16.13. These are interesting motions because
they leave the forward and angular motion of the body unaccelerated
over a stride and therefore lead to steady state travel. Do animals run
with this sort of symmetry? To find out, we are examining film data for
several quadrupedal animals. Preliminary measurements show that the
galloping and trotting cat sometimes runs with symmetric motions [18].
We would like to know:

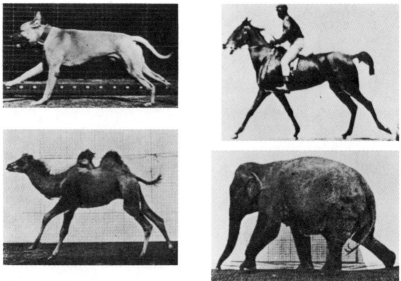

Figure 16.13
Symmetry in animal locomotion. Animals shown in symmetric configuration halfway through the stance phase for several gaits: rotary gallop (top left), transverse gallop (bottom left), canter (top right), and amble (bottom right). In each case the body is at minimum altitude, the center of support is located below the center of mass, the rearmost leg was recently lifted, and the frontmost leg is about to be placed. (Photographs from Muybridge reprinted with permission from Dover Press.)

- How universal is the use of symmetric running by animals, both in terms of different gaits and different animals?

- What is the precision of the observed symmetry?

- Does the symmetry extend to angular motion of the body, as the theory predicts?

- How do asymmetries in the mechanical structure of the body and legs influence motion symmetry?

Virtual Legs. To control the quadruped running machine, the control system synchronizes the behavior of pairs of legs that provides support during stance. The synchronization has three parts requiring that: the legs of a pair exert equal vertical forces on the ground, exert equal hip torque on the body, and displace their feet equal distances from the hip or shoulder. The result of such synchronization is called a *virtual leg* [22] because it makes two legs act like one equivalent leg located half way between the pair. The virtue of virtual legs is that they simplify the control algorithms for balance and dynamic control.

Do animals use virtual legs? To answer this question one must examine the horizontal and vertical forces exerted on the ground by both legs during double support in trotting or pacing. From these measurements, one can find the differential force or impulse. One would expect the differential force to be zero if the system were using a control strategy based on virtual legs. An important manipulation will be to disturb one or both of the feet during stance and to measure the active force response of the legs. Asymmetries in the distribution of mass in the system may require a somewhat generalized version of the virtual leg, in which a fixed ratio of forces, torques and displacements prevails.

Distribution of Body Mass. The distribution of mass in the body can have a fundamental influence on the behavior of a running system. In earlier work we defined the dimensionless group representing the normalized moment of inertia of the body, $j = J/(md^2)$, where J is the moment of inertia of the body, m is the mass of the body, and d is half the hip spacing. As shown in Figure 16.14, when $j = 1$ the hips are located at the centers of percussion of the body. Through computer simulations of a simplified model, we found that when $j < 1$ the attitude of the body in the sagittal plane can be passively stabilized when running with a bounding gait. However, when $j > 1$ stabilization was not passively obtained.

This finding has implications for the interaction between the mechanical structure of an animal and the control provided by the nervous system. Could it be that bounding animals do not actively control pitching of their bodies, but control only forward running speed and direction? A first step toward answering this question is to measure values of j for a variety of quadrupedal animals, and to relate the measurements to their preferred modes of running, trotting or pacing (no pitching) vs. bounding or galloping (pitching). Does the value of j for a quadruped vary with its trot-to-gallop transition speed? Anatomical measurements like those of Fedak, Heglund and Taylor (1982) will provide much of the data needed to answer this question.

Yaw Control. How do human runners keep themselves from rotating about the yaw axis? Control of this degree of freedom in the one-legged hopping machine is difficult because it does not have a foot that can exert a torsional torque on the ground. But humans have long feet that might be used to develop substantial torsional traction on the ground about the yaw axis. A first step in exploring this question would be to measure the torsional torque humans exert on the ground during running

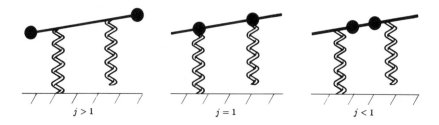

Figure 16.14
The dimensionless moment of inertia, $j = J/(md^2)$, predicts passive stability of the body's pitching motion for a simple simulated model (Left). For $j > 1$, a vertical force on the left foot causes the right hip to accelerate upward. The model has no passive pitch stability. (Center) For $j = 1$, the system acts as two separate oscillators, with neutral stability. (Right) When $j < 1$, an upward force on the left leg causes the right hip to accelerate downward. The model has passive pitch stability. (From Murphy and Raibert 1985.)

and to relate the measurements to yaw motions and yaw disturbances of the body.

16.7.2   Philosophy of Interaction Between Robotics and Biology

It is interesting to combine the study of animals with the study of machines. Biological systems provide both great motivation by virtue of their striking performance, and guidance with the details of their actions. They are existence proofs that give us a lower bound on what is possible. Unfortunately, biological systems are often too complicated to study—there are many variables, precise measurement is difficult, there are limitations on the experimenter's ability to manipulate the preparation, and perhaps, an inherent difficulty in focusing on the information level of a problem.

On the other hand, laboratory robots are relatively easy to build. Precisely controlled experiments are possible, as are careful measurements and manipulations, and the "subject" can be redesigned when necessary. However, the behavior of these experimental robot systems is impoverished when compared with the biological counterpart. They are easy to study, but they do not perform nearly so well as biological systems.

Analysis of living systems and synthesis of laboratory systems are complementary activities, each with strengths and weaknesses. Together, these activities can strengthen one another, leading to fundamental principles that elucidate the domain of both problems, independent of the particular implementation. Because machines face the same physical laws and environmental constraints that biological systems face when they perform similar tasks, the solutions they use may embrace similar principles. In solving the problem for the machine, we generate a set of plausible algorithms for the biological system. In observing the biological behavior, we explore plausible behaviors for the machine. In its grandest form, this approach lets the study of robotics contribute to both robotics and biology, and lets the study of biology contribute to both biology and robotics.

16.8   Acknowledgments

Support for this research was provided in part by the System Development Foundation grant number 86-10-10, and from the Defense Advanced Research Projects Agency of the Department of Defense under contract number MDA-972-88K-0007.

Bibliography

[1] V.S. Gurfinkel, E.V. Gurfinkel, A. Y. Schneider, E.A. Devjanin, A.V. Lensky, and L.G. Shitilman. Walking robot with supervisory control. *Mechanism and Machine Theory*, 16:31–36, 1981.

[2] S. Hirose and Y. Umetani. The basic motion regulation system for a quadruped walking vehicle. In *Proceedings of the ASME Conference on Mechanisms*, 1980.

[3] J. Hodgins. *Legged Robots on Rough Terrain: Experiments in Adjusting Step Length*. PhD thesis, Computer Science Department, Carnegie Mellon University, Pittsburgh, PA, 1989.

[4] J. Hodgins and M.H. Raibert. Biped gymnastics. *International Journal of Robotics Research*, 9(2), 1990.

[5] T. Kato, A. Takanishi, H. Jishikawa, and I. Kato. The realization of the quasi-dynamic walking by the biped walking machine. In *Proceedings of the Fourth Symposium on Theory and Practice of Robots and Manipulators*, pages 341–351, A. Morecki, G., Bianchi, and K. Kedzior editors, Polish Scientific Publishers, Warsaw, 1983.

[6] J. Koechling. *The Limits of Running Speed: Experiments with a Legged Robot*. PhD thesis, Mechanical Engineering Department, Carnegie Mellon University, Pittsburgh, PA, 1989.

[7] R.A. Liston and R.S. Mosher. A versatile walking truck. In *Proceedings of the Transportation Engineering Conference*, Institution of Civil Engineers, London, 1968.

[8] E. Lucas. Huitieme recreation—la machine a marcher. *Recreations Mathematiques*, 4:198–204, 1894.

[9] K. Matsuoka. A mechanical model of repetitive hopping movements. *Biomechanisms*, 5:251–258, 1980.

[10] T. McGeer. Powered flight, child's play, silly wheels and walking machines. In *Proceedings of the IEEE Conference on Robotics and Automation*, Phoenix, 1989.

[11] R.B. McGhee. Some finite-state aspects of legged locomotion. *Mathematical Biosciences*, 2:67–84, 1968.

[12] R.B. McGhee. Vehicular legged locomotion. In G.N. Saridis, editor, *Advances in Automation and Robotics.* JAI Press, 1983.

[13] H. Miura and I. Shimoyama. Dynamic walk of a biped. *International Journal Robotics Research,* 3:60–74, 1984.

[14] S.S. Murthy and M.H. Raibert. 3D balance in legged locomotion: modeling and simulation for the one-legged case. In *Inter-Disciplinary Workshop on Motion: Representation and Perception,* Association for Computing Machinery, 1983.

[15] E. Muybridge. *The Human Figure in Motion.* Dover Publications, New York, second edition, 1955. First edition, 1901 by Chapman and Hall, Ltd., London.

[16] E. Muybridge. *Animals in Motion.* Dover Publications, New York, second edition, 1957. First edition, 1899 by Chapman and Hall, Ltd., London.

[17] M.H. Raibert. *Legged Robots That Balance.* MIT Press, Cambridge, MA, 1986.

[18] M.H. Raibert. Symmetry in running. *Science,* 231:1292–1294, 1986.

[19] M.H. Raibert, M. Chepponis, and H.B. Brown, Jr. Running on four legs as though they were one. *IEEE Journal on Robotics and Automation,* 2, 1986.

[20] M.H. Raibert and I.E. Sutherland. Machines that walk. *Scientific American,* 248:44–53, 1983.

[21] J.F. Schaefer and R.H. Cannon, Jr. *On the Control of Unstable Mechanical Systems,* pages 6c.1–6c.13, International Federation of Automatic Control, London, 1966.

[22] I.E. Sutherland and M.K. Ullner. Footprints in the asphalt. *International Journal of Robotics Research,* 3:29–36, 1984.

[23] M. Vukobratovic and Y. Stepaneko. On the stability of anthropomorphic systems. *Mathematica Biosciences,* 14:1–38, 1972.

[24] K.J. Waldron, V.J. Vohnout, A. Pery, and R.B. McGhee. Configuration design of the adaptive suspension vehicle. *International Journal of Robotics Research,* 3:37–48, 1984.

17 Intelligence in Scientific Computing

Harold Abelson, Michael Eisenberg, Matthew Halfant, Jacob Katzenelson, Elisha Sacks, Gerald Jay Sussman, Jack Wisdom, Kenneth Yip

Abstract

Combining numerical techniques with ideas from symbolic computation and with methods incorporating knowledge of science and mathematics leads to a new category of intelligent computational tools for scientists and engineers. These tools autonomously prepare simulation experiments from high level specifications of physical models. For computationally intensive experiments, they automatically design special purpose numerical engines optimized to perform the necessary computations. They actively monitor numerical and physical experiments. They interpret experimental data and formulate numerical results in qualitative terms. They enable their human users to control computational experiments in terms of high level behavioral descriptions.

As an example of an intelligent computational tool, imagine an ocean engineer designing an offshore mooring tower for large ships. When standing free, such a tower can be modeled in a straightforward way, as an inverted pendulum anchored to the sea bed, driven by wave motion and restored to vertical position by its buoyancy in sea water. However, a massive ship attached to the mooring structure vastly complicates the dynamics: when the mooring line is slack, the restoring force is the same as before; but when the line is taut, the ship also exerts a force through tension in the line. Numerical simulations of such systems have shown that the effect of even small waves can lead to potentially dangerous resonances that can make the structure fail [26]. The goal of the engineer is to design a structure that can withstand the worst conditions that can

Author affiliations appear at the end of this chapter.
This paper appeared in *Communications of the ACM* 32(5), 1989 and is reprinted with permission from the ACM, Inc., New York.

be expected to occur in the environment without making the structure excessively expensive.

The following excerpt of a dialogue shows how we imagine an intelligent computer assistant aiding an ocean engineer in the design of such a structure. Assume that the engineer has already proposed a particular structure, either by drawing it or by combining previously defined structures.

$\vdots$

Computer: The dynamical equations for this model are: *(displays a very large set of equations)*.

Engineer: Call that the `full model`. Try to find a simpler approximate model.

Computer: The time constants for the bending moments and torsional stresses in equations 1 through 25 are very small compared with the period of lowest mode of the structure seen as a pendulum and with the periods of the largest components in our standard wave spectrum for this region of the gulf coast. Because the deflections of the structure are small we can use the following approximate model: *(displays a much smaller number of equations)*.

Engineer: Call that the `simplified model`.

Engineer: Characterize the response of the `simplified model` to the standard wave spectrum.

Computer: State-space analysis shows that the response of this system can be broken into three regions. For very small deflection angles (smaller than 2 degrees) there are stable oscillations, damped with time constants similar to the oscillation frequencies. Significant deflections toward the `boat` show trajectories with competing domains of attraction. There are large subharmonic responses. For deflections larger than about 10 degrees we find complex chaotic motions, but such large deflections violate the assumptions of the model.

Engineer: Characterize the response to the dominant frequency in the spectrum as the amplitude varies from 1 foot to 20 foot seas.

Computer: There are two families of periodic motions here: A and B. Family A is present at the start of the parameter range $s = 1$, with a periodic motion of order 1. At $s = 5.2$ this motion undergoes a symmetry-breaking bifurcation and splits into a pair of motions A_1 and A_2. As s increases, both A_1 and A_2 undergo period-doubling cascades: order 2 ($s = 6.5$), order 4 ($s = 9.8$), order 8 ($s = 10.7$), order 16 ($s = 10.9$). The cascade was not traced past the order 16 motions. Chaotic motions were observed at $s = 12$. Family B begins with a motion of order 1 arising from a fold bifurcation at $s = 8$. This motion persists through the end of the parameter range $s = 20$.

Engineer: How do the maximum stresses affect the structure?

Computer: Family A motions are within the safe operating region for structures of type UG/751 construction, but the family B motions can easily exceed the safe operating region in a 50 year storm.

Engineer: Perform the same analysis, assuming that we triple the buoyancy of the float.

Computer: The qualitative behavior in the two situations differs slightly in the initial phase of growth of oscillations. Once oscillations are established the behavior is approximately the same. The maximum deflections differ by less than 10% between the two situations, but the frequencies are very different.

Engineer: Begin design of an `active stabilizer` to damp the family B motions. Assume we install thrusters at positions halfway up the structure and at 90% of the height of the structure. Expand the `full model` to include drives from these thrusters. ...

$\vdots$

No systems as sophisticated as this engineer's assistant yet exist. However, computer programs incorporating important pieces of it are already in place. Generating stylized natural language is not too hard, although understanding unstructured English text is still difficult, and we will not address that problem in this paper. Additionally, our discussion is not really about ocean engineering; the scenario above is not intended to illustrate good design practice in that domain. Rather, our concern here is with the development of intelligent techniques appropriate for the automatic preparation, execution and control of numerical experiments, and with the automatic interpretation of their results.

- Our envisioned engineer's assistant begins with a description of a mechanism and automatically generates efficient numerical programs that predict its dynamical behavior. This may require more than just straightforward simulation. A stability-analysis task such as "characterize the response to the dominant frequency in the spectrum" requires compiling procedures that evolve, in addition to the state, the variations with respect to changes in initial conditions and the sensitivities with respect to changes in parameters.

- The engineer's assistant automatically prepares high performance numerical experiments. It has extensive knowledge of numerical methods and it can compose appropriate and correct numerical procedures tailored to the specific application. For critical applications, this compilation can be targeted to the automatic synthesis of special purpose hardware.

- The engineer's assistant interprets the results of numerical experiments in high level qualitative terms. This interpretation is based on general mathematical and physical knowledge that constrains the kind of behavior to expect. The interpretation is used to prepare a report to the user, but it is also used in the experimental protocol. The summary of behavior produced from observations of the results of previous experiments is used to automatically select critical values of experimental parameters for subsequent experiments, thus efficiently uncovering the salient phenomena.

The first section of this paper demonstrates significant portions of these capabilities. These include the automatic preparation and monitoring of numerical simulations, the automatic generation of qualitative interpretations of numerical results and the achievement of breakthrough performance on computationally demanding problems with the aid of

specially designed computers. (Our special purpose engine for computing planetary motions has produced the first solid numerical evidence
that the solar system's long term dynamics are chaotic, thereby answering the famous question of the stability of the solar system.)

The second section takes a closer look at the technology behind these
demonstration results. We explain how algorithms from computer vision are applied to interpret phase-space diagrams in dynamics. We
illustrate how knowledge about dynamical systems can be encoded using constraints and symbolic rules. We show how to formulate numerical
algorithms at appropriate levels of abstraction with higher-order procedures and how to combine these with symbolic algebra to automatically
generate numerical programs.

The third section sketches some next steps required to realize the
vision of systems like the engineer's assistant.

17.1 Numerical Modeling Can Be Automated

In a typical numerical modeling study, an investigator repeatedly prepares and runs a series of computations and examines the results at
each step to select interesting new values for parameters and initial conditions. When enough values have been tried, the investigator classifies
and interprets the results. Even with powerful numerical computers,
this process requires substantial human effort to prepare simulations,
and it relies upon significant human judgment to choose interesting values for parameters to determine when a simulation run is complete, and
to interpret numerical results in qualitative terms.

This section exhibits three programs that automate much of the above
process. The *Bifurcation Interpreter* investigates the steady-state orbits
in parameterized families of dynamical systems, classifying the types of
orbits and the bifurcations through which they change as parameters
vary. The *KAM* program autonomously explores nonlinear conservative
systems and produces qualitative descriptions of phase-space portraits
and bifurcations. Both programs automatically generate summary reports similar to those appearing in published papers in the experimental dynamics literature and in engineering studies of artifacts that have
complex dynamics, such as airfoils, ship hulls and mooring structures.
In addition, the capabilities demonstrated by these programs have ap-

plication in the design of intelligent automatic control systems. The breadth of applicability is illustrated by the *Kineticist's Workbench*, a program that models how chemists understand complex chemical reactions. It combines numerical and symbolic methods to characterize reaction mechanisms in qualitative terms that are useful for the working chemist.

We also discuss the place of special purpose numerical engines as scientific instruments and survey significant results in planetary dynamics obtained using the *Digital Orrery*.

17.1.1 Programs Can Discover and Interpret Qualitative Behavior

In a nonlinear dynamical system with a periodic drive, motion starting from any set of initial conditions will typically evolve to a steady-state orbit.[1] For a parameterized family of dynamical systems, tracing the changes in steady-state orbits as the parameters vary provides a valuable summary of the family's qualitative behavior. Much research in nonlinear dynamics is devoted to studying these *bifurcations*, or changes in type, of steady-state orbits. For one-parameter families at least, the bifurcations generically encountered have been classified and are well understood. Some examples are the *fold* bifurcation, at which a stable orbit can appear or vanish, the *flip* bifurcation, at which the period of an orbit doubles, and the *pitchfork* bifurcation, at which an orbit splits into two orbits of the same period. There are also commonly observed bifurcation sequences that occur as the parameter varies. An example is the *period-doubling cascade*, where the order of an orbit successively doubles via a sequence of increasingly closely spaced flip bifurcations, producing chaos.[2]

Dynamicists commonly gain insight into the qualitative behavior of nonlinear systems by developing summary descriptions of steady-state orbits and bifurcations. Figure 17.1 reproduced here from [7] shows a

---

[1] Possible types of steady-state orbits are periodic orbits, quasi-periodic orbits (which have discrete-frequency spectra, but not at rational multiples of the drive period) and chaotic orbits (which, loosely speaking, are steady-state orbits that are neither periodic nor quasi-periodic).

[2] Various authors use different, and sometimes incompatible, terminology to refer to these bifurcation types. For example, the flip is sometimes called a cusp or a pitchfork. We have adopted the terminology used in the book by Thompson and Stewart [27], which provides an introduction to the methods of nonlinear dynamics together with an extensive bibliography.

schematic summary drawn by a physicist based on numerical studies of the two dimensional Navier-Stokes equation for an incompressible fluid. As the Reynolds number of the fluid increases, the steady-state orbits evolve through a sequence of bifurcations. The diagram summarizes how the evolving orbits can be grouped into four distinct families.

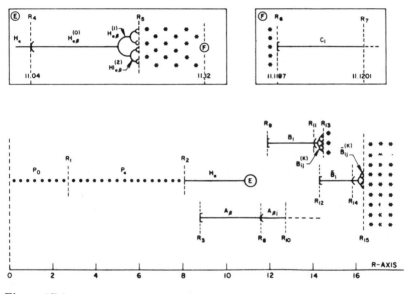

Figure 17.1
This diagram, reproduced from a published paper in fluid mechanics, is a physicist's schematic summary description of an approximation to the two dimensional Navier-Stokes equation for an incompressible fluid. The varying parameter here is the Reynolds number. (Reprinted with permission from *Physics of Fluids*, 26(2), 1983.)

The *Bifurcation Interpreter*, a computer program being developed at MIT by Harold Abelson, automatically generates such summary descriptions for one-parameter families of periodically driven dynamical systems. The dynamical system can be specified by differential equations to be integrated, by a period map that directly computes successive states at multiples of the drive period, or by a description of a physical model such as an electrical network. Given a dynamical system, a parameter range to explore and a domain in state-space, the interpreter discovers periodic orbits, tracks their evolution as the parameter varies, and locates and classifies bifurcations. Using this information, the pro-

gram categorizes the orbits into families and produces a summary report
that describes each family and its evolution through bifurcations.

Here is a sample input to the interpreter:

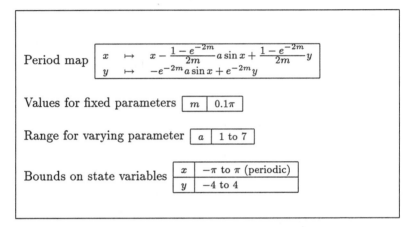

The system to be investigated models the vibration of a hinged bar
with viscous damping subjected to a fixed direction periodic impact
load at the free end. This problem is discussed in [13], which derives the
period map for this motion. Here x is the angular displacement and y
is the angular velocity, a specifies magnitude of the load and m specifies
the damping factor. The interpreter is asked to explore the system as
the load ranges from 1 to 7. With this specification, the interpreter
analyzes the system and generates the following report:

There are two distinct families of periodic orbits, A and B.

Family A is already present at the start of the parameter
range $a = 1$ as a periodic orbit A_0 of order 1. At $a = 4.130$
there is a supercritical flip bifurcation at which A_0 undergoes
period doubling to produce a periodic orbit A_1 of order 2.
At $a = 6.489$ there is a supercritical pitchfork bifurcation
at which the family A splits into subfamilies $A(1)$ and $A(2)$,
beginning with A_1 splitting into two periodic orbits of order
2. As the parameter a increases, each subfamily undergoes
a period-doubling cascade via a sequence of supercritical flip
bifurcations to order 4 at $a = 6.838$, order 8 at $a = 6.891$,
order 16 at $a = 6.901$, order 32 at $a = 6.903$. The period-

doubling cascade was not traced past the order 32 orbit, which apparently period doubles again at $a = 6.904$.

Family B first appears at $a = 3.969$ with an orbit B_0 of order 4 appearing at a fold bifurcation. As the parameter a increases, B undergoes a period-doubling cascade via a sequence of supercritical flip bifurcations to order 8 at $a = 4.239$, order 16 at $a = 4.239$, order 32 at $a = 4.251$. The period-doubling cascade was not traced past the order 32 orbit, which apparently period doubles again at $a = 4.252$.

The program can display this information as a diagram (Figure 17.2) in which this (preliminary version) describes the behavior of a periodically-impacted hinged beam as the load varies, exhibiting the evolution of two different families of steady-state motions. This is similar in style to manually developed Navier-Stokes analysis in Figure 17.1.[3]

17.1.2   Smart Programs Can See What Not To Compute

Dynamical behavior is complex, but it is not arbitrary. There is structure on phase space that restricts the classes of legal trajectories and provides a grammar of legal phase portraits. For example, trajectories of autonomous systems cannot intersect and, as we vary the initial conditions, the trajectories vary smoothly except at isolated places where the behavior changes. As we vary parameters, the phase portrait changes qualitatively only at bifurcations. In Hamiltonian systems, the evolution of the phase space is area-preserving, which greatly restricts the classes of possible structures that can occur in the phase space. This kind of knowledge enables dynamicists to infer a good understanding of a physical system from only a small, but well chosen, set of experiments.

The phase portrait in Figure 17.3, taken from a historically important paper in dynamics by M. Hénon [9], describes how adding a simple quadratic nonlinearity to a linear rotation can lead to dramatic changes in dynamical behavior. Observe how the figure characterizes the dynamics by showing only a few orbits. Presumably, Hénon was able to generate this figure after performing only a few judiciously chosen numerical experiments.

---

[3]The diagram-generation program illustrated in Figure 17.2 was developed by Ognen Nastov.

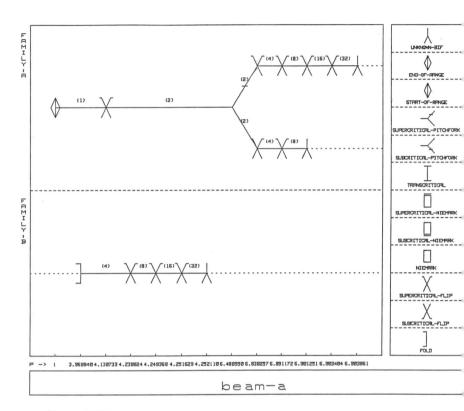

Figure 17.2
The Bifurcation Interpreter automatically generates summary descriptions of dynamical systems similar to those appearing in published papers.

The *KAM* program developed by Kenneth Yip at MIT can analyze systems in the same way [30][31]. It knows enough about the constraints on the structure of phase space to choose initial conditions and parameters as cleverly as an expert dynamicist. KAM's summary description of Hénon's map is shown in Figure 17.4. Observe that this is almost identical to the summary presented by Hénon. Moreover, KAM was able to deduce this description after trying only ten initial conditions.

KAM's ability to control numerical experiments arises from the fact that it not only produces pictures for us to see—it also *looks at* the pictures it draws, visually recognizing and classifying different orbit types as they numerically evolve. By combining techniques from computer

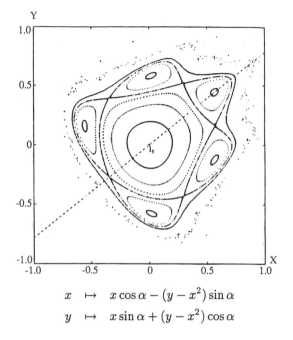

$$x \;\mapsto\; x \cos \alpha - (y - x^2) \sin \alpha$$
$$y \;\mapsto\; x \sin \alpha + (y - x^2) \cos \alpha$$

Figure 17.3
Hénon's summary of the dynamics of the map for $\cos \alpha = .24$. (Reprinted with permission from *Quarterly of Applied Mathematics*, 27(3), 1969.)

vision with sophisticated dynamical invariants, KAM is able to exploit mathematical knowledge, represented in terms of a "grammar" that dictates consistency constraints on the structure of phase space. When it chooses new initial conditions to explore, it does so in an attempt to make the picture consistent with these constraints. In addition to drawing the picture, KAM generates a textual analysis that explains what the program "sees." Here is KAM's description of the picture it generates for Hénon's map.

The portrait has an elliptic fixed point at $(0, 0)$. Surrounding the fixed point is a regular region bounded by a KAM curve with rotation number between 1/5 and 1/4. Outside the regular region lies a chain of five islands. The island chain is bounded by a KAM curve with rotation number between

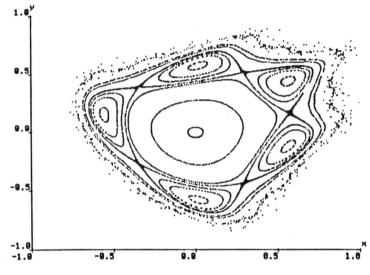

Figure 17.4
The KAM program generates a summary of Hénon's map

4/21 and 5/26. The outermost region is occupied by chaotic orbits that eventually escape.

17.1.3   Programs Can Construct and Analyze Approximations

A powerful strategy for analyzing a complicated dynamical system is to approximate it with a simpler system, analyze the approximation and map the results back to the original system. The approximations must be accurate enough to reproduce the essential properties of the original system, yet simple enough to be analyzed efficiently. Human experts have found that piecewise linear approximations satisfy both criteria for a wide class of models. The PLR program, developed by Elisha Sacks at MIT, exploits this fact to automate the analysis of second order autonomous ordinary differential equations [22][23]. It derives the qualitative behavior of intractable equations by approximating them with piecewise linear equations and constructing phase diagrams of the approximations.

PLR constructs a composite phase diagram for a piecewise-linear system by combining the local phase diagrams of its linear regions. It employs the standard theory of linear equations to ascertain the local phase diagrams. Linear systems have simple, well understood dynamics. Either all trajectories are periodic, all approach a fixed point, or all approach infinity. PLR pastes together the local phase diagrams by determining which sequences of regions trajectories can traverse. It summarizes the results by a *transition graph* whose nodes and links represent regions and transitions. Each path through the transition graph of a piecewise-linear system indicates that trajectories traverse the corresponding regions in the prescribed order. Loops denote trajectories that remain in one region forever, whereas longer cycles denote trajectories that continually shift between a sequence of regions.

As a simple example, PLR can qualitatively analyze the behavior of an undriven van der Pol oscillator, a simple nonlinear circuit consisting of a capacitor, an inductor and a nonlinear resistor connected in series. The current through the circuit obeys the equation

$$i'' + \frac{k}{L}(i^2 - 1)i' + \frac{1}{LC}i = 0$$

with C the capacitance, L the inductance and k a scaling factor. PLR approximates this equation with a piecewise linear equation and constructs the phase diagram and transition graph shown in Figure 17.5. It deduces that the system oscillates from the fact that tracing edges starting from any node in the graph leads to a cycle. Intuitively, the system oscillates because the nonlinear resistor adds energy to the circuit at low currents and drains energy at high currents.

17.1.4 Domain Knowledge Can Guide Numerical Modeling

Mike Eisenberg's *Kineticist's Workbench*, also being developed at MIT, is a program that combines general knowledge of dynamics with specific knowledge about chemical reactions in the analysis, understanding and simulation of complex chemical reaction mechanisms.

Chemists, in trying to model reactions, typically hypothesize a set of elementary reaction steps (corresponding to molecular collisions) that constitute a proposed pathway for the overall reaction. This collection of elementary steps may be large. It usually gives rise to a mathematical model consisting of many tightly coupled nonlinear differential equations. The problem of simulating such a system can be formidable, but a simulation merely provides numerical results. Even more important

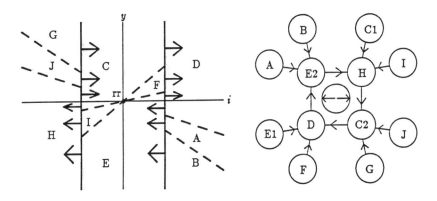

Figure 17.5
PLR's phase diagram and transition graph for its piecewise linear van der Pol approximation. Arrows indicate boundaries that trajectories cross.

to the chemist is to achieve some sort of *qualitative* understanding of the reaction mechanism. The Kineticist's Workbench combines numerical simulation with a variety of symbolic methods in order to characterize reaction mechanisms in terms that are meaningful to the working chemist such as "equilibrium," "steady states" and "oscillations."

The Workbench also suggests ways to simplify complex mechanisms. The key idea here is that the program can use its qualitative characterization of a given mechanism's behavior to determine which steps within the mechanism have an important behavioral effect, and which are superfluous and may therefore be dropped from the chemist's model.

The following scenario shows how the Workbench is intended to interact with a user in the analysis of a chemical process. The initial information is specified as follows:

Step no.	Step	Rate Constant
(1)	$C \to B$	300
(2)	$B \to C$	100
(3)	$A \to X$	1
(4)	$B + X \to Y + D$	1
(5)	$2X + Y \to 3X$	0.333
(6)	$X \to E$	1
(7)	$C \to F$	100

External sources for species C (rate of addition: 100 mmol/ liter-sec).

Concentration of A assumed constant at 1 mmol/liter. Initial concentrations of all species besides A are 0 mmol/liter.

With this specification, the Workbench responds:

The mechanism may be decomposed into two submechanisms. The first may be written as follows:[4]

$$(1.1) \quad [External] \leftrightarrow C \leftrightarrow B \to [External]$$

This submechanism results in a rapid equilibrium between C and B; the final concentrations of both C and B (1 and 3 mmol/liter, respectively) are independent of their initial concentrations.[5]

The second submechanism may be written as follows:

$$(2.1) \quad [External] \leftrightarrow X$$
$$(2.2) \quad B + X \to Y$$
$$(2.3) \quad 2X + Y \to 3X.$$

Since the concentration of B in the first submechanism is constant at 3 mmol/liter, the second submechanism may be further simplified as follows:

---

[4]The notation [External] used in this example is a catchall used to indicate the presence of external sources or sinks for some species. The notation corresponds roughly to the "zero complex" notation of Feinberg [6].

[5]In performing this simplification, the Workbench has treated the original reaction (7) as the presence of an external sink for species C, since the concentration of species F merely grows with time and does not affect any other species. Similarly, reaction (4), being slow compared to all the reactions included in (1.1), may be treated as a slow (but time varying) sink for species B. This reasoning could be exposed at the user's request.

(2.1′)   [*External*] ↔ $X \rightarrow Y$
(2.2′) $2X + Y \rightarrow 3X$.

Simulation of this second mechanism reveals that the concentrations of X and Y oscillate over time. Each oscillation consists of five phases: (1) slow growth in the concentrations of X and Y; (2) more rapid growth in X; (3) large jump in X and decline in Y; (4) large decline in X and increase in Y; and (5) slower decline in X and slow increase in Y. The time between oscillation peaks is approximately 17.8 seconds.

The chemist now asks the program to compare the results of the approximate mechanism (2.1′–2.2′) with the numerically exact results of mechanism (1–7), comparing the qualitative behavior of the two mechanisms as reflected in species X and Y. The workbench responds:

The qualitative behavior of the two mechanisms differs slightly during the initial phase of slow growth in X and Y. Once oscillations begin, the exact mechanism (1–7) displays the same qualitative structure as the approximate mechanism (2.1′–2.2′), and the period is still approximately 17.8 seconds. The concentrations of X and Y at comparable points in the oscillations differ by less than 2 percent between the two mechanisms.

The chemist now tries a different variation on the original reaction, and alters the original mechanism so that the concentration of A is not constant over time, but is rather an explicit function of time, as given by the equation

$$[A] = 1 + \sin t.$$

The workbench responds:

The decomposition into submechanisms is not affected; nor is the constant concentration of B. Again, the concentrations of X and Y appear to be oscillating, but each oscillation now consists of eight phases, instead of five, as before.

It is worth noting some of the key features of this example. First, the Workbench is able to decompose the original mechanism into two submechanisms, each of which is capable of independent simulation; this simplifies both the analysis and simulation of the larger mechanism. Second, the Workbench is able to decompose the first of the two sub-mechanisms in terms of a dichotomy between fast and slow steps; this allows the program to approximate the submechanism as a system in equilibrium. Third, the program uses numerical simulation to derive equilibrium concentrations for this submechanism. Finally, the Work-bench is able to describe the results of simulating the second submech-anism in terms of a succession of qualitative episodes characterized by changing growth rates of the species X and Y.

17.1.5   Fast Computers Need Not Be Large or Expensive

Numerical modeling often requires substantial resources. Scientists and engineers have traditionally obtained these resources either by acquiring large scale computers or renting time on them. However, a specialized computer can be simple and physically small. Indeed, it may be just as easy to design, build and program a special purpose computer than to develop software for general purpose supercomputers. Moreover, the specialized computer can become an ordinary experimental instrument belonging to the research group that made it, thus avoiding the admin-istrative burden and the scheduling problems associated with expensive, shared resources.

The question of the stability of the solar system is probably the most famous long standing problem in astrodynamics. In fact, it was inves-tigations into precisely this problem that inspired Poincaré to develop the modern qualitative theory of dynamical systems. In 1988, Gerald Sussman and Jack Wisdom completed a series of numerical experiments at MIT demonstrating that the long term motion of the planet Pluto, and by implication the dynamics of the solar system, is chaotic [25].

The stability question was settled using the Digital Orrery [4], a spe-cial purpose numerical engine optimized for high precision numerical integrations of the equations of motion of small numbers of gravitation-ally interacting bodies. Using 1980 technology, the device is about one cubic foot of electronics, dissipating 150 watts. On the problem it was designed to solve, it is measured to be 60 times faster than a VAX 11/780 with FPA, or 1/3 the speed of a Cray-1.

Figure 17.6 shows the exponential divergence of nearby Pluto trajec-tories over 400 million years. This data is taken from an 845-million-year integration performed with the Orrery. Before the Orrery, high precision integrations over simulated times of millions of years were prohibitively expensive. The longest previous integration of the outer planets was for five million years, performed on a Japanese supercomputer in 1984 [14]. Even though the Orrery is not as fast as the fastest supercomputer, its small scale and relative low cost mean that it can be dedicated to long computations in ways that a conventional supercomputer could not. To perform the integration that established Pluto's chaotic behavior, the Orrery ran continually for five months.

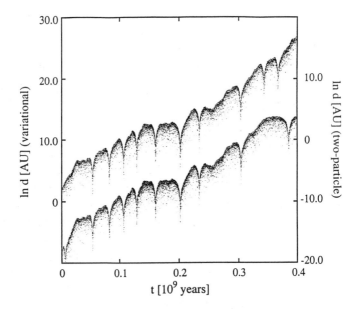

Figure 17.6
The exponential divergence of nearby trajectories is indicated by the average linear growth of the logarithms of the distance measures as a function of time. In the upper trace we see the growth of the variational distance around a reference trajectory. In the lower trace we see how two Plutos diverge with time. The distance saturates near 45AU; note that the semi-major axis of Pluto's orbit is about 40AU. The variational method of studying neighboring trajectories does not have the problem of saturation. Note that the two methods are in excellent agreement until the two-trajectory method has nearly saturated.

The Orrery was designed and built by six people in only nine months. This was possible only because of novel software support for the design process. The simulator for the Orrery is partially symbolic—simulated registers hold symbolic values and simulated arithmetic parts combine these to produce algebraic expressions (in addition to checking timing and electrical constraints). This means that a successful simulation yields a simulated memory containing algebraic expressions that can be checked for correctness.

17.2 Intelligent Numerical Computing Rests on AI Technology

The illustrations above achieve their impressive results by bringing symbolic methods to bear on the problems of numerical computation. Some of these techniques are traditional AI methods, which achieve new power when they are combined with deep knowledge of dynamical systems. The KAM program, for example, uses techniques from machine vision to recognize and classify the relevant geometrical properties of the trajectories. The Bifurcation Interpreter uses algebraic manipulation and knowledge about the local geometry of bifurcations to automatically generate numerical procedures that track periodic orbits. The key to automatically generating high performance numerical algorithms is to express knowledge of numerical analysis at an appropriate level of abstraction. This is supported by a library of numerical methods that is organized around the liberal use of higher-order procedural abstractions. With this organization, one constructs sophisticated numerical methods by mixing and matching standard components in well understood ways. The resulting programs are both more perspicuous and more robust than conventional numerical methods. For example, a procedure by Gerald Roylance that automatically generates special functions has constructed a Bessel function routine that is 40 times more accurate than the National Bureau of Standards approximation, for the same amount of computation.

17.2.1   The KAM Program Exploits Techniques From Computer Vision

Kenneth Yip's KAM program is notable because it applies judgment, similar to that of an expert dynamicist, in directing the course of its numerical experiments. In making judicious choices of what to try next, KAM must interpret what it sees. This process occurs in three phases: aggregation, clustering and classification. The images of an initial point produced by iterating the map forms a set of isolated points. This orbit must be classified. In Hamiltonian systems, there are three types of orbits to distinguish. In a surface of section, periodic orbits appear as isolated points, quasi-periodic orbits appear as closed curves or island chains, and chaotic orbits appear to take up regions of two dimensional space. KAM must also aggregate the components of an orbit so that it can be further classified. It must be able to determine the number of islands in an island chain, as this number gives the period of the enclosed periodic point. KAM must be able to estimate the centroid and area enclosed by a curve and to recognize the shape of a curve. KAM implements these abilities with techniques from computational geometry and computer vision.

KAM classifies orbits using methods based on the Euclidean minimal spanning tree—the tree that interconnects all the points with minimal total edge length—which it constructs by means of the Prim-Dijkstra algorithm [5]. For each subtree of the spanning tree, KAM examines the degree of each of its nodes, where the degree of a node is the number of nodes connected to it in the subtree. For a smooth curve, the spanning tree consists of two terminal nodes of degree one and other nodes of degree two. For a point set that fills an area, its corresponding spanning tree consists of many nodes having degree three or higher (Figure 17.7).

To aggregate points, KAM deletes from the tree edges that are significantly longer than nearby edges, following an aggregation algorithm suggested by Zahn [32]. This divides the tree into connected components. Figure 17.8 shows how the program aggregates points of a quasi-periodic orbit and recognizes it as an island chain.

To compute the area and centroid of the region bounded by a curve, KAM generates an ordered sequence of points from the spanning tree, and spline-interpolates the sequence to obtain a smooth curve. Straightforward algorithms are then applied to compute the area and centroid.

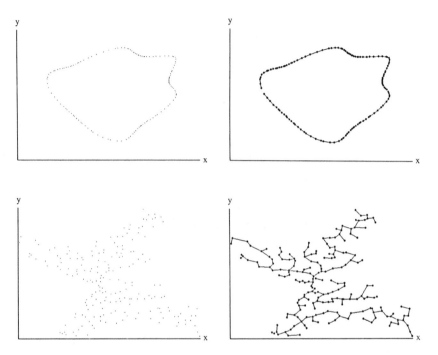

Figure 17.7
Starting with the successive iterates of a point, KAM classifies orbits using algorithms
from machine vision. As shown above, a quasi-periodic orbit can be distinguished
from a chaotic orbit by examining the branching factor in the Euclidean minimal
spanning tree.

Shape recognition is accomplished using scale-space methods pioneered
by Witkin [29].

17.2.2   AI Techniques Can Implement Deep Mathematical
Knowledge

Viewed as abstract examples of AI technology, our demonstration programs are hardly novel. The uniqueness of these programs, and the
source of their power, is that they use classic AI methods to exploit
specific domain knowledge based on rigorous mathematical results.

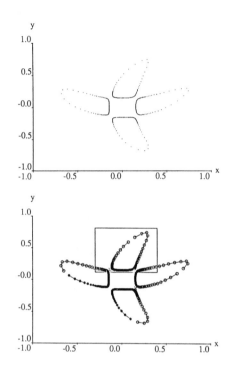

Figure 17.8
KAM uses the minimal spanning tree to cluster orbits into components. The components of an island chain can be isolated by detecting long edges in the spanning tree and deleting these from the graph.

PLR, for instance, combines geometric reasoning, symbolic algebra and inequality reasoning to test whether trajectories of a piecewise linear system cross between adjacent regions in phase space. For a trajectory to cross from region R to S via boundary u, its tangent t at the intersection point with u must form an acute angle with the normal n, as shown in Figure 17.9. This geometric condition is equivalent to the algebraic condition that the inner product $t \cdot n$ be positive. Hence, a transition exists from R to S unless $t \cdot n \le 0$ everywhere on u. PLR resolves the inequality $t \cdot n \le 0$ on u with the BOUNDER inequality reasoner [21].

PLR combines symbolic reasoning with deep knowledge about dynamical systems to interpret the transition graphs that it constructs. For example, the transition graph for the van der Pol equation shows that all trajectories spiral around the origin, but tells nothing of whether they

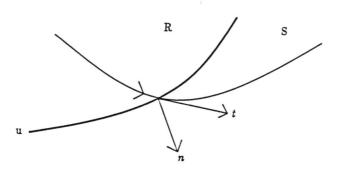

Figure 17.9
Trajectory crossing from R to S via u: the tangent t at the crossing point must form an acute angle with n, the normal to u that points into S.

move inward, move outward or wobble around. PLR invokes a difficult theorem to prove that all trajectories converge to a unique limit cycle. It tests the preconditions of the theorem by proving inequalities and manipulating symbolic expressions.

The KAM program limits the number of phase-space trajectories it must explore by drawing upon constraint analysis, as pioneered by Waltz [28]. As in any constraint analysis, KAM relies upon "grammar" that expresses the consistent ways in which primitive elements can be combined. In KAM's case, the primitive elements incorporate sophisticated mathematical invariants, and the grammatical rules embody deep theorems about the behavior of dynamical systems.

One such invariant, for example, is the *rotation number* of an orbit, a quantity that measures the asymptotic average of the angular distances between any two successive iterates in units of 2π-radians. A rule in KAM's grammar embodies a theorem that the rotation numbers of nearby orbits must change continuously [16]. As an example of how this is used, suppose that KAM has located two nearby almost periodic orbits having rotation numbers ρ_1 and ρ_2 respectively. Suppose ρ_1 is slightly smaller than 1/5, and ρ_2 slightly larger. With only these two orbits, KAM's evolving phase-space picture cannot be complete. By continuity, KAM expects to find a third, nearby orbit with rotation number exactly equal to 1/5, that is, a periodic orbit of period 5, which KAM proceeds to search for and classify.

In a similar manner, Abelson's Bifurcation Interpreter draws upon knowledge of the geometry of typical changes in the steady-state orbits of one-parameter families of dynamical systems. Periodic orbits of a periodically-driven oscillator can be identified as fixed points of the *period map*, which maps a state to the end point of the trajectory starting from that state and evolving for one period of the drive. Stability of an orbit is determined by the stability of the corresponding fixed point. If the interpreter notices that a stable orbit suddenly becomes unstable as the family parameter increases, it attempts to explain this change as the result of a bifurcation. The type of bifurcation can be conjectured by examining the eigenvalues of the period map at the fixed point, and the conjecture can be verified by a search that is tailored to the local geometry for that bifurcation type.

For example, for a stable orbit, the complex eigenvalues of the corresponding fixed point of the period map must lie within the unit circle. If stability is lost with an eigenvalue apparently crossing the unit circle at -1, a classification theorem for bifurcations [11] tells the interpreter to expect that this is a supercritical-flip bifurcation, which corresponds to a period doubling of the orbit. Near the bifurcation one should expect to see a stable orbit just before the critical parameter value and, just after the critical value, an unstable orbit together with a stable orbit of double the period. For this type of bifurcation, the interpreter attempts to locate the new expected orbits using a search technique that detects fixed points by computing the *Poincaré index* of the period map [12]. If these orbits are located, the bifurcation is probably a flip. If a different local geometry is found, the apparent bifurcation may be the result of numerical error, or the interaction of two nearby bifurcations, or it may be a bifurcation of nonstandard type. In any case, the result of the search is passed to a critic that attempts to reconcile the local results for all bifurcations detected and produce a consistent description.

Going beyond general knowledge of dynamical systems, the Kineticist's Workbench program employs a number of techniques specific to the domain of chemical kinetics. For example, the program examines the qualitative history of a reaction simulation, attempting to find periods of time during which concentrations of some species may be treated as constant; this is an automation of the type of steady-state analysis that is a staple of kinetic investigation [15]. Another portion of the program—that portion devoted to spotting fast equilibria within a mechanism—makes extensive use of the *reaction network* formalism developed by Feinberg, Horn, Jackson and coworkers at the University of Rochester [6]. An especially fruitful result of their work is the *zero-deficiency theorem*, which provides a simple algorithmic test for determining whether a reaction mechanism gives rise to stable equilibria. Finally, the portion of the Workbench program devoted to decomposing mechanisms according to mutual influence between species may be used to identify transient species, and to drop those species from a particular simulation as soon as their concentrations are deemed too low to affect the remainder of the simulation.

17.2.3 Numerical Experiments can be Prepared Automatically

Translating high level specifications into high quality numerical routines can be a tedious and error prone process whose difficulty limits the utility of even the most powerful numerical computers. A program by Harold Abelson and Gerald Sussman draws upon a spectrum of computational tools—numerical methods, symbolic algebra and semantic constraints (such as dimensions)—to automate the preparation and execution of numerical simulations [2]. These tools are designed so that combined methods, tailored to particular problems, can be constructed on the fly. One can use symbolic algebra to automatically generate numerical procedures, and one can use domain-specific constraints to guide algebraic derivations and to avoid complexity.

Figure 17.10 shows the wiring diagram for a simple nonlinear circuit, a driven van der Pol oscillator consisting of voltage source, a capacitor, an inductor and a nonlinear resistor with the cube-law characteristic $v = ai^3 - bi$. The figure also shows a description of this wiring diagram in a language formulated for describing electrical networks. This description specifies circuit's parameters, its primitive parts and how the parts are interconnected.

Given this description, the program combines models of the primitive elements to form equations that are then algebraically solved to produce state equations for the van der Pol oscillator. The state equations are compiled into a procedure (the system derivative) that will evolve

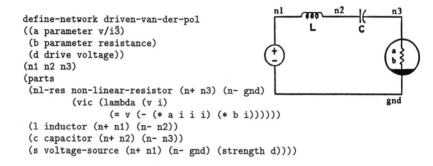

```
define-network driven-van-der-pol
((a parameter v/i3)
 (b parameter resistance)
 (d drive voltage))
(n1 n2 n3)
(parts
 (nl-res non-linear-resistor (n+ n3) (n- gnd)
        (vic (lambda (v i)
               (= v (- (* a i i i) (* b i))))))
 (l inductor (n+ n1) (n- n2))
 (c capacitor (n+ n2) (n- n3))
 (s voltage-source (n+ n1) (n- gnd) (strength d))))
```

Figure 17.10
The wiring diagram of a simple nonlinear circuit is described by means of a special-purpose language of electrical networks. This description can be automatically compiled into numerical procedures that evolve the state of the system.

the system numerically when combined with an appropriate numerical integrator.

These operations can involve a nontrivial amount of algebraic manipulation. Even for systems that are specified in closed form, most nonlinear systems cannot be algebraically solved to produce explicit state equations. In the general case, the program recognizes variables that cannot be eliminated from the state equations and compiles an iterative scheme for approximating these variables. This requires symbolic differentiation to produce a Jacobian that is incorporated into a Newton-Raphson search and to augment the system state so that it will evolve good starting points for Newton's method at each step of the integration.

For applications such as the Bifurcation Interpreter, one must also compile numerical routines that find period orbits and track them as the system parameters vary. Finding and tracking periodic orbits rests upon determining the sensitivity of trajectories to variations in initial state and parameters. This can be done by evolving the variational system, obtained by symbolic manipulation of the state equations, and by evolving various derived systems obtained by differentiating the state equations with respect to parameters.

Figure 17.11 shows a numerical routine, automatically generated from the circuit description in Figure 17.10, that can be combined with a numerical integrator to evolve the states and the variational states of the driven van der Pol oscillator.

```
(lambda (c.c l.l d b a)
  (lambda (*varstate*)
    (let ((t (vector-ref *varstate* 0))
          (v.c (vector-ref *varstate* 1))
          (i.l (vector-ref *varstate* 2))
          (v.c.del.v.c (vector-ref *varstate* 3))
          (v.c.del.i.l (vector-ref *varstate* 4))
          (i.l.del.v.c (vector-ref *varstate* 5))
          (i.l.del.i.l (vector-ref *varstate* 6)))
      (let ((g27 (* a i.l i.l)))
        (let ((g28 (* -3 g27)))
          (vector 1
                  (/ i.l c.c)
                  (/ (+ (* -1 g27 i.l) (* -1 v.c) (* b i.l) (d t))
                     l.l)
                  (/ v.c.del.i.l c.c)
                  (/ (+ (* -1 v.c.del.v.c)
                        (* b v.c.del.i.l)
                        (* g28 v.c.del.i.l))
                     l.l)
                  (/ i.l.del.i.l c.c)
                  (/ (+ (* -1 i.l.del.v.c)
                        (* b i.l.del.i.l)
                        (* g28 i.l.del.i.l))
                     l.l)))))))
```

Figure 17.11
This numerical procedure is the augmented system derivative generator for evolving states for the driven van der Pol oscillator. The procedure was automatically generated from the circuit description shown above.

The result of the physical modeling, algebraic manipulation, and fancy compilation shown above in Figure 17.11 is a higher-order procedure—a *system-derivative generator* for the dynamical system under study. The generator takes as arguments numerical values for the system parameters and produces a *system-derivative* procedure, which takes a system state vector as argument and produces a differential state (a vector that when multiplied by an increment of time is an increment of state). This system-derivative procedure is passed to an *integration driver* that returns a procedure which, given an initial state, evolves the system numerically.

Since all system derivative procedures are constructed to respect the same conventional interfaces, we may choose from a variety of integration methods. Moreover, the integration methods themselves can be automatically constructed from a library of procedures that can be used as interchangeable components in the construction of traditional applications. Going further, we believe that it is not difficult to automatically implement these numerical procedures as special purpose hardware, like the Orrery.

To support the automatic construction of numerical procedures, we are developing a kernel numerical library that is organized around the liberal use of high order procedural abstractions. For example, Figure 17.12 illustrates this mix-and-match construction of numerical routines, expressing Romberg's method of quadrature as a combination of trapezoidal integration and Richardson extrapolation, following the exposition given by Mathew Halfant and Gerald Sussman in [8]. Such a formulation is valuable in that it separates the ideas into several independent pieces. Clever ideas need be coded and debugged only once, in a context independent of the particular application, thus enhancing the reliability of software built in this way. For instance, Gerald Roylance [20] shows how to construct high performance implementations of special functions, abstracting recurrent themes such as Chebyshev economization. His automatically constructed procedure for computing Bessel functions is 40 times more accurate, for the same number of terms, than the approximation specified in the National Bureau of Standards tables [3]. More significantly, Roylance's formulation clearly exposes the underlying approximation methods so that parameters, such as the required precision of the routines, can be changed at will.

Besides providing a convenient target for automatic construction of numerical procedures, powerful abstraction mechanisms help us to express some of the vocabulary and methods of numerical analysis in a form that is close to the mathematical theory, and is thus easy to understand and check. A program is a communication, not just between programmers and computers, but also between programmers and human readers of the program; quite often, between the programmer and him/herself. One power of programming is that it allows one to make the knowledge of methods explicit, so that methods can be studied as theoretical entities. Traditional numerical programs are handcrafted for each application. The traditional style does not admit such explicit de-

composition and naming of methods, thus forfeiting much of the power
and joy of programming.

```
(define (romberg f a b tolerance)
  (stream-limit
    (richardson-sequence (trapezoid-sums f a b)
                         2
                         2)
    tolerance))
(define (trapezoid-sums f a b)
  (define (next-S S n)
    (let* ((h (/ (- b a) 2 n))
           (fx (lambda(i) (f (+ a (* (+ i i -1) h))))))
      (+ (/ S 2) (* h (sigma fx 1 n)))))
  (define (S-and-n-stream S n)
    (cons-stream (list S n)
                 (S-and-n-stream (next-S S n) (* n 2))))
  (let* ((h (- b a))
         (S (* (/ h 2) (+ (f a) (f b)))))
    (map-stream car (S-and-n-stream S 1))))
(define (richardson-sequence seq start-index inc-index)
  (define (sequences seq order)
    (cons-stream seq
      (sequences
        (let* ((2p̂ (expt 2 order)) (2p̂-1 (- 2p̂ 1)))
          (map-streams (lambda (Rh Rh/2)
                         (/ (- (* 2p̂ Rh/2) Rh) 2p̂-1))
                       seq
                       (tail seq)))
        (+ order inc-index))))
  (map-streams head (sequences seq start-index)))
```

Figure 17.12
Romberg's method of quadrature can be built by combining a primitive trapezoidal
integrator with an accelerator that speeds convergence of sequences by Richardson
extrapolation. The result is an infinite sequence (stream) of increasingly accurate
approximations to the definite integral. The same Richardson accelerator can be
combined with other sequence generators to build other classical numerical routines.

17.3   Intelligent Tools are Feasible

The work described in the preceding sections demonstrates much of the
technology required to produce programs that can serve scientists and
engineers as intelligent problem solving partners, programs such as the
engineer's assistant that we envisioned at the beginning of this paper.

We have shown how to use symbolic algebra to compile high level descriptions such as circuit diagrams directly into numerical modeling and simulation programs whose elements can be automatically generated from a library of mix-and-match numerical subroutines expressed at appropriate levels of abstraction. Our experience with the Digital Orrery proves that such numerical programs can be run at supercomputer speeds, without the cost of a general purpose supercomputer. The Bifurcation Interpreter, KAM and PLR demonstrate that intelligent programs incorporating knowledge of dynamical systems can automatically control and monitor numerical experiments and interpret the results in qualitative terms. The Kineticist's Workbench illustrates how these capabilities can be combined with knowledge about a particular domain to produce a sophisticated tool for modeling and analysis.

17.3.1   Higher-dimensional Systems are Hard

Most systems of interest have more than two degrees of freedom, yet the KAM and PLR programs and the Bifurcation Interpreter depend upon special properties of low dimensional systems. The grammar of possible phase portraits and the catalog of generic bifurcations embodied in these programs cannot easily be extended to higher dimensional systems. On the other hand, there are qualitative features of such systems that can be usefully extracted and used to guide numerical experiments.

Exploring the qualitative behavior of high dimensional systems requires a combination of analytic and numeric methods. Analytic methods can provide clear definitive information, but are often hard to apply or unavailable. There are well established methods for deriving the local behavior of trajectories in the neighborhood of fixed points, but few tools exist for determining global behavior. On the other hand, a program could detect a saddle analytically, calculate its stable and unstable manifolds numerically, determine whether the manifolds intersect each other and draw conclusions about global behavior.

Moreover, even in high dimensional spaces, it is still possible to use clustering techniques to examine the set of iterates of a map or the flow of a differential equation and determine if a trajectory is confined to a lower dimensional submanifold of the formal state space. Each reduction in dimension is evidence of an integral of motion, such as conservation of energy. One can also (as people do) apply visual recognition techniques to low dimensional sections and projections of the full space. Despite the fact that orbit types and bifurcations in high dimensional spaces have not been completely classified, nonetheless it is still possible to recognize qualitatively different regions of behavior and to map out these regions in state space and parameter space.

17.3.2 Computers, Like People, Need Imagistic Reasoning

In observing professional physicists and engineers, we are often struck by how an expert's "intuitive grasp" of a field is hard to articulate verbally. This is perhaps indicative of the use of nonverbal reasoning processes as part of the process of solving otherwise verbally presented problems. We observe scientists, mathematicians and engineers continually using graphical representations to organize their thoughts about a problem. The programs we are developing use numerical methods as a means of shifting back and forth between symbolic and geometric methods of reasoning. The programs not only draw graphs and state-space diagrams, but they look at these diagrams and hold them in their "mind's eye" so that powerful visual mechanisms can be brought to bear on what otherwise would be purely symbolic problems.

The idea that problem solvers employing visual, analogue or diagrammatic representations can be more effective than those relying on linguistic representations alone is not new. Even before 1960, Gelernter's Geometry-Theorem Proving Machine [10] used diagrams to filter goals generated by backward chaining. Nevins's [18] forward-chaining theorem prover focussed its forward deduction of facts on those lines explicitly drawn in a diagram. Stallman and Sussman's EL [24] program performed antecedent deductions in circuit analysis by exploiting the finite connectivity of devices, and Novak's ISAAC program [19] used diagrams to solve word problems in physics.

What is provocative, however, is the suggestion that our thought processes are importantly imagistic and that visual thinking may play a crucial role in problem solving. In scientific computation there has been tremendous emphasis on visualization, but this has mostly meant the development of computer graphics technology to aid *human* visualization [17]. We believe that imagistic reasoning is a very general class of problem solving strategies, each with its own appropriate representations and technical support. The programs discussed above suggest that it may be at least as important for scientific computation to develop visualization aids for programs as well as for people.

17.4   Acknowledgments

Support for this research was provided in part by the Defense Advanced Research Projects Agency of the Department of Defense, monitored under Office of Naval Research contract numbers N00014-86-K-0180 and N00014-89-J-3202.

17.5   The Authors

Harold Abelson is an Associate Professor and Gerald Sussman a Professor with the MIT Department of Electrical Engineering and Computer Science, as well as the Leaders of the AI/LCS Project on Mathematics and Computation; Michael Eisenberg is a Ph.D candidate in the MIT Department of Electrical Engineering and Computer Science; Matthew Halfant is a former research scientist with the AI/LCS Project on Mathematics and Computation; Jacob Katzenelson is a Professor with the Technion-Israel Institute of Technology; Elisa Sacks is Assistant Professor with Princeton's Department of Computer Science; Jack Wisdom is Assistant Professor with the MIT Department of Earth, Atmospheric and Planetary Sciences; and Kenneth Yip is Assistant Professor with Yale's Department of Computer Science.

Bibliography

[1] H. Abelson, M. Halfant, J. Katzenelson, and G.J. Sussman. The Lisp experience. *Annual Review of Computer Science*, 3, pages 167–195, Annual Reviews, Inc. Palo Alto, CA, 1988.

[2] H. Abelson and G.J. Sussman. *The Dynamicist's Workbench I: Automatic Preparation of Numerical Experiments*. MIT Artificial Intelligence Laboratory Memo 955, May 1987.

[3] M. Abramowitz and I. Stagun. *Handbook of Mathematical Functions*. Dover Publications, 1965.

[4] J. Applegate, M. Douglas, Y. Gürsel, P. Hunter, C. Seitz, and G.J. Sussman. A digital orrery. *IEEE Transactions on Computers*, September 1985.

[5] S. Baase. *Computer Algorithms*. Addison-Wesley, Reading, MA, 1978.

[6] M. Feinberg. Chemical oscillations, multiple equilibria, and reaction network structure. In W. Stewart, W. H. Ray and C. Conley, editors, *Dynamics and Modeling of Reactive Systems*, pages 59–130, Academic Press, New York, 1980.

[7] V. Franceschini. Two models of truncated Navier-stokes equations on a two-dimensional torus. *Physics of Fluids*, 26(2):433–447, 1983.

[8] M. Halfant and G.J. Sussman. *Abstraction in Numerical Methods*. MIT Artificial Intelligence Laboratory Memo 997, October 1987. Also to appear in *Proceedings of the ACM Conference on Lisp and Functional Programming*, 1988.

[9] M. Hénon. Numerical study of quadratic area-preserving mappings. *Quarterly Journal of Applied Mathematics*, 27, 1969.

[10] H. Gelernter. Realization of a geometry theorem proving machine. In *Proceedings of the International Conference on Information Processing*, pages 273–282, Unesco House, Paris, France, 1959. Also in E. Feigenbaum and J. Feldman, editors, *Computers and Thought*, pages 134–152, McGraw-Hill, New York, 1963.

[11] J. Guckenheimer and P. Holmes. *Nonlinear Oscillations, Dynamical Systems, and Bifurcations of Vector Fields*, Springer-Verlag, Berlin, 1983.

[12] C.S. Hsu. A theory of index for point mapping dynamical systems. *Journal of Applied Mechanics*, 47:185–190, 1980.

[13] C.S. Hsu, W.H. Cheng, and H.C. Yee. Steady-state response of a non-linear system under impulsive parametric excitation. *Journal of Sound and Vibration*, 50(1):95–116, 1977.

[14] H. Kinoshita and H. Nakai. Motions of the perihelions of neptune and pluto. *Celestial Mechanics*, 34, 1984.

[15] K. Laidler. *Chemical Kinetics* (third edition). Harper & Row, New York, 1987.

[16] R. MacKay. *Renormalization in Area-Preserving Maps*. PhD thesis, Princeton University, 1982.

[17] B. McCormick, T. Desanti, and M. Brown, editors. Visualization in scientific computing. *Computer Graphics*, 21(6), 1987.

[18] A.J. Nevins. *Plane Geometry Theorem Proving Using Forward Chaining*. MIT Artificial Intelligence Laboratory Memo 303, January 1974.

[19] G. Novak. Representations of knowledge in a program for solving physics problems. In *Proceedings of the Fifth IJCAI*, pages 286–291, Cambridge, MA, 1977.

[20] G.L. Roylance. *Expressing Mathematical Subroutines Constructively*. MIT Artificial Intelligence Laboratory Memo 999, November 1987. Also to appear in *Proceedings of ACM Conference on Lisp and Functional Programming*, 1988.

[21] E.P. Sacks. Hierarchical reasoning about inequalities. *AAAI*, 649–654, 1987.

[22] E.P. Sacks. Piecewise linear reasoning. *AAAI*, 655–659, 1987.

[23] E.P. Sacks. *Automatic Qualitative Analysis of Ordinary Differential Equations Using Piecewise Linear Approximations.* MIT Laboratory for Computer Science Technical Report 416, March 1988.

[24] G.J. Sussman and R.M. Stallman. Heuristic techniques in computer-aided circuit analysis. *IEEE Transactions on Circuits and Systems*, CAS-22, pages 857–865, 1975.

[25] G.J. Sussman and J. Wisdom. Numerical evidence that the motion of Pluto is chaotic. To appear in *Science*. Also available as MIT Artificial Intelligence Laboratory Memo 1039, April 1988.

[26] J.M.T. Thompson. Complex dynamics of compliant offshore structures. In *Proceedings of Royal Soc. London A*, 387, pages 407–427, 1983.

[27] J.M.T. Thompson and H.B. Stewart. *Nonlinear Dynamics and Chaos.* John Wiley & Sons, New York, 1986.

[28] D.A. Waltz. Generating semantic descriptions from drawings of scenes with shadows. *The Psychology of Computer Vision.* P.H. Winston, editor, McGraw-Hill, New York, 1985.

[29] A.P. Witkin. Cale-space filtering. *Proceedings of IJCAI-83*, 1983.

[30] K. Yip. Extracting qualitative dynamics from numerical experiments. *AAAI*, 1987.

[31] K. Yip. Generating global behaviors using deep knowledge of local dynamics. *AAAI*, 1988.

[32] C.T. Zahn. Graph-theoretical methods for detecting and describing Gestalt clusters. *IEEE Transactions on Computers*, C-20, January 1971.

[33] F. Zhao. *An $O(N)$ Algorithm for Three-dimensional N-body Simulations*, MIT Artificial Intelligence Laboratory Technical Report 995, 1987.

A Highlights of a Quarter Century

Michael L. Dertouzos

Director, Laboratory for Computer Science
Professor, Department of Electrical Engineering and Computer Science

When I was asked to reflect back upon and address our achievements and to pay tribute to the origins of this child called Project MAC on this its 25th birthday, I readily agreed. That was before I did an important calculation—400 x 25 = 10,000, which represents an average of 400 people doing research for 25 years. In equivalent terms, this child started work 6,000 years before the ancient Greek civilization—and has been at it for the last 10,000 years. I will now try to compress 10,0000 years into the few pages of this summary.

As we work today for a future world of million-processor computers interconnected by a new breed of computer networks, we derive inspiration from our development of two of the world's earliest timeshared systems—CTSS and MULTICS. Built by Corbató and his colleagues in the 1960s, these innovations changed computers radically into the commercial timeshared machines that we find today in every bank, every airline and nearly every other place with big machines. This work also brought together, into a unified whole, stronger than its individual pieces, a new set of ideas and techniques that are widely used today in PCs and big machines alike. Some examples include tree-directories, virtual memory, paging, segmentation, access control, secure systems and what was then the revolutionary act of writing an operating system in a higher level language. This early work of Project MAC also pointed the way for newer systems like UNIX, which is apparently *one* of whatever Multics was supposed to be *many* of!

While I talk of computer systems, I should also recognize Jack Dennis' pioneering work on dataflow, along with Arvind's more recent contributions in this area, which have become a major current research thrust in the field. I should also acknowledge our extensive work on computer networks—from Al Vezza's and Bob Metcalfe's ARPANET work to Dave Clark's internetting and ringnet efforts.

Prof. Dertouzos' remarks are those that were given at the Project MAC 25th Anniversary Celebration Banquet, October 26, 1988.

Now, these early days were not devoted exclusively to serious research, as you might surmise from this long list. You could always hit the right key combination on your keyboard and summon all the elevators to the 9th floor. Or, after returning from your weekend away, you might find your office painted in a color of Licklider's choice.

But let me return to my list. In software, as we envision new programming languages and systems that will tie together tomorrow's parallel and distributed computers, we draw inspiration from our early work on Lisp—a great seed sown by John McCarthy before Project MAC was formed. Lisp grew into Maclisp, Gerry Sussman's and Guy Steele's Scheme, Rick Greenblatt's and Tom Knight's Lisp Machines and Halstead's Multilisp. Outside the Lisp family, we have drawn inspiration from Barbara Liskov's Clu and Argus languages, John Guttag's work on abstract data types and from Seymour Papert's and Hal Abelson's Logo.

I know that many of you share our vision of a future world of computational observatories and computational bio-chemical reactors, where scientists will be able to imitate with great precision very small corners of the universe. They will be able to see through their computer simulations what they can never hope to see with their own eyes or even through the most powerful telescopes and microscopes. As we dream of this prospective magic, we draw strength from our earlier work on computer simulation and computer aided design—Cy Levinthal's rotating molecules and John Ward's Kludge display system; Steve Coon's geometric surfaces; Doug Ross' AED language; and more recently, Ed Fredkin's and Tom Toffoli's cellular automata, and Chris Terman's RSIM logic simulator.

Before I recall some of our achievements in intelligent systems, I must remind you of our ambition level: you probably remember the huge hydraulic arm that was capable of demolishing a house. It was being modified and programmed to play ping pong ... first with a human, and later with a machine like itself. After much work, and after the funds for this project were exhausted, the sponsors wanted a demonstration. They came, wearing their military uniforms, to observe what was described as having a slightly degraded performance: the arm was holding a basket and was catching ping pong balls—sometimes.

As we prepare tomorrow's computers to see, hear, walk, work and learn from practice, we stand on the broad shoulders of our colleague's earlier work on intelligent and knowledge based systems—Marvin Minsky's early robots and theory of frames; Joe Weizenbaum's expert psychiatrist Eliza; Joel Moses' widely used Macsyma, with Bill Martin's contributions to that system and to natural language understanding; Pat Winston's learning by analogy; Carl Hewitt's actors; Peter Szolovits' use of deep models in medicine, like the digitalis advisor; ? Marr's and Tomasso Poggio's stereo theory of vision; Horn's vision and robotics results; and Dave Waltz's constraints.

While our renowned group of theorists invents exciting new algorithms for our parallel machines, we look back at Albert Meyer's discovery of inherently hard problems and his subsequent development with Mike Fischer of a notable portion of complexity theory; the extensive work based on prime numbers, like Vaughan Pratt's primes in NP; Michael Rabin's probabilistic primality tests; and more recently, Shafi Goldwasser's nonprobabilistic ones. We also look to the magic of public key cryptography through the work of Ron Rivest, Adi Shamir and Len Adelman; and Silvio Micali's and Shafi Goldwasser's recent work on zero knowledge proofs.

Finally, and I have left this for last because it is the playful part of our work, as we contemplate tomorrow's gadgets, toys, games, hacks and unplanned side effects, we cannot help but remember with awe the game of Space War. Space War was played late at night by almost everyone at Project MAC, and the only people who ever beat us were the astronauts who came to visit from Cape Canaveral. We also remember Rick Greenblatt's chess machine and program, and the long line of editors and formatters—from Teco and Jerry Saltzer's Typeset and Runoff, to Stallman's Emacs. Moving to more recent times, we have Danny Hillis' Connection Machine, and Steve Ward's NuBus, which after nine years and several companies has become a national standard and the hardware base of the Macintosh II and NEXT computers. And, of course, Bob Scheifler's X Window System that is just about everywhere.

Besides generating ideas and helping great people grow, our laboratory has given birth to a few commercial enterprises—Prime Computer with Bill Poduska's dream of putting Multics in a matchbox, Infocom, 3Com, SofTech, Software Arts, Interleaf, LMI, Symbolics, Thinking Machines are only some of the 21 commercial enterprises launched by Project MAC alumni. Of course, these are only the ones we actually know about. While we are gloating, we might as well take some credit (and I repeat, only *some* credit) for helping start a few other MIT enterprises like Project Athena and the Media Lab.

I want you to know that throughout these years, our people have not been overly narrow nor as boring as they are supposed to be according to the stereotype—Marvin Minsky's life story is written up in the New Yorker; Ed Fredkin's in Atlantic Monthly; a photograph of Richard Stallman wearing a Yugoslavian folk-dancing dress appears in Time magazine; Madnick turns an ancient British Castle into a modern hotel; and Sherry Turkle becomes Ms. Magazine Woman of the Year.

In wrapping up these recollections, we are thankful to our institution, MIT, which brought us together and plunged us into that special brand of excitement, hard work, excellence, involvement, teamwork and fun that is our research. We are also thankful to our governmental and industrial sponsors and particularly to DARPA which has been instrumental to our success during our entire 25-year life. We are thankful to you, our colleagues and friends, for your collaboration and support. Finally, we are thankful to the stars. For most of us have been extraordinarily lucky to have had our professional careers in the computer field coincide with the great transition of our society from the industrial to the information age.

Let's admit it: we have had a grand time, and we have every reason to be proud and to rejoice. But let us not leap into the next 25 years believing the nonsense I mentioned about our being 10,000 years old. Judging by the energy, fertility of ideas and determination of our researchers, this child still has a lot of growing up ahead.

Let us then acknowledge this nostalgia, and let us salute the excitement ahead of Project MAC.

B A Timeline History of Project MAC

Peter Elias

Professor, Department of Electrical Engineering and Computer Science
Member, LCS Theory of Computation Group

The following pages contain a historical timeline index of the major events over the past 25 years. It is the result of asking some present and former members of MAC and its descendant laboratories for nominations of significant products, in the form of publications, hardware, software, meetings, company formations, and other transfers of technology to the larger world. The result is heavily affected by whom could be reached and had time to respond, and what references could be easily verified. It is spotty in its coverage of work by recent arrivals, especially in the AI Lab, and of company formations. It lists only some of the MAC and Laboratory alumni and of the others involved in the company foundings. It also includes some work done elsewhere just before or after related work done here.

Even though we have received some additions and corrections to the timeline since its original publication in the Laboratory's Historical Brochure in 1988, you may still see omissions and errors in the data. If you are willing to provide more accurate and/or complete information to remain available in our historical records, please contact me.

Key to Symbols and Acronyms

□   Event
◇   Book
△   Article, report, etc.
*   Denotes motion from the laboratory into the world:
     companies founded by and/or distributing products based
     on work of MAC members or alumni, IEEE standards adoptions,
     etc.

CAD	Computer Aided Design
CTSS	Compatible TimeSharing System
TECO	Text Editor and COomposer
AED	Automated Engineering Design (CAD Language)
ITS	Incompatible Timesharing System
MULTICS	MULTiplexed Information and Computing Service
MAC	Man And Machine, Multi-Access Computer, Minsky Against Corbato

---

1959

Timesharing △ Timesharing memo—The memo McCarthy wrote to Philip Morse, director of the MIT Computation Center, that began the timesharing movement at MIT. [J. McCarthy. A Time Sharing Operator Program for Our Projected IBM 709.]

CAD □ Electronic Systems Lab and Mechanical Engineering Department start CAD project, following Numerically-controlled milling machine project, 1949-55, and Automatically programmed tool project 1956-59.

1960

Timesharing △ Man computer symbiosis—A classic on man-machine interaction. [J.C.R. Licklider. Man computer symbiosis. *IEEE Transactions on Human Factors Electron.*, 1:4–11, March 1960.]

1961

CTSS □ CTSS running on 709.

Timesharing △ Computer utility model—Public utility metaphor for timeshared computer service introduced. [J. McCarthy. Timesharing computer systems. In *Management and the Computer of the Future*. M. Greenberger, editor, pages 221–236, MIT Press.

Timesharing △ Time shared multiprocessor recommended for MIT—Long range computation study group recommended one large timeshared computer to meet MIT's needs. [Report of the Long Range Computation Study Group, MIT.]

Timesharing □ DEC gives PDP 1 to Electrical Engineering Department.

AI △ Steps towards AI—An important prospectus for artificial intelligence. [M. Minsky. Steps towards artificial intelligence. In *Proceedings of the IEEE*, 49:8–30, January 1961.]

AI △ Computer-controlled hand—A computer operated mechanical hand. [J.A. Ernst. *MH-1: A Computer Operated Mechanical Hand.* Ph.D. thesis, MIT Department of Electrical Engineering.]

Mathlab △ SAINT, symbolic integration program—The first symbolic integration program as good as a Freshman. [J.R. Slagle. *A Heuristic Program that Solves Symbolic Integration Problems in Freshman Calculus, SAINT.* Ph.D. thesis, MIT Department of Mathematics.]

CAD □ AED (Automated Engineering Design) language development starts.

1962

CTSS △ First paper on CTSS—First public report on CTSS. [F.J. Corbató, M.M. Dagget, and R.C. Daley. An experimental time-sharing system. In *Proceedings of AFIPS 21*, pages 335–344.

Editors et al □ PDP 1 TECO text editor —The Text Editor and COmposer (TECO) for the PDP 1. [No publication found. D. Murphy credited by Saltzer. See 1964–65 PDP 6 TECO reports below.]

Lisp et al △ Lisp 1.5 manual—The first published manual of the Lisp language. [J. McCarthy, P.W. Abrahams, D.J. Edwards, T.P. Hart, and M.I. Levin. *Lisp 1.5 Programmer's Manual.* MIT Press.]

AI △ Chess program—First MIT chess program? [A. Kotok. *A Chess Playing Program.* AI Memo 41.

1963

Laboratories □ MAC starts with Summer Study.

Laboratories □ Computer aided design (CAD) project moves from Electronic Systems Laboratory (ESL) to MAC.

Laboratories □ Artificial Intelligence (AI) Group moves from Computation Center and Research Laboratory of Electronics (RLE) to MAC.

CTSS □ CTSS running on 7094 at MAC

CTSS □ F.J. Corbató, *The Compatible Timesharing System*, MIT Press.

CTSS △ V. Yngve, COMIT language on CTSS. [Project MAC Memo MAC-M-136.]

Multics □ Multics specifications developed, sent out for bid.

Editors et al □ L. Lowrey's editor "Memo, modify and ditto" on CTSS.

Lisp et al □ Interactive Lisp implemented for CTSS by D. Edwards, S. Russel, T. Hart, and W. Martin. [Project MAC Memos MAC-M-128 and 132.]

Lisp et al △ Garbage collector for PDP 1—First compacting garbage collectors. [M. Minsky. *A Lisp Garbage Collector Using Serial Secondary Storage.* AI Memo 58.]

AI △ Machine perception of 3D solid—Display and rotation of 3D figures with hidden lines removed, developed on TX2 computer at Lincoln Laboratory. [L.G. Roberts. *Machine Perception of Three Dimensional Solids.* Ph.D. thesis, MIT Department of Electrical Engineering.]

CAD □ SJCC session on MIT CAD work included the following five papers in the *Proceedings of AFIPS 23:*

CAD △ CAD requirements. [S.A. Coons. An outline of the requirements for a computer aided design system. Pages 299–304.]

CAD △ Basis of CAD system. [D.T. Ross and J.E. Rodriguez. Theoretical foundations for the computer aided design system. Pages 305–322.]

CAD △ CAD console facilities. [R. Stotz. Man-machine console facilities for computer aided design. Pages 323–328.]

CAD △ Sketchpad—Powerful graphics program developed on TX2 at Lincoln Laboratory. [I.E. Sutherland. Sketchpad: a man-machine graphical communication system. Pages 329–346.]

CAD △ 3D sketchpad. [T.E. Johnson. Sketchpad III: a computer program for drawing in three dimensions. Pages 347–353.]

1964

Timesharing △ PDP 1 timesharing system. [J.B. Dennis. A multiuser computation facility for education and research. *Communications of the ACM*, 7:521-529.]

CTSS □ Kludge (Display console developed at ESL) operates on CTSS.

Multics □ GE bid on Multics accepted.

Editors et al △ Typeset editor, Runoff formatter in CTSS—Typeset, influential early line editor, ancestor of edl and ed on CTSS, edm on Multics: with Lamson's qed was ancestor of BTL qed for Multics, related to qedx and ed on UNIX. A sequence of IBM products—SCRIPT/370, GML, DCF, PROFS— descend in part from Runoff. [J.H. Saltzer in 1964 edition of CTSS Programmer's Guide, personal communications from Saltzer and Madnick (see 1972).]

Editors et al △ PDP 6 TECO text editor—Descendant of PDP 1 TECO used in PDP 6, PDP 10, KL 10 and DEC 20 computers in MAC/AI/LCS. [R. Greenblatt, J. Holloway, and S. Nelson. Project MAC Memos MAC-M-191 (1964) and MAC-M-250.]

Theory △ Complexity of recursive functions—Foundation work on complexity theory. [M. Blum, *On a Machine-independent theory of the complexity of recursive functions*. Ph.D. thesis, MIT Department of Electrical Engineering.]

1965

Timesharing △ Segmentation—Work which influenced Multics and other systems. [J.B. Dennis. Segmentation and the design of multiprogrammed computer systems. *Journal of the ACM*, 8:589–602.]

CTSS ◇ *The Compatible Timesharing System: A Programmer's Guide.* P.A. Chrisman, editor, MIT Press.

Multics □ BTL and GE join in informal collaboration with MIT to develop Multics.

Multics □ FJCC session on Multics objectives included the following six papers:

Multics △ Multics survey. [F.J. Corbató and V.A. Vyssotsky. Introduction and overview of the Multics system. In *Proceedings of AFIPS Conference 27*, pages 185–196.]

Multics △ Timesharing system design. [E.L. Glaser. System design of a computer for timesharing applications. In *Proceedings of AFIPS Conference 27*, pages 197–202.]

Multics △ Multics supervisor. [V.A. Vysottsky, F. J. Corbató, and R.M. Graham. Structure of the Multics supervisor. In *Proceedings of AFIPS Conference 27*, pages 203–212.]

Multics △ Multics file system. [R.C. Daley and P.G. Neumann. A general-purpose file system for secondary storage. In *Proceedings of AFIPS Conference 27*, pages 213–230.]

Multics △ Timesharing communication. [J.F. Ossanna, L. Mikus, and S.D. Dunten. Communications and input-output switching in a multiplexed computing system. In *Proceedings of AFIPS Conference 27*, pages 231–242.]

Multics △ Societal implications. [E.E. David, Jr. and R.M. Fano. Some thoughts about the social implications of accessible computing. In *Proceedings of AFIPS Conference 27*, pages 243–248.]

Labware △ ARDS display specifications—Specifications for Advanced Remote Display Console (ARDS) for MAC, first suggested at 1963 Summer Study. [R.H. Stotz and U. Groneman. *Specifications for a Dataphone-driven Remote Display Console for Project MAC*. Project MAC Memo MAC-M-243.

AI ☐ AMF arm running in AI Lab.

Mathlab △ Iintegrate package integrates rational functions using an algorithm, not heuristics. Its performance in such cases improves on SAINT. Later we use in SIN (see 1967 below). [M. Manove, *Integrate: Online Indefinite Integration*. MITRE Technical Memo TM-04204.]

Mathlab △ Mathlab symbolic math package—Contained Integrate package above. A precursor of Macsyma. [C. Engleman. *Mathlab: Online Symbolic Computation*. MITRE Technical Memo TM-04258.]

1966

Timesharing △ Multiprogramming a multiprocessor—The first systematic multiprocess, multiprocessor task manager. [J.H. Saltzer. *Traffic Control in a Multiplexed Computer*. Sc.D. thesis, MIT Department of Electrical Engineering, and Project MAC Report TR-30.]

Timesharing △ Capabilities and spheres of protection—Capabilities and spheres of protection introduced. [J.B. Dennis and E. Van Horn. *Programming Semantics for Multiprogrammed Computations*. Project MAC Report TR-21.]

Labware △ ARDS display manual. [T.B. Cheek, J.E. Ward, and D.E. Thornhill. *Operating and Programming Manual for the ARDS-1 Experimental Dataphone-driven Remote Storage-tube Display*. Project MAC Memo MAC-M-336.]

Labware □ Moby (1/4 megaword memory) ordered for PDP 6 in 1965 or 1966.

Labware □ ITS running since about 1966.

Lisp et al △ Start of Maclisp—Added bignum integers and a fast compiler. [Anonymous. *PDP 6 Lisp (Lisp 1.6).*]

AI △ Eliza—A script-driven interpreter which simulates a nondirective therapist. [J. Weizenbaum. Eliza—A computer program for a the study of natural language communication between man and machine. *Communications of the ACM*, 9:36–45.]

CAD □ CIRCAL, M.L. Dertouzos; AEDNET, J. Katzenelson; early nonlinear circuit simulation programs with interactive display running in 1966.

1967

Laboratories □ N. Negroponte starts the Architecture Machine Group in the MIT Department of Architecture.

Parallel Computing △ Dataflow graph precursor—The precursor of the dataflow model of parallel computation. [J.E. Rodriguez. *A Graph Model for Parallel Computation.* Ph.D. thesis, MIT Department of Electrical Engineering, and Project MAC Report TR-64.]

AI △ Computer aided diagnosis—Program performs sequential diagnosis as it interacts with user. [G.A. Gorry. *A System for Computer Aided Diagnosis.* Project MAC Report TR-44.]

Mathlab △ Symbolic Mathematical Laboratory—One of three precursors of the Macsyma system. [W.A. Martin. *Symbolic Mathematical Laboratory.* Ph.D. thesis, MIT Department of Electrical Engineering.]

Mathlab △ SIN—A program that integrates like an expert. Another of the Macsyma precursors. SIN, the Symbolic Mathematical Laboratory, and Dendral at Stanford, led to the knowledge based systems concept. [J. Moses. *Expert Symbolic Integration*. Ph.D. thesis, MIT Department of Mathematics, and Project MAC Report TR-47.]

CAD △ Computer aided design of 3D surfaces—Widely used method of describing curved surfaces for CAD. [S.A. Coons. *Surfaces for the Computer Aided Design of Space Forms*. Project MAC Report TR-41.]

CAD □ H.B. Lee and R.D. Thorton use CTSS and AEDNET to teach a circuits course.

CAD △ Graphical display prize paper—A paper which won the IEEE B.J. Thompson award in 1968. [M.L. Dertouzos. Phaseplot: an online graphical display technique. *IEEE Transactions on Computers*, EC-16:2.]

CAD △ The AED approach to CAD—Prize-winning paper on the Automated Engineering Design language (AED) and programming environment. [D.T. Ross. The AED approach to generalized computer aided design. In *Proceedings of the 22 nd ACM National Conference*, pages 367–385.]

Education □ Logo research starts jointly between Project MAC and Bolt, Beranek, and Newman.

Theory ◇ M.L. Minsky. *Computation: Finite and Infinite Machines*. McGraw Hill.

1968

Timesharing △ The working set model—An influential model of paging behavior in a timeshared system. [P.J. Denning. The working set model for program behavior. *Communications of the ACM*, 11:323–333.]

AI △ Recognition of 3D objects—Broad study of dissecting scenes into objects. [A. Guzman. *Computer Recognition of 3D Objects in a Visual Scene*. Project MAC Report TR-59.]

CAD ◇ *D.T. Ross. *Introduction to Software Engineering with the AED-O Language.* SofTech, Inc., Waltham, MA.

Education □ Papert starts Logo project at Project MAC.

Theory ◇ F.C. Hennie. *Finite-state Models for Logical Machines.* John Wiley & Sons.

Companies □ *System Concepts, Inc. started by S. Nelson, P. Sampson, F. Wright—early memory mapping hardware for PDP 10s and CAM-6 in 1987.

Companies □ *Computer Displays, Inc. started by R.H. Stotz and T.B. Cheek—displays based on ARDS-2.

Companies □ *Computek, Inc. started by M.L. Dertouzos—graphics and intelligent terminals.

1969

Multics □ First operational Multics system turned over to the MIT Information Processing Center.

Multics □ Formal BTL participation in Project MAC stopped. Joint work with Honeywell (which as bought GE Computer Department) continued, especially in system security.

Labware △ ITS manual—Operating system for the Incompatible Timesharing System, functioning on PDP 6s in Project MAC in 1966 or earlier. [D. Eastlake, R. Greenblatt, J. Holloway, T. Knight, S. Nelson. *ITS 1.5 Reference Manual.* Technical Report AI-161A and Project MAC Memo MAC-M-377 (revised from AI-161A, 1968).]

Lisp et al △ Multics garbage collector—An algorithm developed from Minsky's for Multics Lisp, now dominant for large-memory systems. [R.R. Fenichel and J.C. Yochelson. A Lisp garbage collector for virtual memory computer systems. *Communications of the ACM*, 12:611–612.]

Lisp et al ☐ Maclisp 97 in being. Includes compiler.

Lisp et al ☐ PAL developed for 6.231—M. Richards simplified Strachey's CPL to BCPL (basic CPL) and used it to implement PAL, an instructional language of great purity and low efficiency used in MIT subject 6.231 (see below). Bell Labs C was based on B which grew from BCPL. [A. Evans, Jr. *PAL Reference Manual and Primer.* MIT Department of Electrical Engineering, June 1969.]

AI △ Planner—First presentation of Planner: more details in 1972. [C.E. Hewitt. Planner: a language for proving theorems in robots. In *Proceedings of the First IJCAI*, Washington, DC.]

AI △ Chess program—The Greenblatt chess program which beat Dreyfus, who had claimed that a computer could not play plausible chess. [R. Greenblatt, D. Eastlake, III, and S. Crocker. *The Greenblatt Chess Program.* AI Memo 174.]

AI ◇ M.L. Minsky and S. Papert. *Perceptions.* MIT Press.

AI ◇ *Semantic Information Processing.* M.L. Minsky, editor, MIT Press.

Mathlab ☐ Macsyma started by Engelman, W.A. Martin and J. Moses.

Education ☐ Logo implemented on PDP 10, 1973 on PDP 11/45 in AI Lab for 11- and 12-year-olds.

Education △ Pioneering programming subject—A pioneering precursor to the Abelson and Sussman Scheme course (1985). [J.M. Wozencraft and A. Evans, Jr. *Notes on Programming Linguistics* (6.231). MIT Department of Electrical Engineering, July 1969.]

Companies ☐ *SofTech, Inc. formed by D.T. Ross et al—software engineering.

1970

Laboratories ☐ AI Group of Project MAC become the AI Laboratory.

Multics □ * UNIX Version 1 running at BTL, influenced by Multics.

Editors et al △ PDP 6 TJ6 text justifier—An ancestor of R, started by R. Greenblatt to evade writing up his chess program and modified by others. [R. Greenblatt, B.K.P. Horn and L. Krakauer. *The Text Justifier TJ6.* AI Memo 164A.

Parallel Computing □ Project MAC Conference on Concurrent Systems and Parallel Computation, J. B. Dennis et al, Woods Hole, MA.

AI △ Turing Award Lecture—1970 Turing Award lecture of the ACM. [M. Minsky. Form and content in computer science. *Journal of the ACM*, 17:197–215, April 1970.]

AI △ Learning from examples—How machines can come to perceive and understand a simple class of visual environments. [P.H. Winston. *Learning Structural Descriptions from Examples.* Project MAC Report TR-76.]

AI △ Shape from shading—Finding shape without binocular vision. [B.K.P. Horn. *Shape from Shading.* Project MAC Report TR-79.]

AI □ The "Copy Demo"—A system by Winston, Horn and Freuder scans a scene, generates a line drawing, identifies objects, recovers spatial relations, plans disassembly of children's block configuration by a modified industrial manipulator (AMF arm) which carries out plan, and then assembles a copy. A 16 mm. film made (see Horn *Robot Vision*, pages 359–362, 1986.]

CAD □ MIT CAD project ends.

CAD □ *Univac announces AED for Univac 1108.

1971

Timesharing △ *Reconfiguring multiprocessors online—The computer utility realized: swapping out processors and other components without stopping service. [R.R. Schell. *Dynamic Reconfiguration in a Modular Computer System.* LCS Report TR-86.]

Timesharing △ Protection ring hardware—Hardware for implementing protection rings. [M.D. Schroeder and J.H. Saltzer. A hardware architecture for implementing protection rings. In *Proceedings of the 3rd ACM Symposium on Operating System Principles*, pages 42–54.

Editors et al □ *SCRIPT/370 marketed by IBM—son of Runoff, later IBM descendants: Generalized Markup Language (GML), Document Composition Facility (DCF), Professional Office System (PROFS). [Personal communication, S. Madnick.]

Lisp et al □ Muddle (MDL) development started by C.E. Hewitt, G.J. Sussman, and C.L. Reeve.

AI △ Micro-planner—Implemented widely, used Prolog-like subset of Hewitt's Planner. [G.J. Sussman, T. Wingorad, and E. Charniak. *Micro-planner Reference Manual*. AI Memo 203a.]

Mathlab □ *Proceedings of the 2nd ACM Symposium on Symbolic and Algebraic Manipulation* included the following seven papers on Macsyma:

Mathlab △ W.A. Martin and R.J. Fateman. The Macsyma system. Pages 59–75.

Mathlab △ W.A. Martin. Computer input/output of mathematical expressions. Pages 78–79.

Mathlab △ J. Moses. Algebraic simplification: a guide for the perplexed. Pages 282–304.

Mathlab △ W.A. Martin. Determining the equivalence of algebraic expressions by hash coding. Pages 305–310.

Mathlab △ R.J. Fateman. The user-level semantic matching capabilities in Macsyma. Pages 311–323.

Mathlab △ J. Moses. Symbolic integration: the stormy decade. Pages 427–440.

Mathlab △ P.S. Wang. Automatic computation of limits. Pages 458–464.

1972

Multics △ The Multics experience—A presentation before public release of the Multics system. [F.J. Corbató, J.H. Saltzer, and C.T. Clingen. Multics—the first seven years. In *Proceedings of AFIPS Conference* 40, pages 571–583.]

Multics ◇ E.I. Organick. *The Multics System.* MIT Press.

Parallel Computing △ Dataflow model—First definitive description of dataflow program graph model. [J.B. Fosseen. *Representation of Algorithms by Maximally Parallel Schemata.* Master's thesis, MIT Department of Electrical Engineering and Computer Science.]

AI ◇ T. Winograd. *Natural Language Understanding.* Academic Press.

AI △ Hakmem—A hacker's classic. [M. Beeler, R.W. Gosper, and R. Schroeppel. *Hakmem.* AI Memo 239.]

Theory △ First provably hard problem—One of the two first problems shown not to be in NP. [A.R. Meyer. Weak SIS cannot be decided. Abstract 72T-E67, *Notice of AMS*, 19(5):A-598.]

Theory △ Second provably hard problem. [A.R. Meyer and L. Stockmeyer. The equivalence program for regular expressions with squaring requires exponential space. In *Proceedings of the 13* th *IEEE Symposium on Switching and Automata Theory*, pages 125–129.]

Theory △ Time vs. space for Turning machines—For 1-tape Turning machines, that which is recognizable in time f^2 is recognizable using space f. [M.S. Paterson. Tapebounds for time-bounded Turing machines. *JCSS*, 6(2):116–124.]

Theory △ The basic paper on "continuations." [M.J. Fischer. Lambda calculus schemata. In *Proceedings of an ACM Conference on Proving Assertions About Programs*, pages 104–109.

Companies □ *Prime Computer, Inc. started by J.W. Poduska—computers.

1973

Laboratories/Education □ MIT starts Division for Study and Research in Education with Logo project as a central focus.

CTSS □ CTSS turned off.

Multics □ *First commercial Multics released by Honeywell.

Distributed Systems □ C.E. Hewitt, Actors first appear in annual progress report.

Theory □ Project MAC Workshop on Concrete Computational Complexity, organized by M.J. Fischer and A.R. Meyer, MIT Endicott House.

1974

Editors et al □ R. Stallman starts Emacs as an improvement of TECO.

Abstraction & Specification △ Abstract data types—Programming with abstract data types, start of Clu design. [B.H. Liskov and S. Zilles. Programming with abstract data types. In *Proceedings of the ACM SIGPLAN Conferences on Very High Level Languages, SIGPLAN Notices*, 9:50–59.

Abstraction & Specification □ Clu named (for "cluster").

Parallel Computing △ A language for dataflow—The first version of a dataflow language. [J.B. Dennis. First version of a dataflow procedure language. *Lecture Notes in Computer Science*, 19, Programming Symposium, B. Robinet, editor, Springer.]

Labware △ Universal arrays for control—Synthesis of control circuits from an array of standard asynchronous cells. [S. Patil. Cellular arrays for asynchronous control. *ACM MICRO 7*. Original work leading to Patil Systems, Inc., 1981.]

Lisp et al △ Maclisp manual—The first full manual for Maclisp, the MAC dialect of Lisp, which grew from Lisp 106 for the PDP 6 (1966). [D. Moon. *The Maclisp Reference Manual, Version 0*, LCS document.

Theory △ Addition decisions are hard—Proves super-exponential complexity of any decision procedure for the first-order theory of the addition of natural numbers. [M.J. Fischer and M.O. Rabin. Super-exponential complexity of computation. In *Proceedings of SIAM-MAS*, 7, American Mathematical Society, pages 27–41.

1975

Laboratories □ Project MAC is renamed the Laboratory for Computer Science.

Timesharing △ Protection review–Widely cited protection survey. [J.H. Saltzer and M.D. Schroeder. Protection of information in computer systems. In *Proceedings of IEEE*, 63:1278–1308.

Abstraction & Specification △ Specifying data types—Specification techniques for data abstractions. [B.H. Liskov and S. Zilles. Specification techniques for data abstractions. *IEEE Transactions on Software Engineering*, SE-1:1.]

Abstraction & Specification △ Specifying data types—Work done at Toronto just before J. Guttag came to MIT. [J.V. Guttag. *The Specification and Application to Programming of Abstract Data Types*. Ph.D. thesis, University of Toronto.]

Abstraction & Specification □ First Clu implementation, data abstraction in a language.

Lisp et al △ Scheme starts—The Scheme dialect of Lisp introduced. [G.J. Sussman and G.L. Steele, Jr. *Scheme: An Interpreter for Extended Lambda Calculus*. AI Memo 349, December.]

AI △ Frames appear in print—-Introduction of frames in knowledge representation. [M.L. Minsky. A framework for representing knowledge. In *The Psychology of Computer Vision*. P.H. Winston, editor, McGraw Hill (initially AI Memo 306, June 1974).]

AI △ Constraint propagation in circuits—Introduced notion of constraint propagation and explanations from recorded dependencies. [G.J. Sussman and R.M. Stallman. Heuristic techniques in computer aided circuit analysis. *IEEE Transactions on Circuits and Systems*, CAS-22:857–865.]

AI △ Visual chip lead bonding—Simple "hand-eye" system aligns chips to bond leads. [B.K.P. Horn. A problem in computer vision: orienting silicon integrated circuit chips for lead bonding. *Computer Graphics and Image Processing*, 4:294–303.]

AI ◇ *The Psychology of Computer Vision*. P.H. Winston, editor, McGraw Hill.

Theory △ Primes are in NP—Every prime p has a proof of its primality of size a polynomial in the number of digits of p. [V.R. Pratt. Every prime has a succinct certificate. *SIAM Journal on Computing*, 4(3):214–220.]

Theory △ Universal codeword sets—One codeword set is almost as good as all Huffman codes, if more probable messages are always given shorter codewords. [P. Elias. Universal codeword sets and representations of the integers. *IEEE Transactions on Information Theory*, IT-21(2):194–203.]

Theory △ Hard problems—Formal publication of details of 1972 results. [A.R. Meyer. Weak monadic second order theory of successor is not elementary-recursive. *Lectures Notes in Mathematics*, 453:132–154, Logic Colloquium, Springer.]

1976

Editors et al □ First Emacs is operating.

Distributed Systems △ Mutual exclusion for unreliable processes—A deadlock-free solution to the problem of mutual exclusion of unreliable processes is given, stimulating a number of papers generalizing and improving the result. [R.L. Rivest and V.R. Pratt. The mutual exclusion problem for unreliable processes. In *Proceedings of the 17th IEEE Symposium on Foundations of Computer Science*, pages 1–8.

Mathlab □ Macsyma consortium formed.

Theory △ Probabilistic primality test—A probabilistic (randomized) test for primality of large numbers. [M.O. Rabin. Probabilistic algorithms. In *Algorithms and Complexity, New Directions and Recent Trends*. J.F. Traub, editor, pages 21–39, Academic Press.

Theory △ First dynamic logic paper—Regular expressions and modal logic combine to form a logic of programs amenable to formal study. [V.R. Pratt. Semantical considerations on Floyd-Hoare logic. In *Proceedings of the 17th IEEE Symposium on Foundations of Computer Science*, pages 109–121.]

Societal Impact ◇ J. Weizenbaum. *Computer Power and Human Reason*. W.H. Freeman, San Francisco, CA.

1977

Multics □ Honeywell-MIT collaboration ends.

Abstraction & Specification △ Data abstraction in Clu—Describes development of the concept of data abstraction and its incorporation into the Clu language. [B.H. Liskov, A. Snyder, R. Atkinson, and C. Schaffert. Abstraction mechanisms in Clu. *Communications of the ACM*, 20:564–576.]

Distributed Systems △ Message passing—An early paper on message passing ideas. [C.E. Hewitt. Viewing control structures as patterns of passing messages. *Artificial Intelligence*, 8:323–364.]

Parallel Computing △ Tagged token dataflow rules—Rules for generating the tags to be attached to the tokens in a tagged dataflow machine. Work done at U.C. Irvine just before Arvind came to MIT. [Arvind and K.P. Gostelow. A computer capable of exchanging processors for time. In *Proceedings of IFIP Congress 77*, pages 849–853.]

AI △ Dependency directed backtracking—Introduced notion of dependency directed backtracking based on recorded dependencies. [R.M. Stallman and G.J. Sussman. Forward reasoning and dependency-directed backtracking in a system for computer aided circuit analysis. *Artificial Intelligence*, 9:135–196.]

AI △ OWL knowledge representation language—A knowledge representation language offering ways to relate classes. [P. Szolovits, L.B. Hawkinson, and W.A. Martin. *An Overview of OWL, a Language for Knowledge Representation*, LCS Memo TM-86.]

Mathlab □ First Macsyma user's conference. W. Gosper, MAC alumnus, implemented a Macsyma algorithm for computing indefinite sums of terms involving rationals, exponentials and combinatorial terms. J. Moses calls it the most important new approach to summation in a century and a half. Four definitive papers by J.L. White and G. Steele on Maclisp also presented.

Theory △ Linear-time string matching—Earliest of several linear-time string pattern matching algorithms developed 1970–75. [D.E. Knuth, J.H. Morris, and V.R. Pratt. Fast pattern matching in strings. *SIAM Journal on Computing*, 6:323–350.]

Theory ◇ F.C. Hennie. *Introduction to Computability*. Addison Wesley.

Theory ◇ J. Stoy. *Denotational Semantics: The Scott-Strachey Approach to Programming Language Theory*. MIT Press.

1978

Distributed Systems □ Workshop on distributed systems organized by LCS groups. [J.L. Peterson. Notes on a workshop on distributed computing. *Operating Systems Review*, 13:18–20, July 1979.]

Distributed Systems △ Accessing shared data in distributed systems —Influential treatment of mutable data as immutable versions in distributed systems. [D.P. Reed. *Naming and Synchronization in a Decentralized Computer System*. Ph.D. thesis, MIT Department of Electrical Engineering and Computer Science, LCS Report TR-205.]

Labware △ Local area nets—A tutorial which influenced IEEE LAN standard. [D.D. Clark, K. Pogran, and D.P. Reed. Introduction to local area networks. In *Proceedings of the IEEE*, 11:1497–1517, November 1978.]

Labware □ S.A. Ward starts Nu Machine project. Led to first C compiler and UNIX port for micros (see 1982) and NuBus IEEE standard (see 1988).

Lisp et al △ A real time garbage collector—A simple real time garbage collector. [H.G. Baker, Jr. List processing in real time on a serial computer. *Communications of the ACM*, 21:280–294.]

Theory △ $K + 1$ head are better than K—Solution to a well known problem about multihead Turing machines. [R.L. Rivest and A.C. Yao. $K+1$ heads are better than K. *Journal of the ACM*, 25:337–340.]

Theory △ The first public key cryptosystem (RSA)—A public key cryptosystem based on the difficulty of factoring large integers. [R.L. Rivest, A. Shamir, and L. Adelman. A method for obtaining digital signatures and public key cryptosystems. *Communications of the ACM*, 21:120–126.]

1979

Editors et al △ First Emacs manual. [R. Stallman. *Emacs—the extensible, customizable, self-documenting display editor*. AI Memo 519.]

Editors et al □ M. Hammer's group names Etude text processor.

Abstraction & Specification △ Clu manual—The second version of Clu implemented and documented. [B.H. Liskov, R. Atkinson, T. Bloom, E. Moss, C. Schaffert, R.W. Scheifler, and A. Snyder. *Clu Reference Manual*. LCS Report TR-225. Also published in *Lecture Notes in Computer Science*, Springer, 1981.]

Distributed Systems △ Distributed system design—A project to design a system which supports distributed applications. [L. Svobodova, B.H. Liskov, and D.D. Clark. *Distributed Computer Systems: Structure and Semantics*. LCS Report TR-215.]

Distributed Systems △ First Argus paper—First paper on Argus design. [B.H. Liskov. Primitives for distributed computing. In *Proceedings of the 7th Symposium on Operating System Principles*, pages 33–41.]

Labware △ Star-shaped ring net—An easily maintained ring network. [J.H. Saltzer and K.T. Pogran. A star-shaped ring network with high maintainability. In *Proceedings of NBS-MITRE LAN Symposium*, May.]

Lisp et al □ NIL starts in Mathlab Group—A forerunner of Common Lisp.

Lisp et al △ The MDL programming language—A description of the MDL (Muddle) programming language interpreter. [S.W. Galley and G. Pfister. *The MDL Programming Language*. LCS Report TR-293.

AI △ Truth maintenance—Based on Sussman and Stallman (1975), introduced "truth maintenance." [J. Doyle. A truth maintenance system. *Artificial Intelligence*, 12:231–272.]

Mathlab △ Probabilistic algorithms for sparse polynomials can be made exponentially faster than for dense ones. [R. Zippel. *Probabilistic algorithms for sparse polynomials*. Ph.D. thesis, MIT Department of Electrical Engineering and Computer Science.]

Theory ◇ D. Harel. First order dynamic logic. *Lecture Notes in Computer Science*, 68, Springer.

Societal Impact ◇ M. L. Dertouzos and J. Moses. *The Computer Age: A Twenty Year View.* MIT Press.

Companies □ *Infocom, Inc. started by M.S. Blank, J.M. Berez, J.C.R. Licklider, S.W. Galley, P.D. Lebling, M.S. Broos, S.E. Cutler, C.L. Reeve, A. Vezza, and T.A. Anderson—computer games.

Companies □ *3Com Corp. started by R. Metcalfe—Ethernet.

Companies □ *Software Arts, Inc. started by D. Bricklin and R. Frankston—VisiCalc.

1980

Abstraction & Specification △ Specifications in program design—Formal specification as a design tool. [J.V. Guttag and J.J. Horning. Formal specification as a design tool. In *Proceedings of a Conference on the Principles of Programming Languages*, pages 251–261.]

Parallel Computing △ Tagged token architecture. [Arvind, V. Kathail, and K. Pingali. *A Dataflow Architecture with Tagged Tokens.* LCS Memo TM-174.]

Lisp et al △ The MDL programming environment—The editors, debuggers, compilers, etc. available to MDL users. [P.D. Lebling. *The MDL Programming Environment.* LCS Report TR-294.]

Mathlab □ Macsyma second most popular computer on ARPANET during several months.

Education □ Microcomputer Logo implementations started: Papert's for TI-99/4, Abelson's for Apple II, then the most sophisticated programs on microcomputers.

Education ◇ S. Papert. *Mindstorms: Children, Computers, and Powerful Ideas.* Basic Books.

Theory △ Communication costs of computation—Precursor of results showing that wires will cost more than devices for many interesting chips. [H. Abelson. Lower bounds on information transfer in distributed computation. *Journal of the ACM*, 27:384–392.]

Theory △ Randomized finite-field—A simple, efficient, randomized algorithm for solving equations and for factoring polynomials in any finite field. [M.O. Rabin. Probabilistic algorithms in finite-fields. *SIAM Journal on Computing*, 9:273–280.]

Companies □ *Interleaf, Inc. started by B. Niamir: it's technical publishing System grew out of Etude.

Companies □ *Apollo Computer, Inc. started by J. W. Poduska—computers.

Companies □ *LMI started by R. Greenblatt—Lisp machines.

Companies □ *Symbolics, Inc. started by W.R. Noftsker et al—Lisp machines.

1981

Distributed Systems △ Nested transactions. [E. Moss. *Nested Transactions: An Approach to Reliable Distributed Computing*. Ph.D. thesis, MIT Department of Electrical Engineering and Computer Science, LCS Report TR-260, MIT Press book, 1984.]

Parallel Computing △ Concurrency for nondeterministic processes—A natural model of concurrency yields counter-intuitive results; this alternative generalization avoids the anomaly. [J.D. Brock and W.B. Ackerman. Scenarios: a model of nondeterminate computation. In Formalization of Programming Concepts. *Lectures Notes in Computer Science*, 107:252–259, Diaz and Ramos, editors, Springer.]

Labware □ *C. Terman starts RSIM logic circuit simulator, used by DEC.

Lisp et al ◇ P.H. Winston and B.K.P. Horn. *Lisp*. Addison Wesley.

AI △ Causal understanding in diagnosis—Models causal understanding of illness. [R.S. Patil. *Causal Representation of Patient Illness for Electrolyte and Acid-base Diagnosis*. LCS Report TR-267.]

AI △ Programs which explain their actions—Expert programs which explain and justify their conclusions. [W.R. Swartout. *Producing Explanations and Justifications of Expert Consulting Programs*. Ph.D. thesis, MIT Department of Electrical Engineering and Computer Science, LCS Report TR-251.]

AI ◇ P.H. Winston. *Artificial Intelligence*. Addison Wesley.

Education ◇ H. Abelson and A.diSessa. *Turtle Geometry: The Computer as a Medium for Exploring Mathematics*. MIT Press.

Theory △ Lower bounds to VLSI costs—Finds asymptotically minimal area shuffle-exchange layout, solving a problem open for some years. [F.T. Leighton. *Layouts for the Shuffle-exchange Graph and Lower Bound Techniques for VLSI*. Ph.D. thesis. MIT Department of Mathematics, LCS Report TR-274, and MIT Press.

Theory △ Mental poker—How to play poker by telephone with untrusted opponents. [A. Shamir, R.L. Rivest, and L. Adelman. Mental poker. In *The Mathematical Gardner*. D. Klarner, editor, pages 37–43, Prindle, Weber and Schmidt.

Companies ☐ *S. Patil starts Patil Systems, Inc. to exploit asynchronous logic ideas developed at LCS in 1974; became Cirrus Logic, Inc. in 1985.

1982

Laboratories/Education ☐ Division for Study in Research in Education ends. Logo and related activities return to LCS.

Labware ☐ *LCS Version 2 10 MBS Ring commercialized by Proteon Associates as ProNet.

Labware ☐ As part of Nu Machine project (1978) S. Ward's Real Time Systems Group developed early microprocessor C compilers (68000 and IBM PC versions) and 6800 UNIX port. These were widely available by 1982 and were the starting point for Sun, Fortune, HP, Masscomp, and many other UNIX-based workstations.

Labware △ The PI custom design system—An advanced Lisp-based placement and interconnect system for automated custom Mead-Conway style NMOS and CMOS designs. [R.L. Rivest. The PI (placement and interconnect) system. In *Proceedings of the ACM IEEE 19th Design Automation Conference*, pages 475–481.

Lisp et al △ The Scheme chip—A one-chip interpreter for the Scheme dialect of Lisp. [J. Batali, N. Mayle, H. Shrobe, G.J. Sussman, and D. Weise. The Scheme-81 architecture—system and chip. In *Proceedings of the MIT Conference on Advanced Research in VLSI*, P. Penfield, editor, Artech House.

AI ◇ D. Mar. *Vision.* W.H. Freeman, San Francisco, CA,

AI ◇ *Artificial Intelligence in Medicine.* P. Szolovits, editor, Westview Press.

Education ◇ *H. Abelson. *Apple Logo.* Byte Books.

Theory △ Exponential complexity of polynomial ideals—revealed unexpectedly large complexity of basic problem in symbolic computation with multivariate polynomials. [E. Mayr and A.R. Meyer. The complexity of the word problems for commutative semigroups and polynomial ideals. *Advances in Mathematics,* 46(3):305–329.]

Theory △ *Models of lambda calculus—Formulated the definition of a "model" of the untyped lambda-calculus. [A.R. Meyer. What is a model of the lambda calculus? *Information and Control,* 52(1):87–122.]

Theory ◇ C. Papadimitriou and K. Steiglitz. *Combinatorial Optimization: Algorithms and Complexity.* Prentice Hall.

Companies □ *S. Papert starts Logo Computer Systems, Inc. which develops a new crop of Logo implementations for PCs.

Companies □ *M. Hammer starts Hammer & Co.—management information technology consultants.

Mathlab □ *Macsyma licensed to Symbolics by MIT.

1983

Abstraction & Specification △ The Larch specification language—The Larch specification language: joint work with DEC. [J.V. Guttag and J.J. Horning. An introduction to the larch shared language. In *Proceedings of the IFIP Congress.*]

Abstraction & Specification □ First distribution of REVE system, R. Forgaard, J.V. Guttag, and P. Lescanne in 1983, used in 30 labs by 1986.

Distributed Systems △ Argus design and implementation—Argus design and implementation. [B.H. Liskov and R.W. Scheifler. Guardians and actions: linguistic support for robust, distributed programs. *ACM Transactions on Programming Languages and Systems*, 5:281—404.]

Parallel Computing △ Multiprocessor emulator—An emulator of dataflow and other parallel architectures. [Arvind, M.L. Dertouzos, and R.A. Iannucci. *A Multiprocessor Emulation Facility.* LCS Report TR-302.]

Labware □ TI delivers 30 Nu Machines to LCS, but stops production before commercializing. NuBus survives.

Lisp et al △ Generational garbage collection introduced. [H. Lieberman and C.E. Hewitt. *Communications of the ACM*, 26(6), June.]

Theory △ Area-efficient VLSI computation. [C.E. Leiserson. Area-efficient VLSI computation. *ACM Doctoral Thesis Award Series*, MIT Press.]

Societal Impact △ The sex barrier in computer science—The difficulties faced by women as students and researchers in LCS and AI at MIT. [Female students and research staff of LCS and AI. *Barriers to Equality in Academia: Women in Computer Science at MIT.* Published by LCS and AI.]

Companies □ *Thinking Machines Corp. started by W.D. Hillis, M. Minsky et al. First Connection Machine announced in 1986.

Companies □ *RSA Data Security, Inc. founded to do cryptographic software based on 1977 RSA scheme.

1984

Distributed Systems △ Data replication in a distributed system— Managing replicated data in type-specific ways does better than less specific methods. [M.P. Herlihy. *Replication Methods for Abstract Data Types.* Ph.D. thesis, MIT Department of Electrical Engineering and Computer Science, LCS Report TR-319, May]

Distributed Systems △ Atomic data in distributed systems—Introduces atomic data types for shared objects in a concurrent system. [W.E. Weihl. *Specification and Implementation of Atomic Data Types.* Ph.D. thesis, MIT Department of Electrical Engineering and Computer Science, LCS Report TR-314.]

Labware □ X Window System development begins, joint effort with Project Athena.

Labware □ *PC/IP communications software release by LCS, including manuals. Led to 1984 J. Romkey development of a PC version, PC/IP. See FTP Software, Inc., 1986.

Labware □ *4th revised release of C. Terman's RSIM, now widely used.

AI ◇ E.C. Hildreth. *The Measurement of Visual Motion.* ACM Distinguished Presentation Series, MIT Press.

AI ◇ P.H. Winston. *Artificial Intelligence.* Second edition, Addison Wesley.

AI ◇ P.H. Winston and K. Prendergast. *The AI Business: The Commercial Uses of Artificial Intelligence.* MIT Press.

Education ◇ *H. Abelson. *TI Logo.* Byte Books.

Theory △ Secure digital signatures—A digital signature scheme secures against all known forms of attack (assuming factoring is hard). [S. Goldwasser, S. Micali, and R.L. Rivest. A 'paradoxical' solution to the signature problem. In *Proceedings of the 25th IEEE FOCS Conference*, pages 441–448.]

Theory △ First hard subclass of Boolean circuits—Boolean Circuits with only constant depth require more than polynomially many gates to compute simple functions like parity. [M.L. Furst, J.B. Saxe, and M. Sipser. Parity, circuits and the polynomial time hierarchy. *Mathematical Systems Theory*, 17:13–27.]

Theory △ Wafer-scale systolic arrays—Algorithms for wafer-scale integration of systolic arrays. [F.T. Leighton and C.E. Leiserson. Wafer-scale integration of systolic arrays. *IEEE Transactions on Computers*, C-34:448–461.]

Theory △ Provably good VLSI layout—The first layout strategy for VLSI with provably good performance. [F.T. Leighton and S. Bhatt. A framework for solving VLSI graph layout problems. *Journal of Computer and System Science*, 28:300–343.]

Theory △ Complexity of elementary algebra and geometry—An exponential space decision procedure for the theory of real closed fields. [M. Ben-Or., D. Kozen, and J. Reif. The complexity of elementary algebra and geometry. In *Proceedings of 16th STOC*, pages 457–464.]

Societal Impact △ Office analysis methodology—How to analyze the operations of an office. [M. Sirbu, S.R. Schoichet, J.S. Kunin, M. Hammer, and J. Sutherland. OAM: an office analysis methodology. *Behavior and Information Technology*, 3:25–39.]

Societal Impact ◇ S. Turkle. *The Second Self: Computers and the Human Spirit*. Simon and Schuster.

Companies □ *InScribe, Inc. started by J. Sieber—computer calligraphy.

1985

Laboratories □ Media Laboratory starts in MIT Architecture Department from Architecture Machine Group et al.

Abstraction & Specification △ Large specification language. [J.V. Guttag, J.J. Horning, and J.M. Wing. The Larch family of specification languages. *IEEE Software*, 24–35.]

Abstraction & Specification △ Unification result—A solution to an important open problem in unification theory. [K.A. Yelick. *A Generalized Approach to Equational Unification.* LCS Report TR-344.]

Distributed Systems △ Fault-tolerant distributed systems—Modular design and implementation of fault-tolerant distributed systems for highly concurrent applications. [W.E. Weihl and B.H. Liskov. Implementation of resilient, atomic data types. *ACM TOPLAS*, April.]

Parallel Computing ◇ W.D. Hillis. *The Connection Machine.* MIT Press.

Parallel Computing △ A digital orrery—A special purpose multiprocessor to compute planetary orbits fast. [J.H. Applegate, M.R. Douglas, Y. Gursel, P. Hunter, C.L. Seitz, and G.J. Sussman. A digital orrery. *IEEE Transactions on Computers*, C-34:822–831.]

Parallel Computing △ Multilisp: a concurrent Lisp. [R.H. Halstead. Multilisp: a language for concurrent symbolic computation. *ACM Transactions on Programming Languages and Systems*, 7:501–538.]

Labware □ *NuBus, first developed at LCS for Nu Machine is used by TI in Explorer.

Education ◇ H. Abelson and G.J. Sussman, with J. Sussman. *Structure and Interpretation of Computer Programs.* MIT Press and McGraw Hill.]

Education □ *A Logo bibliography lists 200 books and 800 papers. There are 25 users' groups.

Education □ Logo activity moves to Media Laboratory.

Theory △ Zero knowledge proofs—How to convince a skeptic that an integer is not a square mod m while giving no other information about the integer. [S. Goldwasser, S. Micali, and C. Rackoff. The knowledge complexity of interaction proof systems. In *Proceedings of the 17*th *Symposium on Theory of Computing*, pages 291–304.]

Theory △ Fat-trees—Any communication performed by an arbitrary network can be efficiently simulated by a fat-tree of comparable volume. [C.E. Leiserson. Fat-trees: universal networks for hardware-efficient supercomputing. *IEEE Transactions on Computers*, C-34:892–901.]

Societal Impact □ Space Defense Initiative (Starwars) debate sponsored by LCS and Computer Professionals for Social Responsibility. D. Cohen, C.L. Seitz, D. Parnas, J. Weizenbaum, M.L. Dertouzos (chair), MIT Kresge Auditorium, October 25.

Companies □ *AI Architects, Inc. started by G. Papadopoulos, R.M. Soley, and D.E. Culler—ships first HummingBoards to Gold Hill to run Lisp fast on PCs in 1986.

Companies □ *Stellar Computer, Inc. started by J.W. Poduska—computers.

1986

Editors et al □ Stallman's GNU Emacs manual is in Edition 5 Version 18.

Abstraction & Specification ◇ B.H. Liskov and J.V. Guttag. *Abstraction and Specification in Program Development*. MIT Press.

Distributed Systems △ Specifications of distributed programs. [B.H. Liskov and W.E. Weihl. Specifications of distributed programs. *Distributed Computing*, 1:102–118.]

Distributed Systems △ Nested transactions. [N.A. Lynch and M. Merritt. *Introduction to the Theory of Nested Transactions.* LCS Report TR-367.]

Distributed Systems △ Community information system operational —A new technology combines digital broadcast and duplex communications and permits your personal computer to provide real time access to AP and New York Times news on your instructions. [J.M. Lucassen, D.K. Gifford, S.T. Berlin, and D.E. Burmaster. *Boston Community Information System User Manual.* LCS Report TR-352.]

Distributed Systems ◇ G.A. Agha. *Actors: A Model of Concurrent Computation in Distributed Systems.* MIT Press.

Parallel Computing △ The Concert multiprocessor. [R.H. Halstead, T.A. Anderson, R. Osborne, and T. Sterling. Design of a multiprocessor development system. In *Proceedings of the 13th Annual Symposium on Computer Architecture*, pages 40–48, Tokyo, June.]

Parallel Computing □ *Thinking Machines Corp. markets the Connection Machine—see Hillis' book, 1985.

Labware □ *X Window System Version 10 released. Basis for numerous UNIX workstation products. [R.W. Scheifler and J. Gettys. The X window system. *ACM Transactions on Graphics*, 5(2), April.]

Labware □ *LCS gateway transfer to Proteon via N. Chiappa completed: complete systems delivered 1986.

AI ◇ M.L. Minsky. *The Society of Mind.* Simon and Schuster.

AI ◇ B.K.P. Horn. *Robot Vision.* MIT Press and McGraw Hill.

Education △ A new paradigm for computer languages for nonexpert users—Introduces Boxer, a new computer medium that integrates text, graphics and programs. [H. Abelson and A. diSessa. Boxer: a reconstructible computational medium. *Communications of the ACM*, 29:859–868.]

Education ☐ Boxer project moves to University of California, Berkeley with diSessa.

Theory △ Almost all primes can be quickly certified—An always correct and almost always fast algorithm for recognizing primes. [S. Goldwasser and J. Kilian. Almost all primes can be quickly certified. In *Proceedings of the 18th Symposium on Theory of Computing*, pages 316–329.]

Theory △ Grid matching—Optimal matching of N^*N random points to an N^*N grid solved a long-standing problem. [F.T. Leighton and P. Shor. Tight bounds for minimax grid matching, with applications to the average case analysis of algorithms. In *Proceedings of the 18th ACM Symposium on Theory of Computing*, pages 91–103.

Theory △ Random functions from random numbers. Pseudo-random number generation from a small random seed. [O. Goldreich, S. Goldwasser, and S. Micali. How to construct random functions. *Journal of the ACM*, 33:792–807.]

Theory ◇ C. Papadimitriou. *The Theory of Database Concurrency Control*. Computer Science Press.

Companies ☐ *Free Software Foundation started by R. Stallman et al—promotes GNU Emacs and other freely modifiable software. Users may copy and redistribute, and may modify if they permit others to copy and redistribute their modified versions.

Companies ☐ *FTP Software, Inc. started by J. Romkey and D. Bridgeham. Wollongong, Bridge, Sun and IBM sell software derived from PC/IP. Micom-Interlan, Proteon, Western Digital, Sytek and Univation all are OEM's of FTP so they sell PC/IP-derived products.

Companies ☐ *GENSYM Corp. started by L. Hawkinson, E. Fredkin, M. Levin, and A. Haffman—real time expert systems.

1987

Multics □ Multics turned off at MIT.

Abstraction & Specification □ First distribution of Larch Prover, S. Garland and J.V. Guttag, (in use at five labs in spring 1988).

Distributed Systems △ Argus manual—First manual for Argus, a language for distributed systems. [B.H. Liskov, M. Day, M. Herlihy, P. Johnson, G. Leavens, R.W. Scheifler, W.E. Weihl. *Argus Reference Manual*. LCS Report TR-400.]

Parallel Computing ◇ T. Toffoli and N.H. Margolus, *Cellular Automata Machines—A New Environment for Modelling*. MIT Press.

Parallel Computing □ *CAM-6 computer, in commercial production by System Concepts, San Francisco.

Parallel Computing △ A Review of dataflow. [J.B. Dennis. Dataflow computation: a case study. In *Computer Architecture: Concepts and Systems*. V. Multinovic, editor, Elsevier.]

Parallel Computing △ FX programming language—The first programming language to include an effect system, FX supports the parallel implementation of applications that perform both symbolic and scientific computations. [D.K. Gifford, P. Jouvelot, J.M. Lucassen, and M.K. Sheldon. *FX-87 Reference Manual, Version 1.0*, LCS Report TR-407.]

Labware □ *X Window System Version 11 released. Eleven major vendors announce their support for X as an industry standard.

AI ◇ W. *AI in the 80's and Beyond: An MIT Survey*. W.E.L. Grimson and R.S. Patil, editors. MIT Press.

Theory △ Correct distributed algorithms. [N.A. Lynch and M. Tuttle. Hierarchical correctness proofs for distributed algorithms. In *Proceedings of the 6th ACM Symposium on Principles of Distributed Computing*, pages 137–151.]

Theory △ Two-writer registers—A two-writer register from one-writer registers with correctness proof. [B. Bloom. Constructing two-writer atomic registers. In *Proceedings of the 6th ACM Symposium on Principles of Distributed Computing.*]

Theory △ Deducing automaton structure—A new, remarkably effective algorithm for inferring the structure of finite automaton. [R.L. Rivest and R. Schapire. Diversity-based inference of finite automata. In *Proceedings of the 28th IEEE FOCS Conference*, pages 78–87.]

Theory △ Dynamic network protocols without timestamps—Solves a longstanding problem of eliminating unbounded timestamps in dynamic network protocols. [Y. Afek, B. Awerbuch, and E. Gafni. Applying static protocols to dynamic networks. In *Proceedings of the 28th IEEE FOCS Conference*, pages 358–370.]

1988

Distributed Computing △ Distributed programming in Argus. [B.H. Liskov. Distributed programming in Argus. *Communications of the ACM*, 31:300–312.]

Parallel Computing △ Id dataflow language manual—A parallel dataflow programming language. [R.S. Nikhil. *Id (Version 88.0) Reference Manual.* LCS Computation Structures Group Memo 284.

Labware □ *Industrially sponsored MIT X Consortium formed to control further evolution of the X Window System.

Labware □ *NuBus accepted as IEEE standard.

Education □ *Logo in use by hundreds of thousands of students. May be MAC's most popular offspring.

Theory △ Distributed random-access machines—A parallel algorithm model that includes communication costs. [C.E. Leiserson and B.M. Maggs. Communication-efficient parallel algorithms for distributed random-access machines. *Algorithmica*, 3:53–77.]

Index

National Research Council, 164
productivity, 159–181
telecommunications infrastructure, 47
Uexküll, J., 255
Unified Medical Language Systems,
   365
University of California at Berkeley,
   87
University of Pittsburgh, 336
UNIX, 4, 20, 65, 70–71, 83–84, 393–
   395
User interface, 20, 39, 64
in X, 78–80, 82
visual, 40

V

Vandevoorde, M., 84
Verifiability, 236
Versions in Argus, 58
Video technology, 39–41
Virtual circuit, 34–35, 37, 44, 47
Virtual circuit abstraction, 34–35
Virtual leg, 390–391, 393, 400–401
Virtual memory, 33
Vision, 163–164, 250–251, 253, 257–
   258, 277–315, 373, 396, 411, 417,
   425–426
Visual user interface, 40–41
Visualization, 41, 437
VLSI, 38, 42, 60, 129–156, 162, 277
Volatile objects, 55
Von Neumann, 93, 106, 108, 125, 130,
   132, 141

W

Wafer, 131
Wallace, S., 86
Waltz, D., 429
Ward, S., 5
Waterfall model, 23
Wavefront computation, 101–104
Weed, L., 338
Weldon, E., 307
Wellman, M., 354, 356
Whirlwind I, 1
Wiener's optimal filtering method, 282
Windowing, 46
Wisdom, J., 423

X

X Consortium, 75, 88–90
goals, 89
membership, 88

X Window System, 63, 71, 75–92
early design, 80–81
history, 83–87
library, 77–79, 82
protocol, 76–79, 82, 86, 90
server, 76–77
toolkit, 78, 81
window manager, 79
Xerox PARC, 4
Xerox, 86

Y

Yaw control, 401
Yip, K., 416, 426
Yngve, V., 2

Z

Zero-deficiency theorem, 431

The MIT Press, with Peter Denning as general consulting editor, publishes computer science books in the following series:

ACM Doctoral Dissertation Award and Distinguished Dissertation Series

Artificial Intelligence
Patrick Winston, founding editor
J. Michael Brady, Daniel G. Bobrow, and Randall Davis, editors

Charles Babbage Institute Reprint Series for the History of Computing
Martin Campbell-Kelly, editor

Computer Systems
Herb Schwetman, editor

Explorations with Logo
E. Paul Goldenberg, editor

Foundations of Computing
Michael Garey and Albert Meyer, editors

History of Computing
I. Bernard Cohen and William Aspray, editors

Information Systems
Michael Lesk, editor

Logic Programming
Ehud Shapiro, editor; Fernando Pereira, Koichi Furukawa, Jean-Louis Lassez, and David H. D. Warren, associate editors

The MIT Press Electrical Engineering and Computer Science Series

Research Monographs in Parallel and Distributed Processing
Christopher Jesshope and David Klappholz, editors

Scientific and Engineering Computation
Janusz Kowalik, editor

Technical Communication
Ed Barrett, editor